CW00339737

POLITICAL CULTURE IN THE REIGN OF ELIZABETH I

Queen and Commonwealth 1558–1585

In Europe, an unprecedented number of female rulers came to power during the period when religious reformation transformed early modern society and culture. The coincidence prompted men, in England and elsewhere, to debate and contest authority relations in strongly gendered terms. In this major contribution to **Ideas in Context** Anne McLaren explores the consequences for English political culture when, with the accession of Elizabeth I, Protestant imperial kingship came to be invested in the person of a queen. She looks at how Elizabeth managed to rule, in the face of considerable resistance, and demonstrates how opposition to female rule was articulated and enacted by parliament, by preachers, by councillors and by favourites. Dr McLaren argues that during Elizabeth's reign men were able to accept the rule of a woman partly by inventing a definition of 'citizen', one that made it an exclusively male identity, and she emphasises the cultural and political continuities between Elizabeth's reign and the outbreak of the English civil wars in the seventeenth century. A work of cultural history informed by political thought, *Political Culture in the Reign of Elizabeth I* makes a significant contribution to Tudor historiography and offers a convincing reinterpretation of the political dynamics of the reign of Queen Elizabeth.

A. N. McLaren studied at Washington University and Johns Hopkins University. She is now a Lecturer in the School of History at the University of Liverpool.

IDEAS IN CONTEXT

Edited by QUENTIN SKINNER (*General Editor*), LORRAINE DASTON,
DOROTHY ROSS and JAMES TULLY

The books in this series will discuss the emergence of intellectual traditions and
of related new disciplines, The procedures, aims and vocabularies that were
generated will be set in the context of the alternatives available within the
contemporary frameworks of ideas and institutions. Through detailed studies of
the evolution of such traditions, and their modification by different audiences,
it is hoped that a new picture will form of the development of ideas in their
concrete contexts. By this means, artificial distinctions between the history of
philosophy, of the various sciences, of society and politics, and of literature may
be seen to dissolve.

The series is published with the support of the Exxon Foundation.

A list of books in the series will be found at the end of the volume.

POLITICAL CULTURE IN THE REIGN OF ELIZABETH I

Queen and Commonwealth 1558–1585

A. N. McLAREN

University of Liverpool

CAMBRIDGE
UNIVERSITY PRESS

PUBLISHED BY THE PRESS SYNDICATE OF THE UNIVERSITY OF CAMBRIDGE
The Pitt Building, Trumpington Street, Cambridge, United Kingdom

CAMBRIDGE UNIVERSITY PRESS
The Edinburgh Building, Cambridge CB2 2RU, UK http://www.cup.cam.ac.uk
40 West 20th Street, New York, NY 10011–4211, USA http://www.cup.org
10 Stamford Road, Oakleigh, Melbourne 3166, Australia

First published 1999

Printed in the United Kingdom at the University Press, Cambridge

Typeset in Baskerville 11/12.5pt [VN]

A catalogue record for this book is available from the British Library

Library of Congress cataloguing in publication data
McLaren, Anne.
Political culture in the reign of Elizabeth I: Queen and Commonwealth 1558 – 1585 / A. N.
McLaren.
p.   cm.
Includes bibliographical references.
ISBN 0-521-65144-1 (hb)
1. Great Britain – Politics and government – 1558 – 1603.   2. Political culture – Great Britain
– History – 16th century.
I. Title.
JN181.N35   1999
306.2'0942'09031 – dc21   99–22403
CIP

ISBN 0 521 65144 1 hardback

For Jennifer, Andrew and Melissa, with much love

Contents

Acknowledgements

I would like to thank J. H. Burns, J. G. A. Pocock and Orest Ranum for their sustained interest in this project and for their willingness to engage with my ideas. My thinking has been very much shaped by their work, and their generosity in attending to mine has been much appreciated. I trust John Pocock in particular knows how much I am indebted to him. I would also like to thank Keith Mason, who has given me practical as well as intellectual assistance. I was told when I started that I should find an intelligent, critical (but supportive) non-specialist who would serve as a sounding-board for my ideas. I have been lucky that he has agreed to play not only that role but an editorial one as well. At several key places my argument is more incisive than it would have been without his comments and suggestions. E. P. H. Hennock showed confidence in my abilities at a critical moment and has continued to take a genuine interest in the project, for which I am grateful. Earlier still, Ann Hughes gave me invaluable encouragement, and stimulated me to think about gender in relation to early modern politics through the example of her own work. Beryl Mason has given unstinting support throughout. Finally I would like to thank the anonymous reviewers at Cambridge University Press and Liz Paton for her intelligent and meticulous attention to detail.

The article upon which parts of chapter 2 are based was published in *History of Political Thought* (1996).

Introduction

In the early modern period, men (and women) thought, wrote and spoke in a cultural context predicated upon the assumption that social order depended upon both hierarchy and patriarchy.[1] As a consequence they read the human male body as an analogue of human experience.[2] And because they regarded hierarchy and patriarchy – social order and male primacy – as interdependent propositions, they did not even, always, distinguish between the two in the way that we would do.[3] As the sixteenth century progressed, reformation ideology brought these assumptions to a level of self-consciousness which led to their articulation and contest, in a debate that permeated European culture, broadly defined.[4] Reformation ideology carried a universal promise: of a new relationship between God and man that would redeem every individual – man and woman, high and low. For contemporaries it posed the simultaneous threat of a profoundly disordered society on the way to the New Jerusalem; one that, for good or ill, would no longer sustain

---

[1] Susan Dwyer Amussen, *An Ordered Society: Gender and Class in Early Modern England* (Columbia, N.Y., 1988), pp. 180–3. Merry Weisner, *Women and Gender in Early Modern Europe*, New Approaches to European History (Cambridge, 1993), pp. 1–7, 239–41. For the French case see Sarah Hanley, 'The Monarchic State in Early Modern France: Marital Regime Government and Male Right' in *Politics, Ideology and the Law in Early Modern Europe: Essays in Honor of J. H. M. Salmon*, ed. Adrianna E. Bakos (New York, 1994), pp. 107–20 and 'Engendering the State: Family Formation and State Building in Early Modern France', *French Historical Studies* 16, no. 1 (1989), pp. 4–27.

[2] Louis Montrose, 'The Elizabethan Subject and the Spenserian Text' in *Literary Theory/Renaissance Texts*, ed. Patricia Parker and David Quint (Baltimore, Md., 1986), pp. 303–40, pp. 307–8; Paul Archambault, 'The Analogy of the "Body" in Renaissance Political Literature', *Bibliothèque d'Humanisme et Renaissance* 29 (1967), pp. 21–53. See also David Freedberg, *The Power of Images: Studies in the History and Theory of Response* (Chicago, 1989).

[3] Lisa Jardine, *Reading Shakespeare Historically* (London, 1996), pp. 70–1, 114–15; Susan Dwyer Amussen, '"The Part of a Christian Man": The Cultural Politics of Manhood in Early Modern England' in *Political Culture and Cultural Politics in Early Modern England: Essays Presented to David Underdown*, ed. Susan D. Amussen and Mark A. Kishlansky (Manchester, 1995), pp. 213–33, pp. 215–16.

[4] For a similar dynamic operating in the context of Enlightenment see Penny Weiss's analysis of Rousseau's thought, *Gendered Community: Rousseau, Sex and Politics* (New York, 1993).

hierarchy or patriarchy and hence any known form of social order.[5] The challenge to any conceivable *status quo* posed by the political doctrine of anarchy, in its late nineteenth- and early twentieth-century manifestations, must be the nearest modern secular equivalent.

Clearly, these conceptual parameters shaped the conduct of politics, especially in the sixteenth century, and particularly in countries that – like France, Scotland and England – experienced both Protestant reformation and female rule. And England, of course, experienced not only an unusually complex reformation process, but fifty years of female rule, under both a Catholic and a Protestant queen. This book began when I read some correspondence between several of Elizabeth's Privy Councillors and prominent ecclesiastics. The letters concerned religious reform and dated from the first decade of the reign. What struck me was their peculiar tone – a kind of baffled frustration that vied with the more conventional obeisances to princely power and authority. These letters summoned up a compelling image of a young woman surrounded on every side by powerful men; men who would presume, on the basis of their status and their gender, that they would have incontestable claims not only to counsel the queen, but also for their advice to be heeded.[6] What happened, I wondered, when a woman succeeded to the imperial crown, that potent symbol and instrument of the Henrician Reformation?[7] What would the political consequences be at this stage in European history, when humanism and religious reformation made Europe a battleground of competing conceptions of social order – but invariably privileged patriarchy as its *sine qua non*?[8]

This book tries to provide some of the answers. In what follows I attend to a range of speakers – the queen, councillors, bishops, parliament men and men 'out of doors', as well as men conventionally and

---

[5] Margo Todd, *Christian Humanism and the Puritan Social Order*, Ideas in Context (Cambridge, 1987); Mary Potter, 'Gender Equality and Gender Hierarchy in Calvin's Theology', *Signs: Journal of Women in Culture and Society* 11, no. 4 (1986), pp. 725–39. For the counter-reformation response see John M. Headley, *Church, Empire and World: The Quest for Universal Order, 1520–1640*, Variorum Collected Studies Series (Aldershot, Hampshire), 1997.

[6] See Louis Montrose's seminal depiction of the cultural consequences of this situation, when all positions of authority – cultural, political, ecclesiastical, familial – were occupied by men, uneasily and intensely aware of their subjection to a woman, in his '"Shaping Fantasies": Figurations of Gender and Power in Elizabethan Culture' in *Representing the English Renaissance*, ed. Stephen Greenblatt (Berkeley, Calif., 1988), pp. 31–64.

[7] J. G. A. Pocock, 'A Discourse of Sovereignty: Observations on the Work in Progress' in *Political Discourse in Early Modern Britain*, ed. Nicholas Phillipson and Quentin Skinner (Cambridge, 1993), pp. 377–428.

[8] See, for example, Donald R. Kelley, *The Beginning of Ideology: Consciousness and Society in the French Reformation* (Cambridge, 1981).

canonically defined as political theorists – as they battled to preserve Protestantism and the imperial crown.[9] Cross-cutting in this way is instructive. First, it shows that in the Tudor polity political discourse, even at the rarefied level of what has subsequently been deemed to be 'political theory', is never gender neutral. In fact it is rarely free from gender-specific references and immediate political application. In Elizabeth's reign these latter can often be recaptured through comparison with 'speech acts' performed by other speakers, in other contexts. This analysis also reveals that the conjunction of consensually shared attitudes towards women, in the ideological context of the godly nation experiencing female rule, and in the age of print, extended the boundaries of the political nation to an extent that would be surpassed only during the English Revolution. Two terms of political debate defined in this way are particularly important to the version of monarchy invented to secure England's Protestant identity under the reign of a queen: 'mixed monarchy' and 'commonwealth'.

Faced with the problem of legitimating a female ruler as holder of the imperial crown, theorists and apologists in Elizabeth's reign drew on and referred to a history of conceptions of political authority that dated from Henry VIII's reign. These conceptions, inseparable from their reformation context, were implicitly – and, in the work of the so-called 'resistance theorists' of Mary Tudor's reign, increasingly explicitly and controversially – imbued with gendered readings of political authority. These readings problematised Elizabeth's claim to 'supreme headship' and made a providential identity, of queen and nation, necessary to her political legitimation. This history also provided a genealogy for the 'mixed monarchy' that was inaugurated at Elizabeth's accession, first articulated and explored in the work of John Aylmer, but, as it transpires, the *lingua franca* of the reign. The 'mixed monarchy' was defined as a corporate body politic; one in which the wisdom of the many (a contested, but gender-specific identity during this period) 'bridled' and imparted grace to a female prince, and thereby preserved both Protestantism and national autonomy. It conjoined the three estates – now

---

[9] In so doing I am following a methodology theorised by J. G. A. Pocock and Quentin Skinner. For Pocock see especially 'The Concept of a Language and the *Métier d'historien*: Some Considerations on Practice' in *The Languages of Political Theory in Early-Modern Europe*, ed. Anthony Pagden (Cambridge, 1987), pp. 19–38; *Politics, Language and Time: Essays on Political Thought and History* (New York, 1973); 'The State of the Art' in *Virtue, Commerce, and History* (Cambridge, 1985), pp. 1–33. For Skinner see 'Meaning and Understanding in the History of Ideas' in *Meaning and Context: Quentin Skinner and His Critics*, ed. James Tully (Cambridge, 1988), pp. 29–67 and 'Motives, Intentions, and the Interpretation of Texts', *New Literary History* 3 (1972), pp. 393–408.

queen, lords and commons, or queen-in-parliament – in a mystical marriage effected at the queen's coronation; a 'marriage' in which, during Elizabeth's reign, both halves vied for the role of 'head' in a cultural context that defined headship as a male role and marriage as a means by which women were made whole through their incorporation in their husbands.[10]

The Elizabethan conception of the mixed monarchy also drew on and appealed to a commonwealth ideology, initiated in the reign of a minor king, Edward VI, that presented godly and patriotic Englishmen as having a vested interest in the 'common weal' as 'citizens' of the True Church. G. R. Elton, in iconoclastic form, refuted altogether the idea that there existed a 'party of commonwealthmen' in Edward VI's reign.[11] But, if we take away his anachronistic use of 'party', we are left with the unexceptionable recognition that evangelical Protestantism (like Erasmian humanism) promoted notions of human spiritual equality – at least among men; even, speculatively and at the fringes, including women as individual creatures in their own right.[12] Men committed to a new Christian order, in Edward's reign as in Elizabeth's, sought to create a society in which all men might be 'brothers' in Christ, and therefore promoted social and economic, as well as ecclesiastical, reform, in England as in other parts of Europe.[13] In a strongly hierarchical society the equation between Christian equality and the progress of reformation proved profoundly disquieting, not least because of the intimation that **all** might refer to women as well as to men. But the fact remains that during Elizabeth's reign what Patrick Collinson has usefully dubbed the 'Protestant ascendancy' largely accepted its necessity, in a True Church alternatively identified as the 'Christian commonweal' and increasingly assimilated to English national identity.[14]

[10] Frances E. Dolan, *Dangerous Familiars: Representations of Domestic Crime in England, 1550–1700* (New York, 1994), pp. 27–9.
[11] G. R. Elton, 'Reform and the "Commonwealth-Men" of Edward VI's Reign' in *Studies in Tudor and Stuart Politics and Government*, 4 vols. (Cambridge, 1983), vol. 3, pp. 234–53. Margo Todd's *Christian Humanism and the Puritan Social Order* is a good corrective, as are G. J. R. Parry's *A Protestant Vision: William Harrison and the Reformation of Elizabethan England* (Cambridge, 1987) and Annabel Patterson's *Reading Holinshed's Chronicles* (Chicago, 1994).
[12] Margo Todd, *Christian Humanism and the Puritan Social Order*.
[13] See Werner O. Packull, 'The Image of the "Common Man" in the Early Pamphlets of the Reformation (1520–1525)', *Historical Reflections* 12, no. 2 (1985), pp. 253–77, and, for the gender dimension, Lyndal Roper, "The Common Man", "The Common Good", "Common Women": Gender and Meaning in the German Reformation Commune', *Social History* 12, no. 1 (1987), pp. 3–21.
[14] For 'Protestant ascendancy', see Patrick Collinson, 'Puritans, Men of Business and Elizabethan Parliaments', *Parliamentary History*, 7 no. 2 (1988), pp. 187–211, p. 190. For 'Christian commonweal' see the entry under 'commonweal' in *The Oxford English Dictionary (Second Edition) on Compact Disc*, Oxford University Press.

These fears and hopes, allied to contemporary convictions about the power balance between men and women, inform the formulation of 'queen-in-parliament' which signalled the mixed monarchy in Elizabeth's reign. This political creation was not narrowly equivalent to the notion of the imperial king ruling *regaliter et politice*, in his own person and conjoined with his realm in parliament, that buttressed Henry VIII's claims to sovereign authority.[15] Instead, 'queen-in-parliament' privileged the potential for political virtue of the body of the realm – (male) inhabitants of the common weal, or 'country', whose zeal and rectitude secured the realm – and of parliament, the institutional means of its expression. Indeed, one of the most significant linguistic developments in this period, which proved to be such a formative one for the English language, was the gradual transition over the second half of the sixteenth century from the interchangeable use of 'common weal' and 'commonwealth' to mean both the general good and (in a secondary sense) the whole body of the people, to the predominant use of 'commonwealth' to signal the latter, potentially a place as well as a people – a gender-specific use that also contained latent antimonarchical implications.[16]

In the context of female rule, the conceptualisation of the commonwealth as potentially socially inclusive, inaugurated in Mary I's reign, led to renewed attention to 'natural' (and God-ordained) differences between men and women, in part as a means of excluding women from direct participation in this political configuration, in part as a concomitant of the ongoing reformation debate about the nature of kingship.[17] On the one hand, therefore, distinct gender identities were articulated, with women allocated a separate and inferior identity as 'other'. This move then allowed, even forced, men to reassess the legitimacy of competing distinctions of status, specifically among men who might be considered 'fellows' and 'brothers', in Christ – and potentially as countrymen and patriots. Here we can see the genesis of the contest over definitions of nobility which acquired political significance in Elizabeth's reign and continued into the reigns of her Stuart successors.[18]

This reinterpretation of Elizabeth's reign throws up a complex of

[15] J. G. A. Pocock, 'A Discourse of Sovereignty'.
[16] 'common weal', 'commonwealth': *The Compact Edition of the Oxford English Dictionary*, 2 vols. (Oxford, 1971), vol. 2, p. 696.
[17] Rebecca W. Bushnell, *Tragedies of Tyrants: Political Thought and Theater in the English Renaissance* (Ithaca, N.Y., 1990), pp. 64–9.
[18] Lisa Jardine, *Reading Shakespeare Historically*; Mervyn James, *Society, Politics and Culture: Studies in Early Modern England* (Cambridge, 1986), esp. 'The Concept of Order and the Northern Rising, 1569', pp. 270–307; 'English Politics and the Concept of Honour, 1485–1642', pp. 308–415; and 'At a Crossroads of the Political Culture: The Essex Revolt, 1601', pp. 416–65.

words whose meanings were contested in politically significant ways, as the queen and her commonwealth jostled to gain political advantage and to preserve the imperial crown. In addition to 'commonweal/ commonwealth', 'policy', 'necessity' and 'effeminacy' were debated in relation to political authority. Another trinity, related to the commonwealth, consists of 'sovereignty', 'state' and 'absolute', with reference to monarchy. This vocabulary expresses some of the 'essentially contested propositions' to which J. G. A. Pocock refers in his description of political languages, and which map Elizabethan political culture.[19] Some, like 'absolute', I use with inverted commas, to insist upon the divergence of the Elizabethan reading of this concept from our own, and, I think, from its meaning in earlier Tudor reigns. For throughout Elizabeth's reign, until the late 1590s, the fear it expressed within the political nation was that Elizabeth would become 'absolute' in possession of the imperial crown; a formulation that alerts us to both the continued disquiet over female rule and the corporate identification of 'sovereignty' that evolved as a solution to its perceived dangers.[20]

Interpreting Elizabeth's reign in this way also sheds new light on the Stuart experience of kingship, from the point at which James VI and I attempted to turn his back on nearly fifty years of English history in order to position himself as the immediate imperial heir to Henry VIII. For, as he announced to his first parliament, 'Precedents in the times of minors, of tyrants, or women or simple kings [are] not to be credited.'[21] The experience of female rule in the context of reformation culture gave men a vocabulary with which to contest 'absolute' kingship in the reigns of James I and Charles I. It also proved to be a necessary precondition for the eventual repudiation of kingship itself, a promise fulfilled when, in 1649, godly Englishmen emerged from the 'country' to execute a tyrannical king and inaugurate the English Commonwealth.

Reassessing Elizabeth's reign by attending to its gender dynamics thus takes us to the heart of early modern English political culture. It also has implications for our understanding of the 'monarchy of council', which began with the Henrician Reformation and lasted until the

---

[19] J. G. A. Pocock, 'The State of the Art', p. 9. He is quoting the philosopher William Connolly.
[20] Katherine Eggert, 'Nostalgia and the Not Yet Late Queen: Refusing Female Rule in *Henry V*', *English Literary History* 61 (1994), pp. 523–50, esp. pp. 528, 542; Carole Levin, *The Heart and Stomach of a King: Elizabeth I and the Politics of Sex and Power* (Philadelphia, 1994), ch. 5, 'The Return of the King', pp. 94–118.
[21] Quoted in J. P. Kenyon, 'Queen Elizabeth and the Historians', in *Queen Elizabeth I: Most Politick Princess*, ed. Simon Adams (London, 1984), pp. 52–5, p. 52.

execution of Charles I in 1649.[22] Yet, surprisingly, Tudor historians have been slow to recognise its centrality.[23] To dismiss this gender dimension by describing Elizabeth I as an early modern version of Margaret Thatcher, as Patrick Collinson has done, does little more than update J. E. Neale's conclusion that Elizabeth's womanly charms solved the problem posed by a woman ruling in a man's world. Reflecting on Elizabeth's relations with her councillors, Collinson writes that 'when we read John Aylmer's apology for Elizabeth's fitness to rule, composed in 1559, along the lines that the government of a woman was tolerable because in England it would not be so much her government as government in her name and on her behalf, we feel sorry for the poor man . . . One might as well justify the government of Mrs. Thatcher on the grounds that her cabinet can be trusted to keep her in order.'[24] The analogy, and the thinking behind it, also limit our understanding of the world that Collinson has so richly described in other works and in other ways. We need to recognise that John Aylmer's achievement, in the tract to which Collinson refers, lay in theorising England as a 'mixed monarchy', and that he did so in direct response to what he perceived as the dangers of female rule. Tellingly, in that tract Aylmer amplifies his definition of the mixed monarchy by describing Elizabeth herself as a 'mixed ruler', by which he meant that she carried within herself elements of the (male) political body as a function of a mystical marriage effected at her coronation and directly superintended by God.[25] Like other apologists – like Sir Thomas Smith, whose concept of a 'monarchical republic' Collinson also draws on – Aylmer wrote to preserve England's Protestant identity, which he saw as inseparable from the imperial crown and threatened by female rule. Men such as Smith and Aylmer translated classical and humanist conceptions of a mixed polity into the context of female rule, with the specific intention of preserving the imperial crown against the return of a king. Their success changed the 'rules of the game' which governed the conduct of monarchical

---

[22] J. G. A. Pocock, 'A Discourse of Sovereignty', p. 408.

[23] To date, attention to gender in this period has been more the province of literary critics, especially Stephen Greenblatt, Richard Helgerson, Lisa Jardine, Louis Montrose, and, in a different vein, Annabel Patterson. Blair Worden is one notable recent exception, in *The Sound of Virtue: Philip Sidney's 'Arcadia' and Elizabethan Politics* (New Haven, Conn., 1996).

[24] Patrick Collinson, 'The Monarchical Republic of Queen Elizabeth I', *Bulletin of the John Rylands University Library of Manchester* 69, no. 2 (1986–7), p. 399. John Guy has recently, and rightly, defined this article as seminal and reprinted it in his edited volume *The Tudor Monarchy* (London, 1997). But he lets the analogy go unchallenged: it is 'superb', he concludes in one of his own contributions to the collection, 'Tudor Monarchy and Its Critiques', pp. 78–109, p. 94.

[25] John Aylmer, *An Harborowe for Faithfull and Trewe Subjects* (Strasbourg, 1559), fol. B2.

authority in England in ways that defined political culture even when a king came again to the throne.[26]

Similarly, John Guy recognises that William Cecil, Elizabeth's chief minister, arrived at a self-definition as a 'public servant of the state' which justified defiance of the queen to preserve the Protestant state of the realm, and did so by recourse to 'quasi-republican' principles. Parenthetically he concludes (quite rightly) that 'probably [Cecil's] line of argument could only have been attempted under a female ruler'.[27] But his formulation – the parenthetical glance at gender – gets the emphasis the wrong way around. In Elizabeth's reign, increasing numbers of men had recourse to 'quasi-republican principles' precisely because their position in reformation history, and in the context of female rule, required them to invent themselves as 'citizens'. The articulation of these 'quasi-republican principles' was allowed for because 'citizen' came to be interpreted as an ambiguous (but specifically male) identity which pointed towards the City of God as much as it did towards Roman republics. The Elizabethan polity achieved a certain stability under these conditions precisely because it allowed men – and **not** women: the exclusion is important – to image themselves as both citizens and subjects; again, in the context of female rule. Over the course of the reign exploration of these identities pushed political engagement in a more socially inclusive direction, and this was one reason for the authoritarian character of the latter years, as well as the politically significant longing for a 'king' – a godly male ruler – to stabilise the body politic.[28] Once more, we see how gender identities and polarities were central to Elizabethan politics.

Guy argues that Elizabeth's reign falls into two parts: the 'first reign' from her accession in 1558; the second (the rather long 'last decade') the period from the late 1580s until her death in 1603.[29] I too see Elizabeth's reign as divisible into two distinct phases. My reasons for arriving at a similar periodisation arise from my reintepretation of the reign, however, and therefore differ from his. In my reading, the 'first reign'

[26] For this understanding of political engagement see Quentin Skinner, 'Meaning and Understanding in the History of Ideas' and J. G. A. Pocock, 'The Concept of a Language and the *Métier d'historien*'.

[27] John Guy, 'Tudor Monarchy and Its Critiques', p. 97. For Cecil's self-identity as a councillor see Richard Helgerson, *Self-Crowned Laureates: Spenser, Johnson, Milton, and the Literary System* (Berkeley, Calif., 1983) and Stephen Alford, 'William Cecil and the British Succession Crisis of the 1560s', Ph.D. Dissertation, University of St Andrews (1996).

[28] Katherine Eggert, 'Nostalgia and the Not Yet Late Queen', p. 546.

[29] John Guy, 'The 1590s: The Second Reign of Elizabeth I?' in *The Reign of Elizabeth I: Court and Culture in the Last Decade*, ed. John Guy (Cambridge, 1995), pp. 1–19. Guy emphasises social and economic factors as precipitants in 'Tudor Monarchy and Its Critiques', p. 99.

attempted to legitimate Elizabeth as a providential ruler, her sex counterweighed by God's immediate intervention in English affairs and by the mediate efforts of godly men engaged in political affairs on His (and her) behalf. The latter part of the reign – the period after 1585 – witnessed attempts to renegotiate that settlement, the radical potential of which had been revealed as a concomitant of the increasingly desperate attempts to secure the imperial crown against the likely succession of the Catholic Jezebel, Mary Queen of Scots.[30]

I would identify the 1584 Bond of Association as the watershed between the two periods. It represented the culmination of processes that caused the transition to what Guy rightly identifies as the embattled, authoritarian culture of the later Elizabethan period. The Bond enabled godly Englishmen from the ranks of the political nation to declare their allegiance to the commonwealth, on the queen's behalf and against her will. It encouraged political action that might extend to the assassination of a ruler judged – by the regime but not by the queen – to be ungodly; in this case Mary Stuart, Elizabeth's cousin, deposed queen of Scotland, and heir presumptive to the English throne. It called up the political *virtù* of godly Englishmen: their ability to act in a military capacity, as individual men and as members of the commonwealth, to preserve their own and other men's liberty, simultaneously religious and political. And it culminated, in 1587, with the execution of Mary Queen of Scots by the regime: a God-ordained event, according to Elizabeth's chief secretary William Cecil, Lord Burghley, 'whose minister this state was in the execution thereof'.[31]

Instance Collinson and Guy as Tudor historians because their work over the past fifteen years has transformed our understanding of Elizabeth's reign and continues to set the standard for others working in the field. We now need to investigate that field anew, using what Anthony Fletcher has called the 'lens of gender', in order fully to comprehend not only the Elizabethan body politic, but also the wider European debate about monarchical authority which so engaged men and women during the early modern period.[32] The present study is a first attempt at that project.

---

[30] I take issue with his assessment that the 'drift to authoritarianism' which characterised the 1590s was 'irrational' ('Tudor Monarchy and Its Critiques', p. 99). Instead, it represented an entirely understandable response to the comprehensive threat to order implicit in the political configuration that allowed for Mary's execution.

[31] John Strype, *Annals of the Reformation and Establishment of Religion and other various occurrences in the Church of England during Queen Elizabeth's Happy Reign*, 7 vols. (Oxford, 1824), vol. III.i, p. 549.

[32] At an Institute for Historical Research conference, 'Gendering History', held in York, September 1996.

Throughout the book I distinguish between 'councillor' and 'counsellor' and their related forms. I do so in order to formalise a distinction that, although important to English political discourse of the period, is often implicit or masked by variable early modern orthography. In the sixteenth century a new distinction began to appear between 'councel' (later 'council') and 'counsel'.[33] The former corresponded to the ecclesiastical *concilium*, extended to cover all cases in which the word meant a deliberative assembly or advisory body. 'Councillor', as in 'Privy Councillor', represented an alteration of the earlier word 'counsellor' through assimilation to 'council', with a new, implicit reference to office-holding that became definitive over the course of the century. At the same time 'counsel' began to be used more generally for the action of providing advice. In the context of reformation England, and especially from Edward VI's reign, 'counsel' carried intimations of its theological definition as any of the advisory declarations of Christ and the apostles, considered not to be universally binding but rather provided as a means of attaining greater moral perfection. The resulting distinction between 'council' and 'counsel' does not correspond to either Latin or French usage. The development points to the politicisation of 'counsel' which occurred in Elizabeth's reign, and which I chart as one of the themes of the book. It provides further evidence that England's debate about monarchical authority was in many ways *sui generis* among European monarchies, not least because of its intersection with contemporary beliefs about gender.

I also use the word 'regime' as Wallace MacCaffrey has defined it: to refer to a cluster of men including but not restricted to Privy Councillors who were drawn together by shared ideological convictions. MacCaffrey rightly sees these counsellors as at least partially responsible to emergent Protestant opinion specifically within the elite but more generally throughout the nation, and as reflecting, in their political initiatives, the changed relations between the crown and councillors which came into being during Elizabeth's reign.[34] I then use 'government' to denote the queen and the regime, on the many occasions when they worked in tandem, in an extraordinary and politically innovative *mariage de convenance*, to maintain Elizabeth's tenure of the crown.

[33] 'council', 'counsel': *The Compact Edition of the Oxford English Dictionary*, 2 vols. (Oxford, 1971), vol. I, pp. 1050–4.
[34] Wallace MacCaffrey, *The Shaping of the Elizabethan Regime* (Princeton, N.J., 1969), pp. 22, 39, 310, 313.

The latter part of the reign, after Mary's execution, inevitably inaugurated a period of reaction, characterised pre-eminently by the attempt to redefine the godly nation as the Elizabethan 'state' and to purge from its ranks, as 'zealots', men engaged in political life primarily on behalf of the True Church. In this period we enter the terrain mapped out by Richard Helgerson in *Forms of Nationhood: The Elizabethan Writing of England*. The political culture of this period was characterised by conflictual and potentially confrontational readings of the key terms 'nation' and 'state' (and, increasingly, 'country'). In this later period, as Helgerson argues, discursive forms that emphasised the state over the nation, and power over custom and the individual conscience, were 'more upper-class and male' (but, I would add, included the queen), whilst those that emphasised nation over state 'include[d] – even identif[ied] with – women and commoners' (but not the queen). In the 1590s, Helgerson concludes, 'Inclusion emerge[d] as an inverse function of power.'[35] I have adopted his use of the terms 'inclusive' and 'exclusive' to analyse English political culture in the period from 1558 to 1585, in part to signal how the 'exclusive' politics of the latter part of the reign – which lie outside the scope of this book – derived immediately and evidently from the 'inclusive' politics of its first decades.

[35] Richard Helgerson, *Forms of Nationhood: The Elizabethan Writing of England* (Chicago, 1992), pp. 8–9, 297–8.

CHAPTER I

'To be Deborah': the political implications of providentialism under a female ruler

Querative: if God should call her majesty leaving issue a daughter . . .
what he thinketh of that Daughter's Right?

Elizabeth to John Knox (1559)[1]

THE DEBATE OVER HEADSHIP

In 1559 Elizabeth's query to John Knox was a telling one. The Henrician Reformation had problematised the relationship of the imperial king to the 'church' (now newly defined as both a universal and a purely English gathered congregation) in ways that also, inevitably, affected the perception and conduct of female rule. What exactly did it mean to be 'Supreme Head of the Church of England next under Christ'? What powers did it entail? Did it necessarily – as many Protestants believed – derogate from Christ's authority? For Anthony Gilbey, writing in Geneva in 1558, before his return to England at Elizabeth's accession, Henry VIII's claim to be Supreme Head left an antichristian remnant in the Anglican Church that impeded further reformation:

This monstrous boar [Henry VIII] for all this must needs be called the Head of the Church in pain of treason, displacing Christ, our only Head, who ought alone to have this title. Wherefore in this point, O England, ye were no better than the Romish Antichrist, who by the same title maketh himself a God, sitteth on men's consciences, bannisheth the Word of God, as did your King Henry, whom ye so magnify . . . So made you your King a god, believing nothing but that he allowed.[2]

---

[1] Elizabeth's annotations on a letter from Knox explaining how she should interpret his *First Blast of the Trumpet Against the Monstrous Regiment of Women* (1558), British Library, Additional MSS. 32,091, fols. 167–9. For Knox's letter see below, chapter 2.

[2] Anthony Gilbey, *An Admonition to England and Scotland to call them to repentance* (Geneva 1558) in *The Works of John Knox*, ed. David Laing, 6 vols. (Edinburgh, 1846–64), vol. VI, pp. 553–71, p. 564.

Reformation ideology in Europe, centred as it was on a true reading of Scripture, collapsed the traditional division between temporal and spiritual authorities (symbolised before the reformation by the relationship between pope and emperor) and called into question the nature and extent of monarchical authority. It also confounded the well-established division between two distinct kinds of ecclesiastical authority: the magisterial power over the church known as the *potestas jurisdictionis* and the sacerdotal, sacramental power, the *potestas ordinis*. The repudiation of ritual observance as necessary to salvation gave a new centrality to the power to declare and expound Scripture. In a Bible-centred theocracy, whether at Zurich or in England, Christ may rule; but He does so primarily through Scriptural pronouncement. In a monarchy – in what Christopher St German called 'the whole catholic church of England' – whose role would it be to interpret Scripture? Was the task of establishing doctrine (as against that of enforcing it) a matter for the temporal or the spiritual authority? For a council, or for the king? What should be the relationship between the two? In a monarchy, if the king, now imperial, fulfilled the role of exegete, did this make him a priest? A prophet?[3] Or, as Gilbey believed, a pope? And did not the concept of an imperial crown, advanced at least in part to repudiate the claims of the supreme pontiff at Rome, logically entail the assimilation of *potestas ordinis* to the crown?[4] As Cuthbert Tunstall warned in 1531, supreme headship would indeed prove to be a *propositio multiplex*.[5]

The conception of empire advanced by the Henrician Reformation also problematised the issue of the **person** who would exercise absolute temporal and spiritual dominion, at a time when contemporary ideological developments in Europe 'personalised' monarchical power, and gendered it as male.[6] J. H. Burns has shown how one influential strand of the scholastic debate over monarchy that occurred over the fifteenth and early sixteenth centuries was the elevation of the status of the monarch, whether pope or emperor, by reference to his reception of authority from, hence identity with, Christ: 'him by whom kings reign'.

[3] One definition of 'prophet' in use in the sixteenth and seventeenth centuries was one who interpreted or expounded the Scriptures; *The Compact Edition of the Oxford English Dictionary*, 2 vols. (Oxford, 1971), vol. I, p. 1473.

[4] This appears to have been Henry VIII's view. See Francis Oakley, 'Christian Obedience and Authority, 1520–1550' in *The Cambridge History of Political Thought 1450–1700*, ed. J. H. Burns (Cambridge, 1991), pp. 159–92, pp. 177–82.

[5] Quoted in C. H. McIlwain, *The Political Works of James I* (New York, 1965), p. xlvii.

[6] Anthony Black, *Monarchy and Community: Political Ideas in the Later Conciliar Controversy 1430–1450* (Cambridge, 1970); Merry E. Weisner, *Women and Gender in Early Modern Europe* (Cambridge, 1993), p. 241.

That political vocabulary – the language of *imperium* and of *plenitudo potestatis*, of secularised equivalents of the perceived relationship between Christ and his Church – subsequently served to legitimate the claims to empire of territorial and national monarchs, like Henry VIII, which proliferated in the late fifteenth and early sixteenth centuries.[7] It was a vocabulary predicated on the assumption that the person who ruled – pope, emperor or king – would be male. In England, where the king's claims to imperial authority were uniquely explicit and far-ranging, the assumption acquired very nearly the status of a categorical imperative, one that helps explain Henry VIII's desperate and constitutionally innovative quest for a male heir.

The rediscovery of classical antiquity too led to and provided authoritative sanction for the perception of monarchical authority as a male capacity, represented by the figure of the 'philosopher-king'. Humanism recovered antique, primarily Aristotelian, gender typologies that classified women as relatively deficient in qualities of reason, judgement and prudence, hence lacking the capacity for political virtue. Even Erasmian humanists depicted women as best able to attain moral virtue through subordination to their husbands, ordained by God to be their 'heads' in the wake of the Fall.[8] On all sides, St Paul's often-quoted injunction prohibiting women from speaking in the congregation was read as confirming a God-ordained spiritual incapacity which denied them authority in spiritual matters and, as a corollary, the exercise of temporal dominion in a godly realm.

From another direction too gender and the problem of monarchical authority were linked. As the religious reformations took hold, especially in Northern Europe, direct obedience to God through His vice-regent Christ became a powerful political ideal: referring back to Christ, as king, the dignity with which terrestrial monarchy had been invested in the course of earlier conciliar controversies. This occurred in the context of a movement that Donald Kelley has rightly identified as 'intensely masculine' in its leadership, rhetoric and imagery: 'God, Pope, priest, king, magistrate, preacher: all were men; so too were the rebels who

---

[7] J. H. Burns, *Lordship, Kingship and Empire: The Idea of Monarchy 1400–1525* (Oxford, 1992), pp. 13–14, 97–100. Dale Hoak, 'The Iconography of the Crown Imperial' in *Tudor Political Culture*, ed. Dale Hoak (Cambridge, 1995), pp. 54–103.

[8] Ian Maclean, *The Renaissance Notion of Woman: A Study in the Fortunes of Scholasticism and Medical Science in European Intellectual Life* (Cambridge, 1980); Margo Todd, *Christian Humanism and the Puritan Social Order* (Cambridge, 1987).

attacked their character and position. All likewise lacked a coequal female partner.'[9]

One solution to the problem this ideological shift posed for monarchical authority lay in eliding the figures of Christ and the king. This was an element of the theory of the divine right of kings as it developed in England in the late sixteenth and especially the early seventeenth centuries, the point at which a king, in the person of James VI of Scotland, was once again in prospect.[10] But it was a solution available (albeit, as events were to prove, profoundly problematical) only to lords and kings, not to ladies and queens. For this was the period that witnessed the resurgence of the 'heresy of Postellus': 'that Christ died only for the salvation of *men*; and that there is a *woman* come, which shall redeem the *women*' – a potent indicator of the ambivalent view of women that emerged from the conflation of humanist and reformation ideologies and the intersection of that view with radical politics.[11]

In England, the role and meaning of 'Supreme Head of the Church of England' was and remained disputable from its inception with the 1534 Act of Supremacy, not least because of the absence of adult male holders of the crown over the period from Henry VIII's death in 1547 until James I's accession in 1603. In this cultural context the role **might** be available to a king, especially one figured as 'king-in-parliament', mystically joined in consultation with the 'whole catholic church of England'

[9] Donald R. Kelley, *The Beginning of Ideology: Consciousness and Society in the French Reformation* (Cambridge, 1981), pp. 75–6. David Freedberg (*The Power of Images: Studies in the History and Theory of Response* (Chicago, 1989), p. 453) argues more generally that in all periods the use of 'man' for 'humankind' 'reflects quite precisely the male orientation of Judaeo-Christian thinking about the relationship between God and his creations'. This insight is particularly valuable for the early modern period, when the processes that gave rise to the religious reformations led to gendered reconceptualisations of 'God's creations', including bodies politic.

[10] J. P. Sommerville, 'Richard Hooker, Hadrian Saravia, and the Advent of the Divine Right of Kings', *History of Political Thought* 4 (1983), pp. 229–45, pp. 239–41.

[11] See, for example, John Strype, *Annals of the Reformation and Establishment of Religion and other various occurrences in the Church of England during Queen Elizabeth's Happy Reign; together with an appendix of original papers of state, records and letters*, 7 vols. (Oxford, 1824), vol. III.ii, p. 348. 'Postellus' was Guillaume Postel (1510–1581), whose insistence that true reformation entailed the marriage of Christ, the new Adam, with the Shekinah, or the new Eve and his identification of her as the holy woman of Venice (and himself as their first-born) led many contemporaries to dismiss him as more mad than dangerous. The misinterpretation of his views, which seem to have been current in England, speaks to anxieties about the future of patriarchy as well as social order in a fully reformed commonwealth. For Postel see William J. Bouwsma, *'Concordia Mundi': The Career and Thought of Guillaume Postel (1510–1581)* (Cambridge, Mass., 1957). John Aylmer in effect accused John Knox of leaving the door open for the widespread acceptance of this heresy in his apologetical work *An Harborowe for Faithfull and Trewe Subjects, agaynst the late blowne Blaste* (London, 1559), fol. Kiii. For the Knox–Aylmer debate see below, chapter 2.

to propound doctrine.[12] It might extend to a minor king, imagined as a new Josiah attending simultaneously to the wisdom of God and of his godly councillors; hence the image of Edward VI as governed by godly preachers propagated in Elizabeth's reign.[13] It would not be available to a queen whose gender, according to contemporaries, disqualified her from exercising authority as either priest or prophet.

During her brief tenure of the throne, Mary I side-stepped some of these issues (and raised others) by marrying and by omitting any claim to the title of Supreme Head. She thereby announced herself as subject in both her persons – as woman and as queen – to the authority of male superiors: her husband and king, Philip II of Spain; and the head of the universal church and vicar of Christ, the Pope. Mary's decisions seemed to contemporaries to allow for a non-violent conquest of England by Spain, as Philip exercised his rights as husband and king over his queen and her realm. This, as much as if not more than the coincident reintroduction of Catholicism, provided empirical evidence that confirmed contemporary theories concerning the dangers of female rule.[14] And this was the immediate context that produced John Knox's famous assertion that 'the empire of a woman is an idol', as well as his wider argument that female rule symbolises, and enacts, the ungodly propensities inherent in kingship itself – the argument to which Elizabeth responded in 1559.[15]

As we shall see, Knox was not alone, albeit in a minority, in his views on kingship. His views on women rulers and their implication in the definition of monarchical authority were, in contrast, much more widely shared throughout Elizabeth's reign, and shared across the confessional divide.[16] The problem of imperial rule therefore re-emerged in a complicated and intensified form at Elizabeth's accession, as godly men attempted to preserve England's autonomous identity – its spiritual and

---

[12] Quentin Skinner, *The Foundations of Modern Political Thought*, 2 vols. (Cambridge, 1978), vol. 2, *The Age of Reformation*, pp. 56–8, 100–8.

[13] See Margaret Aston, *The King's Bedpost: Reformation and Iconography in a Tudor Group Portrait* (Cambridge, 1993) for the cultivation of Edward VI's image in Elizabeth's reign.

[14] See Jennifer Loach, *Parliament and Crown in the Reign of Mary Tudor* (Oxford, 1986), who touches on but does not systematically explore the constitutional consequences of anxieties concerning female rule in Mary's reign. See her discussion of the 1554 Act for the Queen's Regnal Power, pp. 96–7, 217–18.

[15] John Knox, *The First Blast of the Trumpet Against the Monstrous Regiment of Women* (1558), in *The Political Writings of John Knox*, ed. Marvin A. Breslow (Washington, D.C., 1985). For the English face of John Knox in this connection see Jane Dawson, 'The Two John Knoxes: England, Scotland and the 1558 Tracts', *Journal of Ecclesiastical History* 42, no. 4 (1991), 556–76.

[16] John Strype, *Annals*, vol. 1.i, pp. 186–7.

territorial constituents now interpenetrated and powerfully symbolised by the Protestant imperial crown – in the context of female rule.

The resulting tensions are apparent in the debate over the 1559 Act of Supremacy. In that debate a consensus emerged, across confessional lines, that the queen would be Supreme **Governor** of the Church of England, not Supreme **Head**.[17] Geoffrey Elton argued that the new title represented an attempt to satisfy moderate Catholic opinion that Elizabeth had not assumed a title rightly belonging to the pope and also to answer doubts about the 'propriety' of a woman being called Supreme Head of the Church of England.[18] But there is more to the matter than this. By this point in the sixteenth century, again as a consequence of earlier conciliar controversies, the term 'governor' could be used to denote an administrative capacity (read as at least potentially a collective one), and as such contrasted to *imperium*, or the power to command; a distinction that saw four female relations of Philip II enact the role of governor of the Netherlands as a consequence of Philip's fully realised imperial status.[19]

Awareness of a politically significant distinction between 'head' and 'governor' in the context of the royal supremacy undoubtedly informed the debate over Elizabeth's change of title from 'Supreme Head' to 'Supreme Governor' at her accession.[20] In these debates the major faultline over the use of 'Supreme Head' appeared within the Protestant ranks, while Catholic speakers exploited this division, and the ambiguities of the concept of 'supreme headship', to promote the advantages of allegiance to the universal church at Rome. On one side of the line stood those, like William Cecil and John Hales, who regarded Elizabeth's adoption of the title as necessary to differentiate her reign from that of her predecessor queen and convincingly to re-establish Eng-

---

[17] For the debate see John Strype, *Annals*, vol. i.ii, pp. 400, 405–6, 410–11, 419–20.

[18] G. R. Elton, *The Tudor Constitution: Documents and Commentary*, 2nd edn (Cambridge, 1982), pp. 338–45.

[19] J. H. Burns, '*Regimen Medium*: Executive Power in Early-Modern Political Thought', unpublished paper, pp. 3–4; *The True Law of Kingship: Concepts of Monarchy in Early-Modern Scotland* (Oxford, 1996), p. 222. For instances of this use in Elizabeth's reign see William Camden, *The History of the Most Renowend and Victorious Princess Elizabeth Late Queen of England*, ed. Wallace T. MacCaffrey (Chicago, 1970), p. 62, and *The Bardon Papers: Documents Relating to the Imprisonment and Trial of Mary Queen of Scots*, ed. Conyers Read, Camden Third Series vol. xvii (London, 1909), Appendix I, pp. 118–19.

[20] See also F. W. Maitland, who argues the 'etc.' introduced in Elizabeth's style and title represented a deliberate attempt 'in the highest of high quarters' to finesse the problem of 'Supreme Headship'. F. W. Maitland, 'Elizabethan Gleanings', in *Selected Historical Essays of F. W. Maitland*, ed. Helen M. Cam (Cambridge, 1957), pp. 211–46, esp. pp. 211–16. I am grateful to Dr Orest Ranum for this reference.

land's Protestant identity. On the other were ranged those – men like
John Knox and Anthony Gilbey – who regarded both the attempt and
the title as ungodly. Their influence is demonstrated by the fact that it
was Thomas Lever, godly preacher and 'commonwealth-man' in Edward VI's reign, and recently returned Marian exile, who dissuaded
Elizabeth from taking the title of 'Supreme Head'.[21] In the middle stood
those who, like the Archbishop of Canterbury, Matthew Parker, sympathised with both positions, but at heart probably inclined more
toward the latter. Parker was one of the compilers of the 1559 ecclesiastical injunctions designed to support the Acts of Supremacy and Uniformity, although these were edited and put in final form by Cecil alone.
Shortly before his death in 1575 Parker – who, like his successor Edmund Grindal, grew to find service to both God and queen a spiritually
incoherent proposition and regretted his decision to accept ecclesiastical
office – wrote to Cecil (by then Lord Burghley) that 'Whatsoever the
[queen's] ecclesiastical prerogative is, I fear it is not so great as your pen
hath given it in the injunctions.'[22]

In the end, all but one of the Marian bishops refused to take the oath
of supremacy, despite the change in the queen's title. They were deprived of their bishoprics and replaced by Protestants selected by Elizabeth's chief minister, William Cecil. Many had connections with Cecil
dating from their participation in the 'Edwardian moment' of Edward
VI's reign that proved so momentous for later Tudor political culture;
most now returned from godly exile sustained during Mary's reign.[23]
This outcome put in place an ecclesiastical establishment whose views
on imperial kingship were likely to share common ground with those of
men like Gilbey and Knox, even as they recognised the necessity of
protecting the royal supremacy; a necessity that became more compelling with a woman, even a Protestant princess, on the throne.

With regard to the headship issue, these ambiguities persisted as the
reign proceeded. Elizabeth and her Privy Councillors seem to have
wanted to act as though Elizabeth exercised the same theocratic authority as her father had done, whilst holding up the change in title to

---

[21] John Strype, *Annals*, vol. i.i, p. 194.
[22] Ibid., vol. i.i, p. 236. For Parker see Patrick Collinson, 'The Downfall of Archbishop Grindal and
Its Place in Elizabethan Political and Ecclesiastical History', in *Godly People: Essays on English
Protestantism and Puritanism*, ed. Patrick Collinson (London, 1983), pp. 371–97, p. 373.
[23] See William Haller, *Foxe's Book of Martyrs and the Elect Nation* (London, 1963), introduction and pp.
83–6. For the 'Edwardian moment' and its relationship to Scottish political culture see Arthur H.
Williamson, *Scottish National Consciousness in the Age of James VI: The Apocalypse, the Union and the
Shaping of Scotland's Public Culture* (Edinburgh, 1979), ch. 1 and p. 155. I am grateful to Dr Roger
Mason for this reference.

'Supreme Governor' as evidence of their, and her, reforming commitment. Moreover, they seem to have proposed commitment to this expedient position as indicative of loyalty to the regime, at least among the elite.[24] There was, however, one important difference on this issue between the queen and her Privy Councillors. She wanted to exercise imperial authority in her own right, as her father had done. They wanted that authority to be an attribute of the crown, or of the collective capacity of 'her majesty's supreme government', as Thomas Wilson phrased it in 1578.[25] In the parliamentary debates in particular there is evidence that Elizabeth's disclaimer of the title of Supreme Head was partial and occasional. She seemingly adopted a rhetorical strategy of claiming headship of the church in her own person when it appeared she could carry the point, falling back on the well-established trope of the prince as head of the body politic when she could not. The Commons' proceedings were 'not convenient', she responded to one of their numerous petitions urging revision of the prayer book, in 1571. 'Concerning rites and ceremonies she, being supreme head of the Church, would consider thereof as the case should require.'[26] Very often it was a strategy her Privy Councillors were prepared to support, in the interest of managing reforming pressure in the House of Commons. '[S]ince we have acknowledged her to be supreme head, we are not in these petty matters to run before the rule', Mr Controller reminded MPs on the occasion of this debate. To do so, commendable zeal notwithstanding, 'were folly', 'both in the doing and in the probability of offending her Majesty'.[27]

But in 1578 Thomas Wilson, Privy Councillor and the queen's principal secretary, explained his understanding of Elizabeth's position in terms that implied that jurisdictional authority over the affairs of the church lay in the collective capacity of 'her majesty's supreme government' (and avoided the issue of who, within that collective, determined

[24] See, for example, Theodore Beza's 1565 letter to Heinrich Bullinger in John Strype, *Annals*, vol. i.ii, pp. 171–3. For 'regime' see Wallace MacCaffrey, *The Shaping of the Elizabethan Regime* (Princeton, N.J., 1969), esp. pp. 22, 39, 310, 313. Like MacCaffrey, I use 'regime' to refer primarily to the Privy Council and, at points, other of the queen's counsellors. I use 'government' specifically to refer to the queen and her councillors. This distinction needs to be highlighted given the tendency especially of modern-day revisionist historians to use 'the government' as synonymous with the Privy Council – more or less systematically excluding the queen. 'Protestant ascendancy' is Patrick Collinson's useful phrase, indicating the centrality if not the numerical weight of this ideological cohort in Elizabethan affairs. See 'Puritans, Men of Business and Elizabethan Parliaments', *Parliamentary History* 7, no. 2 (1988), pp. 187–211, p. 190.
[25] John Strype, *Annals*, vol. ii.ii, p. 626.
[26] *Proceedings in the Parliaments of Elizabeth I*, vol. i: *1558–1581*, ed. T. E. Hartley (Leicester, 1981), p. 220.   [27] Ibid., p. 250.

doctrine).[28] He made this statement in the course of an episode that is revealing for two reasons. First, it suggests how difficult it would be to promote the sleight of hand proposed by the queen and her councillors – Elizabeth as 'head' or 'governor' of the church depending on political circumstances – to a reformed audience among whom the concept of Christ as king had steadily gained ground in parallel with the progress of the English reformation. It also indicates the sense of engagement in affairs of the realm engendered among godly men by the conflation of these processes.

In 1578 John Wilsford, a devout man 'of some learning', recounted how he had come to harbour doubts about the character of Elizabeth's authority over the church. Engaged in Bible study at home, he had become perplexed upon reading St Paul's Epistle to the Hebrews, which recounted the priesthood of Aaron and Christ.

I perceived that Aaron's pontification and priesthood was earthly, and continued by succession here on earth. But Christ's pontification is celestial, without succession in this world; and not passable ever to any other person in earth . . . And by that means [Christ is the] only mediator between God and man; and *caput ecclesiae*. And thus being in captivity, as Joseph was; who, for his delivery out of the same, took upon him to expound dreams; so I devised with myself to open to the queen's majesty, that it was not lawful for any person to take upon him to be *caput ecclesiae*, except the same person will be Christ's adversary and antichrist, as the pope is.

He therefore took himself off to court to expound this matter to the queen. He got no further than her Privy Councillor, Thomas Wilson, who was able to allay his anxieties (and seemingly warn him against similar prophetic forays in future):

But since being better advised and admonished by Master Secretary Wilson of my rash enterprise therein. For that the queen's majesty assumeth not unto herself, neither to be *summus pontifex*, neither yet to be *caput ecclesiae*, as it is Christ's mystical body: . . . (which the pope doth, hence is antichrist). But her majesty's supreme government is concerning the civil and political government of the clergy and laity of Christ's church and mystical body. Which authority and supremacy, her majesty, with all other princes and potentates, have in their realms and dominions, justly and dutifully, both by Christ's gospel, and all the apostolical doctrine.[29]

In 1583, however, William Cecil, now Lord Burghley, publicly used the

---

[28] For Thomas Wilson as an advocate of militant Protestantism and a prominent member of Philip Sidney's 'party' see Blair Worden, *The Sound of Virtue: Philip Sidney's 'Arcadia' and Elizabethan Politics* (New Haven, Conn., 1996), *passim* and p. 282, n. 10.

[29] John Strype, *Annals*, vol. ii.ii, pp. 625–6.

government's collective disclaimer of the title of 'Supreme Head' on behalf of the queen to shore up loyalty to the crown among the ranks of disaffected Protestants.[30] In *The Execution of Justice in England* he argued what had become a highly disputable and polemically charged case: that Elizabeth's reign inaugurated a new species of reformation, purer and more thorough-going than that which had occurred under Henry VIII and Edward VI, and meaningfully demonstrated by the repudiation of the role and title of Supreme Head.[31] This, he claimed, is the very reason why 'the adversaries' (ambiguously now papists and sectaries) insist that her queenship has become imperial: they 'do most falsely write and affirm, that the Queen's Majesty doth now use [the title of Supreme Head of the Church of England next under Christ]: a manifest lie and untruth, to be seen by the very acts of parliament; and, at the beginning of her reign, omitted in her style'.[32] (At the same time, in a characteristic move, he urged loyalty to Elizabeth on the basis of her descent from the imperial king and the fact that she was not subject to any man: 'King Henry the Eighth's daughter and heir, Queen Elizabeth, a sovereign and a maiden queen'.[33])

Tensions inherent in the position advanced by Wilson, which gave Elizabeth a role as a component element of a Protestant 'supreme government', are also apparent in an episode which began in 1582 with an interchange of graffiti around the Royal Arms in the parish church at Bury St Edmunds. The graffiti exchange itself is revealing. Initially one Thomas Gibson had caused the following Biblical verse to be painted next to the Royal Arms:

I know thy works, that thou are neither cold nor hot. I would thou wert cold or hot. Therefore because thou art lukewarm, and neither cold nor hot, it will come to pass, I will spew thee out of my mouth.

'By advice' the critical words were painted over, substituting after 'I know thy works' the more anodyne *'and thy love, and service, and faith, and thy patience, and thy works; and that they are more at the last than at the first'.*

---

[30] Cecil was ennobled in 1571. In the interest of clarity I refer to him as 'Burghley' in most cases in the remainder of the book.

[31] The case itself was not new. It was made by Laurence Humphrey in his 1559 *apologia* for Elizabeth's accession, the *De Religionis Conservatione et Reformatione Vera*. What is striking is Burghley's use of it to identify as 'adversaries' forward Protestants (now 'Puritans') unable to accept the sleight of hand of Elizabeth as head/governor discussed above. See William Cecil, Lord Burghley [presumed author], *The Execution of Justice in England* (1583), in *The Harleian Miscellany; or A Collection of Scarce, Curious, and Entertaining Pamphlets and Tracts, as well in manuscript as in print, Found in the late Earl of Oxford's Library*, ed. T. Park and W. Oldys, 12 vols. (London, 1808–11), vol. I, pp. 490–513, pp. 495–6. For Humphrey see below, chapter 4.

[32] William Cecil, *The Execution of Justice*, pp. 495–6.   [33] Ibid., p. 503.

Gibson, in consultation with others, then raised the stakes and simultaneously changed the focus from queen to councillor(s) by having the following added:

Notwithstanding, I have a few things against thee, that thou sufferest the woman Jezebel, which maketh herself a prophetess, to teach and to deceive my servants; to make them commit fornication, and to eat meat sacrificed unto idols.[34]

Nor was this the end of the matter. Elizabeth herself seems to have believed that these men expressed sentiments with which her innermost councillors sympathised, and to some extent spoke as their conscience concerning religious reformation. In the next year she alluded to this episode on an occasion when, in company with her principal councillors (including William Cecil, now Lord Burghley), she met with Archbishop Whitgift and representatives of the Lower House of Convocation to accept the clerical subsidy. She used it to imply that her Privy Councillors jeopardised her tenure of the imperial crown, and hence England's Protestant identity, through their lukewarm commitment to her prerogative – defined in terms that only Archbishop John Whitgift, among the Privy Councillors, was prepared to accept without qualification. She first accepted the subsidy 'thankfully, and the rather that it came voluntarily and frankly, whereas the laity must be entreated and moved thereunto'. At this point Burghley interjected, 'Madam these men come with mites, but we will come with pounds.' Ignoring him, she turned to the bishops, saying:

'We understand that some of the Nether House have used diverse reproachful speeches against you, tending greatly to your dishonour, which we will not suffer; and that they meddle with matters above their capacity, not appertaining unto them, for the which we will call some of them to an account. And we understand they be countenanced by some of our Council which we will redress or else uncouncil some of them.'

Then, according to the anonymous recorder of this incident,

[She] told how she had received a letter from beyond the sea, written by one that bore her no good will who wrote that the Papists were of hope to prevail again in England, for that her Protestants themselves misliked her. 'And indeed, so they do', quoth she, 'for I have heard that some of them of late have said that I was of no religion – neither hot nor cold, but such a one as one day would give God the vomit. I pray you, look unto such men . . . Both these [Papists and Protestants] join together in one opinion against me, for neither of them would have me to be Queen of England.'[35]

---

[34] John Strype, *Annals*, vol. III.i, p. 269.
[35] Recounted in J. E. Neale, *Elizabeth I and Her Parliaments*, 2 vols. (London, 1957), vol. 2, pp. 69, 71.

RESTORED PROTESTANTISM AND THE ENGLISH DEBORAH

Elizabeth's equivocal status as Supreme Head of the church, signalled by her investiture as 'Supreme Governor', resulted from contemporary anxieties concerning female rule. Her gender therefore informed, as it shaped, public debate over issues pertaining to the common weal, at that time defined pre-eminently as the maintenance, continuance and extension of Protestant reformation in England and from thence abroad.[36] These anxieties simultaneously promoted her depiction as the 'English Deborah' as a legitimating strategy, one that forwarded the identification of England with Israel that proved so momentous a feature of English history through the mid-seventeenth century. 'Deborah' was an ambiguous monarchical identity, in place from the early days of the reign, and one over which Elizabeth seems to have had little direct control.[37] In the Old Testament, Deborah's role, her 'rule', was providential, ordained directly by God guiding his Israelites. The story was read by many sixteenth-century Englishmen as potentially, if not actually, analogous to Elizabeth's reign. Through Deborah, His instrument, God had intervened directly in Israel's history to protect a godly nation from its enemies; through Elizabeth He had intervened in English history to nullify the Marian apostasy and secure the Protestant nation.[38] 'Deborah' therefore became a powerful emblem of restored Protestantism; at one level, given the taint associated with female rule, in association with and in the service of the crown.

Paradoxically, the analogy with Deborah challenged Elizabeth's personal monarchical autonomy while strengthening her hold on the crown.[39] It did so by allowing the 'Protestant ascendancy' to articulate

[36] G. J. R. Parry, *A Protestant Vision: William Harrison and the Reformation of Elizabethan England* (Cambridge, 1987).

[37] J. N. King, *Tudor Royal Iconography: Literature and Art in an Age of Religious Crisis* (Princeton, N.J., 1989), pp. 183, 227. John Hales described Elizabeth as Deborah in his *Oration . . . to the Queenes Majestie* (in John Foxe *Acts and Monuments of Matters . . . happening in the Church*, 3 vols. (London, 1641), vol. 3, pp. 976–9)), as did John Knox in his 1559 Letter to Elizabeth (see below, chapter 2). Modern historians and literary critics who have recognised the significance of the identification include William Haller in *Foxe's Book of Martyrs and the Elect Nation*, J. N. King in 'The Godly Woman in Elizabethan Iconography' (*Renaissance Quarterly* 38 (1985), pp. 41–84) and John Guy, *Tudor England* (Oxford, 1988).

[38] See the account of the pageant series conducted at Elizabeth's coronation, in which she was explicitly hailed as Deborah, written by Richard Mulcaster as *The Quenes Maiesties Passage through the Citie of London to Westminster the Day before her Coronation* (London, 1559), ed. James M. Osborn (New Haven, Conn., 1960) and modern commentators Sydney Anglo, *Spectacle, Pageantry and Early Tudor Policy* (Oxford, 1969) and David Bergeron, *English Civic Pageantry 1558–1642* (London, 1971).

[39] A. N. McLaren, 'Prophecy and Providentialism in the Reign of Elizabeth I', in *Prophecy: The Power of Inspired Language in History 1300–2000*, ed. Bertrand Taithe and Tim Thornton, Themes in History (Stroud, 1997), pp. 31–50, pp. 39–41.

new kinds of political identity: they used the story of one powerful woman to consider themselves in relation to the rule of another, in ways that delegated authority from king to godly men.[40] According to the Old Testament account Deborah was a judge in Israel before the declension into kingship, when the Israelites, in contrast to the heathen tribes, still recognised God as immediately their king. The story therefore depicted the state of spiritual and political integrity attainable in a truly reformed commonwealth; an ideal that remained a potent political programme through the Interregnum.[41] Moreover, although a 'prophetess' (hence receiving God's command immediately) and a judge, the Biblical Deborah enacted His will through the military commander, Barak. This was a telling feature of the story that achieved political significance during the Essex rebellion, if not earlier, when the Earl of Essex was explicitly identified as Barak in public sermons.[42] (Deborah's pairing with Jael, who finalised the victory by hammering a tent peg through the forehead of the sleeping Canaanite captain Sisera, must also have given contemporaries pause.[43]) It is therefore revealing that the pageant series presented by the City of London to Elizabeth on the day before her coronation climaxed with a tableau in which a figure representing simultaneously Deborah and Elizabeth attended to 'good counsel' proffered to her by her estates. More significant still is the fact that the Deborah/Elizabeth figure presented by the city to their future sovereign wore an open, spiked headpiece, not the closed headpiece of the imperial crown.[44]

   In important ways, then, the identification of Elizabeth with Deborah posited a conception of monarchical authority as God's will devolved to queen and godly nation, and 'spoken' by prophetic utterance – in a culture in which interpreting God's will, except in exceptional circum-

---

[40] For the identification of this phenomenon see Pauline Stafford, 'More than a Man, Or Less than a Woman? Women Rulers in Early Modern Europe', *Gender and History* 7, no. 3 (1995), pp. 486–90, p. 487.

[41] See, for example, one MP's contribution to the 1572 parliamentary debate over the bill for the reformation of rites and ceremonies: 'He believeth those to be nearer Judaism that striveth for ceremony than those which yield to it . . . Few ceremonies in the Apostles' time, and so may also few be suffered in the Dutch or French Church because they were not under any monarchy; but after that Christianity grew to kingdoms, then ceremonies necessary'; *Proceedings*, p. 369.

[42] J. E. Neale, *Queen Elizabeth I* (London, 1934; repr. 1952), pp. 365, 377. *The Geneva Bible* (1560), facsimile edition, ed. Lloyd E. Berry (Madison, Wis., 1969), pp. 110–11.

[43] *Geneva Bible*, pp. 110–11.

[44] Richard Mulcaster, *The Quenes Maiesties Passage*, p. 55. J. N. King argues, I think rightly, that this qualified assertion of Elizabeth's monarchical authority may be the key to interpreting the Deborah tableau (*Tudor Royal Iconography*, p. 227). See also Dale Hoak, 'The Iconography of the Crown Imperial'. For London's political self-identity in this period see Lawrence Manley, *Literature and Culture in Early Modern London* (Cambridge, 1995).

stances, remained a male preserve. Nor were Elizabeth and her councillors likely to welcome any intimation that exceptional circumstances were at hand, given the destabilising potential of the contemporary view of women's rule as 'prodigious' – dangerous, if not entirely unnatural. In this cultural context, therefore, Elizabeth and her ministers were unlikely to assert her immediate prophetic capacity as an element of her queenship. Yet, at least in the years from her accession in 1558 to the mid-1580s, her providential identity constituted by far the most powerful means of justifying subjects in their obedience to the queen; Thomas Norton spoke for many when he declared that 'I have no dealing with the queen but as with the image of God.'[45] Instead, her least contentious claim to a godly monarchical identity – certainly in the early years of her reign – would be that God **informed** her will because she was chosen, the choosing ambiguously providential (as English Protestant queen: a 'Deborah') and historical (because she was a Tudor king). For these reasons a consensual image of Deborah attained currency that identified her, and Elizabeth, as 'handmaids of the Lord' and 'mothers in Israel'.[46] (It is worth bearing in mind too that, as we saw at Bury St Edmunds, perceived declension from the role of Deborah left Elizabeth vulnerable to identification as an alternative Old Testament queen figure, the tyrant queen Jezebel.)

This consensual reading, and the relationship it posited between the queen and her people, underlies one striking feature of the reign: the unprecedented variety and range of unsolicited advice from across the ranks of the (male) political nation that justified Elizabeth's rule by telling her, with varying degrees of explicitness and insistence, how to conduct it in accordance with God's will. In this critique what is most striking is the assumption, expressed over and over in different ways and across a spectrum of opinion right up through the 1580s, that Elizabeth is most godly when she eschews her own will, acting instead as the instrument of God's will as identified by her male subjects.[47] Bishop Pilkington of Durham set the tone when he prayed in 1559 for God to 'Save and preserve our gracious queen as thine own signet', to exercise

---

[45] BL Add. MS 48023, fol. 33r.
[46] Elizabeth did not stake a claim to an overtly prophetic identity even when the political dynamics of the reign shifted in ways that enhanced her monarchical authority. Instead, the latter years of her reign witnessed the maturation of a 'cult' of queenship that cast Elizabeth in pagan and Christian roles symbolic of perpetual virginity, a fusion allowing for an intimated (and politically dangerous) correspondence between the queen and the Virgin Mary. See Helen Hackett, *Virgin Mother, Maiden Queen: Elizabeth I and the Cult of the Virgin Mary* (London, 1995), esp. pp. 198–234.
[47] Margaret Christian, 'Elizabeth's Preachers and the Government of Women: Defining and Correcting a Queen', *Sixteenth Century Journal* 24, no. 3 (1993), pp. 561–76.

government as His representative.[48] She must be at God's work 'in the church but not above', Christopher Foster (alias Colman) told her in a letter of 1569, if she hoped to maintain her worldly position.[49] John Foxe, in 1578, saw England threatened by papists on all sides, with only God's providence, 'somewhat' enacted through his servant Elizabeth, to thank for their miraculous preservation thus far. The qualifier gives force to his prayer, delivered to a public which included Elizabeth, that God would first see to Elizabeth, in the interest of protecting his chosen people. In a speech act that plays on the paradox of associating omnipotence with governorship, and God with the queen, he prayed that God would deign to take queen and country in hand – the first a precondition for the second: 'In this her government be her governor, we beseech thee; so shall her majesty well govern us, if first she be governed by thee'.[50]

Particularly at points when the integrity of the Protestant imperial crown appeared to be under threat, the contingent quality of subjects' allegiance to their 'dear mother' appeared. On these occasions it is notable that Elizabeth was depicted as in danger of departing from her role as Deborah when she was interpreted as threatening to enact her own will – as woman and, more dangerously, in the latter years of the reign, as monarch. In the 1572 parliamentary debates urging the necessity of executing Mary Stuart, Thomas Digges intimated that her 'true and faithful subjects' would be forced to fall out of allegiance if she ignored the 'lamentable cry of her whole realm', in this instance 'pronounced by the mouth of the Parliament':

> The preachers have plentifully poured out vehement reasons, urgent examples and horrible menaces out of the sacred scriptures concerning the execution of justice and shunning of that sugared poison bearing in outward show the countenance of mild pity. The contemning of these yieldeth under God's adversaries great causes of triumph in advaunting our religion to be wicked and our preachers false prophets.[51]

In the next parliamentary session, in 1576, the godly MP Peter Wentworth argued that Elizabeth's refusal to be guided by prophetic address in the 1572 session had drawn down God's wrath on queen and country alike. God had punished His people by taking 'Deborah' from them, leaving a tyrannical female ruler in her place:

---

[48] John Strype, *Annals*, vol. II.ii, p. 598.   [49] Ibid., vol. I.ii, p. 352.   [50] Ibid., vol. II.ii, p. 639.
[51] *Proceedings*, pp. 294–5. See Gerald Bowler, '"An Axe or an Acte": The Parliament of 1572 and Resistance Theory in Early Elizabethan England', *Canadian Journal of History* 19, no. 3 (1984), pp. 349–59.

Well . . . God . . . was the last session shut out of the doors. But what fell out of it? Forsooth his great indignation was therefore poured upon this House. How so? For he did put into the Queen Majesty's heart to refuse good and wholesome laws for her own preservation . . . Since then that her Majesty hath committed great faults, yea dangerous faults to her self and the state love, even perfect love void of dissimulation, will not suffer me to hide them to her Majesty's peril but to utter them to her Majesty's safety.

He proceeded to list these 'faults' in what must have been, for Elizabeth, galling detail, before closing with a characteristic prayer: that she would once more assume the role of an emblem of grace in the body politic; a role that would secure her own authority and the well-being of her subjects:

And I beseech the same God to endue her Majesty with his wisdom whereby she may discern faithful advice from traitorous sugared speeches, and to send her Majesty a melting yielding heart unto sound counsel, that will may not stand for a reason. And then her Majesty [will] stand when her enemies are fallen.[52]

The prospect of marriage to the Catholic François de Valois (duc d'Anjou since his brother Henry's accession to the French throne in 1574) prompted a similar response in the late 1570s. In his incendiary pamphlet *The Discoverie of a Gaping Gulf*, the forward Protestant John Stubbs adjured the queen to set commitment to Protestantism and the godly nation over her own lustful will, bearing in mind specifically that 'relations between men and women' – in which men exercise headship – 'are not countermanded by law or privilege'. Like Wentworth, he stated the regrettable necessity of chastising the monarch, in danger of forfeiting her divinely ordained position as governess of a godly realm (or, in Stubbs's words, she 'in whose hands the Lord hath put and holden a sovereign sceptre'):

We do not love her, whatsoever we say, when flattering her, perhaps, in other vanities, we do not fall down before her with tears, bewailing the wrath of God kindled against her, if by her advised permission, and by means of her marriage, God should be so highly dishonoured in this kingdom wherewith he hath honoured her.[53]

---

[52] *Proceedings*, pp. 430–2. For the political impact and significance of Wentworth's speech see below, chapter 6.

[53] John Stubbs, *The Discoverie of a Gaping Gulf Whereinto England is like to be Swallowed by an other French mariage, if the Lord forbid not the banes . . .* (1579), in *John Stubbs's 'Gaping Gulf' with Letters and Other Relevant Documents*, ed. Lloyd Berry (Charlottesville, Va., 1968), pp. 17, 19–20.

Like Wentworth, Stubbs prayed that God would grant Elizabeth the wisdom to follow godly counsel, 'stop[ping] your Majesty's ears against these sorcerers and their enchanting counsels, which seek to [promote the marriage and hence] provoke God's anger'. At the same time, he reassured her that she was not alone in her struggle to restrain her will. '[P]ray against these dangerous tempters and temptations,' he urged her, ' . . . and know assuredly, to your comfort, that all the faithful of God pray for you, and when you are in your secret, most separate closet of prayer they join with you in spirit'.[54] How consoling such assurance must have been!

To rule as Deborah, then, meant relying entirely on God's grace, serving as His instrument in an ongoing politics ratified and supervised by the men who were committed to her government in two senses: as partisans of Protestantism and, more generally, as men made in God's image and charged to her care in their earthly abode. The latter sense requires emphasis. The reformation context, which celebrated God's promise of redemption to mankind, read man, not woman, as made in God's image, with the promise of their relationship being symbolised through Adam and Christ. This reading extended across the confessional divide and thus problematised female rule for Protestant and Catholic men alike.[55] Moreover, and as a consequence, these values and beliefs extended across the ranks of the political nation, into the court and the Privy Council. Peter Wentworth, for example, was examined in Star Chamber in 1576, after his speech in the House of Commons quoted above. True he was committed to the Tower, but this was a small penalty for implying that Elizabeth ruled as an ungodly tyrant. His release after only one month gives some credence to his account of his examination by Privy Councillors in the wake of his speech. Wentworth implies that the councillors took issue with his decision to identify her Majesty's 'great faults' in the semi-public venue of parliament, not with his identification of those faults or his assessment of their political consequence. According to Wentworth, the Committee told him he might have addressed the queen 'in better terms', and meekly accepted his response that he would not do 'as you of her Majesty's Privy Council do', and express himself 'in such terms as she should not have understood to have made a fault'.[56] Clearly, in

[54] Ibid., p. 30.
[55] See Louis Montrose's delineation of Tudor somatic symbolism in 'The Elizabethan Subject and the Spenserian Text' in *Literary Theory / Renaissance Texts*, ed. Patricia Parker and David Quint (Baltimore, Md., 1986), pp. 303–40, pp. 307–8.   [56] *Proceedings*, pp. 437–9.

the new Israel the line between 'sugared speeches' and *politique* address was a fine one.

John Stubbs was undoubtedly a zealous, even a 'froward' Protestant with radical connections – his sister married Thomas Cartwright in 1577.[57] But he was also part of Burghley's axis, close to his secretary Michael Hicks (a friendship dating back to their time at Lincoln's Inn), as well as to Sir Francis Walsingham and the Earl of Leicester. His 'offence' in writing the *Gaping Gulf* in 1579 led, as is well known, to a sentence condemning him to lose his right hand in 1581. Less well known but more noteworthy in this context is the fact that he continued to enjoy close and cordial relations with these great men until his death, a relationship predicated upon their shared ideological convictions. Burghley later commissioned him to reply to Cardinal Allen's attack on the government's treatment of Catholics, *A True, Sincere, and Modest Defence of English Catholics* . . . of 1584, though there is no evidence the work was actually published, and Leicester conferred the stewardship of Great Yarmouth on him in 1585.[58] At least some contemporaries, including the French ambassador Mauvissière, assumed that Stubbs wrote the inflammatory *Gaping Gulf* with the consent of, if not at the behest of, 'quelques ungs de ce conseil'; an opinion seemingly shared by Elizabeth herself, who banished Walsingham from court in October 1579 for his part in the affair.[59]

Again on the subject of the proposed French marriage, we have the case of Philip Sidney, the Earl of Leicester's nephew, Sir Francis Walsingham's son-in-law, and model of chivalrous Protestantism. His *Letter to Queen Elizabeth*, written at roughly the same time as Stubbs's *Gaping Gulf*, gives a similar reading of the basis of Elizabeth's monarchical authority.[60] Seemingly Sidney too wrote with the knowledge,

---

[57] Patrick Collinson explores the dynamic between 'forward' and 'froward' Protestants in Elizabeth's reign in 'Puritans, Men of Business and Elizabethan Parliaments', pp. 191–5. He denominates as 'froward' men willing to cross the line between ideological commitment and impolitic action, often at the behest of Privy Councillors who believed their calling did not allow them the same freedom of action.

[58] Lloyd Berry, *John Stubbs's 'Gaping Gulf' with Letters and Other Relevant Documents*, introduction; Simon Adams, 'The Protestant Cause: Religious Alliance with the European Calvinist Communities as a Political Issue in England, 1585–1630', D.Phil. Dissertation, Balliol College, Oxford (1972–3), p. 30.

[59] See Susan Doran's account, in *Monarchy and Matrimony: The Courtships of Elizabeth I* (London, 1996), p. 167.

[60] *A Letter Written by Sir Philip Sidney to Queen Elizabeth, Touching her Marriage with Monsieur*, in *Miscellaneous Prose of Sir Philip Sidney*, ed. Katherine Duncan-Jones and Jan Van Dorsten (Oxford, 1973), pp. 46–57. For Sidney, the Sidney circle, and his and their relations with the queen, see Blair Worden, *The Sound of Virtue*.

even at the command, of members of the Privy Council. His Protestant mentor Hubert Languet congratulated him on the widespread circulation of the *Letter*: 'Since you were ordered to write as you did by those whom you were bound to obey, no fair-judging man can blame you for putting forward freely what you thought good for your country.' Perhaps Languet referred to familial obligation – that Sidney was 'bound to obey' those to whom he was joined by blood; perhaps he referred to an equally powerful ideological allegiance to a more extensive coalition amongst the Privy Council. In either case, what comes across powerfully is the sense of ideological solidarity, as Languet adds that Sidney was entirely justified in 'exaggerating some circumstances' in order to put the case against the queen.[61]

What was Sidney ordered to write that he thought good for his country? Very much what Elizabeth had already learned from Stubbs, advanced by a man claiming the status of an aristocratic courtier rather than (or in addition to) that of a prophet. The duc d'Anjou, being a man, 'must needs have that man-like disposition to desire that all men be of his mind' which she, in the context of a marriage, will not be able to resist. More signally there is no reason, 'worldly' or godly, which can support the proposed marriage; to desire it is to endanger her status as Deborah:

[F]or your standing alone, you must take it as a singular honour God hath done unto you, to be indeed the only protector of his church. And yet in worldly respects your kingdom is very sufficient so to do, if you make that religion upon which you stand to carry the only strength, and have abroad those who still maintain the same cause: who as long as they may be kept from utter falling, your Majesty is sure enough from your mightiest enemies.[62]

The hybrid to which Sidney's letter points – providentialism expressed through chivalric discourse – became a feature of the political culture of the latter part of the reign, as did an ensuing contest over the definition and limits of 'expediency', or 'policy'. It was particularly apparent in debates concerned in whole or in part with the fate of Protestantism in the Netherlands. They too, like debates over the fate of Mary Queen of Scots, like debate over godly reformation, revealed the contingent quality of support for the queen, a loyalty dependent upon her enact-

---

[61] Languet to Sidney, 1580, *Miscellaneous Prose of Sir Philip Sidney*, p. 33. It is striking that Languet refers to Sidney's audience for the *Letter* as 'fair minded men', despite its character as a letter specifically addressed to Elizabeth. As so often during the period, once political pressures lead to a recourse to print, the contest being waged has less to do with persuading the queen to reconsider any particular decision than with mobilising public opinion to constrain her in the exercise of her monarchical will. For the role of 'public opinion' in Elizabeth's reign see Patrick Collinson, *'De Republica Anglorum': Or, History with the Politics Put Back*, Inaugural Lecture, November 1989 (Cambridge, 1990), pp. 26–8.   [62] *A Letter to Queen Elizabeth*, p. 56.

ment of her godly role. Or, as Sidney put it in a letter to Sir Francis Walsingham otherwise concerned with household matters relating to the Netherlands campaign:

If her Majesty were the fountain I would fear considering what I daily find that we should wax dry, but she is but a means whom God useth and I know not whether I am deceived but I am faithfully persuaded that if she should withdraw her self other springs would rise to help this action. For methinks I see the great work indeed in hand, against the abusers of the world, wherein it is no greater fault to have confidence in man's power, then it is too hastily to despair of God's work.[63]

THE QUEEN AND THE REGIME

What, then, of the queen? How did she negotiate the role of 'Deborah'? It is impossible to penetrate very far into the personal beliefs of this most private queen. The difficulty is compounded by the intimate, and contested, relationship between Elizabeth and what Wallace MacCaffrey has usefully termed 'the regime': councillors who were partisans of the new queen but even more immediately of common political purposes to which her Protestant identity was central.[64] It seems unexceptionable to conclude that she was like her father in her reading of the relationship between theological conviction and monarchical authority, and that her earlier life prepared her to be 'Deborah' (that is, a Protestant princess) – with an eye always to expediency, or *realpolitik*. For, as John Knox reassured her in a letter at her accession in 1559, it was 'for fear of her life, that [she] declined from religion, and bowed to idolatry' during her sister's reign.[65] That she had 'bowed' was indisputable – but then, too, in one view of the matter, so had everyone who had not fled into exile at Mary's accession, including prominent members of the Privy Council. Whether she had 'bowed' voluntarily was anybody's guess; on this occasion Knox was ostentatiously giving her the benefit of the doubt. At points, as is well known, she claimed that she acknowledged Christ's real presence in the sacrament, and prayed to the Virgin Mary from time to time.

Of necessity, I think, Elizabeth accepted the 'prodigious' or providential character of her reign, and therefore presented herself as an instrument of His will, as in her speech to the House of Lords at her accession:

[63] Sidney to Sir Francis Walsingham in *The Complete Works of Sir Philip Sidney*, ed. Albert Feuillerat (Cambridge, 1968), vol. III, p. 167.
[64] Wallace MacCaffrey, *The Shaping of the Elizabethan Regime*, p. 39.
[65] John Strype, *Annals*, vol. I.i, pp. 2–3.

My Lords, the law of nature moveth me to sorrow for my sister: the burden that is fallen upon me maketh me amazed; and yet, considering I am God's creature, ordained to obey his appointment, I will thereto yield, requiring from the bottom of my heart, that I may have assistance of his grace, to be the minister of his heavenly will in this office now committed to me. And, as I am but one body naturally considered, though, by his permission, a body politic to govern; so I shall require you all, my Lords, two bodies (chiefly you of the nobility, every one in his degree and power) to be assistant to me; that I with my ruling and you with your service, may make a good account to almighty God, and leave some comfort to our posterity in earth. I mean to direct all mine actions by good advice and counsel.[66]

Implicit in this speech – as in many others she made over her reign – was a *quid pro quo*: she will be 'Deborah', eschewing her own will to serve as God's instrument, if (implicitly when) her subjects perform the analogous move by enacting the absolute obedience to her stewardship enjoined by divine example. She also employed another strategy in this speech, one discernible in many of her public and semi-public utterances over the reign, and destined to politicise notions of 'nobility' and 'aristocracy' especially in the latter part of the reign. To make common cause with the nobility she alludes to their participation in the mysteries of government: 'so I shall require you all, my Lords, two bodies (chiefly you of the nobility . . .)'. She reminds them, in other words, that they enjoy a worldly status – at one level one that is in the keeping of kings – and of her and their shared identity as members of the noble caste.

Her most striking appeals to providence, coupled with a recognition of the 'prodigious' nature of her rule, occurred at points when she faced pressure from the political nation, mobilised in parliament and without, which threatened to override her monarchical authority. One such moment produced her well-known closing speech to the parliament of 1576. She followed the Lord Keeper who, in his closing speech on her behalf, had extolled the providential character of God's protection of England under her reign thus far:

I cannot attribute these haps and good success to my device without detracting much from the divine providence [she began modestly], nor challenge to my private commendation what is only due to his eternal glory: my sex permits it not . . . And as for those rare and special benefits [described by the Lord Keeper] which have many years followed and accompanied my happy reign, I

---

[66] Sir John Harington, '*Nugae Antiquae*': *Being a Miscellaneous Collection of Original Papers in Prose and Verse: Written in the Reigns of Henry VIII, Queen Mary, Elizabeth, King James, etc.*, ed. Henry Harington (London, 1775), pp. 114–15.

attribute to God alone the prince of rule, and count myself no better then his hand maid.[67]

She went on to absolve herself of the imputation of expediency, or 'policy'. She argued that her refusal to accede to their demands over marriage and the succession symbolised, had they the 'grace' to see it, her unique status as God's instrument – with the implication that it is they, not she, who are 'worldly' (and potentially ungodly):

If policy had been preferred before truth, would I, trow you, even at the first beginning of my rule, have turned upside-down so great affairs, or entered into tossing of the greatest waves and billows of the world that might, if I had sought my ease, have harboured and cast anchor in most seeming security? It cannot be denied but worldly wisdom rather bade me knit and match myself in league and fast alliance with great princes to purchase friends on every side by worldly means . . . Was I to seek that by man's outward judgement this must needs be thought the safest course? No, I can never grant my self so simple as not to see what all men's eyes discovered. But all these means of leagues, alliances and foreign strengths I quite forsook, and gave myself to seek for truth without respect, reposing my chief stay in God's most mighty grace.[68]

This kind of utterance provides an instance when we see Elizabeth and the regime conjoined – this time through the Lord Keeper's speech, which both framed and prepared the ground for Elizabeth's.[69] But the appeal to providence as enacted exclusively through the mediation of the queen also featured regularly in ministerial pronouncements throughout the reign.[70] The intimation that Elizabeth enjoyed a visionary, if not a prophetic, capacity in her role as queen of England enabled the queen and her ministers to point to rather than insist upon her imperial status. It therefore promoted Elizabeth's monarchical authority. Illuminated by a special relationship with God, she could turn a deaf ear to counsel proffered by men, regardless of its source – and move (as the regime did) in the direction of Catholic iconography to do so.[71]

It was, however, a risky strategy. If it went too far, or was misread by

[67] *Proceedings*, p. 472.
[68] Ibid., p. 472. The strategy she employs here – the list of rhetorical questions – is a very common feature of her recorded speeches.
[69] We know that these speeches were carefully scripted by Burghley, and quite possibly in conjunction with Elizabeth. We know too that speakers occasionally departed from the set text to inform the queen more explicitly of her duty. See, for example, the occasion in 1585 when Speaker Puckering extemporised in this way, in Strype, *Annals*, vol. iii.i, pp. 427–32 and vol. iii.ii, pp. 356–61.
[70] See, for example, the treatise written by either Sir Thomas Smith or William Cecil on the occasion of the 1569 Northern Rebellion, in John Strype, *Annals*, vol. i.ii, pp. 343–4, and William Cecil, *Execution of Justice*, p. 493.
[71] Helen Hackett describes this process in *Virgin Mother, Maiden Queen*.

committed subjects, she stood in danger once more of appearing to imperil England's Protestant destiny and hence losing her legitimacy. That these are the terms in which her public stance was understood, by her and her councillors, is suggested, I think, by the following episode, recounted in a letter from Richard Topcliffe to the Earl of Shrewsbury dated 30 August 1578. Topcliffe, government agent and implacable persecutor of papists, wrote to inform Shrewsbury about Elizabeth's progress in Suffolk and Norfolk. Its most notable feature, in his view, was that 'her Majesty has served God with great zeal and comfortable examples; for by her **Counsel** two notorious Papists . . . were both committed [to prison] . . . and seven more gentlemen . . . were committed to several houses in Norwich as prisoners, . . . for badness of belief'.[72]

How did this glorious outcome transpire? 'Her Majesty' (whose travel arrangements were meticulously supervised and planned in advance with reference to her own wishes by officers of the court) 'by some means I know not was lodged at [Rockwood's] house'. She, seemingly unaware of his religious identity, treated him with affable condescension: when brought into Elizabeth's presence 'her excellent Majesty gave [him] ordinary thanks for his bad house, and her fair hand to kiss'. But at this point, the balance threatening to overtip (Topcliffe informed Shrewsbury that the queen's condescension 'was braved at'), queen and council looked to their Protestant laurels and made a highly visible statement concerning their orthodoxy. First the Lord Chamberlain weighed in, declaring that Topcliffe was 'unfit to accompany any Christian person', let alone the queen, and expelling him from the court to await imprisonment. Then a piece of theatre was enacted, deeply gratifying to Topcliffe and presumably many others, in which Elizabeth herself took the leading role:

And, to decipher the Gentleman to the full; a piece of plate being missed in the Court, and searched for in his hay house, in the hay rick such an image of our Lady was there found, as for greatness, for gayness and workmanship, I did never see a match; . . . Her Majesty commanded it to the fire, which in her sight by the country folks was quickly done, to her content, and unspeakable

---

[72] John Nichols, *The Progresses and Public Processions of Queen Elizabrth*, 3 vols. (London, 1823), vol. II, pp. 216–17. Edmund Lodge (*Illustrations of British History, Biography, and Manners, in the Reigns of Henry VIII, Edward VI, Mary, Elizabeth and James I*, 3 vols. (London, 1791), vol. II, p. 120) modernises the original 'cownsaille' as 'council' – a plausible reading and an instructive instance of the ambiguity of both the term and the relationship of the queen and her councillors. See Helen Hackett, *Virgin Mother, Maiden Queen*, pp. 1–3.

joy of every one, but some one or two who had sucked of the idol's poisoned milk.

And finally, the most weighty evidence of the government's commitment to religious reformation was displayed: the mouths of some godly ministers were unstopped, their licences to preach restored. This obeisance to the Word, was, according to Topcliffe, received with even greater joy than the ritual of iconoclasm which preceded it – significantly (for the implied taint) even among 'most of the court'.[73]

Was Elizabeth perceived, by some of her subjects, as a crypto-Catholic (perhaps 'closet' would be a more resonant term, remembering Stubbs's assurance that her Protestant subjects watched over her even when she was in her 'secret, most separate closet of prayer')? Elizabeth's rooted distrust of Protestant zeal certainly gave scope for speculation. As early as 1565 Beza wrote to Bullinger '[t]hat by the accounts of the ecclesiastical affairs of England . . . popery was not cast out of England, but rather transferred to the queen's majesty; and that nothing else was drove at, than that what had been lately taken away, might be by little and little restored again'.[74] The more heated the political temperature became, as the reign progressed, the more likely it was that her actions would be read as evidence of deficiencies in religion, either in favouring policy' over religion or with regard to what came to be referred to as her 'irreligion' – and that these deficiencies would be charged to both the queen and her councillors. In the parliamentary debates of 1571, for example, one anonymous speaker aspersed the queen's Protestantism and simultaneously attacked the Privy Council for a lukewarm reformation. He thought the name 'papist' should be included among the words of slander constituting treason in the bill under debate, alleging 'that some say in these days there are who do not spare to say her Majesty is of another religion than is published, and that it is the sole doing of her councillors whereby the doctrine (**in sort as it is**) is thus published, and not hers'.[75] This was a powerful indictment of Deborah as heterodox if not heretic which came close to suggesting that England's status as a godly nation was imperilled by the queen herself, and by councillors who adulterated their commitment to enacting God's will with deference to the queen's. How did councillors respond? How did they position themselves with regard to the crown, the queen and the Protestant nation?

---

[73] John Nichols, *Progresses*, vol. II, pp. 216–17.
[74] John Strype, *Annals*, vol. I.ii, p. 171.   [75] *Proceedings*, p. 216, my emphasis.

THE INCORPORATED CROWN: PRIVY COUNCILLORS AND
THE QUEEN

There is no doubt that the great majority of Elizabeth's Privy Council-lors – men like Sir Nicholas Bacon, Francis Russell (second Earl of Bedford), Sir Francis Knollys, and later Sir Walter Mildmay, Sir Ralph Sadler, Sir Thomas Smith, Thomas Wilson, Sir Henry Sidney; and pre-eminently Sir Francis Walsingham, the Earl of Leicester and Cecil himself – shared the ideological convictions voiced by men like Sidney, Stubbs and Wentworth.[76] These convictions continued to inform Eliza-bethan governance, although in complicated ways given councillors' understanding of their position as servants of the queen as well as of the crown, and their commitment to a hierarchical, historically legitimated realm as well as to a godly nation. Moreover, they were, and remained, united in their conviction that, in the last resort, religious reformation depended on a political stability to which her and their maintenance of power were essential; a conviction that gives continuity to the politics of the reign in its entirety. To Thomas Norton's statement that he had 'no dealing with the queen but as with the image of God' we should pair Burghley's deathbed adjuration to his son Robert Cecil – 'Serve God by serving of the Queen' – bearing in mind how circumstances had changed in the twenty years that separated them.[77]

These conflicting pressures institutionalised a novel dynamic between the Privy Council and its various constituencies, including the queen as well as advocates of ongoing religious reform both within and outside the establishment. Councillors were well aware of the destabilising potential of Protestant zeal in the particular context of Elizabeth's reign, from the iconoclastic outbreaks that arose shortly after her accession, if not before. The Catholic merchant Sir Richard Shelly, writing to Burghley after the burning of the cross at Smithfield in 1559 (an event that determined him, like many others, to stay abroad), commented that news of the event

made me call to remembrance that which I heard your lordship say to the old lord Paget . . . to whom, pretending that queen Mary . . . had returned the realm wholly catholic, your lordship answered, 'My lord, you are therein so far deceived, that I fear rather an inundation of the contrary part, so universal a boiling and bubbling I see of stomachs that cannot yet digest the crudity of that time'.[78]

---

[76] Blair Worden, *The Sound of Virtue*. For Burghley, see Stephen Alford, 'William Cecil and the British Succession Crisis of the 1560s', Ph.D. Dissertation, University of St Andrews (1996), pp. 17–23. John Guy, *Tudor England*, pp. 250–89.   [77] J. E. Neale, *Queen Elizabeth I*, p. 350.
[78] John Strype, *Annals*, vol. i.i, p. 261.

And Burghley is forever expressing his fears of the consequences of reforming zeal unalloyed by a due regard for hierarchy and order to members of the ecclesiastical hierarchy, who ought, he feels, to set an example in this regard. (This is a marked feature of the controversy over prophesyings which occurred during the 1570s and led to the suspension of the Archbishop of Canterbury, Edmund Grindal, for his failure to enact the queen's will in the matter.) In Burghley's view, their role required them to temper their own sense of mission with a sense of occasion – expediency? – in the interests of ensuring the stability of the realm, and to communicate the same equipoise to the 'rash young heads', 'so soon ripe to climb into pulpits', whom they patronised. He was often, as he wrote to the bishop of Ely in 1565, 'inwardly afraid' that without this necessary tutelage these young men would 'content them-selves with no limits, either in the church or in the policy. *Ita delectantur verborum monmachia* [so are they delighted with word-combat]'. The sense that the danger is age related, comprehensible and yet potentially disastrous is striking.[79]

One can understand his concern, given the claims made by those who saw themselves as godly and, by virtue of their office, as standing in a sanctified position with regard to temporal authority, particularly that exercised by a woman debarred from 'speaking in the congregation'. Edward Dering, for example, elevated the 'mouth' over the 'head' in a 1572 parliamentary debate over church reform, asking rhetorically what species of authority the government (the queen and her councillors) thought it could confer on men of God:

[T]he minister is but the mouth of God, in whose person Christ himself is either refused or received . . . Seeing all men are subject before the minister, even as himself also is subject to the words of his mouth, what power, what authority will you give unto him?[80]

The table of questions for his subsequent Star Chamber inquisition displays councillors' fears, in the radicalising 1570s, lest the godly nation prove to be one in which there was no room for the queen (or more tellingly for monarchical authority):

XVII. Whether the queen of England hath authority over the ecclesiastical state, and in ecclesiastical matters, as well as over the civil state.

XVIII. Whether the queen of England be chief governor, under Christ, over the whole church and state ecclesiastical in this realm, or but a member of the

---

[79] Ibid., vol. I.ii, p. 158. [80] Ibid., vol. II.i, 404–5.

same. And whether the church of England may be established without a
magistrate.

XIX. Whether the queen of England be bound to observe the judicial laws of
Moses concerning the punishing and remitting of criminal offences.

XX. Whether the queen of England may of herself, and of her own authority, assign and appoint civil officers, or no.[81]

The Privy Council undoubtedly made headway, at least within the
ranks of the ecclesiastical establishment, in insisting that conformity to
authority – in the last instance that of the Privy Council itself – was, as
the bishop of Durham wrote to Burghley in the wake of Grindal's
suspension, 'godly and expedient for the time', if not perhaps obviously
that building of the temple seemingly enjoined on England by Elizabeth's providential accession.[82] But this was a difficult stance, even with
the threat of social disorder attached to the project of thorough reformation, always likely to be read as evidence of their declension from the
godly status that helped justify obedience to a female ruler 'holding', in
Burghley's words, 'the very place of a king'. Mightn't it prove to be the
case that Privy Councillors fought the good fight – but for 'worldly'
motives, whether for personal advancement or solely to secure the
regime? If so, their position compromised the nation's soul and could
not constitute grounds for loyalty to the monarch or to the regime.

Privy Councillors, then, occupied a paradoxical position in the godly
nation inaugurated with Elizabeth's accession. They confronted the
need to defuse Protestant zeal in order to protect the Protestant nation;
the need to admit claims of expediency – not least the necessity to
'manage' the queen – in order to forward godly ends; and the need to
insist upon and enhance the authority of the magistrate, including the
queen, to preserve the imperial crown and accomplish the rebuilding of
the temple. As they pursued this agenda, councillors' actions were read
by other godly Englishmen as to whether they advanced the common
weal or fell short through implication in the coils of worldliness. The
result was a critique of the Privy Council, and especially of the queen's
chief minister William Cecil, Lord Burghley. Analogous to the critique
directed at Elizabeth, it differed pre-eminently in the assumption that, if
her role was to serve as an instrument for God's grace, theirs was to
mould the instrument to be receptive to His will – with the strong
implication that this would be an uphill battle.

These features appear in a letter to Burghley from the bishop of Ely,
Richard Cox, concerning the queen's determination to suppress proph-

---

[81] Ibid., vol. II.i, p. 417.   [82] Ibid., vol. II.ii, pp. 110–11.

esyings and to make her Archbishop of Canterbury acknowledge the supremacy of her will in matters pertaining to the conduct of her church. Cox begins by carefully distinguishing the kind of authority at issue in Grindal's suspension in terms that intimate his commitment to 'public authority' (pronouncements advanced by the queen and her councillors): 'I understand . . . the matter is touching a *conference*, which hath been used, or rather abused, and not by public authority established.' His loyalty declared, he proceeded to his main message: Burghley, like Cox himself, has laboured in God's vineyards in fulfilling his office according to God's will – 'both you and I (God's blessed name be glorified) have constantly, through many bruits, *a dextris et a sinistris*, persevered: and you especially.' Now is not the time to allow Elizabeth's 'will to stand for a reason', in Peter Wentworth's telling phrase. Burghley knows what needs to be done, in this as in other contexts where God's will is manifest, and he well knows the perils of delay and procrastination. Cox adjures Burghley to '*esto fortis, et viriliter age*' [be strong, and perform the part of a man], in bringing Elizabeth to countermand the action against her godly archbishop and the 'needful edifying' of her people that the exercises represented. To fall short in such an important matter would mean that expediency had triumphed over godliness.

In 1579, Parson Prowde, of Burton upon Dunsmore, lectured Burghley in similar terms – or perhaps more accurately analogous terms, from the point of view of the godly populating the nation, not the court. He wrote to alert Burghley to the disquiet felt by 'many' in the area about the regime's failures in godliness. Clearly these are views he shared, despite his recourse to the status of reporter ('some say') when the critique cut particularly near to the bone.[83] His letter is fascinating evidence of the world of Elizabethan politics, in which a lowly parish priest could take it upon himself to lecture the greatest in the land about their and the queen's spiritual deficiencies and their likely political consequences.

Prowde begins by reassuring Burghley that he recognises him as a godly man: 'Your bringing up in true religion; things published by you to the comfort of the brethren . . . hath made me ever to love and reverence you with my heart.'[84] Notwithstanding this promising beginning, however, Burghley has been tainted by his decision to continue in office during Mary Tudor's reign: 'But afterwards the report was, that

[83] Ibid., vol. II.ii, pp. 662–5.
[84] The next five quotations follow each other directly in the letter.

ye did openly revolt from your religion, and fell to go to idolatrous servants: and so, by your dead doings therein, consented to all the blood of the prophets and martyrs that was shed unrighteously in Manasse's [Mary Tudor's] days.' Nor did he make amends in Josiah's days.[85]

And now in Josiah's days ye came not to God's persecuted church, that he builded, maintained and defended . . . against the force of the wolf and the lion; which was not corrupted, nor polluted with idolatry; wherein was the word of God purely preached, and sacraments godly ministered, and discipline without partiality executed: and hearty prayer to God was made for God's afflicted church.

Burghley and his fellows 'came not to God's persecuted church', literally or metaphorically. Clinging to office during Mary's reign they subsequently enacted (at Elizabeth's instigation) an inadequate reformation of the English church:

By the which I persuade my self, and for the suffering of the just of that church, that both ye, and others now in great authority, and the whole land beside, fared the better. Ye came not I say, I say thither (*viz* to Frankfort, Strasburgh, Zurich, etc.) as others did, that were in your faith; confessing there your open falls and sinning in idolatry; asking mercy of God for it, and purposing, by his grace, never hereafter to fall into sin again. And so to have entered into a new league and covenant with him, purposing fully in your heart, by his grace, never to do ill again. But being rid out of idolatrous bondage, it is said and reported, ye gave your consent to the building of God's house or church; that was not builded in all points so perfectly, as the other that he himself had builded, without any lawful or godly magistrate; and left in those days for an example, and I suppose, for you to have followed.

Since then, and as a consequence, things have gone from bad to worse, as Burghley and others in authority have followed the logic of the religious settlement effected in 1559 (and the queen's will) rather than the dictates of God (or the example of pure reformed churches). Their actions, their 'dead doings', threaten the godly nation and suggest that they have bowed to the demands of expediency, in this case through attempting to enact reformation with one eye on the queen's will. Interestingly he seems to take Elizabeth's intransigence as a given,

[85] Interestingly, Prowde does not identify Elizabeth with Josiah – a common identification, used in part as didactic strategy. Instead, for Prowde 'Josiah's days' denote a stage in the progress of the True Church, made available presumably through the godly reformation occurring in Europe from the mid-sixteenth century – a process that involved neither the queen nor her chief ministers. See Margaret Aston, *The King's Bedpost*, pp. 32–4, and, for the influence of the idea of the True Church in Elizabethan England, G. J. R. Parry, *A Protestant Vision*.

implying that Burghley, not Elizabeth, is the party responsible for this dangerous state of affairs:

> Also it is said, that you from time to time, fearing to exasperate the prince, and to make her worse in religion, have spared your plainness, and have not dealt with her so plainly from time to time, as your knowledge hath required, both touching God's church, her own preservation, and the safety and profit of the commonwealth.

Prowde equates godliness with a certain quality of forthrightness in terms of counsel, in effect urging Burghley, as Cox had done, to '*esto fortis, et viriliter age*':

> For he that dealeth plainly with her shall find more favour in the end, than he that flattereth. And when can you do God, your prince, country, and posterity, better service than now, in being courageous in all those good matters that ye know full well may serve these turns; although it should cost you your life?

Moreover Burghley himself appears to have accepted this reading of his role as councillor of the queen. In 1585, he wrote to an anonymous friend complaining of slanders against him that impugned his pursuit of the common weal. It is his mode of action, he claims, rather than his programme, that makes it look as though he is a temporiser. Despite such attacks his conscience is clear – not least because he can assure himself that he has, unlike those proffering 'lukewarm counsel', even offended the queen with his zeal:

> If in any of these I may be proved to have been behind, or slower than any, in a discrete manner, as becometh a servant and a councillor; I will yield myself worthy of perpetual reproach . . . I have dealt with her majesty often, **to the offending of her majesty with my earnestness.**[86]

Finally, in 1584 Thomas Sampson, Marian exile and dean of Christ Church, Oxford, before his deprivation in 1565, assumed a distinction between the queen and her councillors in the matter of religious reformation that made explicit the subtext of 'Supreme Head' as it had been promoted by the regime. In an appeal to the political nation entitled *A supplication*, Sampson advocated the formation of '*A holy league* with the living God'.[87] He argued that past experience – Mary Tudor's reign in particular – showed that laws, no matter how good in themselves, were finally dependent on the variable will of the monarch. What was

[86] John Strype, *Annals*, vol. III.ii, pp. 383–5; my emphasis.
[87] Thomas Sampson, *A supplication, to be exhibited to our sovereign lady, queen Elizabeth, to the honourable lords of her most honourable privy-council, and to the high court of parliament* (1584), given by John Strype, *Annals*, vol. III.ii, pp. 285–94, and, like Prowde's letter, found among Burghley's papers.

required was an 'oath' to sustain a holy league 'after the godly examples of king Asa, of king Josiah, and other godly rulers'; a means by which godly men could secure their destiny in a political arrangement separable from the person of the monarch, should he (or she) prove ungodly. Tellingly he assumes that the 'rulers' (a term that does not include the queen) will be directly responsible for securing this outcome. Is it because his concern is what will happen after the queen's death (a consideration implicit in debates over the Bond of Association as well)?[88] Or does it derive from his perception of Elizabeth as reprobate, of her councillors as therefore standing in a relationship of superior spiritual authority to their 'Supreme Governor', the queen? (My added emphases highlight the distinction he maintains between 'queen' and 'rulers'):

Therefore we humbly desire **our rulers, which are godly**, to devise how by all godly means we all and every one of us may be bound to the true religion of God now received and professed among us . . . It hath been the dutiful and necessary care of **them which do bear rule over us, under the queen's highness**, to prevent all such dangerous practices as have been attempted against her royal person, state, this church, and common wealth. And it hath pleased God to bless their labours so, that all these do stand safe and firm this day. Now we humbly beseech **our queen and the rulers** that she and they will together consult and devise how the kingdom of Christ Jesus may remain fully established among us and our posterity ever . . . [I]t is high time that the **godly rulers** do themselves yield their obedience herein to the Lord God Almighty; and also do both require and exact the same of us, who are the people of God committed to their government and direction.[89]

Significantly, in view of the substance of the debate over supreme headship in the context of female rule, Sampson adduces as one of his articles for the enactment of the holy league the necessity for subordinating the queen's will, even in temporal matters, to God's dictates:

XXV . . . That we the people may both understand what it is that the majesty of God doth command, and what it is that the queen by royal authority doth command; and so to be taught in true understanding, to give Caesar the things which are Caesar's, and to give to God those things which are God's. That we may religiously do that which God commandeth, and also dutifully that which **in this behalf** the queen commandeth.[90]

Here, then, is evidence of one major consequence of Elizabeth's reign: the notion that in significant ways, and especially with regard to for-

[88] Patrick Collinson, '*De Republica Anglorum*', p. 24.
[89] Thomas Sampson, *A Supplication*, pp. 285 and 287.   [90] Ibid., p. 294, my emphasis.

warding reformation, the 'imperial crown' signals a corporate identity and a direct political relationship between godly men in office and their peers abroad in the nation. And it is impossible to ignore the similarities between Sampson's utterance and the terms and language of the Bond of Association, proposed by Burghley and Walsingham in the same year to secure the Protestant nation in the face of the queen's seemingly wilful disregard of the consequences for the nation of her refusal to accede to the execution of Mary Queen of Scots. The congruence provides compelling evidence for the extension of this ideological configuration across the political nation which was so marked a feature of Elizabeth's reign.

CONCLUSION

To identify the 'lords of the Privy Council and the high court of Parliament' as godly and hence charged with 'rule' as explicitly as Sampson did in 1585 reveals important features of Elizabethan political culture. First, it alerts us to the ongoing tension between the two poles of 'queen' and 'regime' – what Patrick Collinson calls the 'pantomime horse' of the queen and her ministers – which continued throughout the reign and, in important ways, defined it.[91] It also points to its concomitant: the politicisation of the godly nation which occurred as men acted to further reformation in a newly conceived role as citizens, of the commonweal and of the kingdom of Christ. Both developments highlight the enduring problematic of Elizabeth's reign: the reconceptualisation of the imperial crown in the context of female rule. What form was this entity to take, how could it be conceived, given a cultural context that privileged the body of the king in relation to the body of subjects and the male body in relation to the female – and read both hierarchies as God-ordained, interdependent propositions that provided the foundation for social order?[92]

The explicitness of Sampson's distinction between the queen and 'the rulers' in the matter of reformation also signals the end-point of a political dynamic that evolved over the period 1558 to 1585. From Elizabeth's accession until the mid-1580s the queen and important elements of the Protestant political nation constructed and negotiated the identification of the queen as a providentially ordained ruler in order

---

[91] Patrick Collinson, 'The Monarchical Republic of Queen Elizabeth I', *Bulletin of the John Rylands University Library of Manchester* 69, no. 2 (1986–7), pp. 394–424, p. 402.
[92] Louis Montrose, 'The Elizabethan Subject and the Spenserian Text', pp. 307–8.

to justify female rule and secure the imperial crown. An important element of that identification centred on a reading of Elizabeth as ambiguously 'Supreme Head' and 'Supreme Governor' of the Church of England – an ambiguity that eventually focused attention on, and politicised, the notion of 'governorship'. By the 1580s it was imbued with intimations of expediency that, in a polarising religious climate, called into question the good faith, simultaneously political and spiritual, of those who advanced it, queen and councillors. Before his execution for treason in 1584, William Parry, a civil lawyer and convert to Catholicism, told the queen to 'forget the glorious title of *supreme governor*. Trouble none that refuseth to swear it; for that cannot agree with your sex. Luther and Calvin did not allow it. The puritans smile at it, and the Catholic world doth condemn it.'[93] This sleight of hand also inevitably advanced the notion of an elect nation in which there would be no king but Christ. Protestants marginalised and persecuted as 'sectaries' in the wake of the Marprelate controversy of 1588, for example, were charged with asserting 'that there is no head or supreme governor of the church of God but Christ; and that the queen hath no authority to appoint ministers in the church, nor to set down any government for the church, which is not directly commanded in God's word' – plausibly their platform, and certainly, by that point, the government's worst-case scenario.[94]

Rule by a woman at this stage of England's reformation history therefore led to a reconceptualisation of monarchical authority, one that simultaneously exacerbated fears of social instability, even anarchy. In the longer run, and as a result, it produced both an aristocratic reaction and a sectarian politics. By the end of the sixteenth century these developments allowed for the naturalisation in England of 'absolutist theories' of kingship, including those advanced by Jean Bodin, as a means of preserving the 'mixed monarchy' invoked by apologists at Elizabeth's accession. There was therefore signal continuity over the reign, the faultline of the events of the mid-1580s notwithstanding. Throughout the reign, players from across the ranks of the political nation – queen and commonwealth – attempted to negotiate issues of monarchical authority inseparable from a reformation context and the

[93] John Strype, *Annals*, vol. III.i, p. 339.
[94] The wording of Sir John Puckering, the queen's sergeant at law and one of the commissioners appointed to investigate these sects. Puckering also states that these sectaries maintain that the Church of England and all its members are false prophets, 'for that . . . they . . . do teach us, that the state of the realm of England is the true church, (which they deny)'. John Strype, *Annals*, vol. III.ii, pp. 102–4.

fact of female rule; their strategies largely defined Elizabethan political culture. In what follows I trace the interaction between ideological conviction and political necessity that shaped the Elizabethan body politic and determined relations between the queen and her subjects from 1558 until the mid-1580s. In the next chapter I begin by moving back to the beginning of the reign to consider the 'problem of counsel' – a feature of political discourse from the establishment of the imperial crown – as it was addressed and altered in the context of female rule.

CHAPTER 2

Announcing the godly common weal: Knox, Aylmer and the parameters of counsel

> I wrote how that me semyd no woman ought soveranly or su-
> premely to reygne upon man.
>
> Sir John Fortescue, Works (1475)[1]

In Elizabeth's reign, and in no small measure because of the influential reading of her accession as providential, an understanding of queenship and English history developed which promoted the characteristic configuration of Elizabethan politics that I described in chapter 1: counsel insistently proposed to, and at points imposed upon, the female ruler by her godly male subjects.[2] In a society that defined women as spiritually deficient and lacking the capacity for political virtue – a view given weight and immediacy by the failures of Mary I's reign – recourse to providentialism constituted a powerful means of legitimating a female holder of the imperial crown.[3] However, reading Elizabeth as 'Deborah' and her 'government' as providentially ordained to secure Protestantism, at home and abroad, inevitably gave rise to political tensions during the reign. It did so because of the ambiguity of the concept of 'prophecy' and the linkage between prophecy and God's expressed will on the one hand, and ongoing fears about the destabilising social consequences of religious reformation on the other. For, in the context of female rule, a providential reading of English history promoted the claims to political consideration of male constituents of the body politic who could claim to

---

[1] Sir John Fortescue, *Works*, 1869 edn., p. 533; cited under the entry 'sovereignly' in the *Oxford English Dictionary* (Oxford, 1971), vol. II, p. 2935.

[2] Throughout the book I use 'councillors' to refer to Elizabeth's official advisers, normally members of the Privy Council, and 'counsellors' to refer to that wider constituency who saw themselves as called upon – by birth, position or vocation – to advise the queen.

[3] The same strategy was adopted in Mary I's reign, tailored to a Catholic reading of English national history and imperial identity. See Cardinal Pole's 1554 speech to parliament in John Foxe, *Acts and Monuments of these latter and perilous days*, ed. George Townsend, 8 vols. (London, 1843–9), vol. VI, pp. 568–71, esp. pp. 570–1.

be 'elders' or 'prophets', hence able to guide the queen and serve, in effect, as interpreters of God's will in part because of their gender.

Another dimension of the 'problem of counsel' in relation to female rule also needs to be borne in mind. This one is suggested by Sir John Fortescue's assumption (given in the chapter epigraph) that sovereignty or supreme rule was 'naturally' a male competence. Expressed through a contemporary commonplace concerning relations between men and women (as such assumptions frequently were), Fortescue's statement points to the intimate connection between gender and issues of regality in the early modern period.[4] The connection itself is unsurprising in an age dominated, in England as in other parts of Europe, by disputes concerning the nature and limits of authority and obedience in matters temporal and spiritual. In these debates the conviction that women lacked political capacity 'by nature' was frequently articulated as a corollary of, indeed as a starting point for, the systematic analyses of political life that featured so prominently in humanist and reformation discourse.[5] This conviction was deeply entrenched. Throughout Europe its articulation led, as Donald Kelley has shown, to the gendering as male of such key terms of political identity and debate as 'virtue', 'headship', and 'majesty', or sovereignty.[6]

In England, the concentration on gender, reformation and imperial identity thus brought to the fore the problem of a being who is inferior to men in her capacity for reason and possessing '*consilium invalidum et instabile*' because of her gender ruling, in Sir John Fortescue's influential formulation, *regaliter et politice*: as mystical head of the body politic which is the imperial realm.[7] It simultaneously proposed a new species of

[4] Merry E. Weisner, *Women and Gender in Early Modern Europe* (Cambridge, 1993), pp. 241, 251–2; Ian Maclean, *The Renaissance Notion of Woman* (Cambridge, 1980); Howard Nenner, *The Right to be King: The Succession to the Crown of England 1603–1714* (New York, 1995), chs. 1–2. For the French case see Sarah Hanley, 'The Monarchic State in Early Modern France: Marital Regime Government and Male Right' in *Politics, Ideology and the Law in Early Modern Europe: Essays in Honor of J. H. M. Salmon*, ed. Adrianna E. Bakos (New York, 1994), pp. 107–26.
[5] R. W. K. Hinton, 'Husbands, Fathers and Conquerors', *Political Studies* 15, no. 3 (1967), pp. 291–300 and 16, no. 1 (1968), pp. 55–67; Gordon J. Schochet, *Patriarchalism in Political Thought: The Authoritarian Family and Political Speculation and Attitudes Especially in Seventeenth-Century England* (Oxford, 1975), chs. 1–3; Constance Jordan, *Renaissance Feminism: Literary Texts and Political Models* (Ithaca, N.Y., 1990).
[6] Donald R. Kelley, *The Beginning of Ideology* (Cambridge, 1981), p. 74. See also his article on 'Elizabethan Political Thought', in *The Varieties of British Political Thought, 1500–1800*, ed. J. G. A. Pocock (Cambridge, 1993), pp. 47–79.
[7] J. G. A. Pocock, 'A Discourse of Sovereignty: Observations on the Work in Progress' in *Political Discourse in Early Modern Britain*, ed. Nicholas Phillipson and Quentin Skinner (Cambridge, 1993), pp. 377–428, pp. 381, 387; John Guy, 'The Henrician Age' in *The Varieties of British Political Thought, 1500–1800*, ed. J. G. A. Pocock (Cambridge, 1993), pp. 13–46, p. 43.

political authority for 'godly men', whether prophets or magistrates, as a solution to the perceived dangers and deficiencies of female rule and hence as a bulwark of order in a reformed commonwealth. This solution was inherently problematical because at one fundamental level, and at a certain political temperature, claims to that status could bypass birth and blood, even breeding and education, to be grounded pre-eminently in the conflation of a male and an English identity: God's Englishmen, chosen successors to His Israelites.

The fusion of these ideological developments thus politicised notions of 'counsel' in particular ways during Elizabeth's reign. On the one hand, it inaugurated a debate over the character of monarchical authority in 'Israel'. It simultaneously rehearsed as a continuing subtext Elizabeth's personal claims, as a female ruler, to monarchical prerogative. John Guy has identified two 'languages' of counsel spoken in early modern England, the 'humanist-classical' and the 'feudal-baronial'.[8] To these we must add a third, which developed as a consequence of the vagaries of the Tudor dynastic succession after Henry VIII's death and which dominated Elizabethan political discourse: the language of godly and prophetic counsel. In important ways this language defined the reign. At all points it informed relations between Elizabeth (a woman, albeit a queen) and the English (male) political nation. It is discernible in proposals for Elizabeth's marriage and the terms in which the succession issue was set and addressed, as it is in MPs' claims for 'freedom of speech' in her parliaments. It surfaced in the related debates over the political problem posed by the continued proximity to the English throne of Mary Queen of Scots. Finally, it allowed for and dictated the form of that extraordinary assertion of national virility on behalf of a female ruler, the Bond of Association of 1584. In this chapter I want to investigate the genesis of this mode of discourse and assess its political implications at the outset of the reign.

A logical place to begin is with the debate concerning queenship in the imperial realm that was conducted at the beginning of Elizabeth's reign by John Knox and John Aylmer (later bishop of London), respectively adopting the roles of prophet and godly councillor. Reading Aylmer's apologetical work, *An Harborowe for Faithfull and Trewe Subjects, agaynst the late blowne Blaste, concerninge the Government of Wemen*, in conjunction with Knox's *The First Blast of the Trumpet against the Monstrous Regiment of Women* (and his subsequent explanation of its applicability to Eliza-

---

[8] John Guy, 'The Rhetoric of Counsel in Early Modern England' in *Tudor Political Culture*, ed. Dale Hoak (Cambridge, 1995), pp. 292–310.

beth's reign) illustrates the interaction between prophets and godly councillors that was to recur in various permutations throughout Elizabeth's reign. It also points to the definition of the 'godly nation' as explicitly a male preserve which came into being in the first decades of the reign. For Knox's and Aylmer's tracts do indeed stand in a dialogic relationship, as historians have customarily asserted. But what is striking is the extent to which their views on queenship and obedience represent variations on a theme: how best to 'bridle' a female ruler acknowledged to be in some sense legitimate, and how to define the grounds of that legitimacy.[9]

A QUEEN CALLED BY GOD: JOHN KNOX'S *FIRST BLAST OF THE TRUMPET*

Knox unloosed his *First Blast of the Trumpet against the Monstrous Regiment of Women* in 1558 because, as he informed readers in his preface, 'I am assured that God hath revealed to some in this our age that it is more than a monster in nature, that a woman shall reign and have empire above man.'[10] The evil consequences are, to Knox's mind, apparent on every hand; 'and yet with us all, there is such silence, as if God therewith were nothing offended'. Nor are the reasons for this silence hard to discover. The majority of men are spiritually unenlightened; to them, 'lawful and godly appeareth, whatsoever antiquity hath received'. They combine with 'the wise, politic, and quiet spirits of this world' – those who know the truth but, wedded to worldliness, acquiesce in the continuance of female rule.[11]

Not so John Knox. He is a 'watchman', like the prophet Ezekiel, and similarly placed by God to watch over His people and flock: '[A]nd

[9] I take the term from Claude de Seyssel's influential work *The Monarchy of France* (tr. J. H. Hexter, ed. Donald R. Kelley (New Haven, Conn., 1981)), frequently republished throughout the sixteenth century. Ann Rosalind Jones's discussion of the sexualised meanings of 'conversation', 'intercourse' and '*cortigliana*' in the world of Castiglione's *The Courtier* suggests some of the resonances the term acquired when applied to women exercising authority; 'Nets and Bridles: Early Modern Conduct Books and Sixteenth Century Women's Lyrics' in *The Ideology of Conduct: Essays on Literature and the History of Sexuality*, ed. Nancy Armstrong and Leonard Tennenhouse, (London, 1987), pp. 39–72, pp. 42–8. Helen Hackett pairs Knox with Aylmer, and describes Aylmer as providing 'faint praise of female rule'; *Virgin Mother, Maiden Queen: Elizabeth I and the Cult of the Virgin Mary* (London, 1995), ch. 2, pp. 38–71, p. 49. See also Constance Jordan, 'Woman's Rule in Sixteenth-Century British Political Thought', *Renaissance Quarterly* 40, no. 3 (1987), pp. 421–51.
[10] John Knox, *The First Blast of the Trumpet against the Monstrous Regiment of Women* (1558) in *The Political Writings of John Knox*, ed. Marvin Breslow (Washington, D.C., 1985), p. 38.
[11] John Knox, *The First Blast of the Trumpet against the Monstrous Regiment of Women* (1558), ed. Edward Arber (London, 1878), pp. 5, 9.

watchmen are they whose eyes he [God] doth open, and whose conscience he pricketh to admonish the ungodly.'[12] God, having opened
Knox's eyes to the enormity of female rule, has thereby placed him in
the characteristically Protestant position of having to choose between
following his conscience or bowing to worldly wisdom: 'But seeing that
impossible it is, but that either I shall offend God, daily calling to my
conscience, that I ought to manifest the verity known, or else that I shall
displease the world for doing the same, I have determined to obey God,
notwithstanding that the world shall rage thereat.'[13] He is fortified in his
resolve by the examples of his fellow 'teachers', Isaiah, Jeremiah and
Ezekiel, who have also shared the gift of prophecy.[14]

Secure in his ordination, Knox then states his case in his well-known
opening sentence of *The First Blast*: 'To promote a woman to bear rule,
superiority, dominion, or empire above any realm, nation, or city is
repugnant to nature, contumely to God, a thing most contrarious to his
revealed will and approved ordinance, and finally, it is the subversion of
good order, of all equity and justice.'[15] Although directed in the first
instance against 'our mischievous Maries' (Mary Tudor and Mary
Stuart), 'Jezebels' to whom 'we find ancient realms and nations given
and betrayed', Knox never deviated from his belief in the prodigious
character of women's rule, even after Elizabeth's accession in 1558.[16]
Instead he exempted Elizabeth from his strictures in acknowledgement
of what he perceived as God's will, providentially manifested, and for as
long as His guiding hand self-evidently (to Knox) maintained her in
obedience to His will. In 1559 he wrote to William Cecil, by then
Secretary of State, to affirm both his (conditional) loyalty to Elizabeth's
rule and his rooted conviction that the views he had expressed in *The
First Blast* were, and remained, those of God Himself:

[N]o more do I doubt the truth of my principal proposition [in the *First Blast*],
than that I doubt [that God pronounced against women at the Fall] . . . And yet
if any think me enemy to the person, nor yet to the regiment of her, whom God
hath now promoted, they are utterly deceived in me. For the miraculous work
of God's comforting his afflicted by an infirm vessel, I do reverence . . . More
plainly to speak, if Queen Elizabeth shall confess, so that the extraordinary

---

[12] John Knox, *Blast*, ed. Breslow, p. 42. In what follows I refer to the Breslow edition unless
otherwise indicated.
[13] Ibid., p. 5.   [14] John Knox, *Blast*, p. 42.
[15] John Knox, *Blast*, ed. Arber, p. 9.
[16] Ibid., p. 66. For the Scottish dimension see Jane Dawson, 'The Two John Knoxes: England,
Scotland and the 1558 Tracts', *Journal of Ecclesiastical History* 42, no. 4 (1991), pp. 556–76.

dispensation of God's great mercy maketh that lawful unto her, which both nature and God's law deny to all women; then shall none in England be more willing to maintain her lawful authority than I shall be.[17]

Knox's mode of argument in the *Blast* is interesting, in terms of the wider reformation debate about the nature of kingship to which it is nearly related. Perhaps because he believed that he was making a universal case concerning women's incapacity for rule, he abandoned his usual practice of relying solely on Scriptural evidence. Instead he drew on a conflation of Biblical and Aristotelian arguments, citing 'ethnics' (and in particular Aristotle) liberally and approvingly.[18] In the introduction he advanced the Aristotelian commonplace that women's 'natural' inferiority proves their political incapacity. But this is 'woman' painted as both effeminate and a virago and hence tyrannical on two counts:

For who can deny but it repugneth to nature that the blind shall be appointed to lead and conduct such as do see, that the weak, the sick, and impotent persons, shall nourish and keep the whole and strong, and, finally, that the foolish, mad, and frenetic shall govern the discrete, and give counsel to such as be sober of mind? And such be all women compared unto man in bearing of authority. For their sight in civil regiment is but blindness, their counsel, foolishness, and judgment, frenzy, if it be rightly considered.[19]

Historical evidence proves that their incapacity continues even up to the present day: 'Nature, I say, doth paint them forth to be weak, frail, impatient, feeble and foolish: and experience hath declared them to be inconstant, variable, cruel and lacking the spirit of counsel and regiment.'[20] In the text he mounts a three-part argument, first proving that women's rule is 'contumely to God', next proving that it subverts civil order, and lastly refuting possible counter-cases that he believes 'worldly spirits' might advance.

He begins by demonstrating the many and varied ways God has pronounced universally – in language as distinct to pagans as to Christians, if they would only heed it – that women are subject to men, and are therefore incapable of office-holding on earth. In essence he argues that God has imposed a two-stage prohibition against women exercising political authority. Even before the Fall, even in her 'greatest perfection', woman was, according to the Holy Ghost (speaking through Saint

[17] *The Works of John Knox*, 6 vols., ed. David Laing (Edinburgh, 1846–64), vol. VI, pp. 18–19.
[18] Jane Dawson, 'The Two John Knoxes', p. 563.   [19] John Knox, *Blast*, pp. 42–3.
[20] John Knox, *Blast*, ed. Arber, pp. 11–12.

Paul), 'created to be subject to man', her progenitor.[21] This was a species of voluntary subjection, allowing woman the exercise of 'free will' in acknowledging the claims to obedience of her superior, man. Having proved herself to be incapable of self-government by 'her fall and rebellion committed against God', however, 'there was put upon her a new necessity, and she was made subject to man by the irrevocable sentence of God'. Moreover, God compounded this new condition by weakening still further woman's capacity for self-control, making her will a prey to her lusts:

As God should say: forasmuch as thou hast abused thy former condition, and because thy free will hath brought thy self and mankind into the bondage of Satan, I therefore will bring thee in bondage to man. For where before, thy obedience should have been voluntary, now it shall be by constraint and by necessity: and that because thou has deceived thy man, thou shalt therefore be no longer mistress over thine own appetites, over thine own will nor desires. For in thee there is neither reason nor discretion, which be able to moderate thy affection.[22]

Nor is the subjection solely that of wife to husband, although Knox acknowledges this is how the injunction is often read. Again, the Holy Ghost, speaking through Saint Paul, teaches that the prohibition bars 'all women' from exercising 'all kind of superiority, authority and power over man'. In effect, each and every woman is subject to all men, although marriage allows women to be primarily subject to one man only, who represents, in his role as husband, both God and patriarchal authority.[23] This is the meaning behind Paul's famous adjuration, 'Let women keep silence in the congregation, for it is not permitted to them

[21] At this point Knox seems to be arguing that man was made directly in God's image, woman only indirectly so through union with man, a reading of the Creation myth common enough to explain the English interpretation of the 'heresy of Postellus' referred to above in chapter 1. I am grateful to Pauline Stafford for pointing out that, although Augustine found the issue a difficult one, he seems to have been trying to assert the fundamental spiritual equality of men and women, rather than making the distinction with which later commentators credited him. Knox clearly follows the interpretation conventionally attributed to Augustine, of defining women as made in God's image only in inferior mode: 'Augustine . . . writeth . . . How can woman be the image of God, seeing she is subject to man and hath none authority, neither to teach, neither to be witness, neither to judge, much less to rule or bear empire? To the question how she can be the image of God, he answereth as followeth. Woman, saith he, compared to other creatures is the image of God, for she beareth dominion over them; but compared unto man, she may not be called the image of God'; John Knox, *Blast*, p. 50.

[22] John Knox, *Blast*, ed. Arber, pp. 15–16.

[23] It is instructive that the term 'common woman' in this period, in England as in Germany, denoted a prostitute – a woman, unprotected by the institution of marriage or the church, who belonged to all men. For paradoxes in the meaning and use of the term, see Lyndal Roper, '"The Common Man", "The Common Good", "Common Women": Gender and Meaning in the German Reformation Commune', *Social History* 12, no. 1 (1987), pp. 3–21.

to speak, but to be subject as the law sayeth.'[24] Speaking 'in the congregation' is a type of office containing both civic and sacramental powers, and the injunction to silence bars women from exercising either. God has taken from her 'all power and authority, to speak, to reason, to interpret, or to teach, but principally to rule or to judge in the assembly of men'.[25] Later on Knox makes the twofold application of this stricture even more explicit. Women are prohibited not only from preaching and administering the sacraments (the conventional understanding of 'the administration of God's grace'), but also from its key concomitant in a godly realm, 'the administration of civil justice, by which virtue ought to be maintained and vices punished'.[26]

God 'hath denied unto [woman] the office of a head' from the dawn of human time. This prohibition attained its original force from God's redemptive plan for mankind, in which it is Christ's office to be head of the church (and Christ is, of course, figured as male): 'Women are commanded to be subject to men by the law of nature, because that man is the author or beginner of the woman, for as Christ is the head of the church, so is man of the woman.' And it is man, God's earthly image, who can deputise for Him on earth: 'So that woman by the law of God, and by the interpretation of the Holy Ghost, is utterly forbidden to occupy the place of God in the offices . . . which he hath assigned to man, whom he hath appointed and ordained his lieutenant in earth.'[27] To promote women to bear rule is therefore, as the worthy early church father Chrysostome recognised, unnatural because ungodly; 'for this cause was woman put under thy power (he speaketh to man in general) and thou was pronounced Lord over her, that she should obey thee, and that the head should not follow the feet.'[28]

Knox then moves on to his next ground, to show that the empire of women 'is the subversion of good order, equity and justice' by exploring the 'natural' order ordained by God. Here he proposes and explores the analogy suggested by Chrysostome between the natural body of man and its analogue in civil society, the 'politic or civil body' of the commonwealth. The idea that the natural (male) body corresponded to, hence informed about, the body politic was not new.[29] Sir John Fortescue had used it in his influential *De Laudibus* (printed in 1537) to describe the imperial authority exercised by a king:

---

[24] John Knox, *Blast*, p. 47.   [25] John Knox, *Blast*, ed. Arber, p. 18.   [26] *Blast*, p. 46.
[27] Ibid., pp. 60, 51, 48.   [28] Ibid., p. 52.
[29] See Paul Archambault's discussion of the history of the comparison, in 'The Analogy of the "Body" in Renaissance Political Literature', *Bibliothèque d'Humanisme et Renaissance* 29 (1967), pp. 21–53.

Saint Augustine, in the nineteenth book of the *De civitate Dei*, chapter 23, said that 'A people is a body of men united by consent of law and by community of interest.' But such a people does not deserve to be called a body whilst it is acephalous, i.e., without a head. Because, just as in natural bodies, what is left over after decapitation is not a body, but what we call a trunk, so in bodies politic a community without a head is not by any means a body. Hence Aristotle in the first book of the *Politics* said that whensoever one body is constituted out of many, one will rule, and the others be ruled. So a people wishing to erect itself into a kingdom or any other body politic must always set up one man for the government of all that body, who, by analogy with a kingdom, is, from 'regendo', usually called a king. As in this way the physical body grows out of the embryo, regulated by one head, so the one kingdom issues from the people, and exists as a body mystical, governed by one man as head.[30]

Knox uses the same metaphor, rooted in the same conflation of Augustine and Aristotle, to describe the unnatural body politic that results when the 'king' is a 'queen':

In the natural body of man God has appointed an order, that the head shall occupy the uppermost place. And the head hath he joined with the body, that from it, doth life and motion flow to the rest of the members. In it hath he placed the eye to see, the ear to hear, and the tongue to speak – which offices are appointed to none other member of the body. The rest of the members have every one their own place and office appointed, but none may have neither the place nor office of the head. For who would not judge that body to be a monster where there was no head eminent above the rest, but that the eyes were in the hands, the tongue and mouth beneath in the belly, and the ears in the feet? Men, I say, should not only pronounce this body to be a monster, but, assuredly, they might conclude that such a body could not long endure.[31]

And a headless body politic exists whenever 'in despite of God' a woman is exalted up to reign over men. (Interestingly, and inevitably, given his earlier discussion, his exploration of the metaphor proposes that the 'offices' of the body politic are a male preserve – perhaps unwitting testimony to the fact that queenship forced men writing about the 'body politic' to acknowledge, if not directly engage with, the fact that in some senses it was composed of both men and women.)

Why then do such empires exist? It is because 'worldly spirits' (now the 'subtle wits of carnal men') advance the idea that women may appoint 'lieutenants, deputies and judges substitute'. Knox is categorical that they cannot, nor can men accept these offices and continue to be on

[30] Sir John Fortescue, *De Laudibus Legum Anglia* (1537), ed. S. B. Chrimes (Cambridge, 1949), p. 31.
[31] John Knox, *Blast*, pp. 55–6.

good terms with God. Female incapacity cannot be effectually compensated for by the activities on her behalf of chosen 'ministers', be they consorts or officers of the church or crown: '[T]he authority of a woman is a corrupted fountain, and therefore from her can never spring any lawful officer . . . whosoever receiveth of a woman office or authority are adulterous and bastard officers before God.'[32] The implication is that the body politic operating according to this arrangement is impotent – neutered – with regard to the attainment of the spiritual ends for which civil authority was instituted. It is, in Knox's famous words, an 'idol':

An idol I call that which hath the form and appearance but lacketh the virtue and strength which the name and proportion do resemble and promise. As images have face, nose, eyes, mouth, hands, and feet painted, but the use of the same cannot the craft and art of man give them. As the Holy Ghost by the mouth of David teacheth us, saying, 'They have eyes, but they see not, mouth, but they speak not, nose but they smell not, hands and feet, but they neither touch nor have the power to go.' And such, I say, is every realm and nation where a woman beareth dominion.[33]

'[I]mpossible it is', he concludes, 'to man and angel, to give unto [a female ruler] the properties and perfect offices of a lawful head.'

The empire of a woman is therefore an 'idol', kept in tune by an unholy alliance of the incapable and the worldly, and potentially or actively antichristian. From this view of the political implications of 'idolatry' derives the idea that so powerfully informed Elizabethan polemic: that a female ruler – Mary of Guise, Mary Tudor, Catherine de Medici, Mary Stuart; even Elizabeth herself – who appears to exercise political authority autonomously is, were we but able to peer behind the façade of majesty, nothing more than the agent or 'countenance' of some ungodly man or men who supply the motor force of the regime.[34]

Knox exempts Elizabeth's rule from these strictures because it is providentially sanctioned. His reading of her queenly authority gave immediacy to the identification of counsel as godly and prophetic, for who but a prophet could claim to support a 'weak instrument' in maintaining a right relationship with God, the precondition for the

---

[32] Ibid., p. 74.   [33] Ibid., p. 56.

[34] The anonymous but highly charged tract *Leycesters Commonwealth* (?Antwerp, 1584) is one of the best-known examples; in *Leicester's Commonwealth: The Copy of a Letter Written by a Master of Art of Cambridge (1584) and Related Documents*, ed. D. C. Peck (Athens, Ohio, 1985). See also Thomas Norton's justification of the proposed execution of the Duke of Norfolk in the parliamentary debates of 1572, in *Proceedings in the Parliaments of Elizabeth I: 1558–1581*, ed. T. E. Hartley (Leicester, 1981), p. 300.

welfare of the commonwealth? In the *Blast*, and in his subsequent explanatory letters to both Cecil and Elizabeth, Knox presents himself as qualified, as a prophet, to pronounce on whether 'evident testimony' exists of God's continuing favour to the queen and to the regime. His stance suggests that Knox finessed Elizabeth's status as a latter-day Deborah (hence at least by analogy both judge and prophetess) by distinguishing, as most of his contemporaries did, between prophecy and illumination.[35] Women could be illuminated by God, but a full prophetic identity – Deborah and Barak combined, as it were – would be, until the latter days, an exclusively male competence. For Knox this means that Elizabeth appears to be God's vessel, but will rule in conformity to His will only by heeding the words of His prophets; her illumination must be secured by their judgement of righteous queenly conduct.[36]

And righteous queenly conduct, it transpired, occurred when Elizabeth humbled herself, as woman and queen, in the presence of God – and John Knox. To maintain her authority, he informs her, she must eschew the role of Jezebel enacted by the 'mischievous Maries' against whom the *Blast* was initially directed, especially their pretensions to 'absolute' monarchical authority.[37] She must forget her birth, 'and all title which thereupon doth hang, and consider deeply how, for fear of your life, you did decline from God, and bow in idolatry' (under Mary Tudor). God has indeed rescued her and raised her up high, but she must recollect always that He has done so 'contrary to nature, and without [her] deserving', and for a particular purpose, 'the comfort of his kirk'. These conditions fulfilled, Knox can unequivocally support this example of female rule – for as long as Elizabeth can withstand the blandishments of worldly power:

---

[35] Ian Maclean, *The Renaissance Notion of Woman*, p. 21.

[36] The bishop of Ross, John Leslie, hit a raw nerve in the English political establishment by claiming in print that Deborah exercised absolute monarchical authority, or sovereignty, by virtue of her status as prophet (and by implication that both Elizabeth and Mary Stuart were similarly endowed): 'I bring, I say, noble Deborah . . ., whom, you cannot deny, was the chief and supreme magistrate, over the people of God . . . She heard, determined, and decided all manner of litigious, and doubtful controversies, as well for bargains and contracts, as for doubts and ambiguities of the law: and that not by other magistrates intermediate, but by herself personally. *Erat autem Prophetissa*. She was a prophetess'; *A Treatise Wherein is Declared, that the Regiment of Women is conformable to the lawe of God and Nature*, Part Three of his *Defense of Mary Queen of Scots* (London, 1571), p. 149. It seems entirely plausible that Elizabeth did indeed, as William Camden claimed, 'connive' at the publication of this work, which advanced a reading of Deborah commensurate with Elizabeth's own views of her monarchical authority; William Camden, *The History of the Most Renowned and Victorious Princess Elizabeth Late Queen of England* (London, 1615), ed. Wallace T. MacCaffrey (Chicago, 1970), pp. 118–19.

[37] John Knox, *Blast*, p. 66.

If thus in God's presence ye humble yourself, as in my heart I glorify God for that rest granted to his afflicted flock within England, under you, a weak instrument, so will I with tongue and pen justify your Authority and Regiment, as the Holy Ghost hath justified the same in Deborah, that blessed mother in Israel. But if, these premises (as God forbid) neglected, ye shall begin to brag of your birth, and to build your authority upon your own law, flatter you who so list, your felicity shall be short. Interpret my rude words in the best part, as written by him who is no enemy to your Grace.[38]

Will such obedience to the divine will maintain Elizabeth in authority as successfully as it did Deborah? Knox refuses to be drawn, saying only he is not minded to 'call back any principal point, or proposition' advanced in the *Blast* 'till truth and verity do further appear'. In other words, he accepts her providential status, but only on a provisional basis – with the implication that the provisional character of his loyalty (and, by extension, that of other godly men) will conduce to the maintenance of her authority by keeping her up to the mark as 'Deborah'. He closes by warning Elizabeth that no good awaits 'such as refuse the counsel of the faithful (appear it never so sharp)', and by praying that Christ's spirit will move her heart 'to understand what is said'. Elizabeth's understanding was certainly acute enough in worldly terms. In her marginal comments on this letter she wrote at one point that Knox's restraints on regal power exercised by a woman were 'false, lewd, dangerous, and the mischiefs thereof infinite'; at another section she demanded passionately, 'Is this to purge or to excuse? . . . your purgation is worse than your book.'[39]

Knox obviously took his role as prophet and counsellor to the queen and the regime seriously. What is equally striking is the character of his connections with the regime, and their participation in this prophetic identity. This emerges clearly in Knox's correspondence with William Cecil, which continued intermittently until Knox's death.[40] In 1559 Knox assumed (seemingly correctly) that he continued, despite the publication of the *Blast*, to enjoy Cecil's favour – 'as it becometh one member of Christ's body to have of another'.[41] In his letter to Cecil he identified himself and Cecil as counsellors, reminding him that they both will stand ultimately before God, 'to make an account of all counsell that we give'. He sent a covering letter to Cecil to accompany his 'purgation' to Elizabeth, asking Cecil to peruse the letter before giving it to Elizabeth 'if you think meet.'[42] He also mentioned John

[38] John Knox, *Works*, vol. VI, pp. 50–1.
[39] The annotated letter is in BL Add. MS. 32,091, fols. 167–9.
[40] John Knox, *Works*, vols. V and VI.   [41] Ibid., vol. VI, p. 15.   [42] Ibid., p. 47.

Aylmer's book ('I hear there is a confutation set forth in print against the First Blast'), and promised to 'communicate [his] judgment' about it to Cecil, when he had had time to read it – reflecting a tone of equality predicated in part, it would appear, on Knox's conviction that the statesman's higher worldly standing was cancelled out by his own superior spiritual stature.[43]

It is a view of their relationship that Cecil appears to have shared. Cecil signs himself 'Yours, as one member of the same body of Christ' in letters to Knox. Later in the same year the Lords of the Congregation in Scotland wrote to Cecil to apologise for Knox's absence on business, knowing, they said, that Cecil had wished to discuss the political situation in Scotland with him.[44] Perhaps most telling was Cecil's response to the *Blast*. Wishing Knox as much prudence as grace, he urged him, as a godly man, to trust in the Lord. Cecil also intimated that Scripture offered an opening that would allow the queen's supremacy, albeit through a door that not many at that time were willing to open, by quoting Galatians 3:28. Perhaps his own ambivalence explains why this section of the letter was in Latin: *Non est masculus neque foemina: omnes enim, ut ait Paulus, unum sumus in Christo Jesu. Benedictus vir confidit in Domino: et erit Dominus fiducia eius.*[45]

The conviction that queens not continuously legitimated by divine providence are tyrants, whatever their 'worldly' claims to rule, exerted a lasting influence on Elizabethan political discourse. It assumed particular meaning given the need to reconceptualise the body politic as both godly and governed by a female monarch which was so prominent a feature of Elizabeth's reign. It is surely significant that both Elizabeth and John Aylmer, responding in different ways to Knox's assessment of her legitimacy as queen, tried only to claim that her 'extraordinary' status as a providential ruler built upon, in a sense completed, her temporal identity. 'God hath made her our prince by due title of birth and law and not by extraordinary miracle without form or right,' Elizabeth wrote, in words she plainly hoped would be used by others on her behalf.[46] And Aylmer saw God's calling – and, significantly, the 'consent of her people' – as indispensable to her claims legitimately to occupy the throne and enact the part of a queen: '[A] woman left by her progenitors, true heir of a realm, having the consent of her people, the

---

[43] Knox accused Cecil of having, like Elizabeth, defected from true religion during Mary Tudor's reign and prayed he would be able to subordinate 'carnal wisdom and worldly policy, (to which both, you are bruited to be much inclined,)' to God's 'simple and naked truth'; *Works*, vol. VI, p. 17.

[44] Ibid., pp. 65–7, 67–70.   [45] Ibid., p. 56.   [46] BL Add. MS. 32,091, fol. 169.

establishment of law, ancient custom, and God's calling, to confirm the
same: may undoubtedly, succeed her ancestors . . . both to inheritance
and regiment.'[47]

Knox's strictures concerning female rule brought forth an almost immediate rejoinder in the form of John Aylmer's 1559 tract, *An Harborowe
for Faithfull and Trewe Subjects*. Aylmer (later bishop of London) was part of
that Cambridge connection so influential in the formation of the Elizabethan regime, shaped in its political and ideological values during the
reign of Edward VI.[48] Like Knox, Aylmer went into exile for conscience
sake during Mary Tudor's reign, thereby avoiding the defection into
idolatry that Knox attributed to those who remained in England.
Returning home at Elizabeth's accession he became archdeacon of
Lincoln and, in 1577, bishop of London. His ideological progression over
the course of the reign, from Marian exile to 'hammer of the conven-
ticles' in the latter years of the reign, paralleled that of the regime itself.[49]
Perhaps it lay at the root of his close relationship with Archbishop
Whitgift in the 1580s.

It is instructive to see, at the outset of the reign, the ways in which
such a figure addresses Knox's arguments and the basis of his 'exhortation to Obedience'. Although Aylmer has often been paired with Knox,
it is generally to contrast the two, with Aylmer given the role of
successfully defending the new *status quo* through arguments based on
Elizabeth's rights of inheritance, her personal attributes, and the overwhelming case for unquestioning obedience to those whom God has
placed in supreme authority. This is true as far as it goes, and recent
historians have increasingly presented a more nuanced picture by indicating the restraints that Aylmer places on Elizabeth's monarchical
autonomy.[50] I want to move the analysis one stage further, however, by

---

[47] John Aylmer, *An Harborowe for Faithfull and Trewe Subjects, agaynst the late blowne Blaste, concerninge the Governmente of Wemen, wherin be confuted all such reasons as a stranger of late made in that behalfe, with a breife exhortation to OBEDIENCE* (Strasbourg, 1559), STC 1004, fols. M–M1.
[48] Winthrop S. Hudson, *The Cambridge Connection and the Elizabethan Settlement of 1559* (Durham, N.C., 1980).
[49] Patrick Collinson, 'Episcopacy and Reform in England in the Later Sixteenth Century' in *Godly People: Essays on English Protestantism and Puritanism* (London, 1983), pp. 154–89, p. 169. Aylmer is both a more complex and a more interesting theorist than his current profile suggests.
[50] Patricia-Ann Lee, '"A Body Politique to Governe": Aylmer, Knox and the Debate on Queen-ship', *The Historian* 52, no. 2 (1990), pp. 242–61, pp. 254, 259–60; Constance Jordan, 'Woman's Rule', pp. 441–2.

arguing that Aylmer's loyalty is engaged primarily by the imperial crown and only instrumentally by its female incumbent. Like other apologists – John Hales, Laurence Humphrey, Sir Thomas Smith – this vantage point leads him to explore the meaning of 'supreme headship' in the context of female rule in ways that reveal more common ground with Knox and his brethren than might at first appear, and that also propose more signal constraints on a female ruler.[51]

Aylmer's intended audience appears to have been godly men among the political nation (especially the elite) who might have been tempted to embrace Calvinist theories of kingship when confronted by a successor queen to Mary I. He argues in effect that the political nation must either preserve the imperial crown by accepting Elizabeth as Supreme Head in some workable sense (details to be negotiated), or allow for a personal, tyrannical and finally antichristian government to be an ongoing feature of English history. This argument explains why much of Aylmer's attention in the text is devoted to describing the 'bridles' that make of the queen not a 'mere' monarch (in this context an effeminate tyrant: a Jezebel) but a 'mixed ruler'. His solution to the problem of female rule – the invention of the 'mixed monarchy' – signalled a paradigm shift in the discourse concerning supreme headship that shaped the contours of political thought from Elizabeth's accession through the English civil wars.[52] Aylmer's text should therefore be read as one sanctioned (and extremely influential) interpretation of supreme headship in the context of female rule; an interpretation that necessarily had implications for the understanding of kingship itself that developed over Elizabeth's reign.

Aylmer does not directly engage with Knox's interpretation of Genesis and its implications for women's nature and status. Perhaps he found it unanswerable. Instead he explores another dimension of Christian history, one that enables him to reverse gender polarities to assert the spiritual superiority of a realm that sustains godly female rule. He emphasises the Christian dispensation revealed in the New Testament to draw attention to the God who works through 'contrarieties' to

---

[51] For Hales see below, chapter 5, and see A. N. McLaren, 'Prophecy and Providentialism in the Reign of Elizabeth I' in *Prophecy: The Power of Inspired Language in History*, ed. Bertrand Taithe and Tim Thornton, Themes in History (Stroud, Glos., 1997), pp. 31–50; pp. 33–5. For Humphrey and Smith see below, chapter 4 and chapter 7 respectively.

[52] For paradigm shift as a historiographical concept, see J. G. A. Pocock, 'Languages and Their Implications: The Transformation of the Study of Political Thought' in *Politics, Language and Time: Essays on Political Thought and History* (New York, 1973), pp. 3–41, pp. 13–15. For the 'monarchy of counsel' and its persistence from the Act of Supremacy of 1534 to the execution of Charles I in 1649 see his 'Discourse on Sovereignty'.

display his power in a process that culminated with the earthly manifestation of Christ, the 'King of Kings', as the lowly Man of Sorrows. '[I]n all ages', he reminds his readers, 'God hath wrought his most wonderful works, by most base means: and shewed his strength by weakness, his wisdom by foolishness, and his exceeding greatness by man's exceeding feebleness.'[53] According to Aylmer, England has benefited already from this divine paradox. He makes Anne Boleyn a type of Christ and the inspiration for the English reformation, in the enactment of which Henry VIII served as instrument, ambiguously of God and the queen: 'Was not Queen Anne the mother of this blessed woman [Elizabeth], the chief, first, and only cause of banishing the beast of Rome?'[54]

To answer Knox directly, Aylmer first argues that God's injunction that woman must be subject to man applies only to the 'office of a wife':

You [Knox] say God has appointed her [woman] to be subject to her husband; . . . therefore she may not be the head. I grant that, so far as pertaineth to the bonds of marriage and the office of a wife, she must be a subject: but as a magistrate she may be her husband's head.

Women's rule is therefore, if less 'convenient' than men's, not 'unnatural', nor utterly prohibited by the Word of God, as Knox asserts. Indeed the Old Testament story of Deborah shows how 'woman as a wife must be at commandment, but a woman as magistrate may lawfully command, for Deborah, we are told, was married to Lapidoth'.[55]

Nor is female rule, as Knox would have it, 'repugnant to Nature'. Here he finds again the picture is not as stark as Knox has painted it. Knox errs, he remarks, in mistaking (in the realm of policy) a lesser good for an absolute evil: 'Just because it is not so convenient, profitable or meet as government by man', he tells Knox, 'you deceive yourself that women's rule is unnatural.'[56] Certainly it is true that women's capacities are less than men's – we have Aristotle's authority for that. But this does not incapacitate them entirely or mean that they are lacking in virtue. The correct analogy to draw, he says, is with the status of the youthful ruler who, although less apt than an adult for the office, is not disbarred

---

[53] John Aylmer, *Harborowe*, fol. C. [54] Ibid.

[55] Ibid., fol. D3. There is scope for ambiguity here. Lipidoth remains a shadowy figure, mentioned only once in the Bible at Judges 4:4.

[56] John Aylmer, *Harborowe*, fol. D. He also introduces an intermediate category, of events so unusual as to be extraordinary but not 'unnatural' – as water running uphill would be, for example. He gives as examples of this intermediate category very old men whose hair remains the colour it was in their youth and the phenomenon of multiple births (fol. D2).

from it. He cites Edward VI, rapidly becoming a Protestant saint at this point, as an example:[57]

But in a woman is wit, understanding, and as Aristotle sayeth the same virtues that be in a man, saving that they differ *secundum maius et minus*, that is, more in the man than in the woman . . . For as Aristotle saith the man's rule is [more meet]. But to reason thus women be not so meet as men, Ergo, it is against nature: is an evil consequent. King Edward for his years and tenderness of age was not so meet to rule, as was his father King Henry: yet was it not against nature.[58]

And St Paul himself (in company with Socrates) provides evidence that the gender prohibition, in the realm of policy, is in fact a product of 'convenience', not God's law or man's:

But you will say there is an aptness in the son to rule, but the woman is ordained to obey, and clean exempt from superiority. This I deny. For both nature and God's words give her a kind of superiority by express words . . . No man I am sure will deny but that the government in the house is a kind of superiority and that over men . . . If then they may govern men in the house by Saint Paul's commission, and a household is a little commonwealth, as Socrates in Xenophon saith: Then I cannot see how you can debar them of all rule, or conclude that to be heads of men is against nature.[59]

Indeed, in the realm of policy an alternative definition of 'natural' suggests itself, according to which a woman ruler's capacity to preserve the commonwealth constitutes the legitimation of her rule, for

It is most natural to preserve and maintain the society of men, seeing man and cities, which consist upon the company of men, be the chiefest work of God by nature, for all other things, be prepared for that, as the chief end: That men living together in a civil company, may peaceably, and quietly honour GOD the author and preserver of that society.[60]

Women's rule therefore is not 'against nature' – insofar as it preserves commonwealths – and Aylmer provides a range of historical and quasi-

---

[57] Margaret Aston, *The King's Bedpost* (Cambridge, 1993), pp. 32–4; J. N. King, *English Reformation Literature: the Tudor Origins of the Protestant Tradition* (Princeton, N.J., 1982), pp. 184–5. Aylmer wants to establish an equivalence between Elizabeth and Edward with regard to their personal qualities, and argues that Edward's premature death was a function of Englishmen's 'folly' (i.e. disobedience); see fol. I2.

[58] John Aylmer, *Harborowe*, fol. C2⁴. Elsewhere he argues, with reference to King Edward, that only the ignorant interpret the Biblical warning 'Unhappy is the realm that hath a child to their King' literally, 'as though this word child were not there a metaphor'. He does so to buttress his assertion that the reformation was fulfilled in Edward's reign, not Henry VIII's – a contentious point throughout Elizabeth's reign and one intimately related to models of kingship.

[59] John Aylmer, *Harborowe*, fol. D.   [60] Ibid., fol. D2.

mythological examples to prove that, on this criterion, their rule is 'not so heinous, and intolerable, or in any way evil as he [Knox] maketh it'.[61]

Aylmer sees Knox's most telling argument against female rule as St Paul's strictures against women speaking in the congregation, which he reads as prohibiting them from exercising an ecclesiastical function. 'This', he says, 'is the Hercules club that beateth all down before it. These be Sampson's locks, that make him [Knox] so strong.'[62] Here, as at other points when he feels himself to be on weak ground (notably when he insists on the separation of ecclesiastical and civil jurisdictions), he intimates he will tackle the whole subject more thoroughly and at greater length at some point in the future.[63] For the moment, however, he responds by refuting Knox's claim that St Paul's injunction is universally applicable: 'St. Paul, nor none of the rest of Christ's guard, meddle not with civil policy, no further than to teach obedience, nor have no commission thereunto in all the whole Scripture.'[64] It becomes apparent here that he is addressing, not Knox, but godly men troubled on theological grounds by a woman acting as Supreme Head of the Church of England, as he urges them to see through the queen to Christ. Articulating the sleight of hand that would have the elite read Elizabeth as Supreme Head of a body politic of which Christ was king, he argues that 'preachers or pulpit men . . . must . . . know their quarter strokes, and the way how to defend their head, their head Christ I say, and his cross'.[65]

He then proceeds to outline the defence such men might make, to themselves and in their public roles. First, he urges that a modicum of forbearance is necessary if divine law is to be enacted in the civil realm under a godly female ruler:

[St Paul] forbiddeth her the greater and more chargeable function, which is the spiritual ministry and preaching . . . No man I think doubteth but that the Ecclesiastical function is greater and more chargeable than [external policy], for the one concerneth the body, and the other the soul . . . But you will say in England she must have both. How can she discharge both, if you make the one [spiritual ministry] so hard?[66]

Aylmer proposes to ease matters by attributing both civil and ecclesiastical competencies to Elizabeth but defining them differentially, such that her exercise of the latter becomes a 'governorship' rather than a 'headship': '[I]ndeed both belong to her but not in one manner. For in the

[61] Ibid., fol. D2r.   [62] Ibid., fol. G3³.   [63] Ibid., fols. D3³, K2¹.
[64] Ibid., fol. G3³.   [65] Ibid., fol. H. For this sleight of hand see chapter 1.
[66] Ibid., fols. I3³–I3⁴.

one (as policy) she hath a function; that is she must be a doer: in the other she hath the authority and oversight but not the function and practice.'[67]

He also finds Scriptural backing for a different distinction – one that allows both kings and, in extraordinary circumstances, male 'Israelites' to be 'doers' in the ecclesiastical sphere – in the commonwealth of the Jews as described in Exodus. There Moses exercised a spiritual compet- ence ordained by God, without displacing Aaron from his role as high priest. Indeed, so did the Israelites themselves, under God's particular care. At this stage in the argument he reverts to the language of kingship, making a general point in relation to godly men that presum- ably he feels would be undercut by continuing his discussion with reference to queens, and possibly in the interest of preserving an integral supreme headship (that is, one in which the distinction between 'gov- ernor' and 'head' would no longer be necessary) for a future godly king:

For [Moses] might do sometimes that extraordinarily, which belonged to the priest, as we read that kings read the book of the law, and yet were no priests. Yea, all the children of Israel, at their coming out of Egypt, did as much as this came to, for every one sprinkled blood upon their door posts in the passover, and yet they could not all be priests. And this sprinkling of blood upon the altar, was but a solemn ceremony, for the time done, and not such a function, as then was properly appointed to the priests. Why may he [the king] not I pray you in like manner, constitute, appoint, correct, and oversee the church men, though he be no church man himself.[68]

Surely, though, this is to present even the male figure of the king as in some sense the representative of the godly, thereby translating Walter Ullman's 'ascending' theory of power into the lexicon of the mixed monarchy.[69]

Given Aylmer's definition of God's will – by one remove, as it were, and in the realm of 'policy' – he can renegotiate Knox's providential stance in support of obedience to the queen, certainly to the regime. When God has so clearly manifested His will in terms of the succession we must 'honor His choice, rather than . . . prefer our own', for, 'when God chooseth himself by sending to a king, whose succession is ruled by inheritance and lineal descent, no heirs male: It is a plain argument, that for some secret purpose he mindeth the female should reign and

[67] Ibid., fol. I3⁴.
[68] Ibid., fols. K²–K2. See Thomas Wilson's 1578 gloss on the relationship between Moses and Aaron in the context of 'governorship'; above, p. 20.
[69] Walter Ullman, *Medieval Political Thought* (London, 1965), pp. 12–13.

govern.'[70] Nor can her subjects exercise their judgement about her role and capacities, for God has pronounced about both and can, through an ongoing providence of which she is the instrument, fulfil His aims in regard to the commonwealth:

> He sendeth a woman by birth, we may not refuse her by violence. He establishes her by law, we may not remove her by wrong. He maketh her a head, we may not make her a hand or foot . . . Placeth he a woman weak in nature, feeble in body, soft in courage, unskilful in practice, not terrible to the enemy, no shield to the friend, well . . . (saith he) My strength is most perfect when you be most weak.[71]

Especially in these latter days, dutiful subjects must follow the advice William Cecil gave to Knox – to trust in God as the shield of the righteous:

> [W]herefore the matter standing so, that whosoever rule, man or child, male or female, God must be our shield, fortress and bulwark: Let us do our duty by trusting him, and he will do his, by helping us, and so much the rather, because that now, it is more like the glory shall be his, if the victory be ours, then if we had some great Goliath, some lusty champion, to take the matter in hand.[72]

Finally, as a signal element of this renegotiation, Aylmer conflates divine law and what he terms 'municipal' or English common law in terms that subordinate the authority of the monarch to the law – and by implication fuse the identities of prophet and councillor in a godly commonwealth. Aylmer concludes his discussion of St Paul's prohibition against women speaking in the congregation by saying that he does not accept its universal character. Even if Knox's reading were correct, however, he argues that female rule would still be allowable in a 'politic weal' (simultaneously Israel and England) in which 'neither the woman nor the man ruleth' but all are subordinate to the law:

> But if this [rule] be utterly taken from them in [St Paul's epistle]: what maketh it against their government in a politic weal, where neither the woman nor the man ruleth. If there be no tyrants, but the laws. For as Plato saith *Illi civitati paratu est exitui ubi magistratus legibus imperat, et non leges magistratui.* 'That city is at the pit's brink, wherein the magistrate ruleth the laws, and not the laws, the magistrate': What could any king in Israel do in that common wealth, besides the policy appointed by Moses?[73]

---

[70] John Aylmer, *Harborowe*, fol. B3. Presumably Aylmer is referring to Edward VI, in keeping with his argument that Englishmen have paid the price since Edward's death for their unwillingness wholeheartedly to embrace reformation during his reign. See above, note 58.

[71] Ibid., fols. C. B2¹–B3   [72] Ibid., fols. M¹–M2.   [73] Ibid., fols. H2–3.

From this starting point in Old Testament tradition, Aylmer proceeds to discuss the constitution of the English commonwealth and the ways in which it 'bridles' a monarch, from here on read as a queen. The evidence is unequivocal that, according to the 'municipal law of England' women can inherit the throne. Moreover, that right is bound up in England's imperial identity:

> For if it were unlawful (as he [Knox] will have it) that the Sexe should govern: yet is it not unlawful that they should inherit . . . And in this point their inheritance is so linked with the empire: that you cannot pluck from them the one without robbing them of the other.[74]

On the other hand, 'It is not in England so dangerous a matter, to have a woman ruler, as men take it to be.'[75] If God offers an enabling providence to the female ruler on the one hand, the English constitution provides built-in safeguards for her natural deficiencies on the other. England, Aylmer announces, is an empire in which the commonwealth bridles the crown:

> The regiment of England is not a mere Monarchie . . . but a rule mixed of all three [monarchy, oligarchy, democracy], where in each one of these have or should have like authority . . . [and in which], if the parliament [Senate and commons] use their privileges: the King can ordain nothing without them.[76]

The queen's will is constrained by their judgement, conveyed through statute (and Aylmer's use of the female pronoun makes it clear he has in mind queens here, his nod in the direction of kings notwithstanding):

> If on the other part, the regiment were such, as all hanged upon the king's or queen's will, and not upon the laws writ: if she might decree to make laws alone, without her senate. If she judged offenses according to her wisdom, and not by limitation of statutes and laws: if she might dispose alone of war and peace: if to be short she were a mere monarch, and not a mixte ruler, you might peradventure make me to fear the matter the more, and the less to defend the cause.[77]

The cause is defensible because a 'mixte ruler' does not exercise sovereignty: 'it is not she that ruleth but the lawes', executed and interpreted by judges, justices of the peace 'and such other offices'. True she appoints such officials – in Aylmer's words 'she may err in choosing such' – but that, he feels, is a species of 'natural' shortcoming which may equally befall a king. It is in any event largely offset by the position of counsellors to the crown: the possibility of a bad choice is why 'they [rulers male or female] have their counsel at their elbow' – presumably

---

[74] Ibid., fols. K3³, B2.   [75] Ibid., fol. H3².   [76] Ibid., fols. H2¹–H³.   [77] Ibid., fol. H3².

both literally and metaphorically.[78] In fact, his earlier characterisation of Elizabeth in the civil realm – that 'she must be a doer' – seems not to be allowed for by the constitution of the realm as he describes it:

[S]he maketh no statutes or laws, but the honourable court of Parliament: she breaketh none, but it must be she and they together . . . If she should judge in capital crimes: what danger were there in her womanish nature? none at all. For the verdict is the 12 men's which pass upon life and death, and not hers: Only this belongeth to her ministry, that when they have found treason, murder, or felony, she utter the pain limited in the law for that kind of trespass.

'What may she do alone,' he demands, 'wherein is peril? She may grant pardon to an offender, that is her prerogative.'[79]

And finally, the ultimate, if in 1559 remote, safeguard – the law itself can be changed to exclude females from inheriting the throne, should that prove desirable or necessary, once a king inherits. For although currently women's inheritance 'is so linked with the empire: that you cannot pluck from them the one without robbing them of the other', Aylmer in the next sentence denies that the linkage is immutable: 'This doubt might better have been moved when the Sceptre was **or shall be** in the hand of the male. And so if it were found evil . . . it might without any wronging of any be reformed.'[80] Indeed he urges Knox to 'do your own country [Scotland] good' by persuading the French king and Frenchmen generally that Mary Stuart's title is unlawful, because she is a woman: 'And as you speed there, you might perchance encourage us [in England] to follow when it may be done lawfully.'[81]

But the extensive sovereignty that Aylmer attributes to the English constitution is, as he acknowledges, not axiomatic, depending instead on the commonwealth being as it 'ought to be (if men were worth their ears)'. The balance – the limitations of the law – requires counsellors of the realm to fulfil their role, whether acquired through birth or office, with wisdom and rectitude:

[I]f the parliament use their privileges: the king can ordain nothing without them. If he do, it is his fault in usurping it, and their folly in permitting it: wherefore in my judgment those that in King Henry the VIII's days, would not grant him, that his proclamations should have the force of a statute, were good fathers of the country.[82]

---

[78] Ibid., fol. H3¹.
[79] Ibid., A 'prerogative' signally overridden in the case of the execution of Mary Queen of Scots, and an element of the negotiations between Elizabeth and her Privy Councillors on the subject; see below, chapter 6. Aylmer also notes that she may, like kings, misspend revenues.
[80] Ibid., fol. B2, my emphasis.   [81] Ibid., fols. F¹, F2.   [82] Ibid., fol. H3.

Nobles, bishops, Privy Councillors, judges, justices of the peace and members of parliament – all must withstand attempts by the prince to exercise exclusive sovereignty, to become a 'mere' monarch. They must be good 'fathers of the country' if they are to avoid such encroachments, whether advanced by the king or (in Mary Tudor's case) the countenance of a queen. This is the thrust of his reading of recent English history, in which England's return to the Catholic fold is finally less the responsibility of the monarch than of those 'inward' councillors who bowed to her will instead of reforming it.[83]

Elizabeth is no Mary. Aylmer makes it clear that his readers are to regard her as a successor to, in some sense a replacement for, the 'blessed Edward VI'. Yet she too will need counsel from across the ranks of the political nation, less because she is likely herself to knock down the safeguards protecting the realm than because her very virtues, allied to her 'womanly nature', make her, like Mary, vulnerable to seduction – a key term in political debate from this point onwards[84]:

[T]he late Queen Mary, . . . bearing, and wearing, a woman's heart, could not (I think) have used such rigor and extremity, in imprisoning, banishing, racking, hanging, drawing, heading, burning, fleasinge [sic], and flaying with all manner of extremity, not sparing her own blood, no not her natural sister: Unless she had been so bewitched, and endoted by her Cardinals, Bishops, and Churchmen . . . It is an easy matter for them that be of devout minds, and godly dispositions, to be brought into error by those whom they think to be godly.[85]

Hence the function of counsel – exercised across the political nation – is doubly necessary in the case of a 'womanly' ruler, for her judgement may persuade her to select as councillors men who are not worthy 'fathers to their country', in Mary's case a coterie of the Catholic hierarchy.

Aware of the dangers – to England, to the godly, at this time – Aylmer sees the way forward clearly. 'We must pray for the Queen's estate and not dispute of her right,' he announces. And as counsellors 'our role is to guide her heart in the choice of her husband' – who will naturally be her 'head' – and to pray God 'to make her fruitful, and the mother of many

---

[83] Ibid., fols. H3–H3¹.
[84] See, for example, Catherine Bates, *The Rhetoric of Courtship in Elizabethan Language and Literature* (Cambridge, 1992), ch. 1, pp. 6–24.
[85] John Aylmer, *Harborowe*, fol. D3¹. Aylmer implies that Mary misinterpreted ecclesiastical authority as both denoting and promoting godliness and may have done so because of her womanly inability to distinguish between form and substance. This is suggestive from the perspective of the controversy over church reform that dominated the later stages of Elizabeth's reign.

children'.[86] I cannot agree with Michael Mendle's assertion that Aylmer is writing this tract ostensibly in support of the monarchy tongue in cheek – that seems to me to misread the political culture of the period – but it does point to the qualified species of loyalty to a female monarch that Aylmer feels can be drawn upon in support of the regime.[87]

Aylmer's tract obviously does not propose unqualified obedience to the queen. Rather, it introduces a new species of obedience. Where Knox professes loyalty and obedience to the queen insofar as her actions can be read as providentially guided, Aylmer proposes loyalty to queen and council, to the queen insofar as she has been counselled – and counselled by men who are themselves godly. Separately, the two texts represent the providential and politic means of reconciliation to female rule; in dialogue we can see Aylmer effecting their fusion. Elizabeth can be led by God, or guided by godly counsel. Either strategy will conduce to the flourishing godly commonweal that will legitimate her rule. Both require of her that she serve in her office as an instrument; in the words of the 'froward' John Stubbs, that she display 'such a tractable and easy sweetness of a yielding nature that [she] readily and humbly may harken to all such good counsels sent [her] from God and such as fear God and love [her] majesty'.[88] Or, as the Privy Councillor Sir Francis Knollys admonished her in 1569, that she put aside 'such affections and passions of your mind as happen to have dominion over you. So yet the resolutions digested by the deliberate consultations of your most faithful counsellors ought ever to be had in most price.'[89]

CONCLUSION: COUNSEL AND SOVEREIGNTY IN THE GODLY NATION

These powerful connectives, between queen and counsel, between providence and patriotism, could conduce to the stability of the regime, as long as the queen's councillors (and pre-eminently those of the Privy Council) were perceived as themselves godly and patriotic. But they also suggest that for councillors, as for the queen, it would be the fruits of

---

[86] Ibid., fol. I2.

[87] Michael Mendle, *Dangerous Positions: Mixed Government, the Estates of the Realm, and the Making of the 'Answer to the xix propositions'* (Tuscaloosa, Ala. 1985), p. 49; see Patricia-Ann Lee, ' "A Body Politique to Governe"', pp. 255–6.

[88] John Stubbs, *The Discoverie of a Gaping Gulf* (London, 1579), pp. 30–1. For the distinction between 'froward' and 'forward' Protestants, see Patrick Collinson, 'Puritans, Men of Business and Elizabethan Parliaments', *Parliamentary History* 7, no. 2 (1988), pp. 187–211, pp. 191–4.

[89] Quoted in Michael Pulman, *The Elizabethan Privy Council in the 1570s* (Berkeley, Calif. 1971), p. 61.

political action that would legitimate the government, not history or even law, and that the reading would be conducted in a court of 'public opinion' composed of godly men across the ranks of the political nation.[90] In conclusion I want to touch briefly on one important political consequence of the centrality of the language of godly and prophetic counsel during Elizabeth's reign: the redefinition of the English kingdom as a 'common weal'.

To do so it is necessary first to look back to Henry VIII's reign. At that point, and especially during the 1530s, the consequences of reformation gave these issues – the basis and extent of regal authority, the role of counsel, the quality and extent of subjects' obedience – new prominence, in both pragmatic and theoretical terms. Writers as significant for Elizabethan political discourse as Christopher St Germain, Thomas Starkey and Sir Thomas Elyot developed theories of limited monarchy that drew on Aristotelian and Thomist ideas of communally beneficial kingship and infused them anew with visions of godly empire. The king, they argued, could be both virtuous and just, rule consensually yet imperially, when supported by the reason of many, especially those members of the community – men of rank – deemed to possess the greatest capacity for reason. Sinfulness, in the person of the king and in the body politic, could be kept in check by such limited and hierarchical communal participation, although its institutional form and framework remained a matter of debate.[91]

That significant decade witnessed (in addition to the appearance in print for the first time of Fortescue's *De Laudibus*), the publication of Sir Thomas Elyot's reflections on the new world appearing in the wake of the break with Rome in *The Book Named The Governor*. There Elyot specifically addressed the question of how the now untrammelled and imperial king could be prevented from becoming tyrannical. He proposed a 'political theology' at the heart of which was to be the relationship of near equality between the king and his counsellors.[92] Elyot defined counsellors as virtuous men whose goodness would be capable of restraining and finally educating the king's will. The conjunction of king and counsellors would therefore institute virtue in the realm. These

---

[90] Patrick Collinson, '*De Republica Anglorum*': *Or, History with the Politics Put Back*, Inaugural Lecture, 9 November 1989 (Cambridge, 1990), pp. 26–8.

[91] Robert Eccleshall, *Order and Reason in Politics: Theories of Absolute and Limited Monarchy in Early Modern England* (Oxford, 1978), Introduction and especially pp. 38–43, and John Guy, 'The "Imperial Crown" and the Liberty of the Subject: The English Constitution from Magna Carta to the Bill of Rights' in *Court, Country, and Culture: Essays in Honor of Perez Zagorin*, ed. Bonnelyn Kunze and Dwight Brautigan (New York, 1992), pp. 65–88, pp. 72–6.

[92] F. W. Conrad, 'A Preservative Against Tyranny: The Political Theology of Sir Thomas Elyot', Ph.D. Dissertation, Johns Hopkins University, Baltimore, Md. (1988).

virtuous counsellors ('lesser magistrates', in the evocative term we also associate with the radical phase of the Protestant reformation) were to be the king's *amici principis*. Their standing would allow them freedom to speak, advise, even 'represent' the king in the exercise of governance. To prove the point Elyot referred at several places to a key passage from Aristotle's *Politics*:

It is by no means easy for one man to superintend many things . . . Indeed, it is already the practice of kings to make themselves many eyes and ears and hands and feet. For they make colleagues [*synarchoi*] of those who are their friends and the friends of their government. They must be friends of the monarch and of his government; if not his friends, they will not do what he wants; but friendship implies likeness and equality.[93]

This new and influential reading of political relations entailed a move away from the older, medieval view of the English monarchy as a corporate enterprise between estates of the realm, and its supersession by a view of it as a collegial exercise, between the king and his 'friends and equals'; not a common weal, but (as Elyot says) a public one: 'It seemeth that men have been long abused in calling *Rempublicam* a common weal', he remarks in *The Book Named The Governor*. 'There may appear like diversity to be in English between a public weal and a common weal, as should be in Latin, between *Res publica*, and *Res plebeia*'.[94] For Elyot, then, what John Guy has called the 'feudal-baronial' model of counsel, in which counsel as a duty is exercised by men of appropriate birth (*consiliarii nati*), must give way to a new aristocratic model, predicated on equality between the king and his counsellors, and informed by 'humanist-classical' rhetoric and assumptions.[95]

Again in the interests of restraining the potentially tyrannical king, newly imperial, Elyot reworked Fortescue's distinction between the two governing capacities of the king (*politice* and *regale*) to emphasise the consensual basis of the latter. In his 1541 political treatise *The Image of Governance* he considered the nature of regal power by drawing on the wisdom of the exemplary third-century Roman emperor Alexander Severus.[96] According to Elyot's translation, Severus argued that the king

---

[93] Aristotle, *The Politics*, ed. Stephen Everson (Cambridge, 1988), Book III, p. 79. See for example Sir Thomas Elyot, *The Book Named The Governor*, ed. S. E. Lehmberg (London, 1962), p. 157: 'Aristotle in his *Politics* exhorteth governors to have their friends for a great number of eyes, ears, hands, and legs; considering that no one man may see or hear all things that many men may see and hear, nor can be in all places, or do as many things well, at one time, as many persons may do.'

[94] Elyot, *The Book Named The Governor*, pp. 1–2. See F. W. Conrad's discussion in 'A Preservative Against Tyranny', pp. 46–54.   [95] John Guy, 'Rhetoric'.

[96] It is unclear whether Elyot was working from a Greek text, supposedly compiled by Severus's secretary, or inventing Severus as a didactic strategy, to persuade Henry VIII to follow his example. Sir Thomas Elyot, *The Image of Governance* (1541), in *Four Political Treatises by Sir Thomas*

ruling *regaliter* did so through recourse to an artificial reason, constructed in his person by his subjects. The person of the ruler contains 'two states or conditions':

> one by nature common with other men, the other by election private and from the people excepted. In the first we be resembled to beasts, for the affections and passions, wherein we communicate with them. In the other we be like unto gods immortal, in supreme dignity excelling all other men.

What is the basis of this godhood? Severus/Elyot continues:

> [It] is to us happened, and not ingenerate, by the prerogative of virtue, which is supposed to be more excellent in us: which virtue is none other thing but disposition and exterior act of the mind agreeable to reason, and the moderation of nature. The supreme dignity that we have received is only in governance of men, which do participate with us in Nature, wherein they always remain equal with us, but by Reason they be made inferior unto us, for they supposing it to be more abundantly given us, have therefore willingly submitted themselves unto our governance.[97]

'Reforming the monarch's will', in accordance with Elyot's model, thus began to look rather different when the monarch in question was a queen, and when the fate of Protestant England was perceived to hang in the balance. Because, of course, to sixteenth-century eyes, women, even queens, were not 'equal' to men; indeed it is doubtful whether friendship as Elyot defined it could exist between a queen and her councillors, depending as it did on a 'likeness' that presumably did not extend across gender boundaries. And who, in the sixteenth century, believed women, even queens, to be superior to men in their capacity for reason? What then was to be the focus of loyalty for the 'inferior governors'? One answer was 'the crown', and it is surely significant that Henry VIII claimed that *imperium* was invested in the ruler alone, whereas Elizabeth derived her power from 'the laws of God and this realm always annexed to the Crown of this realm'.[98]

These views of the relationship between counsel and sovereignty, then, altered profoundly with their translation into the context of female rule, with political consequences adumbrated, in Elizabeth's reign, by Knox's and Aylmer's conceptions of the body politic. The translation explains, I think, why we find that what Starkey and Guy term the 'classic' Tudor Privy Council, born under Henry VIII and with an intellectual pedigree articulated and redefined by humanists at his court, did not survive into the reigns of Mary and Elizabeth Tudor. Neither

Elyot, ed. Lillian Gottesman, Scholars' Facsimiles and Reprints (Gainesville, Fl. 1967), pp. xiii–xiv.
[97] Elyot, *The Image of Governance*, pp. 390–1.   [98] John Guy, 'Rhetoric', pp. 300–1.

exercised the liberty envisaged by Sir Thomas Elyot of choosing her own councillors. Both can be seen as constrained in their choice by what Dale Hoak calls 'political wisdom', articulated through 'professional councillors', generally those who had been active under Edward VI.[99] Elizabeth certainly relied on networks constructed by her Privy Councillors and courtiers to communicate with the social leaders of the country (conceived in bureaucratic terms as *amici principis*), unlike Henry VII and Henry VIII, who communicated with them directly.[100] I do not agree with the view that Elizabeth chose to concentrate all power in the hands of her Council, either in the implication that she chose or indeed that such monopolisation actually occurred. But it is undoubtedly the case that this configuration allowed Elizabeth's councillors to exercise unprecedented autonomy in their role as officers of the crown, in what David Starkey calls an 'eccentric arrangement' lasting until the fall of Robert Cecil in James I's reign.[101]

In the context of the Protestant nation inaugurated with Elizabeth's reign, a move in the direction of 'professional' councillors inevitably meant a move to councillors who were godly, hence 'watchmen' and 'fathers of the country' – men who were perceived as standing in a privileged relationship to the queen as a result. That Elizabeth recognises this fact in choosing to surround herself with councillors who are respectively Marian exiles, former functionaries of Edward VI and prophets is, for John Aylmer, not the least of the indications that she is not a tyrant:

Besides . . . It is not the least token of all to persuade us of her happy and godly proceedings, that she picketh out some such counsellors to serve her (and I trust will do more) as be neither of common wit nor common experience, of whom some by travail in strange countries, some by learning, some by practise and like authority in other rulers' days, some by affliction one way or other: for their gifts and graces which they have received at God's hand, be men meet to be called to such rooms.[102]

Finally, the conflation of female rule and restored Protestantism extended the definition of counsellor, in terms of both who provided counsel and whether it was a duty, or a right.[103] For, if Elizabeth was in

[99] Dale Hoak, 'Two Revolutions in Tudor Government: The Formation and Organisation of Mary I's Privy Council' in *Revolution Reassessed: Revisions in the History of Tudor Government and Administration*, ed. Christopher Coleman and David Starkey (Oxford, 1986), pp. 87–115.
[100] John Guy, 'Rhetoric', p. 296.
[101] David Starkey, 'Court History in Perspective' in *The English Court: From the War of the Roses to the Civil War*, ed. David Starkey (London, 1987), p. 22. [102] John Aylmer, *Harborowe.*, fol. O2.
[103] Stephen L. Collins, *From Divine Cosmos to Sovereign State: An Intellectual History of Consciousness and the Idea of Order in Renaissance England* (Oxford, 1989), pp. 88–91.

some sense constrained to take godly councillors through the dictates of 'political wisdom', she was equally constrained (as were her Privy Councillors) to take counsel from the godly among the political nation. Protestant England, in conjunction with a female ruler, led to a reconceptualisation of the realm as a corporate enterprise: the common weal, read as the godly nation which was potentially the True Church. This is one reason for the emphasis on the 'commonweal' in political discourse during Elizabeth's reign, as well as for the tensions resulting from the conviction politics that dominated the period through to the mid-1580s.[104]

Aylmer set forth the new dispensation in his *Harborowe*, showing how in the body of Christ (now the appropriate analogy for the English body politic) there is no distinction between godly men in the expression of counsel:

I doubt not but her majesty if she could, would choose her counsell of the nobility, she being herself the head of that order and patroness: but if she shall espy out meaner men of greater experience, farther reach, and more science, then they be: [they will be her councillors] . . . [W]ise men by study and noble men by birth will make such an harmony in the common wealth as [no enemy] shall be able to interrupt the concord: and it is to be hoped that neither the one part in respect of their nobility, will condemn the other for their baseness nor envy them for their wisdom: nor the other part through the admiration of their own gifts, set light by the honour and ancientness of the peers . . . Learn a similitude saith Paul (1 Cor. 12) of the body of man, how each member is not the head, and yet hath his necessary use in the body, wherefore if some be wiser, and some nobler, some richer, and some poorer: I doubt not but like good mariners they will all consider, that they must all travail to bring the ship of the common wealth, the Church of Christ, and the Queen's realm, to a quiet port.[105]

At the same time and as a corollary, as we have seen, he defined the queen as a 'mixed ruler', constituted in her regal person by the laws of the realm and their officers (including the office of king), and, as such, Supreme Head of a 'mixed monarchy'. In the next two chapters I want to consider the significance of these formulations for contemporaries during Elizabeth's reign by exploring the ideological origins of the 'mixed monarchy' from the reign of Henry VIII.

[104] David Harris Sacks, 'Private Profit and Public Good: The Problem of the State in Elizabethan Theory and Practice' in *Law, Literature, and the Settlement of Regimes*, ed. Gordon Schochet, The Folger Institute Center for the History of British Political Thought Proceedings, vol. 2 (Washington, D.C., 1990), pp. 121–42, p. 123.   [105] John Aylmer, *Harborowe*, fols. O2¹-O3.

CHAPTER 3

Feats of incorporation: the ideological bases of the mixed monarchy

> It is the whole social order, not merely monarchy, which God hath ordained.
>
> Thomas Starkey, *An Exhortation to the People* (1536)[1]

In *Tudor England,* John Guy dates the emergence of the concept of the 'state' in its modern sense, in England, to the second half of Elizabeth's reign. He sees the deeply ambiguous legacy of Henry VIII's break with Rome with regard to church government as fundamental to this development. As evidence he notes that Henry VIII employed as propagandists two men whose outlooks and conclusions on the definition of imperial sovereignty were 'so fundamentally different that they could not both be right': the caesaropapist Edward Foxe, and Christopher St German, proponent of parliamentary sovereignty in spiritual matters. Yet, as he observes, 'Foxe's theory was muzzled by Elizabeth's Privy Council'. Instead, 'leading Protestant politicians such as Burghley, Lord Keeper Bacon, Leicester, Walsingham, and the earls of Bedford and Pembroke preferred the option of *limiting* the powers of the Crown'.[2]

Given contemporary beliefs about the dangers of female rule, we must ask how much choice they had in identifying England in such a way that the powers of the crown could be limited, pre-eminently by being defined as separable from the person of the monarch. It does not detract from John Aylmer's intellectual achievement to recognise the political necessity to which he responded in articulating his conception of the mixed monarchy. Fears of a 'monstrous regiment' virtually dictated that during Elizabeth's reign England would be defined as a corporation, with imperial sovereignty residing in queen-in-parliament. For increasingly at this time the alternative – 'mere' monarchy, in John Aylmer's terms –

---

[1] Thomas Starkey, *An Exhortation to the People* (London, 1536), fol. 9a.
[2] John Guy, *Tudor England* (Oxford, 1988), pp. 352–78; p. 375; the italics are Guy's.

posited a model of patriarchal kingship which suggested that the king in his own person not only provided the means by which male subjects attained to their earthly identities as husbands, fathers and political beings, but did so because he represented the person of God Himself.[3] This linkage, problematical when applied to a male monarch, was literally inconceivable as a reading of female monarchical identity. Whether couched in terms of the 'cult of kingship', which served to buttress Henry VIII's claims to royal supremacy, or the naturalisation of divine right theories, which, in the 1590s, paved the way for James VI's inheritance of the English crown, 'mere' monarchy presupposed a male incumbent of the throne.[4] 'We are sure women have souls as well as men,' John Donne told James I in a sermon of 1615, 'but yet it is not so expressed that God breathed a soul into woman as he did into man.' And he immediately drew a political parallel of which James, attempting to position himself as a universal king, could only have approved: that, although all governments have 'souls', God 'breathed it more manifestly into monarchy'.[5] James himself announced, in his first speech to parliament as English king, that 'I am the husband, and all the whole isle is my lawful wife; I am the head, and it is my body.' He thus positioned himself as direct successor to Henry VIII, ruling both *regaliter* and *politice*, his recourse to conjugal analogies an attempt to mitigate the tyrannical implications that notions of 'mere' monarchy had by this point accrued.[6] And if the plenitude of power possessed by the imperial king threatened his declension to the status of tyrant (analogous, perhaps, to Lucifer's rebellion against God), for sixteenth-century Englishmen an imperial queen posed a more immediate and intractable threat. Her sexuality – her 'nature' – inclined her towards tyranny, just as her relative imperviousness to reason inured her to the 'bridles' on unjust monarchical authority proposed by conventional political wisdom.[7]

Thus the definition of Elizabeth as a 'mixed ruler' and of England as a

---

[3] R. W. K. Hinton, 'Husbands, Fathers and Conquerors', *Political Studies* 15, no. 3 (1967), pp. 291–300; Francis Oakley, 'Christian Obedience and Authority, 1520–1550' in *The Cambridge History of Political Thought 1450–1700*, ed. J. H. Burns (Cambridge, 1991), pp. 159–92, pp. 180–2.
[4] The phrase is Oakley's in 'Christian Obedience', p. 180.
[5] Quoted in Margo Todd, *Christian Humanism and the Puritan Social Order*, Ideas in Context (Cambridge, 1987), p. 238. For James VI and I and his conceptions of kingship see J. H. Burns, *True Law of Kingship: Concepts of Monarchy in Early-Modern Scotland* (Oxford, 1996), pp. 222–81, esp. p. 281.
[6] For the family as a constitutional model see Donald R. Kelley, 'Elizabethan Political Thought' in *The Varieties of British Political Thought, 1500–1800*, ed. J. G. A. Pocock (Cambridge, 1993), pp. 47–79, pp. 51–2. On one level, of course, James is reminding his auditors that his virility has redrawn the map of Britain by uniting the kingdoms of Scotland and England in his person.
[7] Merry E. Weisner, *Women and Gender in Early Modern Europe* (Cambridge, 1993), pp. 23, 27.

mixed monarchy – invoked by John Aylmer and uncontested until the closing years of her reign – represented an attempt to renegotiate the concept of England as a godly empire in the context of a female Protestant monarch. It drew on theories of corporate political identity which developed in response to the various challenges posed to the imperial crown by its Tudor inheritors: an imperial king, in the person of Henry VIII; followed by a minor king, Edward VI; and, under Mary I, a queen perceived as exercising tyrannical rule as a consequence of her sex. In Elizabeth's reign the 'mixed monarchy' posited a twofold incorporation: of the queen and 'the people' into a sanctified body politic – the godly nation – whose collective consent, enacted in parliament, came to be seen as uniquely preserving of the godly commonwealth.[8] In this chapter and the next I want to investigate why and how 'counsel', 'consent' and 'conscience' became key concepts in the Tudor political discourse that evolved in response to the Henrician Reformation, and suggest how that triad allowed for the invention and acceptance of the 'mixed monarchy' at Elizabeth's accession.

COUNSEL, CONSENT AND CONSCIENCE: THE COMMON GOOD

The exigencies of defining an imperial body politic inaugurated by the Henrician Reformation led in one direction to kingship conceived in hieratic terms: king, not pope, as vicar of God. But they simultaneously promoted theories of corporate political identity, described and debated in terms of counsel, consent and conscience by Christian humanists including Sir Thomas Elyot, Thomas Starkey and, from the direction of the common law, Christopher St German.[9] These men wrestled with the linked issues to which the new imperial identity gave rise: how to prevent 'tyranny' (that is, ungodly rule) in the reformed commonwealth and how to maintain social order.

Sir Thomas Elyot privileged friendship as the mystical ingredient necessary to a reformed kingdom.[10] The king, argued Sir Thomas Elyot,

---

[8] For the centrality of incorporation to English political identity see J. G. A. Pocock, 'Contingency, Identity, Sovereignty' in *Uniting the Kingdom? The Making of British History*, ed. Alexander Grant and Keith Stringer (London, 1995), pp. 292–302, pp. 293–4. See Richard Helgerson, *Forms of Nationhood: The Elizabethan Writing of England* (Chicago, 1992), especially pp. 295–301, for the realisation that, under Elizabeth, 'nation' connotes an inclusive political identity, 'state' an exclusive one.

[9] Quentin Skinner, *The Foundations of Modern Political Thought*, 2 vols. (Cambridge, 1978), vol. 2, pp. 100–7; John Guy, *Christopher St German on Chancery and Statute*, Selden Society (London, 1985), pp. 38–53.

[10] For Elyot see F. W. Conrad, 'A Preservative Against Tyranny: The Political Theology of Sir Thomas Elyot', Ph.D. Dissertation, Johns Hopkins University, Baltimore, Md. (1988).

would eschew tyrannical behaviour because of the quality of intimacy
that would persist between him and his councillors – men in whom
virtue fulfilled the promise of birth. That bond would be forged through
a shared quest for virtue, identified through recourse to reason, and
exercised through the reciprocal act of dispensing and receiving counsel. It would protect the king from the propensity to tyranny – the
exercise of his untrammelled power solely according to the dictates of
his will – inseparable from his position. By the same token, councillors'
consent, signalled by their activities as magistrates on the king's behalf
throughout the realm, would attest to the legitimacy of the king's
political initiatives and hence conduce to social stability. Other members of the body politic, recognising and responding to these patterns of
virtue, at once personal and emblematic of the ordered whole, would by
this means be drawn into Christian obedience. Elyot's humanist vision
in effect sanctified the king by means of his relationships with his
councillors, a move that enabled him to assert the superiority of 'mere'
monarchy to other forms of political organisation as a means of preserving social order.[11]

If Elyot looked to a notion of affinity between the king and his
councillors as the bedrock of a reformed and ordered society, Starkey saw
the king's Great Council as the means to 'bridle' the potentially tyrannical
king. Blending an idealised version of the Venetian constitution with
older English traditions of the nobility's right to restrain bad rulers,
Starkey drew on a medieval tradition which defined the realm as a great
body composed of many men; the king, as head, being a man who differed
from his fellows in degree but not in kind.[12] True, the weighting he gave
this conception was aristocratic, but he identified parliament, as the
institutional embodiment of this council, in terms that stressed its
inclusive, and potentially redeemed, identity.[13] Incorporated into the
corpus misticum of king-in-parliament, the king's judgement would be
cleansed by its 'common counsel'. He would therefore always 'see what is
best' for the country, hence pronounce, as king (through proclamation or
statute), the 'sentence of common authority'. Rejecting the conception of

---

[11] Sir Thomas Elyot, *The Book Named The Governor*, ed. S. E. Lehmberg (London, 1962), pp. 6–7.
[12] Starkey at least raised the possibility of elective kingship in his *Dialogue* from a standpoint that
Margo Todd (*Christian Humanism*, p. 190) identifies as Erasmian humanist. See Thomas F.
Mayer, *Thomas Starkey and the Commonweal: Humanist Politics and Religion in the Reign of Henry VIII*
(Cambridge, 1989), pp. 152–3.
[13] S. J. Gunn, 'Literature and Politics in Early Tudor England', *Journal of British Studies* 30 (1991), pp.
216–21, pp. 217, 219. Like St German, Starkey saw parliament as representing the 'whole catholic
church of England'.

royal supremacy as essentially personal advanced by polemicists such as Edward Foxe and Stephen Gardiner, Starkey approached the common law position in asserting the infallibility in matters concerning the common weal of the 'mixed state' thus embodied. For Starkey, 'the voice of Parliament had become the voice of God'.[14]

Christopher St German too interpreted the royal supremacy as investing imperial status in the corporate identity of king-in-parliament. It was 'king-in-parliament' not the 'vicar of God' that was 'high sovereign over the people'. But it was in effect sovereignty delegated from God to men, enabling parliament to expound scripture and identify (if need be reform) the common law: activities he defined as coextensive and corroborative of God's will. For St German, the rule of conscience – God's voice immediately manifest in each individual soul – represented the means by which the English nation could negotiate the twin perils of papal supremacy and theocratic kingship. The consciences of all men could and should be guided by English common law, which he claimed as *summa lex* on the grounds that it emanated from an immediate relationship between God and nation, relatively untainted by the years of bondage to Rome. He also argued that equity – the legal form of conscience – was contained in the law (pre-eminently common law), rather than representing a means by which the ruler interpreted the law according to the measure of his will; a reading that enhanced the authority of statute law and common law courts as it potentially problematised that of royal proclamation.[15] For St German, as reformation spread throughout the commonwealth, true obedience and good order would arise naturally from the subordination of each man to the dictates of conscience, now informed by common law, safeguarded by the 'whole Catholic Church of England' represented in parliament, and enacted by godly lesser magistrates who filled temporal offices in proximity to the king.[16]

[14] Markku Peltonen, *Classical Humanism and Republicanism in English Political Thought 1570–1640*, Ideas in Context (Cambridge, 1995), pp. 9–10; Quentin Skinner, *Foundations of Modern Political Thought*, vol. 2, pp. 103–4. The quotation, given in Skinner, comes from W. Gordon Zeeveld, *Foundations of Tudor Policy* (Cambridge, Mass., 1948), p. 155.

[15] William Huse Dunham concludes that Henry VIII's statutes reveal 'a simultaneous and illogical exaltation of both statute law and regal power', and several Acts which put prerogative and the common law on a par with statutes; 'Regal Power and the Rule of Law: A Tudor Paradox', *Journal of British Studies* 3, no. 2 (1964), pp. 24–56, p. 36. See above, chapter 2, for Aylmer's view that those prescient enough to deny that proclamations were equivalent to statutes in Henry VIII's reign were good 'fathers to their country', whose example ought to be emulated in Elizabeth's reign.

[16] Quentin Skinner, *Foundations of Modern Political Thought*, vol. 2, pp. 54–5; John Guy, *Christopher St German*, p. 89.

These influential theorists thus responded in innovative ways to a deeply felt need to establish means of 'bridling' a potentially tyrannical ruler: a king who would be a god. At one level this attempt constituted part of the broader reformation debate concerning political authority and more specifically kingship. But it took a unique form in England in the 1530s because of the need to conceptualise the realm as a unitary sovereign state, headed by a king supreme in both church and state and directly superintended by God, which came about as a consequence of the Henrician Reformation. This local circumstance generated a particular political discourse, characterised by bifocal attention to king and commonwealth – the constituent elements of the godly empire – and linked counsel, consent and conscience in ways pregnant with political possibilities. These men's proposed solutions to the problem of imperial kingship, bruited in Henry VIII's reign, presupposed an adult male ruler of unquestioned legitimacy – a being who was not to ascend to the throne again until Charles I in 1625.[17] Nonetheless they provide the context for English conceptions of kingship as they developed in response to the accession of Henry VIII's heirs: a minor king and two (or three, depending on the status one ascribes to Jane Grey) queens.

COMMONWEALTH IDEOLOGY

In this ideological context, Edward VI's status as a minor meant that his reign posed the problem of incapacity on the part of the 'king', including a potential inability to select as councillors, and hence enter into a sound relationship with, men whose virtue controlled their own tyrannical proclivities. On one level, this lacuna gave rise to the vicious power struggles between leading members of the regency Council named by Henry VIII that simmered, and occasionally erupted, during the reign. But it also encouraged a politically significant section of the male elite to define themselves as 'citizens', ambiguously of the True Church and of the godly nation called into existence (from the point of view of convinced Protestants) with England's break from Rome. As a concomitant, Edward's reign also produced a 'commonwealth' ideology that was to be centrally important to the politics of Elizabeth's reign. Articulated by men such as Hugh Latimer, Nicholas Ridley, John Hooper, Thomas Lever,

---

[17] For the disputes concerning the legitimacy of James VI's claims to the English throne see Howard Nenner, *The Right to Be King*, Studies in Modern History (New York, 1995), esp. Introduction and chs. 1–3.

John Hales and Sir Thomas Smith, commonwealth ideology exemplified the mixed ideals of Protestant reformation in linking theological with social reform in a new framework of national election. In this framework, self-interest, whether narrowly economic or more broadly political, began to be perceived not exclusively as a declension from political virtue in the Aristotelian sense but equally as the means by which Antichrist attempted to subvert the True Church and simultaneously the English nation. Its antithesis was a breadth (or community) of vision allowed for by a spiritual capacity which transcended self-interest and caste identity by recognising the claims of the 'commonweal' or 'commonwealth' – a term signalling bonds of brotherhood among the godly as well as, increasingly, an English habitation.[18] And both Edward's and Mary's reigns, in different ways, strengthened the convictions that informed Aylmer's defence of the 'mixed monarchy' at the outset of Elizabeth's reign: that political vision of this order was both a male trait and one demonstrated by men actively and collectively participating in England's national reformation.

The *locus classicus* of the commonwealth movement during Edward VI's reign was the 1549 *Discourse of the Common Weal*. It has been variously attributed to John Hales and Sir Thomas Smith, both of whom were politically active in Edward's reign and again in Elizabeth's: Hales as clerk of the hanaper and informal adviser to William Cecil, Lord Burghley; Smith in various roles, pre-eminently in Elizabeth's reign that of Burghley's right-hand man.[19] The *Discourse* was first published during Elizabeth's reign in 1581, in conjunction with the publication of Smith's depiction of the godly commonwealth under female rule, his *De Republica Anglorum*. The conjunction has been used as evidence for Smith's authorship.[20]

In fact it seems likely that Smith did indeed write the *Discourse*, in view of the common ground it shares with the *De Republica Anglorum*. Confusion over the authorship of the *Discourse* is, however, both understandable and revealing. Hales and Smith (and Burghley) shared an ideological affinity on matters concerning the 'common weal' which historians too often ignore in the interest of assigning them to separate and

[18] For the linkage between commitment to the True Church and 'commonwealth' ideals see G. J. R. Parry, *A Protestant Vision: William Harrison and the Reformation of Elizabethan England* (Cambridge, 1987).
[19] For Hales in Elizabeth's reign see below, chapter 5; for Smith, Burghley and the *De Republica Anglorum* see below, chapter 7.
[20] Mary Dewar argues for Smith's authorship in 'The Authorship of the *Discourse of the Commonweal*', *Economic History Review* 19 (1966), pp. 388–400, pp. 390–4.

incompatible camps: Hales to the backward-looking and politically naive radical Protestants, Smith to the emerging secular rationalist tradition.[21] The difficulty of establishing the authorship of the *Discourse*, as well as its print career in the 1580s, also attest to the signal continuities between the political culture of Edward VI's and Elizabeth's reigns, especially the influence in both of commonwealth values and beliefs. It is therefore worth analysing in some detail.

The *Discourse* takes the form of three dialogues between a Doctor, a Knight, a Husbandman, a Capper (a capmaker), and a Merchant concerning the problems confronting 'this Commonweal that we be in'.[22] 'Dialogue' seems an apt characterisation, despite the large number of parts, since the whole consists of the Doctor (a doctor of divinity) advancing his views, encouraged by the occasional questions and inter-jections of his auditors, who give hearty assent to his pronouncements. Occasionally the Knight – the Doctor's peer – plays devil's advocate. It is interesting as a transitional text, pointing back to Henry VIII's reign as it announces the new dispensation of Edward's, not least in the acknowledgement that prescribing for the body politic, as they are doing, might be a dangerous business. In a section deleted from the print version of 1581 (possibly because by that point in Elizabeth's reign the intimation of repression and defiance struck too close to home), the Knight claims the right to promote their vision of the future: 'What harm is it, though we imagined here a whole Commonweal among ourselves, so it be not set forth as though we would needs have it after our devise?'[23] The *Discourse* is usually read, and accorded significance, because of its discussion of the economic problems afflicting Tudor England: the second dialogue and part of the third discuss enclosures, free trade and the consequences of a debased coinage. What is more striking, in the circumstances of Edward VI's reign, is the self-conscious-ness with which the author uses the term 'Commonweal', and the corporate definition of the body politic which he draws on as the context for his discussion of these issues.[24]

The impression conveyed in the *Discourse* as a whole is of a common-

---

[21] G. R. Elton, 'Reform and the "Commonwealth-Men" of Edward VI's Reign' in *Studies in Tudor and Stuart Politics and Government*, vol. 3 (Cambridge, 1983), pp. 234–53.
[22] Sir Thomas Smith [presumed author], *A Discourse of the Commonweal of This Realm of England* (1549), ed. Mary Dewar (Charlottesville, Va., 1969), p. 11.   [23] Ibid., p. 108.
[24] Mary Dewar approaches it in these terms in 'The Authorship of the *Discourse*'. More recently Neal Wood has argued, against the weight of evidence in my opinion, that the author celebrates avarice as a means of achieving civic unity in 'Avarice and Civil Unity: The Contribution of Sir Thomas Smith', *History of Political Thought* 23, no. 1 (1997), pp. 24–42.

wealth attaining to self-consciousness through the moral education of its 'Commons', defined as the section of the third estate likely to be summoned to sit in parliament, and represented in this conversation by the Doctor and the Knight. The 'Prohemium' consists of two linked statements: 'That no man is a stranger to the Commonwealth that he is in', and 'That of many heads is gathered a perfect counsel'.[25] In the Preface the Doctor justifies his right to prescribe for the body politic because he is 'a member of the . . . Commonweal and called to be one of the Common House':

[A]lbeit I am not of the King's Council to whom the consideration and reformation of [these matters] does chiefly belong, yet, knowing myself to be a member of the same Commonweal and called to be one of the Common House, where such things ought to be treated of, I cannot reckon myself a mere stranger to this matter; no more than a man that were in a ship which were in danger of wreck might say that, because he is not percase pilot of the same, the danger thereof did pertain nothing to him.

The meaning of the latter point is clarified through the careful choice of the occupations of the participants in the ensuing dialogues and by his conclusion that princes, 'though they be never so wise themselves, yea the wiser that they be, the more counsellors they will have; for that that one cannot perceive, another shall'.[26] The Knight too listens eagerly to the Doctor because of his responsibility to provide good counsel to the realm. At one point he begs him to continue in the hope that he may hear some 'sensible reason' from the Doctor, so that 'when I come to the parliament, whereof I am unworthy, I may there declare, which might enter into some men's ears that might do good herein'.[27] Presumably the auditors of lower social standing – the Capper, the Husbandman and the Merchant – are similarly edified, so that they too can both benefit from and advance the moral education of the common weal, in their own social spheres.

Throughout the first dialogue the Doctor argues the case for the political involvement of men learned in moral philosophy in terms that show the conflation of humanist and evangelical Protestant vocabularies. Moral philosophy, he tells his auditors, informs every part of the Commonweal, teaching 'first how every man should guide himself

---

[25] Thomas Smith, *Discourse*, p. 4. The author more commonly uses 'Commonweal' than 'Commonwealth', as, for example, when he uses this statement as a marginal comment in the Preface: 'No man is a stranger to the Commonweal that he is in', p. 11.   [26] Ibid., p. 11.

[27] Ibid., p. 108.

honestly[.] Secondly, how he should guide his family wisely and **prophetically**, and thirdly it shows how a city or realm or any other Commonweal should be well ordered and governed . . . What Commonweal can be without either a governor or counsellor that should be expert in this kind of learning?'[28] Earlier he assigned peculiar value to 'learned men' in the Commonweal because it is they who realise, and enact, the fact that 'we be not born only to ourselves but partly to the use of our country, of our parents, of our kinfolk, and partly of our friends and neighbours'. This corporate identity, awareness of which produces virtuous actions, 'shows forth the image of God in man'. Those who 'study no common utility of other', who seek 'only the conservation of themselves and the propagation of their own kind' – whether men or animals – 'resemble nothing of that godly image'.[29]

The second dialogue largely concerns economic matters. Here too the relationship between the moral education advocated by the Doctor and his self-conscious articulation of a 'Commonweal' is apparent. The discussion of enclosures, for example, focuses on the issue of 'profit'. The Knight puts forward a sixteenth-century version of the 'trickle-down' theory of wealth creation, advanced, he says, by those who support enclosures:

I have heard oftentimes much reasoning in this matter and some in maintenance of these enclosures would make this reason. Every man is a member of the Commonweal, and that that is profitable to one may be profitable to all and so to the whole Commonweal. As a great mass of treasure consists of many pence and one penny added to another and so to the third and fourth and so further makes up the great sum so does each man added to another make up the whole body of a Commonweal.

The Doctor approves of this vision of the Commonweal, which seems to include 'every man'. (Here presumably he includes those represented by the House of Commons, but not themselves able or likely to sit as members.) But he insists on an important proviso: the quest for profit must be controlled by a concern for social justice. 'True it is', he says, 'that that thing which is profitable to each man by himself, so it be not prejudicial to any other, is profitable to the whole commonweal and not otherwise.' He stresses the qualification by reiterating that men 'may not purchase themselves profit by that that may be hurtful to others', before concluding emphatically that 'men may not abuse their own things to the damage of the commonweal'.[30]

---

[28] Ibid., p. 30, my emphasis. I read 'prophetically' as meaning ordered patriarchally, according to the example of Old Testament prophets.   [29] Ibid., pp. 17, 127.   [30] Ibid., pp. 51–3.

This section of the discussion gains point and political resonance from the related discussion eight chapters later which closes the second dialogue, when the 'man' in question is the king. In a chapter entitled 'No league is to be cherished that is not for the Commonweal', the Knight raises the question of what happens when the Doctor's strictures run up against the King's right, a right that is both private and a prerogative of the crown. 'I was one in the parliament when such a thing was moved', he tells the Doctor. 'And then it was answered by a great wise man that it was to be feared lest it touched the league made between the King's Highness and some foreign prince.' The Doctor immediately counters that such a league could have been 'no true league', for its terms of reference were misconceived:

I say to you that I think it is a marvellous league that should let us to make laws to bind our own subjects that might be profitable unto them. And if there were any such league, I had lever it were broken than kept, which being broken it should do us good and being kept should do us harm. And I suppose that when we enter any league the same is meant to be for our wealth and not for our hindrance. Wherefore that league would not be esteemed that might hinder our Commonweal.[31]

Perhaps the most telling evidence for the self-conscious assessment of the envisioned Commonweal as sanctified terrain appears when the Doctor argues that we cannot malign the first inventors of gold and silver, despite the fact that it is 'lucre that drives men to all kind of mischief'. The Doctor accepts this point of view – here voiced by the Knight – and sympathises with his frustration over its damaging consequences for the 'Commonweal' (fellow feeling as well as territorial habitation). Moreover, he clearly sees it as a serious likelihood that 'we' of the Commonweal might do without gold and silver, casting it away along with iron and steel and other 'instruments of much murder and slaughter among men', in a future presumed to be imminent but not yet at hand. He concludes, however, that the abolition of 'lucre' is not possible in a global context in which moral reformation has come first to the Commonweal but has yet to make headway among its neighbours. As the marginal comment puts it, 'That that is universally esteemed must not be rejected of any Commonweal that must have traffic with other.'[32]

Finally, the Doctor's proposals for dealing with the problem of enclosures is instructive, not only for the intimation that the Common-

[31] Ibid., p. 67.   [32] Ibid., p. 112.

weal will be guided by edification to enact a right relationship between profit and social justice, but also for his determination that the way forward lies in incorporating husbandmen into the ranks of the 'Commons'. In this Commonweal, he says, we must understand the limited role of constraints, including the 'straight penalties of the laws'. Negative sanctions (by implication imposed from above, at the level of the crown) can successfully combat only bad behaviour. They cannot play a role in the central task of educating men to embrace a right understanding of 'profit' as a matter both spiritual and economic, and as such pertaining to the corporate body politic. Instead, we must explore the role of 'allurements and rewards', in particular to encourage the use of land for the production of corn rather than for pasturage. He then appeals to both English and Roman history to suggest an alternative social structure to the one currently in existence, one that would institutionalise meaningful 'allurements and rewards'. This social structure, consonant with a reformed Commonweal, would acknowledge the Husbandman's role in the body politic by allowing him a political capacity:

I have read in this realm sometime there was such a law as a man that had trespassed the law of misadventure, might have taken the plowtail for his sanctuary. Also the occupation was had so honourable among the Romans that one was taken from holding the plow to be consul in Rome, who, after his year ended, thought no scorn to resort to the same feat again.

He ends with a paean to the Husbandman's status in which we can detect intimations of that country ideology, celebrating the civic capacity of the yeoman freeholder against the tyrannical legacy of the Norman yoke, which was to flourish in the seventeenth century:

What occupation is so necessary or so profitable for man's life as this is? Or what mystery is so void of all craft as the same is? and how little is it regarded? Yea, how much is it vilified that this late nobility reputes [husbandmen] but as villeins, peasants, or slaves by whom the proudest of them have their livings.[33]

The *Discourse* thus describes social relations in the 'Commonweal' as founded in a species of spiritual equality, recognition of which entailed accepting the capacity for political action of men normally excluded from public affairs. In the society within which Smith wrote, such a radical move could have occurred only in the context of an ongoing religious reformation signalled (to the satisfaction at least of those godly men leading the advance) by God's direct engagement in England's history.

---

[33] Ibid., pp. 119–20.

And for such godly men the experience of a boy king as incumbent of the imperial crown could be, and was, read as providing that confirmation. Imperial kingship in the reign of a child encouraged recourse to a fiction common during the earlier middle ages, last used in the Florentine republic in 1528: that an interregnum – a period when monarchical authority could not be invested in an appropriate figure – was a period during which 'Christ rules expecting a king'.[34] Edward's reign advanced the conception of England as experiencing a species of interregnum as a means of stabilising the realm until he attained his majority. The iconography of the reign, promoted by prominent reformers and councillors – the same personnel as the 'Commonwealth-Men' whose ideological congruence G. R. Elton both identified and derided – displayed the boy king as a saintly conduit for God's will in the commonwealth, his councillors as men with their eyes fixed on God, whose commitment to a reformation signalled by the acceptance of Christ as king attested to their political virtue and hence to their capacity to rule.[35] The move also promoted the millennial expectancy that was so marked a feature of Edward's reign.[36]

This apocalyptically tinged conception of interregnum, like commonwealth ideology, survived Edward's reign, to attain political significance again in Elizabeth's. It is apparent in the seeming equanimity with which William Cecil, Lord Burghley, contemplated the prospect of formalising interregnal arrangements by statute at various points during the reign, from 1563 onwards. In 1584 for example – three years after the first publication of the *Discourse of the Common Weal* – Burghley (who had been personal secretary to Protector Somerset during Edward's reign) helped draft and approved a 'bill for the queen's safety' which outlined mechanisms for the maintenance of government in the event of the

[34] See Ernst H. Kantorowicz, *The King's Two Bodies: A Study in Medieval Political Theology* (Princeton, N.J., 1957), pp. 334–5. In *Tudor Royal Iconography: Literature and Art in an Age of Religious Crisis* (Princeton, N.J., 1989), p. 90, J. N. King notes Edward VI could also be depicted as standing in for Henry VIII, a solution to the problem of minor and female rulers proposed in legal terms through the notion that the 'king never dies'.

[35] John N. King, *English Reformation Literature: The Tudor Origins of the Protestant Tradition* (Princeton, N.J., 1982), pp. 161–206. G. R. Elton, 'Reform and the "Commonwealth-Men"', p. 235.

[36] In Elizabeth's reign the convocation of 1562 found it necessary to amend the explanatory notes accompanying the Lord's Prayer in the Edwardian catechism, to damp down the expectations raised by a too literal interpretation of the petition 'thy kingdom come'. John Strype concludes that the idea of Christ's thousand-year reign upon earth after the destruction of Antichrist was 'doctrine well known and owned among divines in King Edward's days'. *Annals of the Reformation and Establishment of Religion and other various occurrences in the Church of England during Queen Elizabeth's Happy Reign; together with an appendix of original papers of state, records and letters*, 7 vols. (Oxford, 1824), vol. I.i, p. 528.

queen's demise before the succession was assured. In terms that fused the pragmatic with the providential, Burghley envisioned that a parliament would be summoned by a Great Council to determine the queen's rightful successor. This step would be necessary 'because it is likely and very probable that the state of both the Realms [England and Ireland] cannot long endure without a person that by justice ought to be the successor of the Crown shall be known'. The resulting deliberations would be conducted, according to words inserted by Burghley in the text of the bill, 'in the name of God and as it were in his presence' – a text and an interpolation that give some weight to a report circulating in 1602 that after Elizabeth's death the English intended to do without monarchs altogether, governing the kingdom 'by states, as they do in the low countries'.[37]

Commonwealth ideology stressed the desirability of an equitable distribution of resources, including material goods, within a godly community that could be the nation or the True Church. (In the *Discourse*, for example, the Doctor argues that men must not define their economic interests so narrowly that they do not produce as much corn as possible, against the possibility of dearth in other countries.[38]) The economic dimension helps explain the connection between advanced Protestantism or Puritanism and attempts at social welfare or ('social engineering', in Paul Slack's words), both in Edward VI's reign and throughout Elizabeth's.[39] It is apparent in such documents as the 1549 'Policies to reduce this realm of England unto a prosperus wealthe and estate', which proposed a direct link between ongoing church reform and renewal of the commonwealth through secular (primarily economic) reforms.[40] These men unquestionably saw economic reform as a concomitant of the greater programme of reformation of the body politic that would preserve the nation's status as elect.

---

[37] Patrick Collinson, 'The Monarchical Republic of Queen Elizabeth I', *Bulletin of the John Rylands University Library of Manchester* 69, no. 2 (1986–7), pp. 394–424, pp. 420–1; Howard Nenner, *The Right to Be King*, pp. 13, 261. Markku Peltonen (*Classical Humanism*, p. 49) notes that two years earlier John Foord listed *interrex* among 'extraordinary magistrates' in the body politic, defining him as 'a magistrate legally put in the place of the deceased king by the voting assembly' for a specified period of time.

[38] 'Surely common reason would that one region should help another when it lacks? And therefore God has ordained that no country should have all commodities, but that that one lacks, another brings forth . . . to the intent that men may know that they have need one of another's help and thereby love and society to grow amongst all men the more.' Thomas Smith, *Discourse*, p. 62.

[39] Paul Slack, 'Poverty and Social Regulation' in *The Reign of Elizabeth I*, ed. Christopher Haigh (London, 1984), pp. 221–42, pp. 236–7.

[40] *Policie to reduce this realm of England unto a prosperus [sic] wealthe and estate* (1549), in *Tudor Economic Documents*, 3 vols., ed. R. H. Tawney and E. Power (London, 1924), vol. 3, pp. 311–45.

But commonwealth ideology also pointed to a potentially radical reorientation in the basis of monarchical authority, one that associated the monarch, as a member in the body of Christ, with the mission of the True Church. The reorientation was potentially radical for two reasons. First, it posited spiritual goodness as an element in political virtue. The corollary was perhaps even more significant: that, strictly in terms of numbers, the welfare of the many souls constituting the realm might be more important than the well-being of one member alone, even though that member might hold the office of (or be) a king.[41]

Moreover, commonwealth ideology survived through Mary's reign to attain a new political currency in Elizabeth's, the point at which so many men who had 'cut [their] political teeth in the acephalous conditions of Edward VI's minority', and been denied access to office in Mary's, banded together to preserve the imperial crown.[42] The intimations of spiritual and potentially political equality among the godly within the elect nation discernible in the commonwealth ideology which developed under a minor king became more pronounced under an imperial female ruler. That conjunction also ensured that the 'note of apocalyptic nationalism' that Quentin Skinner detects in defences of the Henrician Reformation sounded more powerfully in Elizabeth's reign than it had done in Edward's, this time to legitimate the rule of some male 'multitude' or community which, with God's aid and in conjunction with the queen, would protect the imperial crown in anticipation of a king. I agree with J. G. A. Pocock that the arrival of apocalyptic in England led to a mode of civic consciousness anterior to and a 'far cry from' the classical concept of citizenship, such as developed in England in the seventeenth century.[43] But the definition of England as a mixed monarchy in Elizabeth's reign, buttressed by recourse to a commonwealth ideology that defined the queen's counsellors as godly

---

[41] J. D. Alsop argues that during the 1540s and 1550s reformers such as Hugh Latimer, Thomas Becon and Thomas Smith effected a 'revolution' in the rationale for taxation, justifying claims for supply on the grounds that the sovereign deserved aid 'for the maintenance and conservation of the public weal' rather than more narrowly for the defence of the realm. They thus adduced the sovereign's participation in, and fulfilment of, the common weal rather than military necessity as the basis for taxation in a godly commonwealth. J. D. Alsop, 'Innovation in Tudor Taxation', *English Historical Review* 99, no. 390 (1984), pp. 83–93, pp. 87–8, 90. Or, as the Knight says in the *Discourse* (p. 16), 'the King must be served and the Commonweal'. For related, but distinct, ideological developments in Scotland, see J. H. Burns, *The True Law of Kingship*, especially ch. 3, pp. 93–121.   [42] Patrick Collinson, 'Monarchical Republic', p. 402.

[43] J. G. A. Pocock, *The Machiavellian Moment: Florentine Political Thought and the Atlantic Republican Tradition* (Princeton, N.J., 1975) pp. 333–60. See Markku Peltonen, *Classical Humanism*, for an account that emphasises the availability of these ideas, and their gradual absorption into political debate.

English men enacting the ambiguous role of citizen and prophet on behalf of the commonweal, proved to be an important staging post along the way.

CONQUEST AND CONSENT: THE MARIAN LEGACY

Mary I's rule introduced the wild card of gender. This, as much as the attempt to return England to Rome, had significant consequences for Elizabethan political discourse. Her accession brought into sharper relief conflicting definitions of the relationship between 'king' and 'commonwealth' at the heart of imperial kingship, as attention to the problem of a female monarch produced innovative definitions of what it meant to be a 'king'. Her reign also fused notions of conquest and tyranny and made them appear inseparable from female rule, possibly from the exercise of kingship itself.

Mary's accession to the imperial crown seemed to contemporaries to pose a problem because of her sex, not, initially, because of her religion.[44] Various solutions were advanced, including attempts to naturalise her prospective husband, Philip II, as an English king in his own right, as well as through his marriage to England's queen. The most obvious of these entailed claiming that Philip was a legitimate heir to the crown because of his putative descent from Edward III and John of Gaunt. Genealogies establishing this pedigree circulated widely around the time of Philip's arrival in England, and possibly with official approval.[45] Because of his Catholicism, however, even this solution entailed a wholesale redefinition of the concept of English imperial kingship as it had been articulated during Henry VIII's and Edward VI's reigns. Philip's claims therefore acquired a second-level supporting argument, one that brought the notion of virility centre-stage. This argument proposed that Henry VIII's claims of imperial status for the English crown were spurious, insofar as they were uniquely invested in the Tudor dynasty and linked to Protestantism. Instead, the failure of the male Tudor line denoted in effect a God-ordained reversion to the *status quo ante* in imperial affairs, hence England's incorporation again in the (reformed) Christian empire headed by the pope and the Holy Roman

---

[44] See John Foxe's account, *Acts and Monuments of these latter and perilous days*, ed. George Townsend, 8 vols. (London, 1843–9), vol. VI, pp. 387–89. J. D. Alsop, 'The Act for the Queen's Regal Power, 1554', *Parliamentary History* 13, no. 3 (1994), pp. 261–76, pp. 262–9.

[45] Stephen Gardiner and Lord Paget, at least, claimed to find them persuasive. See John Foxe, *Acts and Monuments*, vol. VI, p. 555; Glyn Redworth, *In Defence of the Church Catholic: The Life of Stephen Gardiner* (Oxford, 1990), p. 318.

Emperor. On this reading, England's past history of conquest could serve as evidence that a true empire had yet to be achieved, and apocalyptic expectancy could attach to the figure of Philip II. As emissary and representative of this true empire – and as virile in his own right – he could thus be figured as redeemer-conqueror; a figuration that perhaps explains his otherwise incomprehensible decision, on disembarking in Southampton in 1554, to unsheathe his sword and carry it 'naked in his hand a good pretty way'.[46]

Protestant polemicists from Mary's reign onwards venomously attacked Mary's Lord Chancellor, Stephen Gardiner, as chief proponent of this perverse, yet undeniably influential, reading of English history. '[T]hat subtle serpent Gardiner', as John Hales referred to him in his 1559 *Oration*, exploited ambiguities in the conception of empire advanced by reformation theorists in Henry VIII's reign to support the case for a return to Catholic orthodoxy.[47] Moreover he drew on Protestant vocabulary concerning kingship and the common weal to do so. Restoration to Catholicism, he argued, was the price that had to be paid to preserve England from the vagaries of dynastic succession, specifically female and minor rule, and to fulfil England's imperial destiny. In his 'Machiavellian' treatise *A Discourse on the Coming of the English and Normans to Britain* written between 1553 and 1555, Gardiner appealed to conquest, 'necessity' and the voice of God to argue that the common good required a renegotiation of the definition of legitimate succession so that a fully competent male would become king of England, on the occasion of his marriage to its queen.[48] Some historians dispute Gardiner's authorship of this treatise, but there can be no doubt that the views it expressed were his own.[49] For this was the man who used the

---

[46] John Foxe, *Acts and Monuments* vol. VI, p. 555.

[47] *An Oration of John Hales to the Queenes Majestie, and delivered to her Majestie by a certain Noble man, at her first entrance to her reign* (1559?), in John Foxe, *Ecclesiastical History: Containing the Acts and Monuments of Martyrs*, 3 vols. (London, 1641), vol. 3, pp. 976–9.

[48] Stephen Gardiner, *A Discourse on the Coming of the English and Normans to Britain* (ed. and tr. as *A Machiavellian Treatise* by Peter Samuel Donaldson (Cambridge, 1975)). Donaldson notes that Gardiner's extensive borrowings from Machiavelli are supplemented by his addition of a new category – the matrimonial prince – to Machiavelli's typology of new princes in *The Prince*. Preface, p. viii; Introduction, p. 24; text, p. 145.

[49] Glyn Redworth, Gardiner's most recent biographer, shares the doubts cast on Gardiner's authorship of this work by Dermot Fenlon (in his review of Donaldson's book in *Historical Journal* 19 (1976), pp. 1019–23) and Sydney Anglo ('Crypto-Machiavellism in Early Tudor England: The Problem of the *Ragionamento dell'advenimento delli Inglesi, et Normanni in Britannia*', *Renaissance and Reformation* 14, no. 2 (1978), pp. 182–93). I find Donaldson's rebuttal persuasive ('Bishop Gardiner, Machiavellian', *Historical Journal* 23, no. 1 (1980), pp. 1–16), primarily because of the congruence between Gardiner's reasoning in the *Treatise* and the views he expressed in other works. See also J. D. Alsop, 'The Act for the Queen's Regal Power'.

very public occasion of a sermon at Paul's Cross in 1554 to celebrate England's return to Rome by maintaining that minor kings and queens could not exercise *imperium*: their deficiency was 'absolute' and different in kind from Henry VIII's waywardness in having set up as emperor in the first place:

> England's separation [from Rome] continued with us these twenty years, and we all that while without a head: for when king Henry did first take upon him to be head of the church, it was then no church at all. After whose death, king Edward (having over him governors and protectors which ruled as them listed) could not be head of the church, but was only a shadow or sign of a head: and, at length, it came to pass that we had no head at all; . . . [f]or . . . the queen, being a woman, could not be head of the church . . . Thus, while we desired to have a supreme head among us, it came to pass that we had no head at all.[50]

In the *Discourse*, Gardiner uses the form of a dialogue conducted between 'Stephen' and 'Alphonso' to argue that kingship came into existence through election. Its genesis indicates the qualities needed to be king:

> By this account, one can see that necessity was the principal reason that moved men in the beginning to chose a king, a man who would be of great authority and reputation among the people and who would in England as in all the other kingdoms of the world conserve unity, administer justice, reduce men to a civil life, bridle insatiable appetites, and finally defend the people against the violence and force of enemies.[51]

Philip, a man who possesses these qualities, can be legitimated by his status as godly prince, in a realm that lost any pretence to conventional dynastic continuity at Edward VI's death:

> Since he [Edward VI] had no bodily heir the kingdom passed to his sister Mary, who with the consent of the lords and in accordance with the procedures of the kingdom took for **husband and king** Philip, son of the Emperor Charles V, for the common good of the kingdom and for the good . . . of all Christendom.[52]

Godly prince . . . and redemptive conqueror. Gardiner figures Philip as both, coming to complete a dynastic sequence begun in 1066 with the arrival in England of William, Duke of Normandy. Gardiner concludes his *Discourse* by apotheosising Philip (ambivalently now conqueror and king) as a Christian emperor whose virtue is attested by his own virility as well as the virility of his emperor father – and by the sentence of common authority[53]:

[50] John Foxe, *Acts and Monuments*, vol. VI, pp. 577–8.
[51] Stephen Gardiner, *A Machiavellian Treatise*, pp. 108–9.   [52] Ibid., my emphasis.
[53] Gardiner appears to follow the contemporary understanding of procreation that Sarah Hanley

William subjugated the realm of England and left it in trust to his successors until the coming of the powerful and most merciful Philip, son of the Emperor Charles V. This I do not call change or alteration in the kingdom, but legitimate succession, confirmed by all orders, for the restoration of religion, the honour of the kingdom and benefit of the people, as augured by the noble blood of the unconquered seed of the most powerful Germany and of that most happy house of the glorious Emperor Charles.[54]

However, the exigencies of Philip's position also led Gardiner to allow him the power of a 'mere' conqueror – as a last resort and for the common good. In the dialogue, 'Stephen' identifies compassion and mercy as salient princely attributes, but only in a king who can also, when the need arises, 'employ the methods of William, Duke of Normandy, in subjugating the kingdom, extinguishing seditions, pacifying rebellions, and leaving the kingdom in faith and peace to his successors'.[55]

Gardiner's strategy brought the issue of conquest into the political arena, in part because of the stage of reformation history in which these events occurred, in part because Philip's main claim to the English throne, disputable genealogies notwithstanding, derived from his possession through marriage of the English queen – and partly because of the related problem of a female incumbent of the crown. In the *Discourse*, Gardiner addressed and strove to defuse the issue of conquest by presenting it as the prerogative of a virtuous male ruler: a godly prince. This interpretation would legitimate Philip as king both in his own right and by virtue of marriage to England's queen. But it also represented an attempt to scotch the idea that an 'absolutist' theory of conquest became relevant in England with the accession of a female ruler, married or unmarried. Married, the realm ran the risk that Mary's husband would 'take upon him the title of Conqueror', unrestrained by his incorporation into the realm through his marriage to its queen. This danger, which Gardiner tried to finesse in the *Discourse*, was inseparable from his virility and possibly from his *virtù*.[56] But the version of English history that Gardiner drew on also implied that a female ruler, married or

calls the theory of 'autogenetic male generation' of progeny. For this, and for its relationship to political theory, see Sarah Hanley, 'The Monarchic State in Early Modern France: Marital Regime Government and Male Right' in *Politics, Ideology and the Law in Early Modern Europe: Essays in Honor of J. H. M. Salmon*, ed. Adrianna E. Bakos (New York, 1994), pp. 107–15.

[54] Stephen Gardiner, *A Machiavellian Treatise*, pp. 149–50.   [55] Ibid., p. 145.

[56] Gardiner insists that, historically, successful princes have been those who ruled according to reason, regardless of the means by which they attained power. Similar attempts to defuse this threat are apparent in the London pageantry welcoming Mary and Philip; John Foxe, *Acts and Monuments*, vol. VI, pp. 557–8S.

unmarried, might occupy the role of a conqueror from the moment she took up the crown, whether the queen in question was Mary or Elizabeth (or Jane Grey). According to William Fleetwood, Recorder of London during Elizabeth's reign and a member of Mary's last parliament, an anonymous author informed Mary early in her reign that she could 'take upon her the title of a Conqueror over all her dominions' because previous statutes did not refer to, hence bind, queens regnant.[57] She might therefore 'at her pleasure, reform the monasteries, advance her friends and suppress her enemies, establish religion, and do what she list', for 'by the law she was not bound'.[58] And of course she might if she chose 'advance' her husband to the status of a conqueror whether he claimed it or not, ceding that identity to him as her superior.

Gardiner undertook to prevent this danger with the 1554 Act for the Queen's Regnal Power, an act that, by identifying queenly power as exactly equivalent to that of kings, sought to restrain the queen within the bounds of law.[59] Gardiner, says Fleetwood, drafted the bill rather 'to remove some scruple out of some simple heads . . . than for any doubt he had' of Mary's legal position as queen-in-parliament. But the 'scruple' re-emerged in Elizabeth's reign. In 1569 Roger Edwards wrote a tract that announced that Elizabeth stood in the same position as had William the Conqueror before he agreed to be bound by English common law – an observation for which he was imprisoned for fifteen months and fined £500.[60] Edwards's tract was fuelled by the same fears of the consequences of female rule that had surfaced in Mary's reign. Ironically its recurrence might have been allowed for because of the efforts of apologists in Elizabeth's reign to assuage those fears, and to nullify the effects of Mary's reign, by arguing that Mary's failure to use

[57] William Fleetwood [presumed author], '*Itinerarium ad Windsor*' or a Dialogue between the Right Honourable Robert Earl of Leicester, Thomas Lord Buckhurst, and William Fleetwood. Written by the said Recorder, BL Harleian MS 6234 fols. 10r–25v, fol. 22r. This would presumably include legislation including Magna Carta which, according to the common law reading, restored and confirmed the immemorial law of Edward the Confessor's time in the wake of William's succession to the English throne and helped serve as a prophylactic against any 'indelible stain of sovereignty upon the English constitution'; see J. G. A. Pocock, *The Ancient Constitution and the Feudal Law: English Historical Thought in the Seventeenth Century* (Cambridge, 1957), pp, 42–55, p. 53.
[58] William Fleetwood, '*Itinerarium ad Windsor*', fol. 22r. See William Huse Dunham's account of this text, in 'Regal Power', pp. 45–6 and, more recently, J. D. Alsop's 'The Act for the Queen's Regal Power, 1554'.
[59] *Tudor Constitutional Documents, 1485–1603*, ed. Joseph Robson Tanner (Cambridge, 1940), pp. 123–4.
[60] William Lambarde's Notes on the Procedures and Privileges of the House of Commons (1584), ed. Paul L. Ward (London, 1977), p. 17.

the title 'Supreme Head' – fully to inhabit her imperial identity as they defined it – invalidated her legislative enactments.[61]

In Elizabeth's reign, as in Mary's, female rule linked issues of marriage, tyranny and conquest. It was a conviction widely shared in the sixteenth century, in England as elsewhere in Europe, that as a consequence of the Fall woman was, in Knox's words, 'no longer mistress over [her] own appetites, over [her] own will nor desires', a state of lust that could be controlled though not rectified by marriage, either to a godly man or, for Catholics, directly to Christ through the agency of a redeemed corporation, the church.[62] This perceived fall into lust, reinforced by the Aristotelian conviction that women desire men more strongly because, like other imperfect things, they strive after perfection, helps explain the view of women as having a stronger sexual drive than men, commonly held, despite the gradual supersession of Galenic scientific theories, until the late eighteenth century.[63] The marriage of a female ruler therefore denoted far more than the means of securing dynastic continuity – itself rendered problematical by the belief that children, in royal as in other marriages, followed their father's blood.[64] It signified the means by which a powerful woman's appetites could be controlled by her head – her husband – such that her rule would secure social order. According to contemporary beliefs, a woman in authority not so constrained would exercise her will according to the dictates of her desires and was therefore more likely than a man to rule a disordered realm as a tyrant. Her fallen state also precluded the possibility of her experiencing, and her will's being reformed or constrained by, pure love of country, an ideal newly reinvigorated by the Renaissance attention to the classical past. This fusion of Biblical and classical motifs informed the rooted distrust of female rule that loomed so large in sixteenth-century political thought. Driven by a twofold expression of lust – for men and for power – an unmarried woman ruler would bring tyranny or conquest in her wake. 'Unbridled' by a head, the law, the reason of the realm, or love of country, she personified political disorder. Her reign was likely to end in *de facto* conquest, either through an excess of disorder, which would attract a conqueror from the ranks of indigen-

---

[61] John Hales and John Aylmer both make this case; see John Hales, *Oration*, p. 978; and John Aylmer, *An Harborowe for Faithfull and Trewe Subject, agaynst the late blowne Blaste* (London, 1559), fol. O.

[62] John Knox, *The Political Writings of John Knox: The First Blast of the Trumpet Against the Monstrous Regiment of Women and Other Selected Works*, ed. Marvin A. Breslow (Washington, D.C., 1985).

[63] Merry E. Weisner, *Women and Gender*, pp. 23, 27.

[64] Sarah Hanley, 'The Monarchic State in Early Modern France', pp. 115–17.

ous or foreign nobility, or if, to satisfy her lust, she ceded her domain to a superior male power.[65]

In this context, Gardiner's attempt to forward the marriage to which Mary was committed appears more patriotic than 'Machiavellian' (defined as contemporaries understood the term). As chancellor (with intimations of a protector's role?), Gardiner's intention seems to have been to position Philip II as the founder of a new English dynasty, as well as Mary's 'head'. In his new role he would rule as if he himself were English, grafting his virility onto the sovereign nation in order to safeguard its imperial identity, his Christian virtue the guarantor against the threat of conquest, variously defined.

Gardiner's response to the problem of a female ruler thus entailed the reversion of the nation to Catholicism as a by-product, almost, of his commitment to Mary's marriage to a godly prince.[66] His commitment arguably derived as much from his fears concerning the consequences of an unmarried female ruler as they did from his desire to ensure a male successor to the crown, immediately and permanently. The tensions and contradictions inherent in this enterprise somewhat paradoxically promoted the claims of the 'commonwealth', or body politic – the voice of the realm inclusively defined – whose confirmation of the new order in parliament would allow Philip to rule as a godly king rather than a 'mere' conqueror. For, as Alphonso reminded Stephen in the *Treatise*,

the Romans and other Christian princes have under their rule subjects and not servants. The Roman plebs had almost equal power with the Senate, and the barons of England and France participate in the state with the king, and they have privileges and authority with the people.[67]

We therefore see Gardiner appealing to the whole body of the realm as well as to the voice of God to legitimate the new imperial crown as an exclusively male identity, and linking virtue and virility in new and politically significant ways in order to do so.

The appeal gives point to an episode recounted by John Foxe in his *Book of Martyrs* concerning an interrogation of the Protestant martyr John Rogers during Mary's reign, an interrogation at which Gardiner

---

[65] John Ponet gives the classic reading of this scenario in his *Shorte Treatise of politike power, and of the true Obedience which subjects are to be kings and other civil Governours* (1556); see below, chapter 4.

[66] Gardiner's position in regard to the marriage is ambiguous. It is unclear whether he was the moving force behind it or whether, defining his role as Chancellor in humanist terms, he sought to enact the queen's will and simultaneously constrain it. The evidence mustered by Glyn Redworth (*In Defence of the Church Catholic*, pp. 312–23) can be read either way. There seems little doubt that he saw Philip's adoption of this imperial identity as the only secure defence against confessional strife.   [67] Steven Gardiner, *A Machiavellian Treatise*, pp. 144–5.

was present. Rogers asked his interlocutors if they really believed in the new order they now professed, seeing that, with parliament agreeing, they had been preaching and writing the contrary for the past twenty years. 'Tush,' said Gardiner, 'that parliament [the reformation parliament] was with most great cruelty constrained.' 'With cruelty,' Rogers replied, 'why then I perceive that you take a wrong way with cruelty to persuade men's consciences.' Another inquisitor explained that Gardiner meant the present parliament has greater authority than the former because 'more condescended to it'. This gave Rogers the opening he (or Foxe, describing Mary's reign to insist that conscience has become consensual in Elizabeth's) needed to privilege conscience over consensus: 'It goeth not, my lord, by the more or lesser part, but by the wiser, truer and godlier part.'[68]

Moreover, there is evidence that the reading of Philip as in some sense England's saviour, whether in his own right or through his presumed ability to father a male child, spoke to a wider audience than Protestant polemicists in Elizabeth's reign were willing to admit, and had more to do with antipathy to female rule than historians customarily recognise. David Loades finds that discontent with Mary's reign after her marriage to Philip was mollified by news of her (false) pregnancy, even though the child would be three-quarters Spanish (and Catholic) and, according to contemporary readings of gender relations, representative of the father not the mother. He concludes that the 'evidence suggests people were prepared to welcome such a child' (assumed to be a boy), and describes how disappointment when the pregnancy proved to be false was much exacerbated by widespread rumours that Mary had been safely delivered of a son.[69]

In the same vein, a tract published in 1555, entitled *Certaine Questions Demanded and Asked by the Noble Realm of England, of her true natural children and Subjects of the Same*, indicates how Mary's tenure of the throne problematised monarchical identities, of 'king' and 'queen' alike.[70] The anonymous author accuses Mary and Philip of subverting the realm – through conquest, not through attempts to reintroduce Catholicism.

---

[68] John Foxe, *Acts and Monuments*, vol. VI, p. 594.
[69] David Loades, *Politics and the Nation 1450–1660* (Oxford, 1974), p. 235; John Foxe, *Acts and Monuments*, vol. VI, pp. 581–3.
[70] *Certaine Questions Demanded and Asked by the Noble Realm of England, of her true natural children and Subjects of the Same* (Wesel, 1555), STC 9981. Gerald Bowler discusses the pamphlet in the context of resistance theory in 'Marian Protestants and the Idea of Violent Resistance to Tyranny' in *Protestantism and the National Church in Sixteenth Century England*, ed. Peter Lake and Maria Dowling (London, 1987), pp. 124–43.

What is striking about the pamphlet is the considerable gender confusion that the author displays in his handling of the terms 'king', 'prince' and 'queen' (and even the pronouns 'he' and 'she'). Mary is a king when he accuses her of acting as a tyrant – in imprisoning Elizabeth, persecuting Sir Nicholas Throckmorton after his judicial acquittal for involvement in Wyatt's rebellion, and executing Lady Jane Grey:

> Item, whether [in these cases] a king becometh a tyrant, in following his will, and forsaking his law ... Item, whether it be a point of tyranny, to kill one of his own blood for fault devised, and done by others. So that none other cause can appear, why he should kill the said cousin, but only that he should not reign after him.[71]

She reverts to being female and a queen, however, when she is placed in proximity to her father or husband, most tellingly with reference to Henry VIII's 'will', which here announces his regality in a flurry of significances:

> Item whether the princess be worthy to be her father's heir (who only by his last will called her unto) will [*sic*] not observe her father's will, and whether of right her father's will ought to prevail.

The confusion culminates in a 'prince' who is ambiguously Philip, Philip and Mary, or Mary – tyrannical (and monstrous) in all three capacities. Is it this conflation that allows the writer to adjure the realm to constitute itself a sovereign power in opposition to the crown?

> Item, whether subjects ought to look to their own safety, and to the safety of the realm and to join themselves wholly together, to put down such a prince as seeketh all means possible to deliver them, their lands, their goods, their wives, their children, and the whole realm into the hands of Spaniards, who be most justly hated like dogs all the world over.[72]

What we see here is an explicit rejection of Gardiner's solution to the problem of female rule, on the grounds not that it is ungodly, but rather that it will prove impossible to restrain Philip from taking on the role of a conqueror. As a man and a king Philip will inevitably seek sole possession of the imperial crown – a possession that will exclude the true nobility from power as surely as it will the queen. If he cannot obtain it by entreaty and fair means he will use the 'foreign power within the realm at his commandment ... and the favour of the Queen' to obtain it by conquest. His charisma makes the queen powerless to stop him,

---

[71] *Certaine Questions*, fols. Aiii.r–v. See Rebecca W. Bushnell, *Tragedies of Tyrants: Political Thought and Theater in the English Renaissance* (Ithaca, N.Y., 1990) for the linkages between tyranny and feminity in the classical world and in the Renaissance.   [72] *Certaine Questions*, fol. Aiii.r.

'though she promise never so fair'. It also draws other members of the nobility to his cause and therefore problematises the status of the nobility as guardians of the realm:[73]

Item: if this word noble, be as much to say as notable: whether the notable wise, or the notable fools of a realm are to be called nobles, and whether of their consents, is to be taken for the consent of the nobility.[74]

It is equally striking that the author couches the problem almost entirely in terms of property rights. The confessional issue makes at most a very low-key appearance, seemingly as a species of property right. Mary's main crime, for which she deserves to be deposed, is that she 'hath and doeth seek all means possible to give away the realm for ever, by Parliament or otherwise, from her right heirs and natural subjects, to a stranger'.[75] Philip has proved himself to be untrustworthy because he has reneged on his promise 'made before his entry to the imperial crown of **his** [sic] realm, to suffer some of his subjects to follow their own religion'.[76] These are the grounds that lead the author to advance his two most radical propositions, asking 'whether the realm of England belong to the queen, or to her subjects', and 'whether there be two kind of treasons, one to the king's person, and another to the body of the realm' – by implication affirming that the realm belongs to the *populus* and that it is incumbent on them to 'join themselves wholly together' to redress treason committed against the body of the realm.[77]

INCORPORATING THE QUEEN

Under Mary, and because of contemporary beliefs concerning female rule, attempts to bridle or **contain** the monarch's potentially tyrannical will thus evolved into attempts to **incorporate** the queen, as a means of preserving the imperial identity of the realm. Incorporation, in Mary's reign as in Elizabeth's, could proceed in one of three directions, each

---

[73] Ibid., fol. Av.v. This view of kingship as a kind of hyper-male identity ordained by God and invested with power to protect and destroy seems to lie behind his reason why women are incapable of rule: 'Item, whether the express word of God in the xxii Chapter of Deuteronomy forbid a woman to bear a sword, or wear spurs, **as kings do in their creation**, or to wear any other weapon, or apparel of man' (fol. Aiii.r, my emphasis). [74] *Certaine Questions*, fol. Avi.v.

[75] Ibid., fol. Av.v. In Scotland, attempts to repudiate George Buchanan's theoretical justification of deposition (provoked by female rule) in *De jure regni apud Scotos* led the jurist Adam Blackwood to argue that kings are heirs to the realm, not to the kings who have preceded them. He therefore posited the *regnum* as an entity separable from both king and *populus*. See J. H. Burns, 'George Buchanan and the Anti-Monarchomachs' in *Political Discourse in Early Modern Britain*, ed. Nicholas Phillipson and Quentin Skinner (Cambridge, 1993), pp. 3–22.

[76] *Certaine Questions*, fol. Aiii.v. [77] Ibid., fols. Av.v and Aii.v.

involving a species of marriage. First, the queen could be incorporated into the imperial crown through a mystical marriage effected at her coronation, the crown understood as comprising the queen and her councillors and as such head of the body politic. This, seemingly, was the path Gardiner attempted to follow with the Regnal Act of 1554 – his fallback and fail-safe for his preferred solution of legitimating Philip as English king in his own right. The continuing acceptability of this avenue sheds light on the interactions between Elizabeth and her Privy Councillors during her reign, specifically over the issue of her marriage. It also helps explain why in Elizabeth's reign *imperium* was defined as being invested in the crown rather than in the person of the ruler – the claim made by Henry VIII.[78] Alternatively, more conventionally, this incorporation could be achieved through the queen's marriage to a godly prince, a 'solution' that became increasingly problematical over the second half of the sixteenth century, as confessional strife raised the spectre of *politique* religious identities and tyrannical kings, and in part because of Philip's intervention into English affairs, which came to be read as Spanish conquest.

Over the same period a third form of incorporation was proposed and explored, one that gained acceptability in direct proportion to the perceived difficulty of arranging marriage to a godly king. The queen could be read as incorporated into the body politic through a mystical marriage that joined her not simply to the crown but to the body of the realm. This union came to be figured as 'queen-in-parliament'. It derived from the influential reading of the imperial crown proposed during the Henrician Reformation: that the king was fully imperial, ruling *regaliter et politice*, when conjoined with the body of the realm in parliament. The redefinition of queen-in-parliament as a new species of incorporation inaugurated under Mary I continued into Elizabeth's reign and transcended, or at least complicated, the confessional divide. It was forwarded by the doctrine of the 'king's two bodies' articulated by Catholic legal theorists Anthony Browne and Edmund Plowden in Mary's reign and into Elizabeth's. F. W. Maitland dates it as having arisen around 1550; Ernst Kantorowicz sees the early 1560s as the point of its most striking formulation in a uniquely English form, in legal

---

[78] See above, chapter 2. It also sheds light on Mary Stuart's characterisation in 1582 of Elizabeth's councillors as 'principal members of this crown' – a taunt designed to insinuate Elizabeth's relative lack of monarchical authority, and to which Elizabeth responded in like terms. See below, chapter 4.

arguments over the Duchy of Lancaster Case.[79] Moreover, it rapidly became popular; common currency, I would argue, as a way of understanding, and possibly accepting, imperial female rule.[80]

Like the notion of king-in-parliament that underpinned Henry VIII's imperial identity, the concept of the 'queen's two bodies' posited a mystical marriage between monarch and realm, embodied in parliament. But this fiction too was one to which the contemporary conception of gender identities and gender relations within marriage were crucial. For in England the notion that a 'king' (or 'queen') was in some respects an artificial body composed of two distinct identities represented not only a means of addressing dynastic discontinuity but also a powerful means of redressing the perceived deficiencies of female rule. By herself, in her 'body natural', the queen was subject to infirmities to which all men (and, with even more dire consequences, women) were prey: infancy, infirmity, error, old age – lust. The 'body politic', however, represented the reason of the realm: pure, immortal, unerring, and invested in the person of the queen through a mystical marriage effected at her coronation. In Elizabeth's reign the doctrine allowed for the definition of the **queen** as a constrained or limited **king**: a 'mixed ruler', in Aylmer's terms. It also – earlier still – advanced a symbolic reading of kingship itself, allowing for the definition of 'king' as a function of 'people' which we associate with theories of resistance that proliferated in Mary's reign, but which was probably more widely and influentially disseminated in Edmund Plowden's Reports (1571). There Anthony Browne reported that 'King is a name of continuance, which shall always endure as the head and governor of the people (as the Law presumes) as long as the people continue . . .; and in this name the king never dies.'[81]

The developments traced in this chapter culminated in what Ernst Kantorowicz has perceptively identified as the 'exclusively English concept of sovereignty, King in Council in Parliament'. That makes sense – as long as we remember that this conception was forced in circumstances where the role of 'king' was played by women. 'King-in-parliament' referred to the marriage between Christ and His Church – the head of the church and the body of Christians – to draw an analogy

---

[79] Ernst Kantorowicz, *The King's Two Bodies*, pp. 406, 446.
[80] Ibid., p. 406; Marie Axton, *The Queen's Two Bodies: Drama and the Elizabeth Succession* (London, 1977), pp. 12–13.
[81] *The Commentaries and Reports of Edmund Plowden, originally written in French and now faithfully translated into English* (London, 1779), cited in Ernst Kantorowicz, *The King's Two Bodies*, p. 23.

about the relationship of the imperial king to his body politic. Given
contemporary beliefs about gender identities, queen-in-parliament denoted a marriage between queen and realm that at some level allowed,
even insisted upon, the 'body' taking the role of head, or husband.[82] But
this reversal was unnatural, threatening established relations of hierarchy and degree, if not, as John Knox asserted, 'monstrous': unholy in
the eyes of God.[83] The fallout from this figuration of the imperial queen
could be counteracted by God's immediate oversight on the one hand,
the patriotic labours of godly men on the other – and by the absolute
rectitude of the queen, signalled by her chastity. It is not surprising that
attempts to define the meaning of these (potentially conflicting) restraining mechanisms loomed large in Elizabethan political culture, throughout the entirety of the reign. Nor is it surprising that Elizabeth reigned as
a virgin queen, notwithstanding her counsellors' determination during
the first decades of the reign to secure an heir of her body as a means of
establishing the succession. At a profound level the insistence upon
Elizabeth's absolute chastity defused some of the tensions inherent in
this reading of the incorporated queen.[84] Finally, the substitution of
'queen' for 'king' in this configuration inevitably encouraged the self-
definition of parliament – Lords and Commons – as the voice of the
body politic, with a brief to protect the integrity of the realm from
conquest effected through the crown.[85] This self-definition in turn
allowed for the emergence of the view, powerfully informed by radical
Protestant conceptions of the brotherhood of men in Christ, that the

[82] Philippa Berry argues (in *Of Chastity and Power: Elizabethan Literature and the Unmarried Queen*
(London, 1989), p. 67) that Elizabethans read Elizabeth's marriage with the realm as the union of
the female with the feminine. Helen Hackett argues the more persuasive case that instead
Elizabethans regendered the nation as male when they used the marriage metaphor during
Elizabeth's reign; *Virgin Mother, Maiden Queen: Elizabeth I and the Cult of the Virgin Mary* (London,
1995), p. 60.

[83] See two classic articles: Natalie Zemon Davis's 'Women on Top' in *Society and Culture in Early
Modern France* (Stanford, Calif., 1965), pp. 124–51, and Louis Montrose's 'The Elizabethan
Subject and the Spenserian Text', in *Literary Theory/Renaissance Texts*, ed. Patricia Parker and
David Quint (Baltimore, Md., 1986), pp. 303–40.

[84] Paradoxically, the fact that it did so successfully allowed her to appropriate her chastity in the
'second reign'; the point at which it became, as several literary critics have appreciated, a
powerful counter in her assertions of monarchical autonomy. See especially Louis Montrose,
'The Elizabethan Subject', Philippa Berry, *Chastity and Power*, and Susan Frye, *Elizabeth I: The
Competition for Representation* (Oxford, 1993).

[85] According to William Huse Dunham's reading of Tudor statutes, from 1554 MPs describe
themselves in preambles as 'representing the whole body of the realm of England and the
dominions of the same, in the name of ourselves particularly, and also of the said body
universally' and repeal laws 'as well for ourselves as for the whole body whom we represent';
'Regal Power', pp. 43–4.

'commons', ambiguously chamber and estate, in some cases and for some purposes exclusively represented the realm which was to attain political significance in Elizabeth's reign.[86]

CONCLUSION

The experience of Mary's reign thus had profound consequences for political culture both in Elizabeth's reign and into the seventeenth century. It made fear of conquest common currency and common ground between those whose concerns were primarily territorial and those who interpreted 'conquest' as the subversion of the realm by the forces of the popish Antichrist. In Mary's reign the 'conquest' had proved all the more insidious because, effected from within the nation and at the level of the crown, it had allowed the 'commonwealth' no redress. Moreover, because women were read as relatively unsusceptible to reason, Mary's reign raised the 'problem of counsel', inseparable from a godly empire, in a new form. As *Certaine Questions* suggests, it problematised the role and status of the nobility, traditionally seen, whether through neo-feudal or humanist eyes, as the order capable of preserving the common weal. It allowed scope for the idea that untainted counsel might be available only from men whose primary allegiance was to the nation (or, as it came to be called in the latter stages of Elizabeth's reign, 'the country'), rather than to its monarchical representative. Mary's reign also advanced the notion that the queen might have to be conquered by her counsellors – men of virtue, ideally also of birth – to preserve the omnicompetence of the crown, for committed Protestants even the sanctity of the church.

These interpenetrating problems and contested definitions culminated, on one timeline, with the Essex Rebellion in 1601; on another with the execution of Charles I in 1649.[87] They also allowed for the emergence of a distinctively early modern concept of the 'state' in the last decades of the sixteenth century, as an attempt at their resolution. In Elizabeth's reign the Protestant ascendancy determined that the queen incorporated in the body of a sanctified nation could most effectively preserve the imperial crown, not least by mustering a broad base of

---

[86] See below, chapter 6.
[87] For the Essex Rebellion see Mervyn James, 'At a Crossroads of the Political Culture: The Essex Revolt, 1601' in *Society, Politics and Culture: Studies in Early Modern England* (Cambridge, 1986), pp. 46–65.

political support for the regime. The determination produced the defining political problems of Elizabeth's reign, problems to which there were no solutions in the context of female rule. We next need to investigate how the radical Protestant critique of kingship articulated by the so-called 'resistance theorists' became implicated in the attempt.

CHAPTER 4

Contesting the social order: 'resistance theory' and the mixed monarchy

[N]o man is king or prince by institution of nature, . . . but every king and kings sonne, hath his dignity and preheminence above other men, by authority only of the common wealth.

Robert Doleman, *A Conference About the Next Succession to the Crown*
(1594)[1]

In 1559 the Archbishop of Canterbury Matthew Parker wrote a letter to Sir Nicholas Bacon complaining that the books of 'ministers of good estimation' – presumably John Ponet and Christopher Goodman[2] – were being 'spread abroad' in London. Parker was concerned about how the *populus* were likely to respond to the ideas these works contained, doubly influential in that they were voiced by men of God, and in the context of female rule:

[T]he doctrine of the one is to prove, that a lady woman cannot be, by God's word, a governor in a Christian realm. And in another book going abroad is matter set out to prove, that it is lawful for every private subject to kill his sovereign, *ferro, veneno, quocumque modo*, if he think him to be a tyrant in his conscience, yea, and worthy to have a reward for his attempt: *exhorrui cum ista legerem*. If such principles be spread into men's heads, as now they be framed, and referred to the judgment of the subject, of the tenant, and of the servant, to discuss what tyranny is, and to discern whether his prince, his landlord, his master, is a tyrant, by his own fancy and collection supposed, what lord of the council shall ride quiet minded in the streets among desperate beasts? What master shall be sure in his bedchamber?[3]

---

[1] Robert Doleman (or Parsons), Catholic controversialist, in *A Conference About the Next Succession to the Crown of England* (1594), pp. 198–9, cited in Howard Nenner, *The Right to be King: The Succession to the Crown of England, 1603–1714*, Macmillan Studies in Modern History (New York, 1995), p. 6
[2] Although possibly John Knox.
[3] Matthew Parker, *Correspondence*, ed. J. Bruce and T. Berowne (Cambridge, 1853), p. 61.

Parker's perception of the extreme point of social dislocation is revealing: 'what lord of the council shall ride quiet minded in the streets among desperate beasts? What master shall be sure in his bedchamber?' For Parker, the egalitarian implications of these men's thought threatened patriarchy, which he read as confirmatory of social order. But it is equally significant that he appears to have been more concerned with the form of expression of 'such principles', and their uncontrolled dissemination, than with the ideas themselves, rooted as they were in Scripture and Christian humanist notions of the sanctity of individual conscience.[4] Presumably in 1559 it was an article of faith for Parker, as for others of the Protestant ascendancy, that edification would lead all men (and, through them, women) to recognise that the Elizabethan body politic was godly.[5] This recognition would, in turn, ensure social order by bringing individual consciences into alignment with, and support of, a reformed polity symbolically enacted (through the common consent of the realm) by the 1559 Acts of Supremacy and Uniformity.[6]

By the early 1570s, however, Parker doubted whether this necessary edification would occur, largely because of Elizabeth's refusal to enact the role of Deborah. Frustrated by what he saw as her attempts to use him in his official capacity to thwart reformation, and to dissociate herself from the resulting political instability, he wrote angrily to Cecil in 1572 that 'If I had not been so much bound to the mother I would not so soon have granted to serve the daughter in this place. And if I had not well trusted to have died ere this time, your honours should have sent thrice for me before I would have returned from Cambridge.'[7] Parker feared that the consequences of Elizabeth's dereliction would be the unedified application of 'resistance theory' to members of the regime, and possibly to the queen. This conviction led him to suspect a clandestine reprinting of Christopher Goodman's *How Superior Powers Oght to be*

---

[4] For the connections between Erasmian social thought, egalitarianism and patriarchy see Margo Todd, *Christian Humanism and the Puritan Social Order*, Ideas in Context (Cambridge, 1987), pp. 115–200.

[5] For the contemporary view that women were 'subsumed' in their husbands, see Frances Dolan, *Dangerous Familiars: Representations of Domestic Crime in England, 1550–1700* (New York, 1994), p. 27.

[6] See John Jewel, *An Apology of the Church of England* (1564), ed. J. E. Booty (New York, 1963), esp. p. 104. For the role of ritual in Elizabethan parliaments see David Dean, 'Image and Ritual in the Tudor Parliaments' in *Tudor Political Culture*, ed. Dale Hoak (Cambridge, 1995), pp. 243–71, pp. 243–6.

[7] Patrick Collinson, 'The Downfall of Archbishop Grindal and its Place in Elizabethan Political and Ecclesiastical History' in *Godly People: Essays on English Protestantism and Puritanism*, ed. Patrick Collinson (London, 1983), pp. 371–97, p. 373.

Obeyed when, in 1573, the lawyer Peter Birchet attempted to assassinate a courtier whom he mistook for Christopher Hatton – Privy Councillor and the queen's favourite – on the grounds that it was lawful to kill those standing in the way of full reformation.[8]

Parker's ambivalence towards the conception of the godly body politic advanced by the 'resistance theorists' – Knox, Ponet and Goodman – was shared by other members of the regime. The influence of these theorists, and the ambivalence, persisted throughout the reign, even when political necessity changed the parameters of the debate.[9] As late as 1584 Archbishop Whitgift of Canterbury – who, as the queen's man, stood in a semi-detached position to the regime – complained that Christopher Goodman was exercising a dangerous and undue influence over the Earl of Leicester, and by extension over public affairs.[10] Moreover, their conception, which in important ways hinged on a critique of imperial kingship, also formed the basis from which early Elizabethan apologists – John Aylmer, Laurence Humphrey, Sir Thomas Smith – attempted, in different ways, to position Elizabeth as a godly prince (princess) and, perhaps more importantly, to present the existing social order as redeemable through reformation. In this chapter I want to consider Goodman's and Ponet's polemic, with specific reference to the gender typologies they deploy.[11] I then want to explore how the godly minister and apologist Laurence Humphrey approached his task, in works addressed to a tripartite audience of the nobility, godly men, and the queen. Like John Aylmer, Humphrey sought to demonstrate how female rule could be consonant with a godly commonwealth. He did so on behalf of the regime and in the framework of the 'mixed monarchy'. And, like Aylmer's *Harborowe*, his apologetical works take us to the heart of the political culture that developed in Elizabeth's reign.

[8] John Strype, *Annals of the Reformation and Establishment of Religion . . . during Queen Elizabeth's Happy Reign*, 7 vols. (Oxford, 1824), vol. II.i, pp. 426–7.

[9] Jane Dawson, 'Revolutionary Conclusions: The Case of the Marian Exiles', *History of Political Thought* 11, no. 2 (1990), pp. 257–72, p. 272.

[10] John Strype, *Annals*, vol. III.i, p. 356. For the influence of Goodman and Ponet throughout Elizabeth's reign see Blair Worden, *The Sound of Virtue: Philip Sidney's 'Arcadia' and Elizabethan Politics* (New Haven, Conn., 1996), esp. pp. 189–90; p. 349; James E. Phillips, 'George Buchanan and the Sidney Circle', *Huntington Library Quarterly* 12 (1948–9), pp. 23–56; and, from a different direction, Michael McGiffert, 'Covenant, Crown, and Commons in Elizabethan Puritanism', *Journal of British Studies* 20, no. 2 (1981), pp. 32–52. I take issue only with McGiffert's assertion that undertakings promoting the 'covenant of works' in the late 1580s and 1590s were 'essentially non-political' (p. 33).

[11] I follow Winthrop S. Hudson's view that Goodman's work functions as a gloss on Ponet's, designed to provide it with a more solid Scriptural foundation and point its direct applicability to the circumstances of Mary's reign; *John Ponet (1516?–1556): Advocate of Limited Monarchy* (Chicago, 1942), pp. 182–3. For Knox see above, chapter 2.

DEFINING A GODLY SOCIAL ORDER: PONET, GOODMAN AND GENDERED KINGSHIP

Both Ponet and Goodman (Ponet more explicitly) use the terms 'common weal' (or 'wealth'), 'body politic', 'congregation' and 'country' interchangeably, pointing to the transition from a perception of England as a godly empire to an elect nation which occurred during Edward VI's and Mary I's reigns.[12] Both define a godly nation as one in which political power is exercised by godly men who serve as executors of God's law on behalf of the common weal. Both therefore disallow an imperial model of kingship.[13] Both see the commonalty – 'the people' extensively defined – as actively or potentially under threat from ungodly magistrates, and regard this as a concomitant of existence in unredeemed time rather than as a result solely of England's retrogression under Mary.[14] Both thus read 'magistracy' as fluid, capable of incorporation into the body of the realm (the repository of the True Church) at points when it and they are godly, but always poised to enact tyranny – possibly at God's behest – as sign and scourge of declension. And both use female rule as a vocabulary with which to discuss the exercise and ends of political power in a godly nation; in the interest I would argue of promoting the general accessibility and acceptability of their conception.[15] Their view of female rule is therefore fundamental to their political thought, not because either or both are necessarily misogynist (there is little direct evidence on this score) but because they use female rule as a means of exploring kingship, the most ambiguous form of magistracy.[16] This point is worth stressing because both men are sufficiently committed to their egalitarian Christian vision explicitly to include (at points) women as well as servants among the individual souls

---

[12] And, of course, to the incursion into English political discourse of the idea of the 'country' that became so politically significant from the 1590s onwards. See below, chapter 5.

[13] In what follows I am very much indebted to J. H. Burns's unpublished work on executive power, '*Regimen Medium*: Executive Power in Early-Modern Political Thought' (see the discussion on pp. 2–4).

[14] Winthrop Hudson argues that Ponet deliberately defined civil power as extensively as he could by constantly referring to the people as the 'poor' people, 'of what state or degree in this world so ever they be'; *John Ponet*, p. 162. Goodman does the same; see pp. 157, 166–7.

[15] Pauline Stafford, 'More Than a Man, or Less Than a Woman? Women Rulers in Early Modern Europe', *Gender and History* 7, no. 3 (1995), pp. 486–90, p. 487; Susan Dwyer Amussen, *An Ordered Society: Gender and Class in Early Modern England* (Columbia, N.Y., 1988), pp. 62–3, 132–3. For Ponet's attempts to propagandise, see E. J. Baskerville, 'John Ponet in Exile: A Ponet Letter to John Bale', *Journal of Ecclesiastical History* 37, no. 3 (1986), pp. 442–7, pp. 445, 447.

[16] Robert M. Kingdon accuses Goodman of misogyny in 'Calvinism and Resistance Theory, 1550–1580' in *The Cambridge History of Political Thought 1450–1700*, ed. J. H. Burns (Cambridge, 1991), pp. 193–218, pp. 196–7.

composing the godly nation; a fact that may well have fuelled Archbishop Parker's fears for patriarchy should they be, from his point of view, misinterpreted by 'the people'.

Ponet begins by asserting that fundamental law is reducible to two propositions: 'Thou shalt love thy lord God above all things, and thy neighbour as thyself. The latter part whereof he [Christ] expoundeth: what so ever ye will that men do unto you, do ye even so to them.'[17] This is the common weal which, after the Fall, is attainable only through grace or through artificial means: the exercise of political power and the constitution in men of a 'second nature', nearly allied to the capacity for reason, which persuades men to accept its exigencies. (It is this distinction that enables Ponet to present women as equal to men under the Christian dispensation, yet in general exclude them from the exercise of political power.) Even 'the Ethnics themselves', led 'only by the law of nature and their own reason', recognised the force of the divine injunction levied on Adam and Eve. With considerable sophistication they learned to prefer a 'mixed state' and, when necessary, to change their government to effect this balance:

[M]en by long continuance have judged [a mixed state] to be the best sort of all. For where that mixed state was exercised, there did the common weal longest continue. But yet every kind of these states [monarchical, aristocratic, democratic, mixed] tended to one end, that is, to the maintenance of justice, to the wealth and benefit of the whole multitude, and not of the superior and governors alone. And when they saw, that the governors abused their authority, they altered the state . . . yet always preserving and maintaining the authority, albeit they altered and changed the kind of government.

They saw, he continues, 'that without political power and authority, mankind could not be preserved, nor the world continued. The rich would oppress the poor and the poor seek the destruction of the rich.'[18]

Under the Christian dispensation, man's fallen nature poses the threat of spiritual declension leading to tyranny, as well as class warfare. And declension is signalled by the failure of Christian egalitarianism, a concept that, for Ponet as for other commonwealth ideologists, was both economic and political. Interestingly, Ponet argues that, when a nation lapses from grace in this way, God will inflict punishment by degrees, beginning with the imposition of a tyrannical head:

[17] John Ponet, *A Short Treatise of politike power* (1556) in *The English Experience*, no. 484 (Amsterdam, 1972), fol. Aiii.r.   [18] Ibid., fols. Av.r–Avi.v

[F]or the time the people followed God, no tyranny could enter, but all the members of the body sought the prosperity and wealth one of another, for God's word taught them so to do . . . And where the people have not utterly forsaken God and his word, but have begun to be weary of it; there hath not God suffered tyrants by and by to rush in, and to occupy the whole, and to suppress the good orders of the common wealth, but by little and little hath suffered them to creep in, first with the head, then with an arm and so after with a leg, and at length (were not the people penitent, and in time converted to God) to bring in the whole body, and to work the feats of tyrants.[19]

We can infer that Ponet refers to a monarch here because of the literalness with which he uses the metaphor of the body politic through-out the *Short Treatise*. It is this exactitude that enables him to attribute the capacity for godly resistance to 'the people' – a term that may include women – or the body of England. The meaning he assigns to 'head', 'legs and arms' and 'body' is most apparent in his conclusion, in which, in prophetic mode, he interprets three contemporary monstrous births as signs from God that refer to contemporary English history and warn of impending catastrophe. One child, born in Oxford in 1552, had two heads and two incompletely developed bodies joined together. Another, born in Coventry in 1555, was born without arms or legs. The third, born 'this year' in Fulham, had a disproportionately large and mis-shapen head, 'bags hanging out at the elbows and heels' and lame feet. Addressing himself to the 'Lords and Commons of England', Ponet interprets these prodigies as follows:

The child at Oxford, what did it betoken, but that our one sweet head, King Edward, should be taken away (as he was indeed) and that there should be in his place two heads, diverse governors and a toward division of the people, but not all together . . . or two people should be knit together, but not in good proportion nor agreement. The child of Coventry without the principle mem-bers to help and defend the body, must needs signify, that the natural body, that is, the people of England, shall be helpless, ready to be trodden under the foot of every creature . . . The child of Fulham, what can it signify, but that the natural body of England shall be weak, the chief members (the arms and legs) which is the nobility, so clogged with chains of gold, and bags of money that the hand shall not be able to draw out the sword, nor the heels to spur the horse to help and defend the body, that is the commons. And as the head of it is the greatest part, and greater than it ought to be, with too much superfluity of that it should not have, wherefore it must pull from the other members to comfort it, and lack of that good proportion it ought to have: so shall the governors and heads of England suck out the wealth and substance of the people (the politic body) and keep it bare.[20]

---

[19] Ibid., fol. Avii.v.   [20] Ibid., fols. Kiii.v–Kv.v, *my emphasis*.

Not only does Ponet use the metaphor of the body politic with great literalness, then, but he also applies to the body politic notions of a double political capacity analogous to the contemporary invention of the 'king's two bodies', discussed above.[21] For Ponet the two capacities, the 'natural' and the 'politic', both inhere in the nation (the 'people of England', or Lords and Commons).[22] They exist as a natural body in their identity as 'true Christian natural English men and women' who live in 'true service of the living God' because of their national identity, if for no other reason.[23] They exist as a politic body when they (now men) meet as a parliament – the point at which their 'wealth and substance' can be redistributed.

This passage should be read in conjunction with another, in which Ponet uses the notion of a double capacity possessed by all men and women as God's creatures to argue that kings attain legitimacy as executors of God's laws only insofar as they are 'contained' by their incorporation in the body of Christ. In a chapter entitled 'Whether kings, princes and other politic governors be subject to God's laws, and the positive laws of the countries' he distinguishes between 'soul' and 'power' as follows:

So then if by this word (soul) is meant every person spiritual and temporal, man and woman: and by this word (power) the authority that kings and princes execute, then can not kings and princes, but be contained under this general word (soul) as well as other. And they being but executors of God's laws, and men's just ordinances, be also not exempted from them.[24]

For Goodman too the Christian dispensation has redeemed 'the people' from enslavement to their rulers, giving them power and liberty to be 'free subjects'; that is, citizens in the body of Christ, all equally obedient to God, our 'chief king and lord'.[25] We see again the ambiguity of the notion of 'citizen', once it is affixed to 'country', in Goodman's statement that such 'free subjects' are stakeholders in the nation, as well as its implications for the relationship between people and magistrates:

[T]he people, which ought not to suffer all power and liberty to be taken from them, and thereby to become brute beasts, without judgment and reason, thinking all things lawful, which their rulers do without exception, command

---

[21] See above, chapter 3.
[22] I omit 'king or queen' here because Ponet also seems to have done so, in keeping with his attempt to define monarchy as an element of the noble order.
[23] John Ponet, *A Short Treatise*, fol. Ivii.v.   [24] Ibid., fol. Cvi.r.
[25] Christopher Goodman, *How Superior Powers Oght to be Obeyed* (1558), The Facsimile Text Society (New York, 1931), pp. 148, 167, 157. Goodman seems to identify 'the people' as a male construct more exclusively than either Ponet or Humphrey does.

them, be they never so far from reason or godliness: as though they were not reasonable creatures, but brute beasts: as though there were no difference betwixt bond slaves, and free subjects: as though they had no portion or right at all in the country where they inhabit: but as they were altogether created of God to serve their kings and governors like slaves, and not their kings and governors appointed of God to preserve his people, whereof they are but a portion and members, albeit they occupy the chief room and office . . . And as the people may be assured by God's word that this liberty apperaineth to them, which becometh members of one body and brethren, because the Lord God himself (from whom kings have their authority and power) calleth their subjects and people their brethren, charging them in no case to lift themselves above them.[26]

And for Goodman, as for Ponet, God has uniquely privileged the English nation. He intimates that this elect status is signalled by the number and variety of magistrates, and by their common recognition that their status derives from submission to God's will. This linkage allows him to describe their function as executive rather than imperial:

God hath no less mercifully dealt with you in England, not only giving unto you his laws and holy word, with far greater light and plainer declaration of his will and pleasure then ever was published to the Israelites: but also hath furnished you with all sorts of magistrates, officers, and governors necessary for the accomplishment, or rather execution of the same.[27]

Thus, for both Ponet and Goodman, magistrates, who are the executors of political power, exist in order to promote God's redemptive plan for mankind. This ordination determines the limits of subjects' obedience, in a cultural context in which it was assumed that, despite human fallibility and the exertions of Antichrist, God's redemptive plan could be known and publicly articulated. It simultaneously privileges the role in political affairs of conscience, conceived of as related to reason, and both individual possession and expression of common consent. Common consent thus emerges as a collective competence, articulated by men, and commensurate with social order in a godly nation of which God is king. For Ponet.

all men whatsoever ministry or vocation they exercise, are but men and so may err. We see councils against councils, parliaments against parliaments, com-

---

[26] Christopher Goodman, *Superior Powers*, pp. 148–9. Ponet obviously views political power as residing in 'the people', insofar as they are godly, who bestow it on their rulers; see *A Short Treatise*, fols. Bv.r, Bvi.v–r. Goodman seems to think of governors as being elected by God and legitimated by His ongoing providence; *Superior Powers*, pp. 44, 122.

[27] Christopher Goodman, *Superior Powers*, p. 214. Earlier he had identified them as 'councillors, noble men, rulers, justices, mayors, sheriffs, bailiffs, constables, or gaolers' pp. 95–6.

mandment against commandment, this day one thing, tomorrow another . . . And therefore Christian men ought well to consider, and weigh men's commandments, before they be hasty to do them, to see if they be contrary or repugnant to God's commandments and justice.[28]

The corollary is that tyrants can be deposed by a private man acting as an instrument of God and the commonwealth. 'Common consent' effects the 'common authority' that allows for this most extreme form of political engagement. His most famous passage states – in gender-specific terms:

I think it cannot be maintained by God's word, that any private man may kill, except (where execution of just punishment upon tyrants, idolaters, and traitorous governors is either by the whole state utterly neglected, or the prince with the nobility and council conspire the subversion or alteration of their country and people), any private man have some special inward commandment or surely proved motion of God: . . . or be otherwise commanded or permitted by common authority upon just occasion and common necessity to kill.[29]

'Common authority', then, is conscience in active, public mode, summoned up by political exigency and ordained by God. It is the voice of the 'country' (the 'body natural' of the godly nation), and it is indisputably, for both Ponet and Goodman, gendered male:

And men ought to have more respect to their country, than to their prince: to the common wealth, than to any one person. For the country and common wealth is a degree above the king. Next unto God men ought to love their country, and the whole common wealth before any member of it: as kings and princes (be they never so great) are but members: and common wealths may stand well enough and flourish, albeit there be no kings, but contrariwise without a common wealth there can be no king. Common wealths and realms may live, when the head is cut off, and may put on a new head, that is, make them a new governor, when they see their old head seek too much his own will and not the wealth of the whole body, for the which he was only ordained.[30]

Goodman argues that 'the word of God freeth you from the obedience of any Prince, be he never so mighty, wise or politic, commanding anything which God forbiddeth, and herein giveth you authority to withstand the same'.[31] And 'you', he makes clear at another place, refers to 'all such as bear the name of Christ and would be taken for the people of God, though they be of the basest and lowest state of subjects' – a potentially socially inclusive (but, in Goodman's handling, a gender-

[28] John Ponet, *A Short Treatise.*, fol. Diii.r. [29] Ibid., fols. Gviii.r, Hi.v, Hii.v.
[30] Ibid., fol. Dvii.r. [31] Christopher Goodman, *Superior Powers*, p. 97.

specific) identity.[32] The special relationship between God and His English people allows them to wield executive power to preserve the common weal:

And though it appear at the first sight a great disorder, that the people should take unto them the punishment of transgression, yet, when the magistrates and other officers cease to do their duty, they are as it were, without officers, yea, worse than if they had none at all, and then God giveth the sword into the peoples' hand, and he himself is become immediately their head (if they will seek the accomplishment of his laws).[33]

What then of kings, queens and nobles? These statements by Ponet and Goodman show them using 'king' or 'prince' to indicate a species of magistrate peculiarly likely to misinterpret the role as an imperial one, not least because of its singularity. From their point of view this means that kings and princes always threaten to appropriate power that belongs to God. This misappropriation constitutes 'tyranny' in the first instance. Of itself, and almost regardless of the political agenda pursued, tyranny endangers the common weal, the attainment and fulfilment of which depends on a right relationship with God. In other words, 'kings' can cede their singularity and be incorporated with the nobility. In this case they can be godly magistrates, provided that they and it are infused with virtue. Alternatively, they can stand alone as tyrants and conquerors – for Ponet figured as Nimrod, the Old Testament despot whose power was, in J. G. A. Pocock's apt phrase, 'not unwilled by God'. Neither man allows for the possibility of a godly emperor.[34] And both use female rule as a means of making this general case and pointing its specific applicability to England under Mary Tudor.

In assessing female rule Goodman takes very much the same line as John Knox. He argues that women's rule is a 'monster in nature, and disorder amongst men' against which God has voiced an absolute prohibition in His treatment of Eve, reinforced by the strictures of St Paul.[35] In 'electing, anointing, and crowning' a woman to be queen of England, Englishmen have been led 'besides your common senses and the manifest word of God'. And God's prohibition is absolute: it includes not only the 'bastard' Mary, but also the 'lawfully begotten' sibling, Elizabeth – 'that godly Lady, and meek lamb, void of all Spanish pride, and strange blood'. Attempts to legitimate women's rule betray only the distance Englishmen have yet to travel before they truly dwell

[32] Ibid., pp. 166–7.   [33] Ibid., p. 185.
[34] J. G. A. Pocock, *The Machiavellian Moment: Florentine Political Thought and the Atlantic Republican Tradition* (Princeton, N.J., 1975), p. 380.   [35] Christopher Goodman, *Superior Powers*, p. 52.

in the house of the Lord, by acknowledging the supremacy of God's law as revealed through Christ:

I know you will say, the crown is not entailed to the heir males only, but appertaineth as well to the daughters; and therefore by the laws of the realm, you could not otherwise do. But if it be true, yet miserable is this answer of such as had so long professed the Gospel, and the lively word of God. If it had been made of pagans and heathens, which know not God by his word, it might better have been borne withal. But amongst them that bear the name of God's people, with whom his laws should have chief authority, this answer is not tolerable, to make the constant and undoubted law of God . . . to give place to the vain and ungodly decrees of men.[36]

The Christian dispensation has freed men to acknowledge only God as their overlord. Yet Englishmen's lack of faith in their destiny, attested to by their concern for inheritance by blood, has led them to 'willingly become as it were, bondmen to the lusts of a most impotent and unbridled woman'. Here he quotes selectively from St Paul (he omits 'neither male nor female', a common elision of the period) to image a political equality that transcends national and familial, but not gender, difference:

For now are we freed from that Jewish yoke to raise up seed to our brethren departing without issue, by the coming of our Saviour Jesus Christ, who hath destroyed the wall and distance betwixt the Jews and Gentiles, and hath no more respect to any tribes (for conservation whereof this was permitted) but all are made one in him without distinction, which acknowledge him . . . For in Christ Jesus there is neither Jew, nor Gentile, Grecian or Barbarous, bond nor free.[37]

Like Knox, however, Goodman believes Englishmen might 'have some pretence . . . to be quiet, and pray for the life' of a female ruler if she devoted herself single-mindedly to the 'peace and protection' of the people. But for Goodman this could be achieved only by a self-reformation that would make her an unflagging champion of God's cause – and even then her rule would be only supportable, not lawful:

To be short, if she . . . could have been satisfied and unfeignedly moved to confess the true Christ and Messiah, and repented her former rebellion in giving contrary commandment to all her dominions, charging them to receive again the true religion and to expel all blasphemous idolatry of the pestilent

---

[36] Ibid., pp. 54–5.
[37] Ibid., p. 97. Gerald Bowler notes that the ideas of such as Knox, Ponet and Goodman, if adopted, would have 'swept away the rule of women, dynastic monarchy, and the possibility of anyone but an enthusiastic Calvinist male sitting on the throne'; 'Marian Protestants and the Idea of Violent Resistance to Tyranny' in *Protestantism and the National Church in Sixteenth Century England*, ed. Peter Lake and Maria Dowling (London, 1967), pp. 124–43, p. 140.

papists: and that none should speak any evil against Christ and his religion . . . then were she more to be borne with, and reverenced as a ruler (if it were lawful for a woman to rule at all).[38]

(It would, presumably, put her in a position of more than usual subordination to godly ministers, to define the 'true religion' and attest to the sincerity of her conversion.)

For Ponet, too, the fetish with legitimate succession which secured Mary's accession reveals declension in the nation. He makes this point by implicitly contrasting the behaviour of Englishmen with that of the Israelites suffering under Queen Athalia:

When that doughty dame Queen Athalia, the woman tyrant . . . had killed all the king's progeny (saving Joas . . .) purposing to reign thereby in security, and to transpose the right of the crown to strangers or some other favourers of her cruel proceedings at her pleasure by the help and subtlety of her traitorous councillors, and so went on in all abomination and cruelty without controlling a great space: Did her subjects suffer her in her wickedness still unpunished though she was the undoubted Queen and chief governor of the land? No, no. But as soon as Joas was a little nursed up, and crept somewhat out of the shell being a child of seven years old: the nobility and commons feeling by experience what misery it was to live under the government of a mischievous woman, not only guarded Joas with men and all decent regal ceremonies unto the house of God and there crowned him solemnly: but also when Athalia came in . . . and perceiving the matter, rent her clothes howling and crying, as the manner of mad women is, especially in the hot seasons of the year: they laid hands on her (for all her crying, treason, treason) and when they had carried her out of the house of God, they slew her. And so was the realm rid of a tyrant, the right inheritor possessed in his regal state, the people made a new bond with God to serve him sincerely according to his word, and banished all idolatry and false religion (which the queen had set up and used), and the common wealth flourished afresh.[39]

It is interesting that the right inheritor is a male child and, like Edward VI, surrounded by godly men as ministers and councillors. One cannot help but also think of the implications of this well-rehearsed story for English as well as Scottish politics once Mary Stuart gave birth to a son in 1566.[40]

---

[38] Christopher Goodman, *Superior Powers*, p. 131.   [39] John Ponet, *A Short Treatise*, fols. Hii.v–r.
[40] John Aylmer recounts the story of Athalia in his *Harborowe for Faithfull and Trewe Subjects, agaynst the late blowne Blaste* (London, 1559), but argues (as one would expect) that her reign was illegitimate and therefore inapplicable to Elizabeth's queenship. Job Throckmorton identified Mary Stuart as 'that wretched Athalia' in commending her execution and insisting it be a preliminary to 'reform[ing] the house of Goddan, to settl[ing] the Crown to the bliss of posterity' in a parliamentary speech of 1588; J. E. Neale, *Elizabeth I and Her Parliaments*, 2 vols. (London, 1957), vol. 2, pp. 150–1.

'Kings, princes and other governors . . . are ordained for the people', Ponet claims, yet to acknowledge this requires a level of spiritual attainment incompatible with imperial kingship and unobtainable by women unless immediately informed by grace.[41] Again Ponet uses female rule (in this case Mary's) to make the point, refuting views he attributes to Edmund Bonner, bishop of London in Mary's reign and one of the archfiends who populate his book:

> But thou wilt say: it [the realm] is the Queen's own, and she may lawfully do with her own what she lusteth. What if it be denied to be her own? But thou wilt say: she hath the crown by inheritance, and may dispose of the realm, and every part of the realm, as it pleaseth her. But I answer: that albeit she have it by inheritance, yet she hath it with an oath, law and condition to be kept and maintain it, not to depart with it or diminish it . . . For albeit the king or queen of a realm have the crown never so justly, yet may they not dispose of the crown or realm, as it pleaseth them. They have the crown to minister justice, but the realm being a body of free men and not of bondmen, he nor she can not give or sell them as slaves and bondmen.[42]

Finally, Ponet intimates that 'king' may denote Nimrod in a modern guise, again by means of an anecdote concerning female rule. This one recounts the actions of Cacanus, a king of Germany, and Ramilda, wife of a Venetian duke and, after his death in battle, sole possessor of his domain. In this anecdote, which points explicitly at England under the rule of Philip and Mary, the language of conquest is central, and the woman figures both female lust and the city degraded by female rule. After killing the duke in battle, Cacanus besieges the city where Ramilda is lodged. Perhaps because of his superior manliness, manifested in his ability to kill her husband, she develops a passionate attraction to him: 'She wisheth, that she might feel him enter into her own hold. Meat nor drink could do her no good, she could not sleep, she sobbeth, she howleth, . . . she teareth her hair, and is more than half mad, for lack of her lust.'[43] Ramilda has 'no regard of the love that every honest **creature** ought to bear to his country'; the indeterminate noun allows Ponet to glance at godly women without derailing his typology. Her disregard is evinced by her conviction that she possesses the city, just as she seeks to possess Cacanus. Inevitably, dishonourably, 'she promiseth to give him city, country, jewels, goods, and whatsoever she could pull off her subjects . . . so that he would marry her'. This he did, for the twofold

[41] John Ponet, *A Short Treatise*, fol. Gvii.v.   [42] Ibid., fols. Eiii.v–r; Eiiii.v.
[43] Lena Orlin refers to this anecdote in her discussion of the treatment meted out to the wayward wife of Faversham, Alyce Ardern; *Private Matters and Public Culture in Post-Reformation England* (New York, 1994), pp. 79–84.

purpose of punishing her and warning the city of the dire consequences of female rule. After a night of conquest (he 'took pains to shake up her lecherous rotten ribs'), he departed, leaving 'her gates open free to every man: and (as some, God give them grace to repent in time, did to the wicked woman of Feversham in Kent, that not long since killed her husband) he gave every man liberty that would, to offer his devotion in to her corporesse [sic]'. Cacanus then 'caused her to be thrust on a stake naked, that all men might see those ugly parts, which to satisfy she was content to betray her natural country: and that it should be an example to all others, to take heed to do the like, he causeth the whole city to be clear overthrown.' Dispassionately Ponet points the moral, in terms that establish an unambiguous equivalence between the figure of a king and the figure of Nimrod: 'This [sic] may ye see, that kings spare neither male nor female, great nor small, that for any respect betray their own natural country.'[44]

Ponet and Goodman use the dangers and inadequacies of female rule, instanced by Mary's reign among others, to urge spiritual reformation on their countrymen; a reformation that, once effected, will make England God's nation, indisputably and perpetually. This move allows them to appeal to the nobility (a term they tend to use as synonymous with magistrates excluding 'kings and princes') on the basis of its corporate identity as a virile and potentially virtuous estate. The nobility are ordained by God to protect the common weal. They do so by constraining the king's will (more powerfully now 'kings' and queens' will'[45]) and protecting the 'people of God'. Ponet argues this is the only ground upon which the differentiation of the nobility from the rest of mankind can be justified:

Whereof came the name of nobility, or how were those that be called heroical or noble personages divided from others, and had such honour and reverence, seeing all men came of one man and one woman? Was it for their lusty hawking and hunting? for their nimble dicing and cunning carding? for their fine singing and dancing: for their open bragging and swearing? for their false fliering [sic] and flattering? for their subtle piking and stealing? for their cruel polling and pilling? for their merciless man murdering? for their unnatural destroying of their natural country men, and traitorous betraying of their country? No, no, there was no such thing. The respect only of their virtue and love to their country brought them thereto. Because they revenged and delivered the oppressed people out of the hands of their governors, who abused their authority, and wickedly and cruelly and tyrannously ruled over them.[46]

[44] John Ponet, *A Short Treatise*, fols. Iii.r–v.   [45] Christopher Goodman, *Superior Powers*, p. 144.
[46] John Ponet, *A Short Treatise*, fol. Gvii.r.

Goodman argues that in Mary's reign the nobility have been deceived about their true role because of the unholy alliance of pope and queen:

> The nobles also (though unworthily will be so called) hearing no other preaching, but that they must obey their Prince, neither knowing whom, wherein, nor how far, have in like manner, as men disguised upon a stage, turned their nobility to open shame amongst all nations . . . seeing they are made instruments of impiety, and destroyers of their native country, which first were ordained in realms to stand in defence of true religion, laws and wealth of their nation, and to be a shield (to their power) against their enemies in time of war, and a bridle at home to their princes in time of peace: neither to suffer them in this sort to rage against God, and utterly to condemn the wholesome laws of the realm, to satisfy their filthy lust and vainglory.

'Wicked councillors', 'plain Gnatos and flatterers' have persuaded the nobles that true obedience requires that they 'compass nothing but that which their princes lust after, or may at the least please them'. These wicked councillors 'have hitherto sought and yet appearingly do, how to accomplish and satisfy the ungodly lusts of their ungodly and unlawful governess, wicked Jezebel [Mary]'. Those who join their ranks, whether through an inability to see the truth or through pride of birth, 'most wickedly betray[ ] Christ, their country, and themselves (so much as lieth in them) to become slaves'.[47] Here again, as with Ponet, we see how tyrannical 'lust' can be expressively, but not exclusively, figured as the attribute of a female ruler, and how this critique of kingship positions 'true' nobility as enacted through opposition to imperial pretension.

Ponet and Goodman set out a commanding view of the godly commonwealth, informed by militant Christian humanism and delineating the role of the godly in circumstances of tyrannical (read as female) rule. They did so through an appeal to the nobility which simultaneously valorised 'the people', defined in socially extensive (if gender-specific) terms as 'the country'. They proposed radical commitment on the part of all men to God and the common weal as the sole guarantor of a right relationship between God and His people – men and women – in the godly nation and the True Church. Their understanding of magistracy presented kingship as inherently problematical and likely to degenerate into tyranny, and depicted the nobility as ambiguously positioned with regard to Christian, hence political, virtue. In part Ponet's and Goodman's appeal to the nobility is evidence of what Mervyn James calls the

---

[47] Christopher Goodman, *Superior Powers*, pp. 34–5. I take 'so much as lieth in them' to mean that they still remain God's creatures – in implicit contrast certainly to the pope and possibly to Mary herself.

'moralisation of politics' which occurred during the Tudor period, attested to by the concern of Protestant expositors that 'nobility' become synonymous with 'virtue', defined in Christian terms, rather than solely with reference to blood and military capability.[48] But the appeal has been rendered militant by its articulation in the context of female rule. Their cry (on behalf of the nobility) is not 'Serve God and King', but rather 'Serve God as King' and use the sword in their hand to protect the common weal. Moreover, their ideas would have been generally accessible. Drawing on contemporary commonplaces concerning women's nature and their incapacity for rule that achieved a new and widespread currency during Mary I's reign, Ponet and Goodman communicated their vocabulary of political relationships in a popular idiom, one that continued to command assent even after England's providential deliverance from her rule.

REDEFINING THE SOCIAL ORDER: LAURENCE HUMPHREY'S APOLOGETICAL WORKS

The re-establishment of Protestantism under a female ruler at Elizabeth's accession was therefore a difficult proposition, not least because of the ways in which reactions to female rule under Mary I – across the confessional spectrum – had problematised monarchical authority. At this stage in England's reformation history it required the renegotiation of the central tenets of the 'resistance theorists' so that the support of the godly could be mobilised on behalf of a female monarch and in defence of a social order wedded, until such time as further reformation transformed it, to the maintenance of socially determined hierarchy and degree. This balancing act was all the more difficult, and necessary, given the lack of widespread support for the reformed position, certainly among the ranks of the long-established aristocracy.[49] Laurence Humphrey, whose time in exile under Mary was spent helping John Foxe compile and publish his *Acts and Monuments* and who became regius professor of divinity at Oxford in the 1560s, grappled with these paradoxes in two apologetical works produced in the early years of Elizabeth's reign. Humphrey's efforts to effect this renegotiation are worthy

[48] Mervyn James, 'English Politics and the Concept of Honour, 1485–1642' in *Society, Politics and Culture: Studies in Early Modern England* (Cambridge, 1986), pp. 316–20.
[49] Lawrence Stone, *The Crisis of the Aristocracy 1558–1641*, abridged edn (Oxford, 1977), p. 335; Patrick Collinson, 'The Elizabethan Exclusion Crisis and the Elizabethan Polity', *Proceedings of the British Academy* 84 (1994), pp. 51–92, p. 56.

of attention, partly because he, like John Aylmer and Sir Thomas Smith, sought to claim Ponet's and Goodman's image of the godly common- wealth as the basis for Elizabethan political arrangements. Moreover he, like them, spoke on behalf of the regime to explore and explain the meaning of the 'mixed monarchy'.[50]

Humphrey produced two works instructing his readers of their rights and responsibilities in the godly commonwealth, the *De Religionis Conser- vatione et Reformatione Vera* and *Optimates sive de Nobilitate*, printed in Basle in 1559 and 1560 respectively. In the *De Religionis Conservatione* Humphrey spoke, in Latin, to an assumed audience of elite men, addressing 'Fathers and Noblemen' and 'most noble and beloved citizens'.[51] The *Optimates sive de Nobilitate*, dedicated both to the queen and to the 'Christian Gentlemen' of the Inner Temple, was clearly designed to be more widely accessible, as its translation into English as *The Nobles or of Nobility* in 1563 suggests.[52] The gender typologies that Humphrey em- ploys as he attempts to delineate the rights and responsibilities of the three estates of the realm – queen, lords and commons – are particularly instructive in view of the relationship between his envisaged common- wealth and that of Ponet and Goodman.

In *De Religionis*, Humphrey, like John Aylmer, faced the task of redefining 'obedience' so that it could be seen as the godly duty of every subject. In the wake of Goodman and Ponet's works this also entailed justifying female rule and disallowing the proposition that a private man could, at God's calling or upon 'common authority', kill a ruler deemed tyrannical. Humphrey's first move therefore was to emphasise the universal and socially inclusive character of the new dispensation – in terms that appeal exclusively to men:[53]

I shall show how great it is to those who at least confess the boon yet belittle it with words; and I shall try to convince those, who altogether do not believe,

---

[50] He enjoyed the support of Burghley, Leicester, Edwin Sandys and Matthew Parker, who used him to promote the government into the 1570s. For information about his life and his links with Elizabeth's councillors see Janet Kemp, 'Laurence Humphrey, Elizabethan Puritan: His Life and Political Theories' (Ph.D. dissertation, West Virginia University (1978).

[51] Janet Kemp translates it as an Appendix to her dissertation, 'Laurence Humphrey, Elizabethan Puritan'. All cited references are to her translation see pp. 186 and 189.

[52] Laurence Humphrey, *The Nobles or of Nobility. The Original nature, duties, rights, and Christian institutions thereof* (London, 1563), STC 13964. All quotations are taken from this edition.

[53] In the text it is obvious that Humphrey is very aware of the problem of whether and when inclusive social identifiers – 'the people', 'the multitude' – refer to women as well as men. For the most part he presents these terms as referring specifically to men, in keeping with his emphasis on England's institutions as instrumental to her salvific history. But I think it is fair to detect a broader definition of 'the people' – as a gender-inclusive identity – operating as a subtext in his discourse; an attempt, in evangelical Protestant terms, to have his cake and eat it too.

that the reason why they should rejoice, give thanks to God and embrace this new change with their whole minds was given, not to one party or faction of men, but to many, indeed not only to many but to the multitude.[54]

This new change is doctrine led and providentially directed – a status betokened by the consent of the 'whole people': it has been 'made holy and confirmed by the public deliberation of the whole commonwealth'.[55] Significantly, Humphrey's conception of this new, true process of reformation positions the queen as a godly magistrate – a governor – by pointing an implicit contrast with the imperial reformation effected by Henry VIII ('you' are the 'Fathers and Noblemen' whom he addresses):

If the Old Christ . . . had been the most perfect Messiah and Christ, there would have been no need, after the matter had been raised again and subjected to a reckoning, to annul the old decrees and to establish a new one and to abolish the previous decrees with the consent of the assemblies and the honourable council. But your wisdom saw that this other Christ had been thrust upon you by force . . . established more by command than truth, advanced by the evil of the time and the blindness of men . . . And so you prefer to run back to the Christ whom the voice of the father, calling from Heaven, ordered you to hear . . . For this reason the matter was settled openly and transacted in Parliament and in the assembly of all ranks, by agreement of the nobles, clergy and people with all parts agreeing. In this matter, while you, at the instigation of the Holy Spirit, by the declaration of sacred scripture, by the new and most fortunate guidance and command of her Majesty, with a change in direction, are reforming previous acts with later ones (which usually are wise and more mature), you . . . testify . . . by one universal act . . . that you consider private affairs and consideration of names less than the Christian commonwealth and the true dignity of the whole people.[56]

Elizabeth can therefore be a queen, insofar as godly men remain in obedience to the 'new Christ'. Humphrey pleads with 'English fathers and brothers . . . by our common father and brother Christ' to preserve the doctrine that they themselves have received and promoted by acknowledging themselves to be subjects of a godly governess, beneficiary and benefactor of their godly endeavours. He posits an 'ascending' model of edification (to use Walter Ullman's terminology) among the male body politic, a move that enables him to harness reforming zeal to the service of the regime.[57] Their obedience – to God through the queen – attests to their sanctified status, as it will promote hers:

[54] Laurence Humphrey, *De Religionis*, pp. 169–70.   [55] Ibid., p. 211.
[56] Ibid., p. 183.   [57] Walter Ullman, *Medieval Political Thought* (London, 1965), pp. 12–13.

Since I believe that your divinely inspired courage, together with your devout and outstanding prudence, should be proclaimed in all centuries . . . you who in your counsels and opinions led back Christ into parliament, into the realm and Commonwealth, so I think your obedience which spreads abroad on everyone's lips, by which you follow the queen, the true heir and most worthy prince most wonderfully brought forth by God to reveal the glory of his name and for the inviolable administration of religion, should [also be commended] . . . [I]t is the part of men who reject all religion to wish her ill, who is the strongest founder and promoter of religion.[58]

But Humphrey does not find it possible to insist on obedience to magistrates, including the queen, at all costs. Clearly he shares Ponet's and Goodman's conviction that such unqualified obedience not only threatens true religion but also reduces 'men in Christ' to brute beasts. He therefore argues against tyrannicide – the killing of a tyrant by a private individual – on the grounds, not that such an outcome is forbidden, but rather that it is the prerogative of the 'whole people'. Their collective deliberation allows for the deposition of kings as it preserves against the 'disturbance of the public order and anarchy'.

As we go back to the sources themselves, it is not written here that a private individual should strike his king from his midst but whoever made the law . . . ascribes clearly and distinctly the place, the form of judgment, witness and judges . . . And does this not intend that the whole people shall be the judge? Does not this speak about legitimate examination and punishment? . . . We are sheep and lambs, not wolves or bears.[59]

Here, as throughout, he attempts to renegotiate Ponet's and Goodman's vision of the commonwealth in pacific mode. He argues that virtue, and 'true nobility' is figured, until the Second Coming, by the 'new Christ', not the 'old' – an antithesis in which the latter term points ambiguously, if bizarrely, to both Jehovah and Henry VIII.[60] This move allows him to define kingship as a form of popular election and to privilege the 'common consent of the realm' as the means of edification of both king and Commons.[61] Here again, as with Thomas Starkey, we encounter parliament as the 'voice of God', but presented in a form that shows how far English political thought had travelled by the time of Elizabeth's accession. The depiction of the 'whole people' as 'statute and plebiscite' is particularly striking:

If the statute and plebiscite agree in choosing someone and confirming him, it is unjust for him, who is admitted by the council, to be taken away by force and it

---

[58] Laurence Humphrey, *De Religionis*, p. 197.   [59] Ibid., p. 220.
[60] In *The Nobles* he attributes this martial competence to Jehovah; see below, pp. 126–7.
[61] Albeit with the characteristic slippage from 'people' to 'councillors'.

is unjust for him to be overwhelmed by the force of arms when he has been approved by considered decisions, especially if those who inaugurated him knew before the decision was given that he was impious. What now remains except to bear patiently what you have entered into, if it cannot be otherwise avoided? Or to emend by further deliberation what has been foolishly admitted. For if whoever is put in charge of the greatest things becomes guilty of divine treason, this is not to be at all tolerated, if he can be corrected.

The message is clear: the correct moment for civil disobedience is before the installation of a ruler recognised to be ungodly. Resistance is permissible only when a ruler charged with executing God's will renounces his or her obligation – and in that event correction (including deposition), not necessarily assassination, is the appropriate remedy:

Thus they [statute and plebiscite] are permitted to use whatever remedies they need, which are the most gentle to him and the most healthy for all. The matter should be called to the vote and should not come to blows. It should be fought with free votes not with violent arms. It should not be decided with the keen point of a sword but with the keenness of the mind so that calm deliberation rather than a turbulent warfare should break up the controversy.

Parliament, representing the voice of the whole people, is crucial in this process of edification. It symbolises and enacts what Sir Thomas Smith calls the 'common doing' for which commonwealths were created. For Humphrey this means it can even (pacifically) constitute itself to resolve the problem of an ungodly ruler, because thwarting this common doing is itself a sign that the king has become a tyrant. He continues:

For to what purpose is the nobility, the people and the whole body of the commonwealth unless to consult together on common plans, as individuals and as a whole, the weak and the great together? But, you may say, the ordinary people cannot be called together unless the king dictates and orders it. Yes, if he is really a king, he will not deny or prevent it but if he is a tyrant, they can and ought to come together.[62]

If we take the *De Religionis* as representing Humphrey's attempt to win the support of other members of the elite for and to instruct them about the new dispensation, it is illuminating to consider his second-stage pronouncement, this time to the 'whole people', including the queen. As in *De Religionis*, in *The Nobles* he is at pains to nullify the threat of war, or social disintegration, which he sees as having occurred in actuality in Mary's reign and as being in effect celebrated as a preservative against tyranny by warriors in God's cause like Ponet and Goodman. Again this

[62] Laurence Humphrey, *De Religionis*, p. 214.

entails an inclusive strategy, one that cuts across social and confessional boundaries (but not, I think, the gender divide) to identify a consensual basis for the Elizabethan regime. In this work however, as one might expect, he adopts a more conservative stance, signalled in part by his attention to the nobility rather than the whole body of the common weal. (Interestingly, in contrast to Goodman, he identifies noblemen who have attained spiritual enlightenment as 'judges of ministers', hence the final court of appeal in the godly nation.[63])

The change in audience also explains his recourse to explicitly providential rhetoric, both to describe the process of reformation and to affirm Elizabeth's legitimacy. It is extremely revealing to see how little room for manoeuvre he has to negotiate the problem of preserving social order and degree in a reformed body politic presided over by a queen – the radical quality of this conservatism – in a context in which, for example, he feels he must find grounds to defend the continued existence of a noble caste against the conclusion of 'some learned' men – not 'Anabaptists or Libertines either' – who hold they have proved themselves to be 'unprofitable members' of the commonwealth and should be 'cut off.'[64]

There are three main planks in the consensus Humphrey promotes. First, he presents the queen as incorporated in the nobility. She is not 'singular' (hence predisposed to tyranny) in her exercise of monarchical authority. He also celebrates her personal qualities in order to argue that she is the pattern of the Christian virtue that the nobility enact in their role as magistrates. Both are therefore executors of God's will in modes consonant with their genders. This species of equality, enacted under God's immediate providence, signals that in England magistracy is godly (and enjoys an aristocratic bias). Secondly, the nobility, defined by virtue as well as by blood, now includes gentlemen as well as Christian nobles; we can see the significance of his second dedication of this work to the 'Christian Gentlemen' of the Inner Temple. Both terms – nobility and virtue – are potentially socially extensive, although, in keeping with his agenda in this work, Humphrey suggests that examples of the very base being lifted to the highest degree are so remarkable as to denote God's specific intervention.[65] Thirdly, as in the *De Religionis*, he is forced to argue that the queen's incontestable virtue and the fact that reformation is ongoing validate the regime, with the implication (more

---

[63] Laurence Humphrey, *The Nobles*, fol. Riii.v.   [64] Ibid., fols. Bvi.r–Bvii.v.
[65] See, for example, fols. Ev.v–Evi.v.

to the fore in the *De Religionis*) that a lapse in either constitutes grounds for its collapse or dissolution.

For Humphrey, the spiritual reclamation of the nobility is therefore a task of some urgency. The existence of a body of godly men whose corporate identity publicly announces a virtue attested to by 'common consent' provides the means whereby the commonwealth can continue in existence, and with it social order, should the queen and her familiars lose their way.[66] Humphrey also clearly believes that this model serves as a powerful reason why unreformed members of the nobility should identify themselves with the godly, at least in their 'politic' capacity, as a preservative of social stability and political order.

Humphrey dedicates *The Nobles* to Elizabeth, lauding her queenship in the providential language with which, by 1563, she must have been all too familiar. Englishmen have been mightily blessed: their liberty recovered, the Church renewed, religion restored 'to her ancient sincerity and primitive pureness'. They have entered a quiet harbour: a 'clear calm, ensuing the tossings, and troublesome storms of later times' has ensured the 'prosperous, and quiet settling all things, as well abroad as at home'. Who to thank for these blessings?

[W]e ought first render heartiest and immortal thanks to almighty God. And next your godly travail, singular endeavour, and faithfullest service (O most Christian queen) ought to be registered in every book, and spread to all posterity. For what hitherto, nor force, nor power, nor all the fetches of man's wit or policy could compass, that now to have happe[ne]d not through the manhood, might, or government of a manly king: but under the conduct, of a woman queen, without tumult, quietly, and even by God's hand . . . Who not roll in amazed thought?[67]

God is indeed not only English but sovereign head of this body politic:

Wherein (O Queen) we advance not your might, nor your arm, not your wisdom: but wonder at your weakness and infirmity. We praise not man's power: but ascribe it to the bounty and mercy of God. To whose beck, word, and providence, all and whole this wondrous fact . . . must freely and wholly be imputed. Therefore that hymn and triumphant song, which Moses and the children of Israel sang in the desert, after the burial of Pharaoh in the red sea: in

---

[66] I cannot agree with Quentin Skinner's conclusion that *The Nobles* provides the 'clearest formulation of th[e] widespread, convenient belief that whilst virtue is essential to true nobility, it happens to be found most fully displayed in the traditional ruling classes'; *The Foundations of Modern Political Thought*, 2 vols. (Cambridge, 1978), vol. 1, *The Renaissance*, p. 238. It seems to me that Humphrey's attempt to reconsider and redefine this correspondence is essential to his argument, as is his anxious consideration of the relationship between virility and virtue.

[67] Laurence Humphrey, *The Nobles*, fols. Aii.r–v.

the congregation of the godly, ought always resound, singing with one tune and joined hearts. The lord is our strength and praise, and he is become our salvation . . . The lord is a man of war, his name is Jehovah.

As he has scattered the powers of darkness that oppressed England under Mary Tudor, so too will He, through His handmaiden Elizabeth, enlighten the dark corners of the globe. Humphrey ends his dedication by informing Elizabeth of his wish 'That by your godly precedent, and Scotland now in faith our sister: The other neighbour nations France, Spain, Flanders, and all realms and kingdoms may at length awake from their long slumber, to take light of the Gospel.'[68]

Humphrey then lays out the main purpose of his book, which is to call the nobility to a recognition of their obligations as an estate in the godly commonwealth. For the nobility, necessary to the maintenance of good order, are 'chosen' but as yet unreformed. That is, they hold an office by right of birth which they must make their calling, internalising Christ's message that 'the vaunters of their blood, . . . vaunt but gore':[69]

I thought, this chosen order once seasoned with right and Christian opinions, and reformed by the uncorrupted [doctrine] of antiquity, both princes shall more soundly govern their subjects and ecclesiastical ministers more faithfully perform their charge, and the people execute all their bounden duties more diligently, and so the whole common wealth more strongly breath, live and recover, since their counsels all these seem to follow, and on these authorities lean and stay.[70]

This is all the more important because for Humphrey – moving on from Sir Thomas Elyot – the king's *synarchoi* are in effect themselves kings, in a godly realm where 'mere' monarchy denotes ungodly rule. He addresses himself to the nobility because, he says,

they be the heads, they be the stomachs and hearts of common weals. So that who [wants] the safety of the other parts, must of necessity first minister to these. That they may . . . spread as through veins into every other part, parcel of their commodities. For they be the eyes, and ears of princes, to see, hear, and foresee, such things, as be not only profitable to themselves, but also commodious and wholesome to others. And as they be the subjects of kings: so be they in manner the lords of the people.[71]

They are 'princes, lieutenants, and wardens and ministers of the laws',[72]

---

[68] Ibid., fols. Bi and Bii.v.   [69] Ibid., fol. Ci.r.   [70] Ibid., fols. Aiii.r–v.   [71] Ibid., fols. Aiii.v–r.
[72] An equation that leads Humphrey to extol the Roman age, 'wherein noble men were lawyers . . . this profession, was peculiar to gentlemen. Which would it were renewed, that they themselves might order judgment . . . For, a right and noble prince, and guarder of the laws, is a beneficial and earthly god to common weals'; *The Nobles*, fol. Qvi.v.

the motor power of a commonwealth in which the queen's role is to symbolise God's superintendence and to example moral virtue:

And presently who swarm in princes' courts but noble men? Who their councillors but they? Who wield the chiefest dignities, who are present? who presidents as well in private as public affairs, but the highest and noblest? Who leadeth in the parliament, overweigheth in the law, swayeth both far and near? Even princes and nobles. Who bids, forbids, doeth, undoeth, twineth, untwineth, all things? Who maketh and unmaketh laws? Who wieldeth the common wealth in peace, or wageth war against the enemy, but great and noble men?[73]

Indeed, according to the reckoning of antiquity, both classical and Biblical, they would have been counted kings: 'In [Homer's] age those were counted kings whom now we term nobles. Which we also gather by the Scriptures, naming kings, of Sodom, Gomorrah, and other cities in Genesis. Whose territories perhaps had no larger limits, than in these days the possessions of our nobles.'[74]

Humphrey sets out his view of true nobility when he considers what the word 'noble' means. Here we can see the parameters within which the maintenance of degree can be justified in a godly commonwealth. In terms very like those used by Sir Thomas Smith to describe degree in his *De Republica Anglorum*,[75] Humphrey argues that it is a necessary concomitant of unredeemed society. It can be cleansed, however, by relating it strictly to virtue, so that the reformed order of the nobility becomes itself the instigator of reformation. For Humphrey this entails a move in a socially inclusive direction. First he argues that the word itself, derived from the verb 'nosco', means simply anyone who is famous, 'either for virtue or vice: or for any other cause renowned or notable'. He then appeals to classical precedent to argue both that 'degree' is a constant feature of civil society; and that, rightly understood, the term 'noble' includes the social order the English denominate as 'gentlemen':

For every estate and civil society, though it consist of many nevertheless was parted of Romans, after the manner of the Athenians (who severed it twixt the Lords and husbandmen) into two degrees, and forms as it were. Accordingly it may among us be divided to the nobles and commons. The one part contains the Prince, and men of greater part and substance, surmounting far the other in living and lineage. The other the inferior multitude, the mean and baser sort. But though we commonly term those nobles, who are next to the prince and council: yet the Latins name him noble, whom the Italians, French men, and we otherwise term a gentleman. Whereby it appeareth, this word with his

[73] Ibid., fol. Ciii.v.   [74] Ibid., fol. Qvi.v.   [75] See below, chapter 7.

largest reach containeth not only the highest estates and callings: but whatsoever worthies, of whatsoever power or place: as also the Germans name their Junkers.[76]

And this discussion leads him to consider 'new sprung nobility', the 'new men' who, in God's cause, can become as praiseworthy as any of the ancient nobility: 'God it is, who raiseth the poor from the dunghill . . . Marry, that only arbiter and dispenser of human haps, maketh of slaves Lords, of Rhetors, Consuls: from base estate and fortune, lifteth to the highest rooms and honours whom him listeth.'[77]

He summarises his argument in a passage which describes social relations in the reformed commonwealth, as it adjures all men to enact their roles as brothers in Christ – in its public manifestation a virtuous and not a virile identity (I think it is fair to read this as referring solely to men, with their socially determined competencies of physical strength and intellectual capability):

Be this therefore the sum of all. That the commons win the nobles with service: the nobles the commons with benevolence. They obey lowly, the other rule favourably. They strive to excel in justice, the other in obedience. They know they govern free men not beasts: The other think themselves not bond by nature, but by the law and Gospel aids and helpers. They rule with counsel, the other be pressed with their travail. They perform their charge with the practice of their wit: the other with the toil of their body. Either rule and serve other in the lord. That so they wholly apply and frame themselves in sweet consent to the glory of Christ, the honour of the realm, and their own safety. So shall there be no care no thought of arms.[78]

What then of the queen? If we return to Humphrey's dedication to Elizabeth we can see how he identifies her as incorporated in the reformed nobility, her governorship consisting largely of setting it a moral example. In the dedication Humphrey looks to Elizabeth as governor (that is, God's handmaiden) for solutions to the political problem posed by the nobility's current unreformed status. The rhetorical strategy he adopts is an interesting one, for it allies Elizabeth with the godly by publicly assuming that she actively promotes and participates in the definitions of nobility (and reformation) that he advances. He first looks to Elizabeth in her role as 'patroness' of the order of the nobility. She is, he tells her, 'already mindful enough' of what true Christian nobility entails. Similarly she knows 'how expedient this knowledge is, how profitable, necessary and meet, for these times'. The 'weight and authority' of her acceptance of this dedication will persuade other

---

[76] Ibid., fols. Div.r–Dv.v.   [77] Ibid., fols. Ev.v–Evi.v.   [78] Ibid., fols. Diii.r–Div.v.

nobles that they 'need not condemn' his book; further that they should amend their ways in accordance with its contents.[79] He then attributes to Elizabeth 'nobility' and virtue in a Platonic form. Consonant with her gender, she acts as a Christian model for the nobility: a model of virtue, not virility. He cites 'Plato in his Book of common wealth' to 'propose your majesty [as the] pattern of the ancient dignity, image of the old honour, and pillar of true nobility'.[80] What can the nobility do but follow her example?

> Whether they weigh your upright justice, welcome to the good, dreadful to the enemy: or the singular learning . . . or your fervent zeal, love, and furthering of religion, or your noble and haughty courage: who in greatest tempests and storms, both a woman and sole, wield and steer, most wisely and stoutly, the stern of so great a kingdom.[81]

In this scenario the 'haughtiness of stomach' conventionally attributed to nobles (and famously awarded to herself, as king, by Elizabeth in her speech at Tilbury in 1588[82]), like a 'princely mind', figures in a novel definition of what it means to be an English monarch. It becomes a means by which 'a maiden Queen' can withstand the blandishments and threats of the unredeemed remnant, whether they be the 'few' or the 'many', to complete the work of reformation begun by Edward VI, 'your brother a child, and king'.[83] He continues:

> Which haughtiness of stomach, to confirm and keep I see I need not exhort you. For may we doubt . . . if yet any dregs remain [in the church] . . . [you] will with all help, care, counsel, speed, provide for it, withstand it, and reform it? For neither will who began this good work in you, not finish it (to whom only belongeth to give princely minds to princes). Nor is your wisdom ignorant, what you do is God's work, not your own. His the house, yours the building. Wherein not the fear of few nor murmuring of many, ought withdraw you from your forward foundation. For, his will it is, his temple should be raised, the walls of Jerusalem repaired.[84]

This ongoing reformation, the chief jewel in Elizabeth's crown, will effect the spiritual reclamation of the nobility; whether by God's direct intervention or indirectly, through her 'perfect' example, is left ambiguous. Once this renovation has occurred, God will, according to Hum-

---

[79] Ibid., fol. Aiiii.r.   [80] Ibid., fol. Av.v.   [81] Ibid., fol. Avii.r.

[82] And possibly apocryphally. In the reigns of the Stuart kings, the 'myth of Tilbury' became a yardstick with which to measure their perceived monarchical incapacities (including a propensity towards tyranny). See Susan Frye, 'The Myth of Elizabeth at Tilbury', *Sixteenth Century Journal* 23, no. 1 (1992), pp. 95–114. Frye is particularly good at relating these changing depictions to issues of gender.   [83] Laurence Humphrey, *The Nobles*, fol. Aviii.v.

[84] Ibid., fol. Aviii.r.

phrey, give signs of His approbation. He will speak as follows:

We greet well . . . our Christian Nobility, who provoked by your [Elizabeth's] princely precedent, and inflamed with gentlemanly courage, doubted not to follow the call, and authority of their guide and captain. Yea, so to follow, as they blushed not, to set their hands, to employ their counsel and travail, to repairing this heavenly frame.[85]

Until that day comes, Humphrey begs her to accept counsel only from the 'true nobility', men who, like Thomas Norton, have 'no dealing with the queen but as with the image of God'.

[C]hiefly furnish your court, (as most painfully and politicly you do) with men famous for commendation of justice, godliness, and learning, And studious and earnest appliers and practicers thereof. Continue to cherish and honour true nobility, wherewith your kingdom swarmeth, and now your court flourisheth. Since it is the keep of your reign, the light of your realm, and the safest guard of your person. But [banish] mockcourtiers and counterfeit nobles, if any such yet lurk . . . by your grave councillors' advice, and other nobles, and your own precedent.[86]

With Humphrey's address to Elizabeth and his redefinition of 'nobility' we can see the parameters of incorporation – queen in sanctified nation represented in parliament – which defined political engagement during her reign. This is the Elizabethan 'mixed monarchy' that made the queen, in Aylmer's telling phrase, a 'mixed ruler': godly – and 'bridled' – through her marriage to, hence inclusion in, a godly commonwealth.

CONCLUSION: NOBILITY AND VIRILITY IN THE COUNTRY

Humphrey's apologetical works, like John Aylmer's and, as we shall see, Sir Thomas Smith's, suggest that the most significant achievement for Elizabethan politics of the so-called resistance theorists – John Knox, Christopher Goodman and John Ponet – was their success in using existing distrust of female rule to focus attention on the problem posed by imperial kingship in the context of reformation ideology. They did so by dwelling upon the dangers of female rule and insisting upon the fundamental continuities between queenship and kingship. Their discourse thus problematised attempts to legitimate queenship, eventually even kingship itself. Knox and Goodman in particular injected what Donald Kelley calls a kind of Bible-based political fundamentalism into

---

[85] Ibid., fol. Aviii.v. Ambiguously, of course, God and the queen.
[86] Ibid., fol. Avii.r. The distinction between 'councillors' and 'other nobles' is a telling one.

concepts of the godly empire current from Henry VIII's reign.[87] This move presented Mary less as 'Spanish Mary' than as Jezebel, making her a stalking horse primarily for the Romish Antichrist, with Philip II in the role of the pope's minion. John Ponet's articulation of the 'country' as a specifically male identity, associated with patriotism and possessing, as a latent capacity, the 'common authority' that would allow it political competence when leaders were reprobate, was equally significant. Central to their polemic was the Protestant emphasis on the brotherhood of men in Christ, which, in the context of female rule, acquired a host of new resonances. Their orthodoxy in exile became common currency when Elizabeth ascended the throne, partly because of the prominence of Marian exiles and sympathisers among the ranks of the regime. And, paradoxically, identifying Mary's commitment to Rome as her culpable offence opened up a loophole that allowed the men who were to become Elizabeth's ministers, councillors and apologists – men who undoubtedly shared contemporary views about female rule and were themselves ambivalent about imperial kingship – to justify, to themselves and others, the accession to the imperial crown of a godly female princess: a Deborah. Finally, given contemporary beliefs concerning female rule and specifically its propensity to degenerate into tyranny, these theorists' recourse to, and elaboration of, notions of Christian egalitarianism among men as the guarantor of the godly commonwealth subverted by ungodly magistrates continued to be relevant, albeit increasingly contentious, as long as there was a woman on the throne.

On one level, then, Ponet's, Goodman's and Knox's views are both 'resistance theory' and a repudiation of imperial monarchy, powerfully articulated in the circumstances of female rule and drawing on contemporary views of women to enforce their effect. And it is important to stress that Mary's reign only made these ideas available; it did not make them normative. Nonetheless, as my readings of John Aylmer and Laurence Humphrey indicate, their implications for subsequent English history were dramatic. The prophetic conception of the godly body politic, and its renegotiation by first-generation apologists in Elizabeth's reign, provide a necessary background for understanding the tensions of Elizabethan politics which I explore in the following chapters. In the longer term, this dynamic points inevitably to the English civil war. For, over the period from Elizabeth's accession to the mid-seventeenth

[87] Donald R. Kelley, 'Ideas of Resistance before Elizabeth' in *Law, Literature, and the Settlement of Regimes*, ed. Gordon J. Schochet, The Folger Institute Center for the History of British Political Thought Proceedings, vol. 2 (Washington, D.C., 1990), pp. 5–28, p. 9.

century, such ideas did become normative. Moreover, their fundamental ambiguities and paradoxes concerning social order remained unresolved, despite the efforts to define women's nature, nobility and kingship which permeated especially late Elizabethan and Jacobean culture.[88] This debate, conducted with reference to concepts of virtue and virility, effeminacy and tyranny – from the 1590s 'court' and 'country' – encouraged the development of the profoundly rich and ambiguous 'cult' of Elizabeth, which, in the period after 1585, both promoted her authority as queen and challenged it. It provided a vocabulary for godly men such as Sir Philip Sidney and Edmund Spenser to consider their position as virtuous Englishmen, constrained in the expression of their true nobility by the equivocal figure of their queen.[89] It allowed others to forge an alternative oppositional identity, defining themselves, through their capacity for virtue, as citizens of the 'country': patriotic in their commitment to God and England's common weal.[90] As a result it prepared the ground for the abolition of kingship in 1649. This was the point at which the reading of imperial kingship as inherently tyrannical, ungodly and at war with the common weal – a reading initiated in Mary's reign and reformulated, not repudiated, in Elizabeth's – was finally deemed to be applicable to an English male incumbent of the imperial crown.

[88] Susan Amussen, *An Ordered Society*, pp. 122–3; 182–3; Blair Worden, *The Sound of Virtue*; Rebecca W. Bushnell, *Tragedies of Tyrants: Political Thought and Theater in the English Renaissance* (New York, 1990).
[89] Richard Helgerson, *Forms of Nationhood: The Elizabethan Writing of England* (Chicago, 1992), esp. pp. 49–59; Blair Worden, *The Sound of Virtue*.
[90] Richard Helgerson, *Forms of Nationhood*, p. 126. See below, chapter 6.

CHAPTER 5

Godly men and nobles: the bicephalic body politic

> The queen's majesty hath no surety but as she hath been coun-
> selled.
>
> Lord Burghley to the Earl of Leicester, (1572)[1]

The 'mixed monarchy' enacted in Elizabeth's reign was rooted in a theoretical framework of revived Aristotelian and Polybian ideas of a mixed constitution, infused with theological terminology and metaphors, and newly prominent in the wake of the conciliar movement and the reformation.[2] But it would have been inconceivable without the local habitation provided, in England, by the regnal sequence after Henry VIII of one short-lived minor king and three queens. In Elizabeth's reign, one anonymous writer explicitly recognised the unprecedented character of England's history since the Henrician Reformation. The author of *The History of the Reign of King Henry the Eighth, king Edward the Sixth, Queen Mary, and part of the Reign of Queen Elizabeth*, dateable on internal evidence to the late 1570s, justifies the interest of his work on the basis of the innovative enactments of kingship which have occurred since the advent of the Tudor dynasty:

> Then if you shall restrain your consideration to the state of this monarchy; first there will occur unto you changes rare, and altogether unknown unto antiquity, in matters of religion, and the state ecclesiastical. Then to behold the several reigns of a king, that first, or next the first, became absolute in the sovereignty;[3] of a king, in minority, of a queen, married to a foreigner; and lastly, of a queen that hath governed without the help, either of a marriage, or of any mighty man of her blood.[4]

---

[1] Quoted in Michael Pulman, *The Elizabethan Privy Council in the 1570s* (Berkeley, Calif., 1971), p. 52.

[2] Donald Kelley, 'Elizabethan Political Thought' in *The Varieties of British Political Thought, 1500–1800*, ed. J. G. A. Pocock (Cambridge, 1993), pp. 47–79, p. 51.

[3] I take this to mean Henry VIII was 'next the first' in regard to blood (being the second Tudor monarch), but 'first' in regard to the 'new', reformed monarchy.

[4] Anon., *The History of the Reign of King Henry the Eighth, King Edward the Sixth, Queen Mary, and part of the Reign of Queen Elizabeth*, in *Cabala Sive Scrinia Sacra, Mysteries of State and Government: in Letters of Illustrious Persons and Great Matters of State* (London, 1663), p. 255.

134

The author implicitly defines an established, legitimate succession as one composed of male rulers, of full age, of the Tudor line. He suggests that the historical sequence that he describes – a minor king and two queens – might betoken England's providential status. This possibility is indicated by his evident conviction that either legitimate succession as he defines it or providential intercession was necessary to sustain a monarchy that, with Henry VIII, had become 'absolute in the sovereignty', and particularly in the case of a queen 'governing without the help, either of a marriage, or of any mighty man of her blood'.

For this anonymous historian the fact that England under Elizabeth was not simply what he termed a 'hereditary monarchy' also meant that it was prone to political instability and social disorder, as it had been under her sibling predecessors: 'Besides, there have not wanted examples . . . neither of an usurpation, nor of rebellions under heads of greatness, nor of commotions merely popular, nor of sundry desperate conspirators (an unwonted thing in hereditary monarchies).'[5] His conviction that England was experiencing a succession crisis, and one that threatened the maintenance of social order, was widely shared among the political elite. Nor was it simply a function of Elizabeth's refusal to marry and establish the succession, although historians have generally focused on these specific issues.[6] These broader concerns found political expression in the redefinition of the three estates of the realm as queen (or crown), lords and commons and, as we have seen, in the simultaneous recourse to providentialism as a legitimating strategy, bruited in Mary's reign and enacted in Elizabeth's.

Various historians have recognised, if they have not explored, the significance of this redefinition of the three estates in Elizabeth's reign.[7] It signalled the transformation of the Fortescuean notion of 'king-in-parliament' that occurred when 'kingship' came to be embodied in a queen. The queen as an estate became, with the lords and commons, constituent elements of the godly body politic and, to that extent, *primum inter pares* with reference to the other estates. Nor was the primacy of the

---

[5] Ibid.

[6] Mortimer Levine, *The Early Elizabethan Succession Question, 1558–1568* (Stanford, Calif., 1966); *Tudor Dynastic Problems 1460–1571*, Historical Problems: Studies and Documents (London, 1973).

[7] Vernon Snow, *Parliament in Elizabethan England: John Hooker's 'Order and Usage'* (New Haven, Conn., 1977), p. 106; G. R. Elton, 'Arthur Hall, Lord Burghley and the Antiquity of Parliament' in *Studies in Tudor and Stuart Politics and Government*, vol. 3 (Cambridge, 1983), pp. 254–73; pp. 271–2.; G. R. Elton, 'Parliament' in *The Reign of Elizabeth I*, ed. Christopher Haigh (London, 1984), pp. 79–100. Richard Jackson traces the antithetical process, whereby commitment to notions of blood identity eventually privileged princes of the blood as quasi-kings in 'Peers of France and Princes of the Blood', *French Historical Journal* 7, no. 1 (1972), pp. 27–43.

monarchical estate in this arrangement inviolable. Instead, the queen became a godly magistrate (insofar as that role could be seen as consonant with female identity), her authority invested in the office rather than in her person. This reorientation, proposed by both John Aylmer and Laurence Humphrey, raised the prospect of an equality of political virtue between the queen and her counsellors, in the first instance those of the Privy Council. It therefore produced a novel political dynamic during the reign, in which the relationship between crown and counsel was contested across the ranks of the political nation.[8]

In 1566, in the highly charged parliamentary debates over the succession (the first since Mary Queen of Scots gave birth to a male heir), an anonymous MP described the relationship between the queen and her counsellors by defining the office of a 'king'. In his utterance we see the fusion of humanist and godly languages of counsel, used to elucidate the body politic in its new manifestation:

The word or name of a king doth signify a ruler or governor, an high office . . . and may well be termed an head. Now, what is the office of an head? The office of the head consisteth in these two points: first, carefully to devise and put in execution all things most commodious for the whole body and every member thereof; then, wisely to foresee and prevent the evils that may come to any part thereof, and to that end God hath placed therein the brain to devise, and every member giveth place thereunto, and patiently perform their duties. He hath also (for helps) placed therein the eye to look about and the ear to hearken for all things, either beneficial or discommodious. And lastly, to his great glory he hath created the tongue to utter the same, where the good may be received and the evil prevented. This king, this head, with the consent of the whole body and through the providence of God, weighing that his eye and ear cannot be in every corner of his kingdom and dominions at one instant . . . hath established this honorable counsel of every part of the same absent from the king's eye and ear, the which is termed a parliament, that is, a speech uttered from the heart, from the mind, yea a free speech wherefore this counsel was ordained to be absent from the king's eye and ear . . . for the prince and commonwealth joined together make a perfect man consisting of head, body and members, and cannot be separated.[9]

In this redefinition the gender identities ('king', 'perfect man') are significant, as is the body analogy of which they form part. They imply that the queen becomes a 'king' when she 'marries' the realm (that is, when she is subsumed within it) by accepting its counsel.[10] This marriage, effected through the provision of counsel, marks the point at which she (it) can enact kingship: conjoined in this way, they make 'a perfect man'. It is also worth noting that on this reading counsel is given by the 'consent of the whole body', which exists in a permeable relationship with parliament. (And 'parliament' itself is presented as ambiguously act – 'a speech uttered from the heart . . . a free speech' – and institution.) The anonymous MP goes on to adjure the queen, or her councillors, to act the part of a king – he instances Henry VIII – in establishing the succession:

> So that to conclude, both these I do affirm: that the Queen's Majesty is bound, both in honour and in conscience, to establish the succession; and it is the best and surest way for her Majesty's present safety, for she cannot stand without the hearts of her people. And as to that said, that it toucheth the Counsel [the Privy Council] in honour and conscience to move her Majesty to provide a known successor, forasmuch as by the scriptures kings and magistrates ought all to run one course and be guided by one rule. The reasons before rehearsed concern them as nearly as the prince; howbeit much more are they to be blamed than the prince for that this great and universal inconvenience hath not been prevented before this time.[11]

Nor was his utterance an isolated one. In the wake of this parliament, 'certain lewd Bills [were] thrown abroad against the Queen's Majesty for not asserting to have the matter of succession proceed in Parliament', and (the inescapable concomitant) 'bills also to charge Sir William Cecil the Secretary with the occasion thereof'.[12]

QUEEN AND COUNSEL IN THE BICEPHALIC BODY POLITIC

The relationship between prince and counsellor envisaged by earlier humanist theorists – predicated on the assumption that the prince would seek counsel from virtuous men, and that his noble councillors would disinterestedly provide it – did not, in England, survive the recourse to providential modes of legitimation which inaugurated and sustained

---

[10] In Scotland the Lords of the Congregation used this language, but with an aristocratic accent, to justify their refusal to accept Mary of Guise's authority as regent. She had failed to 'joune her self to us, to consult upon the affairs of our common-weal, as we that be born Counsallouris to the same, by the ancient laws of the realm'. See J. H. Burns, *The True Law of Kingship: Concepts of Monarchy in Early-Modern Scotland* (Oxford, 1996), p. 164.   [11] *Proceedings*, pp. 134–5.
[12] *A Collection of State Papers relating to Affairs in the Reign of Queen Elizabeth, From the Year 1571 to 1596*, ed. William Murdin (London, 1759), p. 762.

Elizabeth's rule.[13] As an individual, Elizabeth might be presented as having attained to a 'politic' (and exceptional) capacity for rule that promoted her above her sex. This was one reason for the paeans to her learning and intelligence which were characteristic of panegyric during her reign, as well as her frequent insistence on her exceptional status.[14] But the conjunction of reformation views concerning women's spiritual incapacity and classical, especially Aristotelian, convictions about women's inferior status as rational beings left open what the relationship between Elizabeth and her counsellors was to be, just as the progress of reformation after Henry VIII's death left open, in various ways, the issue of who they were to be.

For much of the reign, the 'rules of the game' outlined in chapter 2 dictated that the queen must take counsel and that it should be 'approved' counsel. Yet she had sufficient room for manoeuvre that the threat of 'unofficial' counsel was one her Privy Councillors referred to time and time again. This voiced a very real fear that Elizabeth would ally herself with advisers (including potentially a husband) whose views or whose relationship with the queen might distort the balance of the composite mixed monarchy, and hence jeopardise the godly nation.[15] Their fears appeared to be realised in 1576, when Elizabeth moved to deprive Edmund Grindal of his archbishopric for his refusal to suppress prophesyings – that potent symbol of the nation's commitment to thorough reformation.[16] Grindal's exclusion from the ranks of the queen's counsellors was a significant moment in the reign. Arguably it was the first at which Elizabeth asserted the primacy of her will, in the face of conciliar opposition, as a step towards enacting her own conception of monarchical authority. Unable to rely on her Privy Councillors, who refused to support her in the matter, she turned to her Italian physician, Giulio Borgarucci, to arrange legal advice. Dr Julio, as he was known, was a member of the queen's privy chamber. According to contemporary opinion he therefore stood in a different – more intimate and servile – relationship to the queen than did her Privy Councillors.[17]

[13] J. G. A. Pocock, *The Machiavellian Moment: Florentine Political Thought and the Atlantic Republican Tradition* (Princeton, N.J., 1975), pp. 338–9.
[14] Allison Heisch, 'Queen Elizabeth I and the Persistence of Patriarchy', *Feminist Review* 4 (1980), pp. 45–54.
[15] See Blair Worden's account of the Anjou marriage negotiations in *The Sound of Virtue: Philip Sidney's 'Arcadia' and Elizabethan Politics* (New Haven, Conn., 1996), especially chs. 6 and 7.
[16] Patrick Collinson, 'The Downfall of Archbishop Grindal and its Place in Elizabethan Political and Ecclesiastical History' in *Godly People: Essays on English Protestantism and Puritanism* (London, 1983), pp. 371–98.
[17] Pam Wright, 'A Change in Direction: The Ramifications of a Female Household, 1558–1603' in

Her initiative led Burghley to write to Walsingham that on this occasion 'he was more of her Majesty's council than two or three that are of present council'.[18] Later Sir Francis Knollys wrote to Thomas Wilson about Grindal's troubles in terms that suggested the queen was effecting a revolution that would subvert the common weal. His words reveal how intimate, in his mind, was the connection between the Protestant imperial crown and the provision of godly counsel: 'But if the bishop of Canterbury shall be deprived, then up starts the pride and practice of the papists. And then King Richard the Second's men will flock into court apace, and will show themselves in their colours.'[19] 'King Richard the Second's men', for Knollys, would be those who defined their role narrowly and exclusively as effecting the monarch's will and could be referred to, abusively, as flatterers or 'courtiers'.[20]

Conversely, this tension also helps explain the persistent lampoon of the regime as a *regnum Cecilianum*, or alternatively 'Leycester's Commonwealth'. In this cultural context doubts about Elizabeth's status as 'Deborah' imperilled her monarchical authority, even her claim to be queen. They also, inevitably, compromised the godly identity of her 'inward' councillors. Failure to enact a role of transparent virtue left councillors vulnerable to the charge that their standing derived too much from the queen's favour, too little from their identification with the common weal. In the context of female rule, what could this mean but that such 'great ones' took it upon themselves to act the role of king, and possibly through the seduction of the queen?[21]

A revised perception of the relations between councillors and their princes was not an exclusively English development. By 1559 it was increasingly apparent in diplomatic relations throughout Europe, as minority and female succession complicated authority relations already

The English Court: From the War of the Roses to the Civil War, ed. David Starkey (London, 1987), pp. 147–72.

[18] 31 May 1577: BL Add MS. 5935, fol. 68. Burghley concluded, 'These proceedings cannot but irritate our merciful God, [and I hope that] He shall show mercy to his afflicted church.

[19] Patrick Collinson, 'The Downfall of Archbishop Grindal', p. 381.

[20] Knollys's fear of the subversion of the Protestant imperial crown triggered by Grindal's downfall led him to argue, in the 1580s, that legislation passed in Henry VIII's reign and revived in Elizabeth's made bishops subject not only to 'the supreme government of her Majesty: But also subject and answerable to the councillors of estate in its behalf'. By this point it was too naked an assertion that the queen and her councillors, and the councillors themselves, were frequently at odds over fundamental theological matters. Knollys found himself isolated among the Privy Councillors (although Burghley continued to be sympathetic to both his fears and his position). See W. D. J. Cargill Thompson, 'Sir Francis Knollys's Campaign Against the *Jure Divino* Theory of Episcopacy' in *Studies in the Reformation: Luther to Hooker* (London, 1980), pp. 94–130, pp. 120–1.

[21] See *Leicester's Commonwealth: The Copy of a Letter Written by a Master of Art of Cambridge (1584) and Related Documents*, ed. D. C. Peck (Athens, Ohio, 1985).

problematised by the radicalising currents of religious reformation.[22] Mary Queen of Scots struggled to assert her monarchical authority in a political context sufficiently similar for her to point to the tensions between Elizabeth and her councillors in her dealing with them – as a means, perhaps, of asserting an identity between her and her sister queen.[23] In contrast to Elizabeth, Mary often argued that as a female ruler she exercised little autonomy, being bound by the dictates of her male counsellors (including, during her French career, her father-in-law and husband). But she could use this plea of female incapacity as a means to forward her immediate political ends, and, like Elizabeth, deploy the threat of recourse to 'unofficial' counsel in order to do so.

We can see one example of this strategy in 1561, when she was engaged in negotiations with Elizabeth and her councillors over her request for free passage through England into Scotland. In her letter to Sir Nicholas Throckmorton, the English ambassador in France, Mary couched her request for permission to travel through England in terms of her need to seek counsel. She assures Throckmorton that she seeks only counsel that she knows will be acceptable to the regime, but argues that she must be physically present in Scotland to achieve this end. Even more illuminating is the subtext of her utterance, which positions Elizabeth as constrained in her monarchical autonomy by her Protestant councillors. I think it is permissible to read Mary as addressing both Elizabeth and councillors, despite her frequent and exclusive references to 'the Queen your Mistress', given her direct address to Throckmorton and her use of irony:

[S]ince his [her husband's] death, my interest failing in the realm of France, I left to be advised by the Council of France, and they left me also to mine own Council; indeed . . . my uncles being, as you know, of the affairs of this realm [France], do not think meet to advise me in my affairs; neither do my [Scottish] subjects, nor the Queen your Mistress, think meet that I should be advised by them, but rather by the Council of my own realm; here are none of them, nor

22 H. G. Koenigsberger, George L. Mosse and G. Q. Bowler note that by 1559 government in the Netherlands, France, Scotland and Portugal as well as England had passed into the hands of children or women – rulers whom they assume would be unable to confront the challenge to monarchical authority posed by Calvinism; *Europe in the Sixteenth Century* (London, 1968; 2nd edn, 1989), p. 303. For the attempts of the young French king Charles IX to position himself as king, and hence as superior to his councillors, using strategies similar to those of Elizabeth, see Sir Dudley Digges, *The Compleat Ambassador* (London 1655), pp. 7–8.
23 For this Scottish context see J. H. Burns, *The True Law of Kingship*, esp. pp. 156–67. Mary Stuart wanted to be named Elizabeth's *filia adoptiva* or her *soror reginae* at the latter's accession; John Strype, *Annals of the Reformation and Establishment of Religion*. 7 vols. (Oxford, 1824), vol. 1.ii, p. 95, and *A Collection of State Papers*, p. 758.

none such as is thought meet that I should be counselled by; . . . I do not think it meet in so great a matter to take the counsel of private and unexpert persons, and such as the Queen your Mistress knoweth be not most acceptable to such of my subjects, as she would have me be advised by.[24]

She alludes to her willing submission to 'good' counsel: 'such as . . . [would be] most acceptable' – not only to Elizabeth, but also to those of her (Mary's) subjects whom Elizabeth would wish to see exercising political influence ('such of my subjects, as she would have me be advised by'). The insistence on an affinity between Elizabeth and a faction of Mary's subjects must be ironic, in view of the tension between Elizabeth and her Privy Council at this point, as at others during the reign, over whether regard for monarchical prerogative or commitment to global Protestantism should determine English policy toward Scotland and its queen.[25]

Mary also intimates that what Elizabeth and her councillors define as true council is nothing more than their words in the mouths of men who are notionally her own servants. We see this in part through the implied contrast with the disinterested counsel of her French uncles (through marriage) and the Council of France; in part through her suggestion that she has councillors in France, but that their adherence to her personal interests renders them unacceptable to Elizabeth and her councillors ('here are none of them, nor none such as is thought meet that I should be counselled by'). Her seeming deference to Elizabeth's will harbours a tacit threat: that she, as an uncounselled queen, may have recourse to 'private and unexpert persons' – rather in the vein of nature abhorring a vacuum – should she not be allowed to return to her own realm and its sanctioned Council.[26]

And it is in this context that one should read Elizabeth's 1582 insistence upon her monarchical authority (conveyed via Sir Francis

---

[24] *Cabala Sive Scrinia Sacra*, p. 376.

[25] Wallace MacCaffrey, *The Shaping of the Elizabethan Regime* (Princeton, N.J., 1969), pp. 68–9.

[26] In a letter of 1569 Elizabeth put forward a counter view of Mary's relations with her counsellors. Writing to Mary about a newly discovered plot, she suggests that Mary's counsellors might have overstepped the line, so difficult to establish across the gender divide, between **enacting** the monarch's will and **presuming** to enact it: 'I neither doubt your honour nor your faith in writing to me that you never thought of such a thing, but that perhaps some relative, or rather some ambassador of yours, having the general authority of your signature to order all things for the furtherance of your affairs, had adjusted this promise as if it came from you, and deemed it within the range of his commissions.' Ironically this became Mary's defence in her trial for treason, when she argued that she had no real control over her secretaries, who could and did write in her name and not always with her knowledge or approval. William Camden, *The History of the Most Renowned and Victorious Princess Elizabeth Late Queen of England*, ed. Wallace T. MacCaffrey (Chicago, 1970), p. 252.

Walsingham) again to Mary Stuart, who, as we have seen, challenged it, and not only in the obvious ways that modern scholars generally focus on. In this utterance Elizabeth insists that her counsellors are not 'principal members of the Crown', but that she herself, as monarch, is 'absolute'; that is, that she stands in the same relationship to her councillors as her progenitors had done:

[S]he [Elizabeth] doth find it strange that she [Mary] should direct her letters unto her Counsel, as unto principal members of this Crown (for so doth she in her said letters term them, a course that heretofore hath not been held), whereof her Majesty cannot other conceive but that there she doth not repute her to be so absolute as that without the assent of such whom she termeth 'principal members of the Crown' she cannot direct her policy; or else, that . . . she [Elizabeth] were by them to be called to an account. Of which misconceit of the said Queen and misunderstanding of the absoluteness of her Majesty's government she thinketh meet she should by your Lordship be better informed . . . For although her Highness doth carry as great regard unto her Council [Privy Council] as any of her progenitors have done, and hath just cause so to do in respect of their wisdom and fidelity, yet is she [Mary] to be let understand that they are councillors by choice, and not by birth, whose services are no longer to be used in that public function than it shall please her Majesty to dispose of the same; and therefore her Highness cannot conceive to what end a complaint should be made unto them, unless either she repute her to be in her minority or else doth mean to use her Counsell as witnesses against her.[27]

Elizabeth's relations with her counsellors, then, had as an unmistakable subtext the question of where sovereignty resided in a godly nation under female rule. This is not to argue that Elizabeth had no say in political decision-making, or that she was 'controlled' by her councillors. But it does indicate some of the powerful constraints on her princely autonomy that operated at the heart of court politics. As Patrick Collinson notes, it was characteristic of Elizabethan politics that 'any degree of political incapacity in the Crown, actual or threatened, strengthened rather than diminished the political capacity of the Crown's servants'.[28] To 'actual or threatened' I think we would need to add 'perceived', because of the deeply rooted conviction permeating European society at this time, occurring in a particularly acute form in England, that women were at least relatively incapable of supreme command.

Throughout the first decades of the reign, therefore, we can see Elizabeth's 'inward councillors' – those of the Privy Council, and

---

[27] Edmund Lodge, *Illustrations of British History* (London, 1791), vol. ii, pp. 276–7; quoted in Patrick Collinson, 'The Monarchical Republic of Queen Elizabeth I', *Bulletin of the John Rylands University Library of Manchester* 69, no. 2 (1986–7), pp. 394–424, p. 424.
[28] Patrick Collinson, *'De Republica Anglorum': Or, History with the Politics Put Back* (Cambridge, 1990), p. 24.

specifically those nearest the queen – attempting to secure 'sound' (that is, godly) policies. They did so in a political context in which her failure to enact policies deemed necessary by the political nation – achieve a thorough reformation, advance the interests of international Protestantism, secure England's future through establishing the succession – would be read as proof of her (and their) deficiencies, moral and political. Their success, paradoxically, jeopardised the delicate equilibrium of the 'mixed monarchy', especially as the queen's distinctive gloss on these consensual goals became both more apparent and more rooted.[29] If they, in the words of the bishop of Ely, Richard Cox, 'perform[ed] the part of a man' and contested the queen's will, when necessary, to safeguard the godly nation, they did so at the risk of endangering existing monarchical authority by opening the door to religious radicalism, thus to political and social instability. These were dangers of which Elizabeth's councillors were well aware, as elite men of the period would be. As we shall see, they were dangers to which Elizabeth frequently referred in her negotiations with them, as a means of buttressing her personal authority as queen.

OFFICERS AND NOBLES IN THE GODLY NATION

In her 1582 message to Mary, quoted above, Elizabeth speaks of councillors holding their office by (her) 'choice, and not by birth'. Here she seemingly refers to the humanist and Protestant definition of councillor of the realm as a calling enjoyed by men of virtue.[30] She did so to attempt a characteristic inversion, arguing that 'choice' (or election) was absolute, and absolutely in her own gift. Certainly it was part of the dynamic of her reign that she attempted to make appointments her 'prerogative' – that aspect of royal majesty pertaining exclusively to the person of the monarch.[31] For much of the reign, however – arguably until 1583, when William Whitgift replaced Edmund Grindal as Arch-

[29] Patrick Collinson characterises Elizabeth's outlook on these matters as 'eccentrically dispassionate'; 'Puritans, Men of Business and Elizabethan Parliaments', *Parliamentary History* 7, no. 2 (1988), pp. 187–211, p. 191. It is more plausible to see her as passionately committed to the maintenance of kingly authority, but constrained in her ability to act on this commitment by the need to preserve her political legitimacy as queen.
[30] John Guy, 'The Rhetoric of Counsel in Early Modern England' in *Tudor Political Culture*, ed. Dale Hoak (Cambridge, 1995), pp. 292–310; and Dale Hoak, 'Two Revolutions in Tudor Government: The Formation and Organisation of Mary I's Privy Council' in *Revolution Reassessed: Revisions in the History of Tudor Government and Administration*, ed. Christopher Coleman and David Starkey (Oxford, 1986), pp. 87–115.
[31] Simon Adams, 'Eliza Enthroned? The Court and Its Politics' in *The Reign of Elizabeth I*, ed. Christopher Haigh (London, 1984), pp. 55–78, pp. 60–1. For contested readings of the term 'prerogative' see below, chapter 6.

bishop of Canterbury – this could be little more than a statement of intention. For the most part Elizabeth's 'choice' involved selection from a slate of godly councillors consensually arrived at, 'men meet to be called to such rooms', as John Aylmer has it. It did not necessarily (or primarily) include members of the nobility who traditionally proffered counsel to the king by right of birth, or the favourites whose access to power depended entirely upon the monarch's will (or fancy).[32] The notion that both favour and virtue were necessary elements in the councillor's election, and that their correct ratio was a matter for negotiation and debate, was itself integral to and a product of the enactment of the 'mixed monarchy', as was the consequent necessity for the nobility to reinvent itself as a political estate.

The appointment of men deemed godly to official positions represented the regime's attempt to protect the commonweal by marginalising those who, through personality or position, were believed to incline to some version of the *status quo ante*, or to be susceptible to the charisma of the crown. One revealing example occurred in 1566 when John Hales, commonwealth man, author and, under Elizabeth, Clerk of the Hanaper, wrote to William Cecil to suggest that the godly George Bromley be placed as Attorney of the Duchy of Lancaster. Hales tells Cecil that Bromley is a man who 'for his religion and knowledge of the law ought above many to be preferred'. More importantly, given the purported Catholic (certainly legitimist) bias of many lawyers, his appointment would 'win the hearts of a good many Protestants who, now discouraged, will take some hope if they may hear a Protestant lawyer beareth some authority in Westminster Hall.'[33] Bromley was duly appointed. What is remarkable is that Hales penned his letter in circumstances in which Elizabeth was attempting to marginalise him (and the Privy Councillors he represented) for flouting her monarchical authority: he wrote from the Tower, where he had been imprisoned for writing a book explicitly rejecting the claims of Mary Stuart to the English throne.[34]

[32] See, for example, the memorandum written by Sir Nicholas Throckmorton at Elizabeth's accession, in which he drew up a list of appointments that he proposed she should make to fill important offices of state, as well as a speech for her to use on the occasion of her first meeting with Mary's Privy Councillors. J. E. Neale found his 'presumption' baffling; 'Sir Nicholas Throckmorton's Advice to Queen Elizabeth on Her Accession to the Throne', *English Historical Review* 65 (1950), pp. 91–8.

[33] Quoted in Mortimer Levine, *The Early Elizabethan Succession Question*, p. 178. See Brian Levack, *The Civil Lawyers in England 1603–1641: A Political Study* (Oxford, 1973) for Elizabeth's attempts to buttress her authority by appointing a majority of civil, rather than common lawyers, and the association of the former with Catholicism.

[34] The offence was twofold: firstly, too 'precisely' writing against the Scottish queen's title; perhaps even more offensively, appealing to international Protestantism to do so. Hales solicited the legal

And what of the nobility? The evidence suggests that the emergence of the concept of a mixed monarchy produced a 'legitimist' reaction to which the concept of nobility as a virile and martial identity tied to birth and blood, and succession through 'right' so defined, were central. This strand found expression at various points in the reign, from the Northern Rebellion in the early years of the reign to the Earl of Northumberland's short-lived rebellion at its close.[35] For, as we have seen, the regime (but not, I think, the queen) not only subscribed in some measure to the ambivalence concerning 'nobility of blood' which became a concomitant of the godly nation, it also privileged a definition of 'virtue' as a 'second nature' attainable (by men) primarily through their Christian commitment, in a cultural context in which noblemen, as well as the queen, had 'two bodies': one their souls, the other their caste identities.

The declaration of the earls of Northumberland and Westmorland, in which they justified their actions in the Northern Rebellion of 1569, made their case in legitimist terms. It referred to the 'disordered and evil disposed persons about the queen's majesty' who, seeking to advance themselves, have 'overcome . . . the true and Catholic religion . . . and abused the queen'. Now, lastly, they 'seek [to] procure the destruction of the nobility'. For the 'ancient nobility' have, through their representatives the earls of Northumberland and Westmorland, sought to 'make manifest and known to all manner of men, to whom of mere right the true succession of the crown appertaineth'. But this 'godly, good, and honourable' attempt has been 'prevented by certain common enemies of this realm about the queen's person', leaving the earls – the 'true remain' of the nobility's 'virtuous counsel and intent' – in danger of their lives and liberties.[36] There are intimations in the declaration of the alternative, Catholic, conception of England's godly and imperial identity as promoted by Stephen Gardiner in Mary I's reign, now allied to a 'feudal-baronial' conception of the nobility's role as kingmaker.[37] Sig-

opinion of foreign Protestant lawyers to assert the legitimacy of the Earl of Hertford's marriage with Lady Catherine Grey. Cecil's correspondence with Sir Thomas Smith, then in France, makes it clear that Hales was working on behalf of the Privy Council. Elizabeth targeted Nicholas Bacon, the Lord Keeper, as exemplar and meted out a characteristic punishment, restricting him to an official (not a counselling) capacity narrowly defined. He was 'kept from the court, and from intermeddling with any other thing but the chancery'. John Strype, *Annals*, vol. i.ii, pp. 117 and 121.

[35] Linda Levy Peck, 'Kingship, Counsel and Law in Early Stuart Britain' in *The Varieties of British Political Thought 1500–1800*, ed. J. G. A. Pocock (Cambridge, 1993), pp. 80–115.
[36] John Strype, *Annals*, vol. i.ii, pp. 313–14.
[37] For Gardiner, see above, chapter 3; John Guy, 'The Rhetoric of Counsel', p. 297.

nificantly, it occurred when a 'king' of sorts was in prospect – after the marriage of Mary Queen of Scots to the flower of the English peerage, the Duke of Norfolk.

The official response, in a tract addressed to the earls' followers, is also revealing. Sir Thomas Smith, William Cecil's godly adjutant, responded first by arguing the traditional case that councillors serve as agents of the monarch's will, although the context of the utterance – female rule – perhaps qualifies these conventional assertions:[38]

> Is there any greater falsehood than thus to defame the queen's most noble government? Are you so blind not to see the queen touched, though . . . her name be spared? Came they, whom you call *disordered*, to the queen uncalled? Are they not of her majesty's council by her wise and good choice? Deal they not in the causes of the realm, to such ends and with such means as her majesty appointeth? Do they anything without her authority and good liking? . . . In causes out of parliament, is aught put in execution without her highness's will and pleasure?

He innovates however in differentiating 'council' from the nobility. In so doing he defines the collective endeavour of the body politic in a way that responds to the ambiguity contained in the earls' characterisation of the queen's 'evil councillors' as 'certain common enemies of this realm about the queen's person': whether they are numerous; share a common maliciousness; or are of non-noble stock. For Smith, as for Laurence Humphrey, nobility pertains to those who follow the truth:

> Cease then to be so beguiled. Take that shadow away; and take it as truth is; that your earls' proclamation indeed saith, though not in the selfsame syllables, that the queen's majesty, with her nobility, parliament, and council, have done these mischiefs, that my lord of Westmorland and his fellows must redress in haste.[39]

The tensions and paradoxes that resulted from this configuration surfaced time and again in interactions between the queen, her councillors, and members of the nobility. They appeared in 1571, when Henry Percy, Earl of Northumberland – and, at points, both a convinced Protestant and a stout supporter of the regime – was arrested for intrigues in support of Mary Queen of Scots. Acting as intermediary between Elizabeth and Burghley over Percy's forthcoming trial, the Earl of Leicester wrote to Burghley in terms that clearly conveyed Elizabeth's distrust of Burghley's intentions in this important matter. According to Leicester, Elizabeth had expressed her concern lest Percy escape pun-

---

[38] The tract is anonymous, but John Strype plausibly attributes it to Sir Thomas Smith in his *Annals*, vol. I.ii, pp. 332–3.   [39] John Strype, *Annals*, vol. I.ii, pp. 332–3.

ishment, and her greater fear lest the verdict given at his trial – whether
for or against the defendant – be seen to be taken at Burghley's behest,
rather than her own:

> I brake with her Majesty also about Sir Henry Percy; she was in some doubt
> what as best to do, but in the end she concluded that he should have his trial.
> She gave me great charge to will your Lordship to have great and special care to
> have it substantially done, least there be some packing and partial favour
> shewed . . . And, my Lord, I must tell you her words, In any wise, sayth she, bid
> my Lord Treasurer show himself as he should do in this case of Percy's . . . I
> trust, the matter being so manifest, and he so lewd, there will be consideration
> had accordingly; and therefore, least some may think to please Burghley, for
> that he hath matched with him, let him [i.e. Burghley] deal with the attorney
> and my learned Counsel the more earnestly, that they may perceive that he
> looks only to my service.[40]

Michael Pulman regards this document as evidence that Elizabeth and
her councillors 'assumed juries could be tampered with' and that 'such
interference was legitimate when the interests of policy demanded it'.[41]
This is not wrong, but a less anachronistic formulation would be that
they operated in the context of a deferential society. More striking is
Elizabeth's assumption that in key cases the political will being deferred
to would be that of her chief councillor, rather than hers. And because
deference regards perceived or informal power relations as much, if not
more, than institutionalised ones, she was particularly concerned with
how Percy was displayed. Hence her next point of attack was the terms
of Percy's imprisonment. Leicester's letter continues:

> Beside, she said, she was informed that Sir Harry Percy had as it were the
> liberty of the Tower, and walked openly upon the Hill at his pleasure, and who
> list talked with him. She would needs have me send for the Lieutenant
> forthwith to come hither, to know how he had this liberty more than others, for
> that she never heard of it, and with great offence willed me, in any wise, that
> your Lordship should call the Lieutenant before you, to inquire from whom the
> liberty grew, and why he had it, and that she would understand his answer.
> This manner of special favour shewed to him above the rest (sayth she) will
> cause some folks to think, that it is for Burghley's sake, and perhaps when
> further matter shall now come in question, the like opinions may procure him
> that which I doubt not but both he and the rest will foresee, and therefore let
> him have special care to give charge, both to my learned Counsel and the
> Judges, to have regard to the proceedings with him.[42]

[40] *A Collection of State Papers*, pp. 228–9.
[41] Michael Pulman, *The Elizabethan Privy Council in the 1570s* (Berkeley, Calif., 1971), p. 181.
[42] *A Collection of State Papers*, pp. 228–9.

On this occasion Elizabeth reacted against what she saw as her councillors' conflicting loyalties, primarily by reminding both Leicester and, through him, Burghley, of her power and their duty to her. The Leicester–Burghley axis is particularly significant in this regard, because she defined Leicester as her 'creature' and 'favourite', hence bound to her by ties of allegiance more personal than those that allied her and her other Privy Councillors. Presumably, however, she doubted her ability to counteract the powerful influence of her chief councillor, perhaps especially in a case such as Percy's, where virility as well as nobility was in play. (Perhaps she felt that such a case marked a point at which her 'haughty stomach' differed in essence from the virility of her nobles, leaving her in *terra incognita*.) For whatever reason, her next move was to warn Burghley to make sure that the 'right' verdict was returned and that it was known to be her will rather than his – accompanied by a refusal to commit herself about what that outcome should be. Her refusal is announced, characteristically, in evasive language, this time as she refers to future events: 'This manner of special favour shewed to him above the rest (sayth she) will cause some folks to think, that it is for Burghley's sake, and perhaps when further matter shall now come in question, the like opinions may procure him that which I doubt not but both he and the rest will foresee.' Perhaps this was a means of leaving it to Burghley's conscience to determine whether his actions in regard to Percy's trial promoted the mixed monarchy, the godly commonwealth, or his own noble pretensions.[43] And this refusal to commit herself – so marked a feature of Elizabeth's behaviour as queen – led on this occasion to Leicester's response:

I told her Majesty what you said to me this morning, and what you thought best, which was to proceed even as she hath willed, only her pleasure was required to be understood; for that at our last dealing with her about the prisoners, her majesty was so offended as we could not certainly resolve or agree what her pleasure was, either for him or some others. But I knew your Lordship thought it best to let the course of her laws to take place.[44]

In a passage such as this we can see how the enactment of the bicephalic body politic gave rise to a contest between Elizabeth and her

---

[43] The Scottish minister Andrew Melville provides this possible gloss on Cecil's motives. According to Melville, Cecil asked Norfolk about his views on the rightful incumbent of the English crown. Norfolk replied 'that he would serve and honour the queen his mistress [Elizabeth] as long as she lived. But after her decease he would set the crown of England upon the queen of Scotland's head, as lawful heir.' He then told Cecil to 'go and prattle that language again to the queen'; to which Cecil allegedly responded that 'he would be no taleteller to the queen of him, but would concur with him in any course, and serve him in any honourable thing wherein he would employ him'. John Strype, *Annals*, vol. II.i, p. 192.   [44] *A Collection of State Papers*, pp. 228–9.

godly councillors, one element of which was the attempt to 'capture' the nobility in the interests of advancing their sometimes conflicting political interests. It is also possible to get an immediate sense of the contested quality of Elizabeth's relations with even her 'inward councillors', as well as the ramifications of the enactment of the mixed monarchy for issues of law.

Throughout the reign too, and as a consequence of this novel equation of 'zeal' with virtue, the claims of parliament as an alternative centre of counsel and law-making in the godly nation were advanced: by members of the House of Commons; by nobles and bishops sitting in the House of Lords; by Privy Councillors participating, directly or indirectly, in the proceedings of the two Houses – by godly Englishmen self-consciously participating in England's national redemptive mission.[45] Linda Levy Peck notes that from at least the 1570s some members of the House of Commons claimed to be not simply representatives of their localities, but public officials and advisers to the monarch.[46] MPs become as it were auxiliary councillors – a role allowed for in the first instance by Privy Councillors' recourse to their godly colleagues as a means of exerting semi-public pressure on the queen to preserve the regime in its Protestant integrity in the 1560s and 1570s.[47]

The political consequences of this move appear in a 1566 tract entitled *The Common Cry of Englishmen Made to the Most Noble Lady, Queen Elizabeth, and the High Court of Parliament*. The author petitions the queen to settle the succession, depicting the dangerous condition of her subjects whilst it remains unsettled. He changes focus however and speaks as a counsellor to his fellows in pushing for a solution to the impasse Elizabeth effected in 1563 through her refusal to act. The queen is either 'timorous', of her womanliness, or 'singular', perhaps impervious to common reason. It is therefore incumbent on her counsellors, in the Privy Council and in parliament, to see to the preservation of the realm. Nor does he see an absolute division between the two types of counsellors:

And if the Queen either of timorousness to attempt a matter of so great weight or of any other singular respect should seem not to be willing to hear and help

---

[45] See T. E. Hartley, *Elizabeth's Parliaments: Queen, Lords and Commons 1559–1601* (Manchester, 1992). For a useful definition of 'national culture' at this time see Susan Dwyer Amussen, *An Ordered Society: Gender and Class in Early Modern England* (New York, 1988), p. 35.

[46] Linda Levy Peck, 'Kingship, Counsel and Law', p. 98.

[47] John Guy, *Tudor England* (Oxford, 1988), pp. 322–3. See also M. A. R. Graves, 'Managing Elizabethan Parliaments' in *The Parliaments of Elizabethan England*, ed. D. M. Dean and N. L. Jones (Oxford, 1990), pp. 37–64, p. 45.

. . . then we turn our cry to you our Lords and Commons assembled now in Parliament. Though the delay made upon your last most godly request in this behalf [i.e. in the 1563 session] did daunt and grieve the hearts of you and of thousands which loved you for your good attempt, yet assay again . . . If it should happen [despite] the peril that hangeth thereon, as you do know what your authority is, so beshow your wisdom and power to put your country out of such peril. [Princes sometimes act unwisely and go astray.] Then do not only wise councillors stand instead, but chiefly such great assemblies of such persons so authorized and therewith privileged as Parliament men are. [Parliament is the place of free speech.] Speak there![48]

This speech brings us face to face with what Donald Kelley has called the 'mythical and mystical' conceptions of parliament, and the potentially radical connections between godly counsel and free speech.[49] Their development, so prominent especially during the 1570s and 1580s, was allowed for in part by an innovative reading of a 'constitutional' distinction proposed by Mary Tudor (and followed by Elizabeth): that state affairs were not the proper sphere for parliamentary initiative, but that commonwealth matters were.[50] With the revival of commonwealth ideology under Elizabeth it is hard to overestimate the significance of this innovation. Appropriation of matters of commonweal by parliament allowed for intimations that parliament, possibly even the House of Commons, was the true locus of counsel, godly MPs the legitimate counsellors of the elect nation. And such counsellors might find themselves in a position in which the demands of the True Church conflicted, not only with those of the monarch, but also with those of councillors of erstwhile virtue, who had lost the battle to subsume their private interests in the good of the common weal.

SPEECH ACTS IN THE MIXED MONARCHY[51]

I explore the extension and radicalisation of 'counsel' in the 1570s in chapter 6. I raise it here as a necessary context for understanding the

[48] Quoted in Mortimer Levine, *The Early Elizabethan Succession Question*, p. 169. Levine notes that the tract was with Thomas Sampson's papers and speculates that he may have been its author.
[49] Donald Kelley, 'Elizabethan Political Thought', pp. 75–6.
[50] G. R. Elton, 'Parliament', pp. 96–7.
[51] For 'speech act' see J. G. A. Pocock, 'Languages and Their Implications: The Transformation of the Study of Political Thought' in *Politics, Language and Time: Essays on Political Thought and History* (New York, 1973), pp. 3–41 and, more recently, 'The Concept of a Language and the *Métier d'historien*: Some Considerations on Practice' in *The Languages of Political Theory in Early-Modern Europe*, ed. Anthony Pagden (Cambridge, 1987), pp. 19–38; and Quentin Skinner, 'Meaning and Understanding in the History of Ideas' in *Meaning and Context: Quentin Skinner and His Critics*, ed. James Tully (Cambridge, 1988), pp. 29–67.

relations and interrelations among the estates of the realm in the provision of counsel that characterised Elizabethan politics from very early in the reign. This complex is illuminated, and some of its tensions adumbrated, in an episode of 1566 that I want to explore in some detail. In that year, again in the context of parliamentary and conciliar attempts to resolve the matters of the queen's marriage and the succession, a delegation from both houses waited upon the queen, to add the weight of their presence to the parliamentary petition. Perhaps it was because Elizabeth recognised and feared the political implications of a unanimity of counsel across the two houses and into the court that she reacted so vehemently when, as on this occasion, that consensus appeared to be in prospect. The episode consists of four parts: Elizabeth's reaction (recorded by the French ambassador) upon being informed that this united front was in prospect; her speech to the delegation; her speech as vetted by the delegation; and a final exchange in print on the subject in the form of the Commons' preamble to a subsidy bill and Elizabeth's hand-written response to it.

Seemingly aware that they were venturing into uncharted terrain with the proposed joint suit concerning settlement of the succession, a small party of lay peers and some bishops spoke to the queen in private about the Commons' approach. According to the French ambassador, Elizabeth was very angry. The Commons were 'very rebellious'; they would not have attempted 'such things during the life of her father'. She then turned on the peers, attempting perhaps to stave off the upcoming joint petition by threatening to 'uncounsel' them if they persisted in this new alignment:

My Lords, do what you will; as for myself, I shall do nothing but according to my pleasure. All the resolutions which you may make have no force without my consent and authority; besides, what you desire is an affair of much too great importance to be declared to a knot of hairbrains. I will take counsel with men who understand justice and the laws, as I am deliberating to do; I will choose half a dozen of the most able I can find in my kingdom for consultation, and after having their advice, I will then discover to you my will.[52]

Her speech, more measured than the outburst captured by the French ambassador, did not differ fundamentally in content. It shows some of the rhetorical strategies she consistently adopted over the course of the reign, and translated into political action when opportunity

---

[52] Quoted in Mortimer Levine, *The Early Elizabethan Succession Question*, p. 176. Levine thinks she's bluffing, asking, with justice, where such alternative counsel was to be found in the political circumstances of the 1560s.

offered. She begins (characteristically) with an implied threat, joined to an implied claim that she, not the men on whose behalf they attend her, is the true possessor of 'wit' (here wisdom or judgement). She also suggests that they have been imposed upon, if not duped, by those 'bridleless colts' who have mistaken her princely magnanimity for weakness. Interestingly, she draws on the notion of a 'king' as a potentially tyrannical figure to intimate their good fortune in being subject to a queen:

If the order of your cause had matched the weight of your matter the one might well have craved reward and the other much the sooner satisfied; but when I call to mind how far from dutiful care and, yea, rather how nigh a traitorous trick, this tumbling cast did spring, I muse how men of wit can so hardly use that gift they hold. I marvel not much that bridleless colts do not know their rider's hand, whom bit of kingly rein did never snaffle yet.[53]

Unable however to dismiss the importance of the matter, given the consensual front they represented, she stakes out an alternative position. First she argues that the issues are of such moment that discussion in parliament is inappropriate: 'Whether it was fit that so great a cause as this should have had his beginning in such a public place as that, let it be well weighted.'[54] (Here she uses 'public' not, as Sir Thomas Elyot would have it, in relation to *res publicae*, but as the antonym of 'private', the meaning that became conventional over the late sixteenth century.) Secondly, she suggests that their speeches on the subject impugn her own word, because she herself had stated that she would marry. This is part of an ongoing attempt to portray their 'speech' as insignificant, if not actually counterproductive to the common ends of 'her realm', her 'word' (which need not be communicated in language) as its true counter:

Well, the matter whereof they would have made their petition (as I am informed) consists in two points: in my marriage, and in the limitation of the succession of the crown, wherein my marriage was first placed, as for manner sake . . . I did send them answer by my counsel I would marry (although of my own disposition I was not inclined thereunto,) but that was not accepted nor credited, although spoken by their Prince. And yet I used so many words that I could say no more. And were it not now I had spoken those words, I would never speak them again. I will never break the word of a prince spoken in public place, for my honour sake. And therefore I say again . . . A strange order of petitioners that will make a request and cannot be otherwise ascertained but by the prince's word, and yet will not believe it when it is spoken.

[53] *Proceedings*, p. 145.   [54] Ibid.

Again, the motives of those who attempt to wrest meaning from her must be suspect: 'There have been some that have ere this said unto me they never required more than that they might once hear me say I would marry. Well, there was never so great a treason but might be covered under as fair a pretence.'[55]

Some among them – specifically the nobles – are wise enough to realise that, when the petitioners (now identified as members of the lower house) moved on from marriage to the limitation of the succession they breached fundamental propriety, for it is 'a strange thing that the foot should direct the head in so weighty a cause'. She does not, however, blame the upper house (though this does not prevent her using sarcasm to bring home to its representatives how they have been 'seduced'). Instead she blames two bishops, whom she presents as adulterating the caste identity of the noble estate through their zeal:

And further to help the matter, ['those unbridled persons'] must needs prefer their speeches to the upper house, to have you, my Lords, consent with them; whereby you were seduced and of simplicity did assent unto it, which you would not have done if you had foreseen before considerately the importance of the matter . . . But there, two bishops with their long orations sought to persuade you also with solemn matter, as though you, my Lords, had not known that when my breath did fail me I had been dead unto you, and that then, dying without issue, what a danger it were to the whole State: which you had not known, before they told you it! . . . But we will not judge that these attempts were done of any hatred to our person, but even for lack of good foresight. I do not marvel though *Dominii Doctores* with you, my Lords, did so use themselves therein, since after my brother's death they openly preached and set forth that my sister and I were bastards.

Indeed zeal – which she tries to paint as subverting the notion of Christ's headship – lies behind all such motions concerning the succession: 'They would have twelve or fourteen limited in succession, and the more the better. And those shall be of such uprightness and so divine as in them shall be divinity itself.'

This counsel is tainted, not least because their petitions ignore entirely her own status ('wherein was nothing said for my safety, but only for themselves'). She can therefore ignore it – but only to have recourse to 'true' counsel. By this point she has evidently consulted those anonymous 'men who understand justice and the laws' as she threatened to do when confronted by the 'knot of hairbrains' engaging in parliamentary speeches. Not surprisingly, the counsel of these shadowy figures (who

[55] Ibid., pp. 146–7.

might be, in Mary Queen of Scots' words, 'private and unexpert', but wedded to the interests of the queen) consists of a statesmanlike silence:

> I have conferred before this time with those that are well learned, and have asked their opinions touching the limitation of succession, who have been silent; not that by their silences after lawlike manner they have seemed to assent to it, but that indeed they could not tell what to say considering the great peril to the realm, and most danger to myself.[56]

She, not they, has the necessary qualities – of reason, foresight, majesty – to pronounce upon matters material to her realm, and will do so at a time and after a manner suitable in her judgement. (Even here however she can only, rhetorically and politically, postpone the issue.)

> You would have a limitation of succession. Truly, if reason did not subdue will in me, I would cause you to deal in it, so pleasant a thing it should be unto me. But I stay it for your benefit . . . I am your anointed Queen. I will never be by violence constrained to do anything. I thank God I am endued with such qualities that if I were turned out of the realm in my petticoat I were able to live in any place of Christendom. . .
>
> Your petition is to deal in the limitation of the succession. At this present it is not convenient, nor never shall be without some peril unto you, and certain danger unto me . . . [But as soon as convenient despite dangers she will do it] and offer it unto you as your prince and head, without request. For it is monstrous that the feet should direct the head. And therefore this is my mind and answer, which I would have to be showed in the two houses.[57]

Lord Chief Justice Sir Robert Catlyn or Sir James Dyer were then named to report this answer back to the upper house, Cecil for the House of Commons. According to the diarist recording proceedings, at this point the representatives of the lower house objected that they had not brought their Speaker with them, not realising that his offices would be called for. Although the pronouns become extremely ambiguous at this point (which leads Hartley to amend the manuscript 'he' to 'she'), the diarist writes that 'she said that he was a speaker indeed, and there ended'.[58] I read this as Elizabeth asserting her capacity to assign office – Cecil is a speaker if she says he is – while reminding these delegates that the Speaker is a servant of the crown.

In a sense, at this point, the assertion was immaterial. Cecil duly reported back to the House the following day in a speech that, endorsed by the whole delegation, is more striking for its divergence from Elizabeth's meaning than for the superficial similarity of its wording:

---

[56] Ibid., p. 148.   [57] Ibid., pp. 148–9.   [58] Ibid., p. 149.

But now for further satisfaction of such as have taken her former speeches that she would marry to be but a phrase of speaking, she remembered of what weight the word of a prince was, spoken in a public place; . . . And further assurance she could not make but by speech . . . And so in this matter she concluded that she could not use any further means to satisfy them which desired her marriage but by speech, and therefore required to be believed.

The other matter, for limitation of the succession, she said as she could not deny but that it was necessary and profitable, so had it also great perils therein to enter at this time into the decision thereof.[59]

Finally, perhaps buoyed by the reasonableness of the queen's response as conveyed through the delegation (but more likely still following the agenda of which it was an instance), the Commons drafted the following preamble to the subsidy bill:[60]

We cannot but . . . thankfully remember to your Majesty that it pleased the same to signify unto us that you did not mislike of us for our desire in this Parliament to have the succession of the crown declared . . . And signified further of your godly disposition and natural love toward us, to our great comfort, that rather than your realm should threat ruin for lack of declaration of succession – which you trusted Almighty God would show of your own body in due time after your marriage – you would by God's help, though it should appear some peril to yourself (which God defend), declare the succession in such convenient time as your Highness, with the advice of your council and assent of your realm, should think meet in such person as in whom the right thereof according to law and justice ought to be settled and remain.[61]

Elizabeth's response, hand-written on the folio, insisted that at the least her words must remain her property, unfixed in print:

I know no reason why my private answers to the realm should serve for prologue to a subsidies book. Neither yet do I understand why such audacity should be used to make without my license an act of my words. Are my words like lawyers' books, which nowadays go to the wiredrawers to make subtle doings more plain? Is there no hold of my speech without an act compel me to confirm? Shall my princely consent be turned to strengthen my words that be not of themselves substantives?[62]

Here she was successful, and the offending preamble was revised. This episode, unusually well documented, was by no means atypical. Elizabeth's relations with her parliaments (and councillors) may not have been helped by what Geoffrey Elton called her 'inclination to lose her

[59] Ibid., pp. 150–1.
[60] For the role of Privy Councillors in drafting these preambles see J. D. Alsop, 'Innovation in Tudor Taxation', *English Historical Review* 99 (1984), pp. 83–93.
[61] J. E. Neale, *Elizabeth I and Her Parliaments*, 2 vols. (London, 1957), vol. I, *1558–1581*, pp. 174–5.
[62] Ibid., pp. 192–3.

temper over all that unsolicited advice, no matter how well meant' – but to enact (controlled) rage is also to play the part of a king.[63]

The episode also sheds light on the politicisation of speech and silence that was so marked a feature of the period and that was allowed for only in the context of print culture. For it was characteristic of this age that the prince's will was still communicated through others, as a sign of his power, but that printing had weakened the control that even powerful speakers could exercise over their words. Sir Francis Walsingham, for example, spoke to Mary Stuart as Elizabeth's mouthpiece in the 1582 exchange cited above.[64] There, and in countless similar episodes, we can see reflections of an enduring cultural archetype of relations between masters and servants, of which relations between king and counsellor are one variety (relations between husbands and wives another). In this model – still very much alive in the early modern period and newly invigorated by humanism – servants serve as vessels, filled with the word and will of their masters, in a way analogous to the ideal relationship between man and God: a relationship mediated by the Word. This quality of intimacy, reflected through referred speech, informed the analogy between the body politic and the human body to which men of the sixteenth century so often had recourse. At this time it attained a new political significance in the context of parliament. Here, in theory, Speakers, like mediums, expressed the wisdom of their estates, whilst in Elizabeth's reign in this period some MPs began to agitate for 'free speech'. In the late sixteenth century, controversy over free speech in parliament had many dimensions. One, to which insufficient attention has been paid, is that a claim to freedom of speech, in the context of female rule, constituted an implicit assertion of civic capacity in Aristotelian and Pauline terms: the same terms that allied speech to reason, disallowed women the status of reasonable beings, and exhorted them to silence.[65]

This cultural pattern also underpinned conflict over issues of speech and silence, oral and print modes of transmission that arose in the course of Elizabeth's reign. For if Elizabeth could threaten to 'uncounsel' her councillors, or seek counsel elsewhere, her councillors could equally threaten to withdraw from the copulative 'queen and counsel', leaving her to announce her political isolation in particularly damning terms: as an uncounselled queen. In the closing session of the 1563

[63] G. R. Elton, 'Parliament', pp. 99–100.   [64] See above, pp. 141–2.
[65] Donald Kelley, *The Beginning of Ideology: Consciousness and Society in the French Reformation* (Cambridge, 1981), p. 73.

parliament this is exactly what the Lord Keeper Nicholas Bacon did, over the same issue of marriage and the succession. On other matters he had, as was customary, responded verbally to the Speaker and the assembled MPs on the queen's behalf. But on this particular issue he read out a statement she herself had drafted, for reasons he explained to the House:

> And touching your request before this made unto her for her marriage and succession, because it is of such importance, whereby I doubted my own opening thereof, and therefore desired her majesty that her meaning might be written, which she hath done and delivered to me to be read.[66]

What was this, if not a politic announcement that in this matter the queen had refused to accept the advice of her councillors?

'You know my mind', Elizabeth frequently concluded her letters to those whom she trusted, with the clear implication not only that this was a privileged position but also that, knowing her mind, the recipient would proceed to enact her will. During Elizabeth's reign that confidence, fundamental to the traditional servant/counsellor axis, often proved to be unfounded – often enough to make the terms of the relationship between the king and his servants a prominent element of political discourse through Elizabeth's reign and into the reigns of her immediate successors.[67] This was one important consequence of the bicephalic body politic over which Elizabeth reigned, when men could be loyal to a female ruler through obedience to God's will, even when God's will diverged from the queen's.

CONCLUSION

John Guy argues that Francis Bacon followed a long tradition when, in 1612, he approvingly attributed to the ancients the view that 'Sovereignty is married to Counsel'. (In this marriage, significantly, sovereignty or *imperium* is figured as male, counsel – *consilium* – as female.[68]) What he does not explore, and what looms large in these disparate readings of counsel, is their authors' awareness that, deriving from a context in which *imperium* is invested in a female prince, the relationship – the 'marriage' – between sovereignty and counsel becomes a matter both more complex and more contested than had been the case under

---

[66] Ibid.,, p. 112.
[67] See, for example, the three-way correspondence between Walsingham, Cecil and Leicester over marriage negotiations with the French court in 1570–1 in Dudley Digges, *The Compleat Ambassador*, pp. 37–55. [68] John Guy, 'Rhetoric of Counsel', p. 292.

the early Tudors.[69] During Elizabeth's reign the contest produced two competing readings of where sovereignty resided in the English polity, readings forged in the context of female rule and articulated through definitions of 'counsel'. On the one hand the Protestant ascendancy reread English history and political institutions as having produced a 'mixed monarchy', in which sovereignty resided in the three equal estates of king, lords and commons, and the 'crown' symbolised the enactment of their collective will, articulated in some form in parliament. This collective identity came to be termed, with an increasingly specific meaning over the period, the 'commonwealth'; by the 1590s, in some cases, the 'country'.[70] On the other side it is possible to trace the attempt by the queen to insist on the pre-eminence of the crown; to claim, as king, a sovereign capacity in matters of state and the role as head of the body politic in regard to affairs of the commonweal. In this reading the crown was not, as Edward Coke would have it, a 'hieroglyphic of the laws', but rather an emblem of the king's majesty; a reading that, in France, was to lead to an ideology of divine right kingship centred on the absolute identification of the state with the person of the monarch.[71]

During Elizabeth's reign, the relationship of counsel to sovereignty was therefore a contested proposition, in regard to both the queen's relationship to her Privy Councillors and their relationship (individually and collectively) to parliament and more broadly to the nation. For much of the reign, 'counsel' was defined extensively in terms of its providers, yet was still considered to be a duty, not a right. It could refer to traditional councillors (the nobility and/or the queen's chosen councillors, especially of the Privy Council) or to 'godly' counsellors from the ranks of the political nation (who might be members of the nobility, or Privy Councillors, or Members of Parliament, or ministers, or 'good Englishmen'). And parliament – the place of parity where collective wisdom assembled to determine the common weal, as John Hooker defined it in his 1572 book *Order and Usage* – came to be perceived as the institutional organ of godly

---

[69] I am following J. G. A. Pocock's description of political language as 'by its nature ambivalent', consisting in the utterance of "essentially contested concepts" and propositions, and in the simultaneous employment of languages favouring the utterance of diverse and contrary propositions'; 'The State of the Art' in *Virtue, Commerce, and History* (Cambridge, 1985), pp. 1–33, p. 9.

[70] Stephen Collins, *From Divine Cosmos to Sovereign State: An Intellectual History of Consciousness and the Idea of Order in Renaissance England* (Oxford, 1989), p. 192, and see below, chapter 6.

[71] Coke made this claim in the 1608 Calvin's Case. See Ernst Kantorowitz, *The King's Two Bodies: A Study in Medieval Political Theology* (Princeton, N.J., 1957), p. 16. For the French case see H. C. Dowdall, 'The Word "State"', *Law Quarterly Review* 39 (1923), pp. 98–125; Herbert H. Rowen, "L'État C'est à Moi": Louis XIV and the State', *French Historical Studies* 2, no. 1 (1961), pp. 83–98.

counsel.[72] At points during the reign, especially during the period 1570–85, the exigencies of enacting God's will for the English body politic allowed for counsel (another term for which, in this context, was 'free speech') to be conceived of as both a duty and a right, possibly even a right peculiarly the province of councillors in the lower house.[73] This formulation also implied that it was the monarch's duty, as one of the three estates, to allow her will to be informed by such collective wisdom, or run the risk of becoming a tyrant.

Concentration on the role of parliament in a mixed monarchy thus led, during this period, to a politically significant reading of specifically the House of Commons as *primus inter pares* in the mixed monarchy because of its connection, not with the crown, but with the 'country': ambiguously county, locality, countryside – and True Church.[74] This reading, and its political implications, are the subject of the next chapter. Yet at the same time a bifurcation occurred. The same pressures that led to militancy led inevitably to the political reorientation that characterised the last eighteen years of the reign. The prospect of the permanent extension of the political nation beyond the House of Commons 'out of doors' – and the threat of egalitarian radicalism as a constituent of the godly nation so defined – led increasing numbers of godly men (including, eventually, most Privy Councillors) to follow the queen *some way* in the struggle for sovereignty described above. That is, they defined the queen as (symbolically) a king, and as such 'sovereign' among the three estates. This move led to a controversial, and related, attempt to cleanse the definition of 'courtier': to present a courtier as a counsellor who enacts the will of the monarch as the best means of advancing the public (not common) weal.[75] 'Serve God by serving of the queen', in Burghley's words – but only once the crown had been secured for the godly nation by the execution of Mary Queen of Scots.

It was the *mariage de convenance* between this tendency – what might be termed the *politique* wing of the Protestant ascendancy – and the queen and her party (her views less idiosyncratic with the rise to power of her 'creatures' and in the wake of Mary's execution) that announced what John Guy has termed the 'second' reign, the period after 1585.[76] Not

---

[72] Vernon Snow, ed., *Parliament in Elizabethan England*, pp. 182–3.

[73] Stephen Collins, *From Divine Cosmos to Sovereign State*, pp. 88–9.

[74] For a reading of some of the ambiguities of the term 'country', and a sense of their cultural consequence, see Richard Helgerson, *Forms of Nationhood: The Elizabeth Writing of England* (Chicago, 1992), p. 136.

[75] And emphatically rejected by such as William Harrison. See G. J. R. Parry, *A Protestant Vision: William Harrison and the Reformation of Elizabethan England* (Cambridge, 1987), esp. pp. 262–8.

[76] John Guy, 'The 1590s: The Second Reign of Elizabeth I?' in *The Reign of Elizabeth I: Court and Culture in the Last Decade*, ed. John Guy (Cambridge, 1995), pp. 1–19.

surprisingly, Elizabeth marked this sea change in her closing speech to
the 1589 parliament by disallowing the definition of counsel that had
been dominant since her accession. In a speech which does not survive,
but which Sir Edward Coke referred to in the 1593 parliament, she told
MPs that they had misunderstood their function in the realm: 'Many
come hither *ad consulendum, qui nesciunt quid sit consulendum*' [many come
hither to counsel, who are ignorant what counsel means].[77]

She made the point again, through the mouth of Speaker Puckering,
in the course of a parliamentary debate over free speech in the 1590s, as
she gained the political initiative. The role of those who 'take upon them
to be counsellors and procurators of the Commonwealth' (here members of the House of Commons) are not called 'to speak there of all
causes . . . and to frame a form of religion or a state of government, as to
their idle brains shall seem meetest. She saith, no king fit for his state will
suffer such absurdities'.[78] Arguably at this stage in the reign she could
plausibly identify herself as a 'king'.[79] She did so, characteristically, in a
speech act that insisted upon the change in the political balance of the
'mixed monarchy' which she claims to have effected: 'counsellors and
procurators of the Commonwealth' ratify the reason of state which it is
her prerogative to identify and enact in order to effect the common
weal. The attempt to occupy this political high ground had a particular
end in view. It allowed Elizabeth to assert that she was 'head' of the
body politic, even as her father had been, and that as such she stood
above the three estates in a form of government that James I was to
define as 'a mixed polity created by kings' – successor state to the
Elizabethan mixed monarchy.[80]

---

[77] J. E. Neale, *Elizabeth I and Her Parliaments*, vol. II, *1584–1601*, p. 220.
[78] Ibid., pp. 249–50, my emphasis.
[79] Leah S. Marcus, 'Erasing the Stigma of Daughterhood: Mary I, Elizabeth I, and Henry VIII' in
Daughters and Fathers, ed. Linda E. Boose and Betty S. Flowers (Baltimore, Md., 1989), pp. 400–17
pp. 411–15. Marcus describes how Elizabeth's self-references changed over the course of the
reign, in parallel with this 'winning of the initiative', so that by the last decade she very
commonly used the term 'king' in place of 'lady', 'princess', 'Queen', or 'prince'.
[80] See George L. Mosse's discussion of the early years of James I's reign in *The Struggle for Sovereignty
in England from the Reign of Queen Elizabeth to the Petition of Right* (New York, 1968), chs. 3 and 4.

CHAPTER 6

Godly men and parliamentarians: the politics of counsel in the 1570s

> But if he [Member of the House of Commons] range in evil words, then [it is necessary] to interrupt him, saying, 'I pray you to spare these words. They become not this place that is a place of state and counsel.'
>
> William Lambarde, *Notes on the Procedures and Privileges of the House of Commons* (1584)[1]

In the ninth parliament of Elizabeth's reign (1597–8), in the course of a heated debate on monopolies, MP Sir Edward Hoby was shocked by the appearance outside parliament of 'a multitude of people who said they were commonwealth men and desired [the House] to take compassion of their griefs'.[2] In the parliament of 1601 Robert Cecil similarly complained that 'Parliament matters are ordinarily talked of in the street. I have heard myself, being in my coach, these words spoken aloud: "God prosper those that further the overthrow of these monopolies. God send the prerogative touch not our liberty."' He reminded his auditors 'that whatsoever is subject to a public exposition cannot be good', and implicitly blamed those in the House of Commons who, he suggested, shared the secrets of the House with men out of doors. They 'would be glad that all sovereignty were converted into popularity'.[3] The anonymous speakers 'out of doors' appealed to MPs in the House of Commons on the basis of a common collective identity as godly Englishmen – an identity that had come to be increasingly marginalised after the

---

[1] *Lambarde's 'Notes on the Procedures and Privileges of the House of Commons'*, ed. Paul L. Ward (London, 1977), p. 64. Lambarde began his *Notes* in the mid-1570s and completed them by 1587 although they did not appear in print until 1641.

[2] J. E. Neale, *Elizabeth I and Her Parliaments*, 2 vols. (London, 1957), vol. II: *1584–1601*, p. 383.

[3] *Ibid.*, p. 386.

execution of Mary Queen of Scots through its associations with religious radicalism and the related threat of social disorder.[4]

By the late Elizabethan period we enter a world in which Englishmen endeavoured to forward their political ends by identifying themselves and their programmes as 'aristocratic': socially exclusive as well as godly. In many ways the contest waged over attempts to delimit the political nation in these terms defined the latter part of Elizabeth's reign, as it informed the debate over sovereignty, godliness and female rule which continued in the new political circumstances of the period after 1585. Richard Helgerson, who identifies and explores this contest principally in its literary manifestations, rightly pinpoints the 1590s as the decade of 'maximum tension'.[5] But latent tension over the constitution of 'the nation' marked English culture from Elizabeth's accession, when apologists defined the realm as a 'mixed monarchy'. For the mixed monarchy was conceived of as a corporate body politic in which the wisdom of the many, variously defined, 'bridled' and imparted grace to a female prince whose assumed deficiencies in reason and spiritual capacity predisposed her to ungodly, or tyrannical, rule.

As we have seen, this conception emphasised the collective capacity of the realm (read as the male political nation) and left open both its extent and how its voice was to be heard. No doubt Elizabeth's advisers assumed that the 'best men' would continue to represent the wisdom of the many, perhaps as the *amici principis* envisaged by humanist thinkers. They were, however, sufficiently committed to evangelical Protestantism, and sufficiently anxious about the dangers of female rule, to look to the creation of a 'godly nation' to preserve the imperial crown, and to appeal, at least rhetorically, to its egalitarian presuppositions as a basis of support for Elizabeth's tenure of the throne. The same conflation of hope and fear prepared them, as recent historians have increasingly realised, to extend the hand of brotherhood to godly MPs in the House of Commons in order to persuade the queen to attend to the wisdom of the realm. This innovation was tellingly symbolised by the invitation issued in 1572 to a French diplomatic delegation – on what must have

---

[4] See David Harris Sacks for the recognition that the debate over monopolies 'engaged [MPs'] sense of public morality', and that for Englishmen complaining about monopolies, both within and without the House, 'the operative word was "Bondage"'; 'Private Profit and Public Good: The Problem of the State in Elizabethan Theory and Practice' in *Law, Literature, and the Settlement of Regimes*, ed. Gordon J. Schochet, The Folger Institute Center for the History of British Political Thought Proceedings, vol. 2 (Washington, D.C., 1990), pp. 121–42; pp. 129–30.

[5] Richard Helgerson, *Forms of Nationhood: The Elizabethan Writing of England* (Chicago, 1992), pp. 9–10, 203. See also Annabel Patterson, *Reading Holinshed's 'Chronicles'* (Chicago, 1994), pp. 10, 187–212.

been the Privy Council's initiative – to enter and witness a debate in the House of Commons.[6]

In the 1570s the Protestant ascendancy, and the queen, explored the parameters of the 'mixed monarchy' in the face of threats to its existence posed by resurgent Catholicism and the continuing proximity to the throne of Elizabeth's sister queen. The 1570s witnessed the first enactment of the concept of public counsel in the House of Commons, in debates over Mary Queen of Scots,[7] and – a concomitant – the first recorded use of the term 'commonwealthsman', in John Stubbs's alarum to the godly nation, *The Discoverie of a Gaping Gulf*.[8] It also produced, and in response, the articulation of a concept of royal 'prerogative' as separable from the common law.[9] More generally, the extensive definition of 'counsel' which was articulated and enacted in the 1570s allowed for the radical political acts of the 1580s: the Bond of Association and the execution of Mary Queen of Scots.

It is the origins and political implications of the innovative definition of 'public counsel' that I want to explore in this chapter. I shall first consider John Hooker's reflections on parliament in his 1572 work, *Order and Usage*, as ideological context. I shall then analyse the 1572 parliamentary debates over the fate of Mary Queen of Scots. In these debates MPs and the queen engaged in 'speech acts' designed to advance their conflicting definitions of the mixed monarchy.[10] They did so in a situation in which Elizabeth's refusal to act against Mary threatened her status as Deborah, hence its consensual basis, and hence her tenure of the crown.

---

[6] J. E. Neale, *The Elizabethan House of Commons* (London, 1949), p. 402.
[7] See the epigraph to this chapter.
[8] 'Commonwealthsman' is defined as 'One devoted to the interests of the commonwealth; good citizen, patriot', and the first cited quotation comes from Stubbs's *Gaping Gulf*: 'More like Basciaes to the great Turke, then Christian commonwealthmen'; *The Compact Edition of the Oxford English Dictionary*, 2 vols. (Oxford, 1971), vol. I, p. 696.
[9] This is the first stage in a contest that would feature John Cowell's definition (in his 1607 law dictionary *The Interpreter*) of the prerogative as free from the ordinary constraints of common law and one of the defining marks, as a personal possession, of an 'absolute' king. See David Harris Sacks, 'Private Profit and Public Good', pp. 125–6, for Elizabeth's attempt to define the prerogative as an attribute of her monarchical competence in the context of monopolies.
[10] For 'speech acts' see J. G. A. Pocock, 'Languages and Their Implications: The Transformation of the Study of Political Thought' in *Politics, Language and Time: Essays on Political Thought and History* (New York, 1973), pp. 3–41 and, more recently, 'The Concept of a Language and the *Métier d'historien*: Some Considerations on Practice' in *The Languages of Political Theory in Early Modern Europe*, ed. Anthony Pagden, (Cambridge, 1987), pp. 19–38; and Quentin Skinner, 'Meaning and Understanding in the History of Ideas', in *Meaning and Context: Quentin Skinner and His Critics*, ed. James Tully (Cambridge, 1988), pp. 29–67.

JOHN HOOKER'S *ORDER AND USAGE*

As a young man John Hooker entered the service of Miles Coverdale, stalwart of the Henrician Reformation and, under Edward VI, bishop of Exeter. According to Vernon Snow, the modern editor of *Order and Usage*, Hooker's commonplace book reveals his own commitment to the ideals of the Edwardian reformation.[11] Presumably this ideological affinity explains why Francis Russell, Earl of Bedford, became his patron. Bedford – former Athenian, Privy Councillor and friend of the French 'resistance theorist' François Hotman – was one of the half dozen aristocrats and Privy Councillors whose social status and Protestant fervour gave men who shared their ideological convictions easy access to print during the early decades of Elizabeth's reign.[12]

Perhaps it was Bedford's influence that allowed Hooker to publish his book, despite its obvious debt to the ideas of the resistance theorists and specifically John Ponet.[13] Alternatively, Hooker may have been articulating a reading of political relations within the mixed monarchy still sufficiently consensual, in the early 1570s, to be relatively uncontroversial. In this regard it may have benefited from the fact that it was written during the Admonition Controversy. Hooker's most radical assertions – the equality in 'nobility' between members of the House of Lords and the House of Commons while parliament is in session, the superiority of the Commons over the Lords in its capacity to represent the nation and withstand seduction by the crown – were part of an analysis that still insisted upon the godliness and legitimacy of a representative institution, in a context in which other godly men (such as Thomas Cartwright) began to intimate that parliament itself, and the House of Commons, might be reprobate.[14]

In *Order and Usage* Hooker built on and elaborated the apocryphal fourteenth-century work *Modus Tenendi Parliamentum* to elevate the place of parliament in English society and the role of the Commons in parliament.[15] He did so by defining 'counsel' as geographically extensive and potentially socially inclusive. He also identified parliament, and

[11] Vernon Snow, ed., *Parliament in Elizabethan England: John Hooker's 'Order and Usage'* (New Haven, Conn., 1977), p. 29 (hereafter *Order and Usage*).

[12] Lawrence Stone, *The Crisis of the Aristocracy 1558–1641*, abridged edn (Oxford, 1967), p. 339. The others include the Earls of Leicester, Huntingdon and Warwick and Lord Rich. Hotman dedicated a book to Bedford in 1559. For Hotman's English connections see Donald R. Kelley, *François Hotman: A Revolutionary's Ordeal* (Princeton, N.J., 1973), p. 92.   [13] *Order and Usage*, p. 49.

[14] Thomas Cartwright [presumed author], *A Second Admonition to the Parliament* in *Puritan Manifestos: A Study of the Origin of the Puritan Revolt*, ed. W. H. Frere and C. E. Douglas (London, 1907), pp. 81, 88–9, 129–31.   [15] *Order and Usage*, p. 49.

specifically the House of Commons, as embodying, and, through its legislative capacity, enacting, the common good. Hooker's project also gives evidence of a growing sense of identity amongst Protestant men as participants in affairs of the common weal, whether in office or out of doors. For, as Snow notes, although Hooker sat in the parliaments of 1571 and 1586, he began his work before he had ever served as an MP.[16] This development, as much as the evidence of Ponet's direct influence, sets the scene for the politics of this decade.

Hooker begins his book by establishing a pedigree for English parliaments that extends before the Norman Conquest to the reign of Edward the Confessor; indeed, through example, back to classical antiquity. He identifies members of both houses as 'elders' and 'senators' (which he presents as equivalent terms) because of their participation in that consultative assembly. They are therefore equal, through virtue, to their king. According to Hooker, exemplary rulers have always observed the 'wisdom and policies' of their councillors by acknowledging this equality: 'as Moses had his elders, Licurgus his Ephoros [sic], the Atheniensis [sic] the Councels, the Romans their Senates.'[17] Perhaps the recourse to the pattern of Israel under Moses – or his familiarity with Calvin's ideas – enabled him to recast this model of council in an even more unconventional direction.[18] For in Hooker's model the exemplary ruler and his councillors go one step further by drawing on the collective wisdom of the nation. They assemble 'all the wise, grave, expert and prudent men from out of all parts of their realms' to add to their deliberations. It is this collective assembly, fully embodying the wisdom of the realm, that constitutes 'a Senate or Parliament'.[19]

Hooker evidently subscribed to the conventional Christian view, given new immediacy by the Protestant reformation, that only Christ enacts perfect government unaided. Temporal rulers are imperfect, even Moses, David, Solomon 'yea and Saint Paul'. Their exemplary character – their status as godly magistrates – derives not least from their recognition of this central Christian tenet. Their deficiencies are, however, rectified, and perfect (that is, godly) earthly government is allowed for by the consultative assembly of the 'Senate or Parliament'. This assembly makes in effect a perfect man, attentive to God and informed by the collective wisdom of the nation. By dint of its collective identity

[16] Ibid., p. 15. [17] Ibid., p. 208.
[18] See Quentin Skinner's discussion of Calvin's idea of 'ephoral' authority in *The Foundations of Modern Political Thought*, 2 vols. (Cambridge, 1978), vol. 2, *The Age of Reformation*, pp. 232–3.
[19] *Order and Usage*, p. 208.

this 'perfect man' is truly made in God's image, no longer in Adam's, a transfiguration effected by grace and signalled by the fact that the multiplication of faculties and body parts which he describes is not (as Knox would have it) 'monstrous'. It/he is therefore possessed of virtue, a quality that is both spiritual and political:

> But many wise, learned, grave and expert men assembled together (out of all places of the realm) they become as it were one man having many wits, many eyes, many hands and many feet. *Qui omnia cernunt, omnia que provident. Nihil eis obscurum, Nihil inopinatum, Nihil novum, Nihil inauditum, Nihil que magnum videri potest.* [To those who comprehend all things and foresee all things, nothing can seem dark to them, nothing unexpected, nothing new, nothing unusual, nothing overwhelming.][20]

King, lords and commons therefore enact, as in the form of parliament they embody, the common good, in a mystical – and egalitarian – process of which law is the material product. Their deliberations reflect the disembodied participation of 'all parts' of the realm; they promulgate 'good orders devised as before the common and public weal'. And England – 'this little isle and realm' – has surpassed past examples because her ancient 'kings and rulers' have bound themselves to the law, the embodiment of collective wisdom:

> For the Kings and rulers [of England] (not for a short time: but in the course of many hundreds of years) have not been so valiant as wise, not so courageous as prudent, not so puissant as learned, and not so politique in the fields: as grave in the Senates. Likewise the laws, in equity most upright, in judgments, most true, and in conscience most reasonable. The observation and keeping of which laws hath heretofore preserved this realm from foreign enemies, defended it from civil seditions, and kept the people in safety, so that is vrified [sic: verified?] which Melanchthon writeth of Solon: *Denique vita hominum, tranquilla et honesta manetit: servandi leges, dum pia cura manet.* [Then will the life of men be quiet and virtuous when the conservation of laws remains a pious duty.][21]

Hooker's account emphasises the equality of all men in their Christian duty of obedience to the law: they are **all** executors of the law. This reading moves away from the conventional distinction between the ruler and the ruled in their relationship to the law, according to which the former both enacts and observes what the latter merely obey:

> Archidamus saith, that in all well governed commonwealths all degrees and estates of people are like obedient to the order of the laws: as well the magistrate as the inferior, and the King as the subject. Saint Paul saith, that he is not the

---

[20] Ibid., p. 209.   [21] Ibid., p. 121.

just man, which only knoweth the laws: *Sed qui factis legem exprimit* which living under the law doth obey and keep the same.[22]

Here we can see evidence of that conflation of English or common law and God's law, articulated as parliamentary statute, which assumed political significance at this point in Elizabeth's reign.[23] It is related to, and it allowed for, the growth of the view that **all** English subjects, regardless of degree, were bound by acts of parliament because they participated in its deliberations; they consented to its enactments.[24] (It appears that for Hooker 'the people' are men, their wives included, under their headship, in their consent.[25]) Parliament thus symbolises a harmony of counsel, consent and conscience that encompasses 'all degrees and estates of people' and which, in an immediate relationship with God, constitutes the godly nation.[26] For Hooker this inclusive definition of the body politic defines civil society: the 'common and public wealth'.[27]

Hooker then proceeds to consider relations among the three estates, to see where responsibility lies for preserving the 'common weal'. He begins by ascribing *de facto* nobility to the 'wise, grave, expert, and prudent' men who are called to the House of Commons, while parliament is in session. For Hooker, the division into two houses, Lords and

---

[22] Ibid., p. 122.

[23] Speaker Richard Onslow, in the closing proceedings of the 1567 parliament, distinguished between common law and statute law, identifying the former as 'so grounded on God's laws and nature that three several nations governing here [in England] have all allowed the same, which is not inferior but rather superior and more indifferent than any other laws'. He also argued that it is through the common law that 'the prince is provided [with] many princely prerogatives'. *Proceedings in the Parliaments of Elizabeth I*, ed. T. E. Hartley (Leicester, 1981), vol. 1: *1558–1581*, pp. 169–70.

[24] *A Discourse upon the Exposition and Understanding of Statute* (1567–71?), ed. Samuel E. Thorne (San Marino, Calif., 1942), Introduction, p. 30.

[25] An assumption made explicit in 1632, in a political climate again polarising over issues of commonweal – but now with a king on the throne. *The Lawes Resolutions of Womens Rights* (unknown author) explains that, because they are incorporated in their husbands, 'Women have no voice in Parliament, they make no laws, they consent to none, they abrogate none. All of them are understood either married or to be married and their desires [are] subject to their husband' (sig. B3v).

[26] This is the definition advanced by Sir Thomas Smith in his celebrated description 'Of the Parliament and the Authority Thereof' in the *De Republica Anglorum* of 1565; see below, chapter 7. Ernst Kantorowicz argues that the notion of the 'king's two bodies' in England 'cannot be severed from the very early development and lasting momentum of Parliament in English constitutional thought and practice. Parliament, was, by representation, the living "body politic" of the realm. That is to say, the English Parliament was never a *persona ficta* or *persona repraesentata*, but always a very real *corpus repraesentans*. "Body politic of the realm", therefore, had in England far more than in any other European kingdom a uniquely concrete meaning'; *The King's Two Bodies: A Study in Medieval Political Theology* (Princeton, N.J., 1957), p. 447.

[27] *Order and Usage*, pp. 207, 118.

Commons, occurred only recently and merely 'for the avoiding of confusion'. In reality, members of both houses are 'of like and equal authority, every person of either of the said houses being named, reputed, and counted a peer of the Realm' both because of their participation in parliament ('for Par', he explains, 'is equal') and because they are fathers of their country ('for *Pier*, is a father'). Members of the Lower House 'are also called Councillors,' he adds, 'because they are assembled and called to the Parliament, for their advice and good counsel in making and devising of such orders and laws as may be for the common wealth'.[28]

This definition of political virtue – of 'nobility' as a product of either birth or breeding up in the country, pertaining equally to all men who are 'fathers of their country' – allows him to assert the primacy of the House of Commons over the House of Lords specifically because it represents the 'commons of the whole realm'. The three estates 'jointly and with one consent' can 'establish and enact any laws, orders, and statutes for the common wealth'.[29] Nor can any one estate act on its own. If, however, they are divided, 'one swerving from the other' (he intimates because of declension in the Lords), 'the King with the consent of his Commons (who are represented by the Knights, Citizens and Burgesses) may ordain and establish any Act or Law, which are as good, sufficient and effectual as if they [sic] Lords had given their consents'. The Lords 'cannot **by their folly** abridge the King and the Commons of their lawful proceeding in Parliament'.[30] The reverse does not apply: 'But of the contrary, if the Commons be summoned, and will not come, or coming will not appear, or appearing will not consent to do anything, alleging some just weighty and great cause: [t]he King (in these cases) cannot with his Lords devise, make or establish any Law.'

Hooker advances two reasons for this state of affairs. The first is historical. '[W]hen Parliaments were first begun and ordained: there were no prelates or barons of the parliament, and the temporal lords were very few or none, and then the King and his Commons did make a full Parliament, which authority was hitherto never abridged.' The second reason derives from the representative character of members of the House of Commons. They, not the Lords, articulate the collective

---

[28] Ibid., pp. 182–3.
[29] He intimates that members of the House of Commons are more likely to retain their political virtue, whether through engagement in their localities, with the virtue of the 'godly and forward people', or through distance from the corrupting influence of the court is unclear; *Order and Usage*, p. 181.   [30] Ibid., p. 182, my emphasis.

wisdom of their locality. He continues:

> [A]gain every Baron in Parliament doth represent but his own person, and speaketh in the behalf of himself alone. But in the Knights, Citizens and Burgesses are represented the Commons of the whole realm, and every of these giveth not consent only for himself: but for all those also for whom he is sent.[31]

Its representative character means the Commons can, if necessary, incorporate with the king alone to act as sovereign, to enact the common good.

It would seem that for Hooker virtue emanates from a godly people, in a society in which hierarchies of age and gender, but not degree, will continue to be unconditionally sanctioned. He defines 'elders' as men moored in virtue through their relationship with 'the country' (ambiguously county, countryside, nation, and its inhabitants) and hence able to represent and enact this relationship in the 'body of all England', as parliament was also known. In contrast, he presents the nobility's relationship with the 'country' as a voluntary one. They can be 'fathers of their country', but birth places them in an ambiguous position, nearer to the crown, which sustains their worldly privileges, than to the country.[32]

The mystical corporate identity of the 'Commons' within a Parliament read as a godly assembly also explains Hooker's emphatic identification of the danger to the nation posed by 'young men' in positions of responsibility, whether as 'favourites' to the queen or as representatives in the House of Commons. Significantly, it is only when he discusses the dangers of 'young men' that he alludes to the tyrannical propensities of 'mere' monarchs:

> If Solomon's wise and ancient senators ought to have place in Parliament: what shall the rash and young councillors of Rehoboam do there? [I Kings 12.6] If Moses by the advise of such ancient elders of Israel as were wise, valiant, dealt truly, feared God, and hated covetousness, did direct the people in judgment and govern them in justice: what shall children, young men, and such as neither fear god nor hate iniquity, which are of no experience or knowledge: sit in

---

[31] Ibid., p. 182. The same point was made in the contemporaneous *Discourse upon the exposition and understanding of Statute* (p. 93): 'But what if all the bishops make default, or what if all the lords spiritual and temporal be absent, yet it is said that the King with his commonalty may keep the Parliament alone, for the Commons have every of them a greater voice in Parliament than hath a lord or bishop.' T. F. T. Plunknett attributes the tract to Sir Thomas Egerton, later Baron Ellesmere; 'Ellesmere on Statutes', *Law Quarterly Review* 40 (1944), pp. 242–9.

[32] *Order and Usage*, p. 125. This reading of virtue as inhering in the 'country' is recognisably descended from Ponet's work (see above, chapter 3). It takes on a new form in Elizabeth's reign, as I explore below. See also Richard Helgerson, *Forms of Nationhood*, pp. 105–147, especially pp. 136–7.

Senate of the wise, and give judgment among the grave and learned? Finally if the old Senators and wise Fathers, ought there to sit in ancient order and in grave manner: what place is there for punies, rash heads and young men, who having no learning, and less experience, are carried away (as a feather with the wind) with every light toy, making no account nor having any regard at all to the public weal?[33]

'Young men' are those who, like Rehoboam's councillors, identify with and advance the will of the monarch rather than the common weal. They lack the capacity for political virtue which Aristotle attributed to adult males. Nor are they patriarchs, the 'wise fathers' whose wisdom and experience confirm them in godliness. They are neuters, divorced through choice or circumstance from the qualities of virtue that are necessary to citizenship – qualities symbolised by and achievable through true virility.

In 1572, Hooker assumed that 'grave and learned' MPs, would, like the patriarchs of old, act as the conscience of the body politic. He thus interpreted age and gender as symptomatic of rectitude in a way characteristic of early modern (and latterly non-western) culture.[34] It needed a more polarised political climate for this assumption to be attacked, in a reading of the estates paradigm systematically marginalised by the queen and her councillors after the execution of Mary Queen of Scots. This reading, recognisably descended from Hooker's delineation of the godly nation in 1572, was provided by Job Throckmorton in the parliament of 1586–7. His speech made the House of Commons both the domain of privilege and an appendage of the court, and located godliness in denizens of the 'country' (ambiguously 'young men' or the 'inferior sort'):

Ye shall speak in the Parliament House freely, provided always that ye meddle neither with the reformation of religion nor the establishment of succession . . . In these causes . . . that reach so high and pierce so near the marrow and bones of Church and Commonwealth, if any of the **inferior sort** here amongst us do happen in some zeal to overstrain himself, surely you that are honourable . . .

---

[33] *Order and Usage*, pp. 123–4. In I Kings 12.6–12 the 'old men' who had been Solomon's councillors advised Rehoboam to 'be a servant unto' his people, who would then be his servants for ever. But Rehoboam rejected their wisdom. Instead he consulted with 'young men that were grown up with him'. They advised him to secure his state by enacting the part of a tyrant.

[34] Elizabeth made a contrary case proceeding from the same assumptions. She argued that the House of Commons was dominated by young men as a means of disallowing its claims to represent the wisdom of the realm. T. E. Hartley, *Elizabeth's Parliaments: Queen, Lords and Commons 1559–1601* (Manchester, 1992), p. 170. For the significance of this age dimension among the godly see G. J. R. Parry, *A Protestant Vision: William Harrison and the Reformation of Elizabethan England* (Cambridge, 1987), especially chs. 2 and 3.

ought in equity to bear with them, because the fault is in yourselfs . . . When grey hairs grow silent, then **young heads** grow virtuous.[35]

Order and Usage thus sheds light on what historians now generally accept as one of the key phenomena of Elizabethan politics in the 1570s: the confident recourse by Privy Councillors to the House of Commons as an institutional forum peculiarly well positioned to exert quasi-public pressure on Elizabeth to forward the godly enterprise – or at least allow it to go forward in her name. As I have suggested, Hooker was not alone.[36] His stance was, broadly speaking, a consensual one among the political elite. The conviction that England under Elizabeth was potentially the True Church meant that the 'great men' could, and did, look for political virtue among the ranks of the godly in the body of the nation. As political pressures mounted, therefore, Elizabeth's councillors came to look to the support of the 'commonalty', represented by the third member of the 'parliamentary trinity': the House of Commons and the godly 'gentlemanly' MPs it contained.[37] Their hope must have been that deliberation in the common forum of parliament – the emblem, as Sir Thomas Smith declared, of the mixed monarchy – would preserve that hybrid in godliness and degree. Hooker's analysis therefore provides a necessary background for understanding the political significance of parliamentary debates during the 1570s, debates that explored the limits of that consensus and marked, in Peter Wentworth's 1576 speech, the beginning of its end.

CONTESTING CONSENT: SPEECH ACTS IN PARLIAMENT, 1571–1572[38]

The parliamentary debates of 1571 and 1572 were held in the wake of, and specifically in response to, the twofold threat to the nation posed by the 1569 Northern Rebellion and the 1570 Papal Bull excommunicating

---

[35] J. E. Neale, *Elizabeth I and Her Parliaments*, p. 150, my emphasis. The equation between youth, virtue and non-noble status is notable.

[36] Vernon Snow, for example, suggests that Hooker followed John Aylmer in his understanding and uses of the term 'mixed monarchy' and details possible lines of contact, primarily through the Earl of Bedford and their Strasbourg connection; *Order and Usage*, p. 105.

[37] T. E. Hartley, *Elizabeth's Parliaments*, p. 166.

[38] By using the term 'speech act' I am both adopting a Pocock–Skinner analytical technique and taking issue with G. R. Elton's assertion that political debates in parliament, especially under Elizabeth, 'served little if any purpose when the monarch chose to ignore them'; *The Parliament of England, 1559–1581* (Cambridge, 1986), p. 321. See J. G. A. Pocock, 'Languages and Their Implications' and 'The Concept of a Language'; and Quentin Skinner, 'Meaning and Understanding in the History of Ideas'. For information on the MPs mentioned in the following discussion see P. W. Hasler, ed., *The House of Commons 1558–1603*, 3 vols. (London, 1981).

Elizabeth. The speeches that survive possess a discernible subtext concerning the political implications of the incorporation 'queen-in-parliament' and the definition of sovereignty in the mixed monarchy at a point when godly Englishmen first mobilised to protect a Deborah whose main concern was to ensure that the crown, and the majesty it represented, remained the monarch's prerogative.[39] They give evidence of contested readings of 'consent', a contest that was to culminate, in this round, with the queen's strategic retreat from her right to an absolute power of veto of legislation proposed by the House of Commons. In these debates the main axes of contest concerned law, prerogative, and parliament's role and definition. The debates also produced politicised definitions of the terms 'justice' and 'mercy' which were to resonate through the deliberations leading to Mary Queen of Scots' eventual trial and execution. Two other features are noteworthy: first, the appeal to a corporate identity enacted in parliament and specifically in the House of Commons; secondly the reinterpretation of Scottish identity caused by Mary Stuart's proximity to the English throne. From being, as they had been deemed by earlier apologists, brothers in Protestantism, the Scots became 'strangers' (a term employed with equal venom to describe recusants within England) and 'barbarians', an identification that underpins the language of conquest which features so prominently in these debates.

In response to the threat posed by the 1570 Papal Bull, which declared Elizabeth a heretic and released subjects from their obedience to her, the 1571 parliament proposed a bill 'For the preservation of the Queen's Majesty in the royal estate and crown of this realm', the effect of which was to make treasonous speeches or actions intended to remove her from the throne, dispute her lawful status as queen or call into question her religious orthodoxy. Thomas Norton approved of the proposed bill, declaring 'that her Majesty was and is the only pillar and stay of all safety, as well for our politic quiet as for the state of religion, and for religion the very base and pillar throughout Christendom'. He then promptly sought to extend the bill's scope in two significant directions, first by pointing the finger of treason in the direction of the Stuart line, secondly by providing 'that whosoever shall say the court of Parliament hath not authority to enact and bind the title of the crown [that is, to declare the succession], to be adjudged a traitor'.[40]

---

[39] It is interesting, and possibly significant, that the journals that remain from the 1571 parliament are the first surviving unofficial accounts of parliamentary proceedings under Elizabeth; *Proceedings*, p. 301.   [40] *Proceedings*, p. 204.

In a separate debate – about reforming the Book of Common Prayer – Christopher Yelverton illustrated the connections between religion, counsel and prerogative in language very like that used by Hooker in *Order and Usage*, building on Norton's proposed amendments to the earlier bill to do so. Parliament's role in Elizabeth's election – her accession through grace to the English throne – is the best evidence of a 'fullness of power' that makes parliament omnicompetent – within certain limits:

He further said that all matters not treason or too much to the derogation of the imperial crown was tolerable there, where all things came to be considered of, and where there was such fullness of power as even the right of the crown was to be determined, and by warrant whereof we have so resolved that to say the parliament had no power to determine of the crown was high treason. He remembered that men were not there for themselves but for their countries, and showed it was fit princes to have their prerogative but yet the same to be straitened within reasonable limits. The prince, he showed, could not of her self make laws, neither might she by the like reason break laws.[41]

What constituted too much derogation of the imperial crown', when the nation was threatened with conquest by a female Catholic Scot? In this section of the debate we can see in outline the image of Mary Stuart that was to develop and become consolidated over the session. Because she was a woman, Catholic and Scottish, she became a polymorphous symbol of conquest attempted for her own or others' ends and effected through various means: through force of arms (by the 'barbarous' Scots), through Catholic treachery (the pope working through his minion, Mary) and/or through female lust (Mary's lust for power, allied to her capacity to seduce men, like the Duke of Norfolk, from their allegiance to the godly nation).[42]

Robert Newdigate made the connection between Mary's Scottish identity and her likely status as a conqueror explicit by comparing her to William the Conqueror. (Interestingly, for Newdigate, the 'conquest' was exactly that, and witnessed the complete subversion of the realm.) He argued that Elizabeth had misinterpreted God's will by taking her continuing survival as a sign of divine providence. She has not recognised the 'miraculous' opportunity that God has offered her to preserve the whole realm, forever, in a future in which she will play no part. They are the 'children' whose future welfare she must preserve:

[41] Ibid., p. 239.
[42] The strands were brought together in the bill passed against the Queen of Scots on 25 June. See *Proceedings*, pp. 302–3.

He feareth she [Elizabeth] depend too much upon God's providence, refusing the means now miraculously by God offered unto her. Mary Stuart by nature a Scot, enemies to England by Nature. William Conqueror when he first invaded England made a surmised title to the crown . . . but after he had achieved the same, he then claimed it as a conquest. What followed? He deposed all the English nobility, placed Normans, changeth councillors, magistrates and all kind of governors, disheriteth every man, altereth the whole state, and finally the realm brought to such misery that it was counted detestable to be counted an English man. He looketh for no ther in [sic; naught therein?] but to follow this pattern. Though she pretend a title for the present, if she may prevail she will claim by conquest and then all our lands be lost, all our goods forfeit . . . I have heard [Elizabeth] delighteth to be called our mother. Let us desire her to be pitiful over us her children who have not deserved death.

Thomas Atkins imaged the pope as Antichrist and Mary ('the burden of the earth') as his minion to argue that her execution would purify the nation, allowing it to repel any other form of attack: 'No foreign prince to be feared, she being dejected.'[43]

In the interest of forwarding this necessary endeavour MPs embarked on a series of linguistic manoeuvres, redefining in the first instance the meaning of, and relationship between, those conduits of collective consent in the English body politic, 'petition' and 'prerogative'. In the debate on 28 May, Recorder William Fleetwood addressed this issue directly after a few obligatory disclaimers ('we ought to deal modestly when we deal with them that carry the sword. He will only talk of orders and form, and would not have his speech drawn to any other purpose'). Petition and prerogative, he claimed, have ever been two sides of the same coin, signalling the reciprocal relationship between king and commonalty. In this reading *le Roy voet* betokens the common mind denoted in another guise by the concept of king-in-parliament:

Petitions have been made by the Speaker in the name of the House in kings' days for small causes. In King Edward the Third's time a petition made to remove some of his Council, and the king agreed to the same. In the time of Henry IVth the [?Speaker] sent to desire the King to advance his sons to honour . . . It was granted by Parliament to Henry the VIIth to restore any man in blood by his prerogative, and yet after, upon a petition, he was content to depart with his prerogative. And to all these petitions was said *le Roy voet*.[44]

On 9 June he used Tully to refer to a higher law – that of godly, and now national, necessity. Again he defined the Scots as 'strangers' in the course of arguing that it is the duty of MPs to secure the imperial crown:

This matter we now treat of a very weighty cause, concerning the crown of

<hr />

[43] Ibid., p. 377.   [44] Ibid., p. 383.

England. He is amazed with a sentence of Tully. If breach of laws a man should undertake, then break them boldly for kingdom's sake. Causes of kingdoms cannot be pleaded by way of estoppel. If any person hap the crown, he doubteth what exposition they would make . . . He hath heard it notoriously argued that those which are born in Scotland are English born; but their error is great. It is judicially adjudged in the time of Richard the second, that the Scots be *accolini no incolini* . . . The law of the crown made 25 Edwardi 3 hath declared it.

Although Fleetwood's prose is rather hard to follow, it seems he is making a three-stage argument. First, he wished to disallow the succession 'by law' of Mary Stuart. He therefore asserted that private laws of inheritance do not apply when the case concerns the kingdom ('Causes of kingdoms cannot be pleaded by way of estoppel'). Perhaps because he regarded this as a disputable, or at least debatable, proposition, he then argued that Mary, should she acquire the crown, would reverse that precedence to define the crown (and the realm) as her 'property' – one of the prerogatives of conquest. To answer this case he appealed to a 'higher' law, that of Edward the Confessor. According to that law, all those born in Scotland were 'strangers', regardless of their pedigree.[45] Fleetwood used this law to claim that Mary could not lawfully succeed to the English crown either through right of succession or through right of inheritance. Perhaps it was because this argument was so widely accepted that MPs gradually moved to a consensual view that Mary would ascend the English throne only by violence – a view that determined their growing conviction that only a pre-emptive strike to secure her death, whether through execution or assassination, would safeguard the imperial crown.[46]

In a situation of such peril, yet so full of potential promise for Christendom, MPs concluded that parliament – the deliberative forum of the three estates of the realm, the 'common mind' – was to have a

---

[45] And in the process disallowed Robert Newdigate's reading of William's conquest as 'absolute'. The reading Fleetwood offers had to be renegotiated after James's accession. This was effected in part through the debate over the 1608 Post-Nati case. For the status of Edward the Confessor in relation to conquest theory see J. G. A. Pocock, *The Ancient Constitution and the Feudal Law* (Cambridge, 1957), pp. 42–4; for his exemplary status in Elizabeth's reign see Annabel Patterson, *Reading Holinshed's 'Chronicles'*, pp. 106, 270.

[46] Reading the parliamentary debates it becomes quite clear that at this point MPs hoped for Mary's execution, and that it would be enacted by the crown: the queen and Privy Councillors. They were, however, prepared to countenance, and even encourage, Mary's assassination by any 'honest, zealous and true' subject if that outcome did not materialise. See especially the bill against the Queen of Scots, 25 June (*Proceedings*, pp. 303–10, p. 310). The situation that developed in the 1580s – when Elizabeth's councillors insisted on execution whereas she herself preferred the option of assassination – occurred only once it became apparent that her opposition to Mary's destruction would be overridden. See below, chapter 7.

decisive voice in matters concerning 'the crown of England'. This was a conclusion shared, indeed forwarded, by the queen's councillors partici- pating in these debates, including Sir Francis Knollys, treasurer and senior Privy Councillor sitting in the House of Commons, Sir Thomas Smith (principal secretary and future Privy Councillor) and Sir Thomas Wilson (Master of Requests and future Privy Councillor). They implied in different ways that these deliberations were final, it remaining only to 'reason' with the queen in such a way that she would draw her own mind to accept their conclusions. It explains Thomas Norton's signifi- cant clarification of Fleetwood's reference to the 'law of the crown', in which he implicitly identified monarchical prerogative as an element of, hence subject to, the ancient common laws:

He would not have words lately spoken by the Recorder to be mistaken, in speaking of the laws of the Crown. That no man should thereby imply other but the common laws and statute laws concerning the Crown: no other particular law of the Crown varying from these.[47]

What is striking in these parliamentary debates is the articulation of a corporate identity – extending from the Privy Council, through the Lords and into the Commons – in which the House of Commons can speak for the godly nation, which is the body of Christ. For, as Richard Bedell said in the debate on 9 June, it was 'as necessary to provide for the feet as the head, for if the feet be taken away the head is in danger', especially when the 'head' was, for reasons of gender, so liable to political miscalculation.[48] One telling example occurred in responses to Robert Snagge's horrified report that 'some' had informed the Lords that he had 'uttered speech tending to that end that they had not [naught] to do with the common wealth, but that we in the common house had only the care thereof; they came for their own persons only'.[49] The course of MPs' responses to this problem is interesting, in that the focus rapidly shifted from dissension sown between the three estates of the realm to the heart of the matter, potential rifts between Commons and Lords. Christopher Yelverton opened with the first ('What can be a more detestable act then to set dissention and debate or to procure displeasure between the Queen, the nobility, and us which represent the commonalty?'[50]), but Fleetwood spoke to the nub of the matter in focusing on relations between Lords and Commons as he advanced the view that such attempted subversion was a popish practice:

[47] *Proceedings*, p. 398.   [48] Ibid., p. 399.   [49] Ibid., p. 403.   [50] Ibid., p. 404.

These tale tellers very ripe in Queen Mary's time. It was the practise of papists, and they were traitors. Some of them be dead since and some of them walk now in Westminster Hall. Messages were sent to the Houses, great trouble grew; some men troubled by speaking, some men by silence, and generally every man offend[ed]. He is assured, whensoever the tale teller is found, it shall appear he is an errant papist that seek to set dissension . . . Surely it is great treason to set dissension between [the Lords] and this House.[51]

Robert Mounson agreed, 'fully resolved' the culprits must be papists, 'to breed an uproar between the Lords and us', which because of its moment (and here he referred not solely to the legislation about Mary Stuart but also to the potential dissension between Lords and Commons) is 'a public cause'.[52]

And it transpired that an appropriate medium for corporate resolution was the written record, voicing the collective wisdom of the realm simultaneously to the queen and (at least potentially) to opinion 'out of doors'. This move represented an opening out of communal deliberations, on the one hand, and an extension of 'free speech', on the other. Or, as an anonymous journalist phrased it:

After this it seemed good that a further conference should be had with the Lords about this matter, which being had, it was by them agreed that every man should set down in writing such reasons as he thought were best able to move the Queen herein . . . It was agreed that the most principal reasons should be chosen and they alone set down in the writing which should be presented to the Queen's Majesty. It was thought better that these reasons should be thus delivered by writing rather than uttered by the mouth of any one person. For though the one way move more for the time, yet it is gone strait, and the reasons soon forgotten. Whereas the other way they are read with pausing and are considered upon, and so the better imprinted in the mind, and thereby so much the more do move.[53]

But this was disingenuous. Writing connoted resolution, in contrast to deliberation, as well as signalling an intention to reach outside the parliament to 'counsellors' out of doors, as many MPs were aware. This was after all the justification for John Field's and Thomas Wilcox's publication of the inflammatory *Admonition to the Parliament* during the sitting of this parliament. Identifying 'parliament time' as an extension of parliamentary debate beyond the institutional confines of the assembly, they argued it should be the occasion for 'free speech': they 'wrote it in parliament time, which should be a time of speaking and writing freely'.[54] It was no accident of reportage that Recorder Fleetwood began his

---

[51] Ibid., p. 405; the brackets are Hartley's. [52] Ibid., p. 405. [53] Ibid., pp. 331–2.
[54] *Puritan Manifestos*, ed. W. H. Frere and C. E. Douglas, introduction, p. xiii.

reflections on law, kingdoms and the crown, quoted above, by noting that '[i]n Queen Mary's time men were not suffered to write what was said'. At another point he rejected a proposed alternative strategy that would have MPs' views, no matter how strongly or collectively held, 'come to the Queen but by way of opinion'. It was in response to this idea that Fleetwood defined the prerogative as essentially consensual, concluding:

> There was talk also of opinion. Opinion he thinketh is nothing; may change every day. Now whether it may be changed he doubteth not whatsoever it were it might be altered during the session: it is all but one day . . . He misliketh this word 'opinion', and would have it brought to a resolution, for that the gravity of this House is not to deal with opinions but to make conclusions.[55]

The question left unasked, although it reverberated through these debates, is what happened when the 'common mind' did not include the queen's. The dichotomy became pressing with her message of 28 May, forbidding MPs to continue their deliberations over the fate of Mary Queen of Scots and suggesting that they drop the subject altogether until such time as they were presented with a disabling bill 'which she liketh best to be drawn by her learned council'.[56] The queen, announced Thomas Wilson, 'desireth to proceed more mildly [in punishing Mary], not seeing the danger she standeth in'. This was as much as to say, as T. E. Hartley recognises, that Elizabeth 'was incapable of taking correct or appropriate political action on this issue, and that parliament knew better'.[57] A few days later, when he and Knollys went to see Elizabeth about bills on religion currently before the House, he in effect said as much to her face (or so he informed the House):

> It pleased her to demand of me what matters were now in the House. I desired pardon, for that the same were matters of secrecy. She was important [sic; importunate?]. I declared how upon declaration of her message yesterday I saw great mourning and lamenting, yet to the shedding of tears, that her Majesty would leave so notorious treasons and conspiracies unpunished. She confessed the offence was heinous: so she thought the disablement would be a great punishment to her. I replied, if farther proceeding were not, no safety could follow, the protestants in great danger.[58]

Stymied, temporarily, in the quest for Mary Stuart's execution, MPs turn to the pending matter of the Duke of Norfolk's execution. This was regarded as a poor second to executing Mary, but a more meaningful blow at her than the 'disablement' proposed by the queen. Peter Wentworth spoke for many when he argued, in the wake of the queen's

---

[55] *Proceedings*, pp. 382–3.   [56] Ibid., p. 382.
[57] T. E. Hartley, *Elizabeth's Parliaments*, p. 73.   [58] *Proceedings*, p. 379.

message, that they now had no alternative but to press ahead on this front, for, 'since she will not alwholy [all wholly?] provide for remedy hereof, that at least it be done in part, in executing of the Duke, and so cut off half her [Mary Stuart's] head'.[59] Sir Francis Knollys, then, as though thinking aloud, embarked on a calculation about the most effective way of presenting a petition asking Elizabeth to act in the matter of the Duke's execution, in which he considered the logistics (and likely impact?) of the 'whole House' (the nation?) appearing to make this 'request' of the queen.[60]

Three days later, Knollys adopted a different strategy to achieve the same end. Intimating that he knew Elizabeth's mind because of his position as an 'inward counsellor', he implied an assurance that she was at the point of signing the warrant for the Duke's execution. He told MPs:

I perceive your intent is to make motion for the execution of the Duke, which I perceive proceedeth of very love and care you have to the Queen's person . . . And although I do know nothing is more convenient and needful than execution, and that with speed, yet I know the disposition of princes is rather of themselves to do such things than by way of pressing and urging. It may be, and it is like enough, her Majesty is of her self already disposed sooner to do it than you do perhaps think or believe. And I would not wish we should attempt her of his hasty execution, for that I know already her mind partly therein . . . The words that I speak, I speak upon good reason, and I would wish you all to consider what moveth me thereunto, and what may cause me to have and use this speech.[61]

But this strategy for 'managing' the House of Commons was surely directed as much at the queen as it was to the House, not only stating the necessity of the Duke's execution, but intimating that Elizabeth could not count on retaining subjects in obedience without at least this evidence of a godly disposition. His emphasis on the nature of princes was nothing more than a sweetener for the pill he suggested she had no alternative but to swallow: if not Mary, then the Duke – but (if done quickly) at a time when it should appear to be her own initiative. Here we can discern councillors' amphibious quality, constituents of the court and the country, and see how their position gave them leverage to speak to the queen by means of the public forum provided by parliament.

Burghley spoke to Elizabeth directly on the same subject, in his role as councillor at court. He told her that her failure to fulfil her godly role threatened her status as queen, showing her to be weak and challenging her identification as God's vessel: 'What more hope can be given to the

---

[59] Ibid., p. 382.   [60] Ibid.   [61] Ibid., p. 313.

evil than to see impunity which some interpret to fearfulness of the Queen, some to lack of power in her hand, by God's ordinance; yea, some to the Scottish queen's prayers and fasting?'[62] Burghley also wrote to Walsingham about the Duke of Norfolk's execution in terms that highlight the dynamic at play here. Two things are notable. First, Burghley refers to 'majesty' as a quality separable from the monarch; an understanding of it that presumably Elizabeth shared.[63] Secondly, one senses that, for Elizabeth, these circumstances have created a situation in which the 'danger' posed to 'her Majesty' emanated from the political nation as much as from the Duke himself:

I cannot write you what is the inward cause of the stay of the Duke of Norfolk's death, only I find her Majesty diversely disposed, sometime when she speaketh of her Majesty's danger, she concludeth that justice should be done; another time when she speaketh his nearness of blood, of his superiority in honour, etc., she stayeth.[64]

If **all**, bar the queen, agreed to a course of action both 'just and lawful', MPs found only truly fearful possible explanations (apart from incapacity associated with her gender) for the failure to enact the common mind.[65] Perhaps she was misled by 'evil counsellors', men seeking their own private interests rather than forwarding the common weal, or actively in the service of the pope. Robert Snagge raised this possibility in immediate response to Elizabeth's message of 28 May, in which she forbade MPs to continue their deliberations on the bill calling for Mary Stuart's execution. He obviously could not believe that this message, so contrary to the collective will, reflected anything other than duplicity amongst some of the queen's counsellors: 'Those that have persuaded with the Queen to stay the former proceeding never to be liked of: to do one thing here openly and persuade another secretly.'[66]

[62] Quoted in Wallace MacCaffrey, *The Shaping of the Elizabethan Regime* (Princeton, N.J., 1969), p. 280.
[63] National monarchs – Henry VIII, Francis I, Charles I of Castile – deliberately claimed *majestas* as an element in their kingships to support their imperial pretensions in a process which, according to John M. Headley, culminated in the 1530s. See 'The Burden of European Imperialisms, 1500–1800', *International History Review* 18 (1996), pp. 873–87, pp. 878–9. Its location and definition was then contested in the context of Protestant reformation. See Donald R. Kelley, *The Beginning of Ideology: Consciousness and Society in the French Reformation* (Cambridge, 1981), pp. 309, 316; and J. H. M. Salmon, *The French Wars of Religion in English Political Thought* (Oxford, 1959), p. 51 for the debate in France during the 1570s.
[64] Sir Dudley Digges, *The Compleat Ambassador* (London, 1655), p. 164.
[65] Robert Snagge believed that Elizabeth 'will not be offended with our importunateness' in continuing to push for Mary Stuart's execution, despite her express command, 'although for maidenly modesty she draw back'; *Proceedings*, p. 382.   [66] Ibid., p. 382.

And papist and traitor were near allied, as Fleetwood suggested. Subversion, then, could take the form of misleading the queen, or undermining the consensual basis of the commonwealth – from within, and potentially from above, at the level of the crown. The latter point is ironic (or pointed, depending on one's reading of it) in view of Elizabeth's attempts at various points to do exactly that, in the interests of maintaining and enhancing her monarchical autonomy.

Indeed, it is impossible to read MPs' speeches in these debates without realising how they glanced at the queen, who either did not receive or chose to ignore godly counsel. In the last resort, her consent to proposed measures was necessary in the mixed monarchy, and the failure to enact the common mind inevitably pointed at her. For it was her wilfulness that admitted evil counsel, her blindness that permitted popish seeds to take root in the elect nation. What could this mean except that Elizabeth was, at least potentially, reprobate? And if this was the case, was it not their duty, as godly men, to enact the common mind in despite of the queen? This was the conclusion that Peter Wentworth reached, and too forcefully articulated, in his first speech to the next parliamentary session, in 1576.

Why then did Elizabeth consistently, even ostentatiously, argue that in this affair it was incumbent on her, as a female ruler, to act according to a code of honour which decreed that mercy rather than justice was the appropriate virtue of a noble woman: a queen if not a king? Was it political miscalculation? Why did she highlight her inability to be a 'king' as her most compelling reason for holding out against this political consensus? On the one hand I think we can see Elizabeth making a virtue of necessity, and operating in the terrain staked out by Laurence Humphrey in order to do so. That is, she described herself as inhabiting by 'nature' (gender) a pacific, even Christ-like identity, one befitting the stage of reformation history whose onset was signalled by her accession. Equally significant was her evident belief that her self-portrayal as embodiment of this quintessential Christian virtue elevated her above the political fray in a way that protected her 'majesty', if it did not immediately advance her political autonomy. It suggested that she voluntarily (though not necessarily) 'straiten[ed]' her monarchical prerogative 'within reasonable limits' and in conformity to the view of mixed monarchy expressed in these parliamentary debates. As Burghley wrote to Walsingham in 1572 about these linked measures for execution: 'The Queen's Majesty hath always been a merciful lady, and by mercy she hath taken more harm than by justice, and yet she thinks that she is more beloved in doing herself harm.'[67] Her commitment to mercy also constituted a counter by which she could assert, emblematically but powerfully, that she was not tyrannical, neither Jezebel nor a conqueror – an important statement, at a point when violent action was under discussion. Claiming the right to be merciful as her prerogative by status, character and gender was therefore, within limits, an effective strategy, although one of steeply diminishing returns over the session. It allowed Elizabeth to withstand the corporate consensus (which she rightly saw as threatening her political autonomy) without forfeiting her subjects' loyalty as godly citizens. But this was a high-risk strategy and subjects' love, like their obedience, was conditional – a qualification that historians who focus on the passionate affection shown to Elizabeth by her subjects too readily overlook.[68]

Indeed what is apparent during the 1570s, and exemplified in these debates, is a process whereby events urged the primacy of justice over mercy, and the queen's counsellors, in the Privy Council and in parliament, became the agents of justice under a female ruler. Thomas Wilson suggested that 'justice', defined by this 'company called together', could override the queen's will, on the occasion when he associated her desire for clemency with her political incapacity. He argued that her clemency was appropriate to her gender but could not be (in the words of another MP) 'prohibitive': '[S]ince the queen's mercy is such as is admirable, we ought importunately to cry for justice, justice.'[69] And on the occasion of the third reading of the bill, Thomas Norton explicitly redefined 'mercy' to make it the prerogative of justice, exemplified and articulated by the queen's (male) counsellors:

> But to all the world appeareth manifestly she [Mary Stuart] is a very unnatural person, and no repentance found in her; and mercy hath no place where there is no repentance. If ye [MPs] will be merciful, extend mercy to the best prince that liveth, and not extend mercy to the worst, to the danger and destruction of the best. Let mercy be showed to the good Christians whom she seeketh to destroy; be merciful to ourselves . . . [It has been argued that Mary's activities have not been such as to allow her execution to be 'honourable'.] But he thinketh law and justice to be always honorable. The matter hath been considered by the bishops, according to the word of God, by the civilians and by the judges of the common law, and all have agreed that it is just and lawful. God forbid we should prefer the vain name of honor before the safety of the Queen's Majesty.[70]

[67] Sir Dudley Digges, *The Compleat Ambassador* (London, 1655), p. 164.
[68] See for example Thomas Atkins's speech, *Proceedings*, p. 377.   [69] Ibid., p. 365.
[70] Ibid., p. 408.

'You will say', he concluded, elevating Elizabeth over Mary because of her status as Henry VIII's daughter and creation of the Protestant nation, that 'she [Mary] is a Queen's daughter and therefore to be spared; nay then spare the Queen's Majesty that is a King's daughter and our Queen'.[71]

Englishmen found themselves in an unprecedented situation in the 1570s, besieged by Antichrist attacking the godly nation through the equivocal figure of its queen. The grounds and extent of a collective response are revealed in these debates. There were, of course, counter-vailing voices to the common mind, for the consensual front which figures so prominently here and in other forms of contemporary reflection on England's status as elect nation was at least partly rhetorical. These voices advanced an alternative interpretation of mixed monarchy that gave more weight to monarchical regality, almost certainly in response to what were perceived as the destabilising consequences of the kinds of utterances discussed above. This is the final variable in the political equation 'queen-in-parliament' in the 1570s and can be seen at various points in the 1571 and 1572 sessions.

In the parliament of 1571, for example, Henry Goodyear took exception to Thomas Norton's proposed additions to the Treason Bill, specifically the article affirming parliament's role in the settlement of the crown. 'He . . . said that the penning of [this addition] was clouded, involved with secret understandings, not to be understood but of such who more curiously would and more cunningly could look therein than he. For matters of title to the crown he said he neither knew any, neither durst to entermeddle or cause to take knowledge of any.'[72] In the same debate Sir Nicholas Arnold expressed an awareness of and ambivalence about the political consequences of public speech and its committal to writing. He 'liked of the whole tenor of both bills, but to have so slanderous words imprinted of her Majesty [as those contained in Norton's addition] . . . , he would not have it to be left to posterity, but that in general words the same might be reached'.[73] He also wanted to know if the same or similar speeches featured in former laws. And in 1572 Francis Alford suggested that MPs accept Elizabeth's dismissal of the bill proposing Mary Queen of Scots' execution in terms that need not be (I would argue should not be) read as 'absolutist': 'The Queen's Majesty is wise, she knoweth and considereth more than every one of us doth know or can consider. It is better in consul-

---

[71] Ibid.   [72] Ibid., p. 213.   [73] Ibid., p. 204.

tations to give credit to one wise person than a number of others.'[74]

We do not have to follow the consensualist stance of contemporaries, assimilated to cold war Europe by J. E. Neale, and regard such speakers as defectors from the common good, if not crypo-Catholics.[75] Alford, for example, was a Marian exile, and Cecil identified Goodyear, along with Thomas Norton, Robert Bell, Thomas Wilson and Anthony Cook, as 'public spirited' members of the House of Commons in the 1560s.[76] G. R. Elton's view – that controversy in parliament stemmed largely from faction and in-fighting at court, transported into another forum through long-standing networks of clientage – is limited, flawed by the insistence that ideological conviction played little if any role in political affairs.[77] Instead we should recognise that the uncharted political territory in which the English nation found itself in the 1570s threw into relief issues of regality, majesty and sovereignty which were susceptible of different, and potentially conflicting, interpretations within conceptions of the mixed monarchy that developed over Elizabeth's reign.

'LE ROIGNE SE AVISERA'

The extent to which such alternative voices were on the defensive in the debates of 1572 is best exemplified in the speech act with which Elizabeth prorogued the first session of this fourth parliament. In this speech we can see one of the well-known instances of the reign where Elizabeth stood alone, ranged against a solid phalanx of her godly counsellors who, in the 1570s, populated 'every corner of the establishment', as T. E. Hartley has shown, but who found their voice in parliament, the public forum or 'great council' representing, now, the three estates of the realm and the nation.[78]

At the end of the session, the tally of bills passed by both houses was read out for Elizabeth's consideration. In his *Journal* Thomas Cromwell described both the procedure and the 'strange answer' it gave rise to upon this occasion. '[T]o those which the Queen allowed the Clerk pronounced upon the reading of the titles, "*Le Roigne le voit*"; to the other

---

[74] Ibid., p. 328.

[75] J. P. Kenyon, *The History Men: The Historical Profession in England since the Renaissance* (London, 1983), p. 208.

[76] John Strype, *Annals of the Reformation and Establishment of Religion and other various occurrences in the Church of England during Queen Elizabeth's Happy Reign*, 7 vols. (Oxford, 1824), vol. i.i, p. 440.

[77] See, for example, Geoffrey Elton, 'Arthur Hall, Lord Burghley and the Antiquity of Parliament' in *Studies in Tudor and Stuart Politics and Government*, 4 vols. (Cambridge, 1983), vol. iii, pp. 254–73.

[78] T. E. Hartley, *Elizabeth's Parliaments*, p. 74.

whereto she gave not her consent the Clerk said *"Le Roigne se avisera".*[79] Last of all came the most important bill, the focus of most parliamentary energy in the preceding six weeks and an important step along the road that would lead to Mary Queen of Scots' execution in fourteen years' time, 'the bill against Mary commonly called Queen of Scots'. At this point, customary practice was broken with in quite a signal form, for 'before any answer [was] made the Queen's Majesty called the Lord Keeper unto her, who thereupon pronounced thus much in effect following'.

'The Queen's Highness's pleasure is, I wish you not to be moved though upon a strange occasion a strange answer have been made.' **Here the Queen interrupted him and told him that no answer at all was made as yet.** He then proceeded, turning his speech to the answer which should be made, which was *'Le Roigne se avisera'*; wishing them not to take the same in such sense as it hath heretofore been common understood, applied, and taken. That manner of speech in times past taken as rejecting of a bill; which she meaneth not to reject or refuse, she liketh so well of the substance thereof. Some points notwithstanding are contained in the same whereof she is not yet fully resolved, some things so excluded, some so concluded as hath not as yet her whole and perfect liking. But the greatest part thereof is to her contentation, and therefore, the time of the year considered, she is compelled to prolong the performance thereof to a farther deliberation. And for that purpose her pleasure is the parliament be prorogued.[80]

So little, however, did Elizabeth 'like' the proposed legislation (acquiescence in which would have constituted, in T. E. Hartley's words, 'victory for the Privy Council, Commons and Lords') that the parliament was prorogued, not for the matter of months she implied in her speech at this point, but for three and a half years.[81] Nor was the political nation able to carry its point for a further fourteen years, in the most notable instance in Elizabeth's reign of the queen's will being overridden to preserve Deborah and her godly nation from the menace of 'Jezebel', Mary Stuart, 'the whole hope of that called holy, but indeed unholy league of Trent' headed by the pope.[82]

The political implications of the speech are revealing. It is noteworthy, for example, that Elizabeth found it necessary to interrupt the Lord Keeper in order to insist on the ambiguity of her response: 'Here

[79] *Proceedings*, p. 418.
[80] Ibid., my emphasis. Hartley notes 'prorogued' replaces 'purged' in the original. Perhaps Cromwell, the diarist, was subliminally attuned to Elizabeth's unvoiced desires: she may well have wanted to 'purge' parliament at this point, rather than merely prorogue it.
[81] See T. E. Hartley's discussion in *Elizabeth's Parliaments*, pp. 63–7. [82] *Proceedings*, p. 377.

the Queen interrupted him and told him that no answer at all was made as yet.' (She was to attempt the same manoeuvre, again on the subject of Mary Queen of Scots' proposed execution, in the parliament of 1586–7, when she begged parliament in her speech at the end of the session to 'take in good part my answer-answerless'.[83]) The speech also stands in marked contrast to the one delivered on her behalf by Lord Keeper Bacon at the end of the 1571 parliament, in implicitly recognising the solidly unified character of the opposition. In 1571 she attempted to manoeuvre within the estates paradigm by hiving off 'certain of the lower house' from their dutiful colleagues, but equally the Commons from the Lords:

[L]ike as the great number of them of the lower house have in the proceedings in this session showed themselves modest, discreet and dutiful as becomes good and dutiful subjects and meet for the places they be called unto, so there be certain of them . . . which . . . have showed themselves audacious, arrogant and presumptuous . . . And like as her Majesty allows and much commends the former sort for the respects aforesaid, so doth her Highness utterly disallow and condemn the second sort for their audacious, arrogant and presumptuous folly, thus by frivolous and superfluous speech spending the time and meddling with matters neither pertaining unto them nor within the capacity of their under-standing. And thus much concerning Parliament men of the nether house.

And as to my lords here of the upper house, her Majesty hath commanded me to let them know that her Highness taketh their diligence, discretion and orderly proceedings to be such as redoundeth much to their honour and commendations, and much to her comfort and consolation.[84]

If she hoped the seeds of division between Lords and Commons sown on this occasion would have borne fruit by 1572, and therefore agreed, reluctantly, to summon a parliament, the hope proved misplaced – or at least premature.[85]

More significant than the ambiguity of her opening gambit in the 1572 speech or the corporate body to which it was directed was her redefinition of monarchical prerogative in regard to the power of veto. '*Le Roigne se avisera*', she says, no longer means rejection of a bill, but a

[83] J. E. Neale, *Elizabeth I and Her Parliaments*, p. 129.

[84] *Proceedings*, p. 188. Hartley says that 'the Lords' support was not automatically available to Elizabeth . . . and it must have seemed to her that the "natural" props of her regime were not wholly reliable' (*Elizabeth's Parliaments*, p. 121). This is no doubt true, but it is worth bearing in mind that in exchanges like this one she is using language strategically. She acts as if the lords are her natural allies (as they should be), and as if there are meaningful divisions between them and the 'commonalty', to exploit potential faultlines (especially relating to the definition of nobility and the threat of social instability) within the united front that parliament was capable of mustering at points when the godly enterprise appeared to be in danger.

[85] T. E. Hartley, *Elizabeth's Parliaments*, p. 66.

postponement of its enactment to allow for fine-tuning – for it to 'be drawn . . . toward the law', as she said on another occasion.[86] Elizabeth's word play was allowed for by the law French formula, turning on the verb 'se avisera'. Historically it represented the royal veto. The House of Commons informed the king of the condition of his realm in the form of petitions airing specific grievances. Through this formula the king acknowledged the legitimacy of their complaint but left open the manner in which it would be redressed, by 'taking thought, reflecting, bethinking (him)self'. That is, in the case of a veto he stated his intention to deliberate (which might involve consultation with others) as to the means by which the stated wrongs might be rectified.

But there is an ambiguity latent within the English use of the French term, which, like the enactment of majesty to which it referred, came to be explored in the reign of Elizabeth, for 's'aviser' could mean (and came to mean, before its obsolescence in the seventeenth century) 'to consider in company, to hold a consultation, to take counsel' – a small but significant shift that occurred during the late sixteenth century.[87] This definition of veto should be located between Sir Thomas Smith's confident assertion in the 1565 *De Republica Anglorum* that the laws or bills proposed by parliament of which the king disapproved were 'utterly dashed, and of no effect' and Richard Hooker's attempt, at the end of the sixteenth century, to define the power to veto parliamentary legislation as an essential element of the royal prerogative. The reason Hooker gives – 'which not to give them, were to deny them that without which they were but kings by mere title, and not in exercise of dominion' – speaks to issues of sovereignty generated by Elizabeth's reign, in which the exercise of dominion, by a female ruler, was not simply or easily the other face of an empire also signalled by parliament's statutory role.[88] For at this point in the debate we see how political necessity drove Elizabeth to a strategic redefinition of monarchical prerogative, which in effect ceded headship to the body politic, leaving open only the question of its institutional representation.

In this political context how was the 'fine-tuning' to which Elizabeth referred going to occur? On what terms were the queen and her counsellors to be reunited? In 1572, in the speech quoted above, Elizabeth implied that she would 'take counsel' – but do so by deliberating in

---

[86] *Proceedings*, p. 332.   [87] 'Advise', *Oxford English Dictionary*, vol. 1, p. 140.
[88] Sir Thomas Smith, *De Republica Anglorum* (1565), ed. Mary Dewar (Cambridge, 1982), p. 58. W. D. J. Cargill Thompson, 'The Philosopher of the "Politic Society": Richard Hooker as a Political Thinker' in *Studies in the Reformation: Luther to Hooker* (London, 1980), pp. 141–91, p. 173.

a more private forum with men whom she chose to consult. That, at least, was her public proposal. In actuality the weight of consensus about Mary's danger to the realm being what it was, 'deliberation' seems to have meant being subjected to 'advice' urging the necessity of execution proffered by men whose offices gave them ready access to the queen. Burghley, for example, enacted his advice on the subject in a fashion that Elizabeth could hardly ignore, although he claimed that political exigency prevented him from openly venting his views. Writing to Walsingham he claimed the strain of counselling Elizabeth on this matter made him 'overthrown in heart', so enfeebled and oppressed that he had to be carried both to the parliament house and to Elizabeth's presence, 'being every third day thrown down to the ground'. After her final (equivocal) pronouncement he wrote:

> For the Parliament I cannot write patiently. All that we laboured for, and had with full consent brought to fashion, I mean, a law to make the Scottish queen unable and unworthy of succession to the crown, was by her majesty neither assented to nor rejected, but deferred . . . But what all other wise and good men may think of it, you may guess.[89]

She attempted an analogous move when the stakes were yet higher, in the 1580s, by drawing on the second definition and identifying MPs sitting in the House of Commons as themselves councillors. Through the mouth of the Lord Chancellor, Christopher Hatton, she defined them as virtually her peers in their ability to find alternatives to execution:

> [M]oved with some commiseration towards the Scottish Queen, in respect of her former dignity and great fortunes in her younger years, her nearness of kindred . . . and also her sex, [Elizabeth] could be pleased to forbear the taking of her blood, if by any other means, to be devised by her Highness's Great Council of this realm, the safety of her Majesty's own person and of the State might be preserved . . . without peril or danger of ruin and destruction; and else, not.[90]

She then urged them in effect to act on this newly (by her) proposed identity by breaking ranks and approaching their Privy Councillor colleagues or the Speaker as individuals with their 'private conceits' about alternatives. This time around, however, MPs were attuned to the

---

[89] John Strype, *Annals*, vol. ii.i, pp. 200–1.
[90] J. E. Neale, *Elizabeth I and Her Parliaments*, pp. 122–3; see also Christopher Hatton's brief, drawn up for use in parliament: 'She hath thought meet to use you as a council (for so you be) to be made acquainted with such things as may touch merely both her and yourselves'; *The Bardon Papers: Documents Relating to the Imprisonment and Trial of Mary Queen of Scots*, ed. Conyers Read, Camden Third Series vol. xvii (London, 1909), p. 93. The 'merely' insists upon their indissolubility.

game she was playing. Some of the speakers in the debate which followed, recalling 1572 and the 'se avisera' episode, read the Queen's message as 'a peremptory proposition' excluding them for continuing their suit for Mary's death – which, in the circumstances of the 1580s, it was not.[91]

CODA: PETER WENTWORTH'S SPEECH, 1576

Finally, we need to examine a coda to these parliamentary debates: Peter Wentworth's famous speech in the 1576 parliamentary session.[92] Wentworth's speech was evidently written in 1572, as part of the debate described above. The unexpected prorogation gave him time to hone it in preparation for the next parliamentary session, which occurred in 1576. In the speech Wentworth argued, as other historians have shown, that freedom of speech was necessary to the well-being of the realm.[93] But he claimed it as an adjunct of conscience, in a speech in which he asserted the sovereign power of godly men in parliament over a queen who he intimated had become reprobate, hence a tyrant. He therefore asserted, far too explicitly for the continued stability of the mixed monarchy, that parliament, the 'body of the realm', could constitute itself as the head of the body politic in deference to God's will and in opposition to the queen's. He also privileged parliament as the place of law specifically to render illegitimate the extra-parliamentary means that Elizabeth – a personal monarch in a deferential society – might use to effect her will.[94]

Wentworth began his speech with an extended paean to the virtues of free speech, concluding that free speech was necessary to the maintenance of members' political virtue. Without freedom of debate, constrained by 'rumours' and 'opinion', they became courtiers, not counsellors:

[S]o that to this point I conclude that in this House which is termed a place of free speech there is nothing so necessary for the preservation of the prince and state as free speech, and without it it is a scorn and mockery to call it a parliament house for in truth it is none, but a very school of flattery and

---

[91] J. E. Neale, *Elizabeth I and Her Parliaments*, pp. 122–3.

[92] *Proceedings*, pp. 421–34. Hartley analyses the speech in *Elizabeth's Parliaments*, ch. 7, 'Peter Wentworth Revisited'.

[93] J. E. Neale, 'The Commoners' Privilege of Free Speech in Parliament' in *Historical Studies of the English Parliaments*, ed. E. B. Fryde and E. Miller (Cambridge, 1970), pp. 147–76.

[94] David Starkey, 'Court History in Perspective' in *The English Court: From the War of the Roses to the Civil War*, ed. David Starkey (London, 1987), pp. 1–24. In what follows I concentrate on the section of the speech that Wentworth actually delivered before being silenced by the House; T. E. Hartley, *Elizabeth's Parliaments*, p. 131.

dissimulation and so a fit place to serve the Devil and his angels in and not to glorify God and benefit the commonwealth.[95]

How then was their speech constrained? '[S]ometimes a message [from the queen] is brought into the House either of commanding or inhibiting, very injurious unto the freedom of speech and consultation.' Even more pernicious, in Wentworth's view, were the informal controls which left MPs ambivalently positioned between their desire to enact God's will and their desire to serve their queen:

> The one is a rumour that runneth about the House and this it is: 'take heed what you do, the Queen's Majesty liketh not of such a matter; whosoever preferreth it, she will be much offended with him.' Or the contrary: 'Her Majesty liketh of such a matter, whosoever speaketh against it she will be much offended with him.' . . . I would to God, Mr. Speaker, that these two were buried in Hell, I mean rumours and messages, for wicked undoubtedly they are: the reason is, the Devil was the first author of them, from whom proceedeth nothing but wickedness.

In suggesting why these techniques were ungodly, his use of the conditional tense indicates his fear that Elizabeth, in her own person, has withdrawn from the mixed monarchy:

> Now I will set down reasons to prove [these manoeuvres] wicked. First, if we be in hand with any thing for the advancement of God's glory, were it not wicked to say the Queen's Majesty liketh not of it, or commanding that we shall not deal in it? Greatly were these speeches to her Majesty's dishonour. And an hard opinion were it, Mr. Speaker, thus to conceive of the Queen's Majesty. And hardest of all were it, Mr Speaker, that these things should enter into her Majesty's thought. Much more wicked and unnatural were it that her Majesty should like or command any thing against God or hurtful to her self and the state. The Lord grant this thing may be far from her Majesty's heart.[96]

Wentworth also alleged that, because of her official position, Elizabeth has been able to take the bishops with her. For they now cut the cloth of God's word to the measure of their mistress's will, with potentially fatal consequences for the godly nation[97] (I take his reference

---

[95] *Proceedings*, p. 426.   [96] Ibid., p. 428.

[97] Later in the speech, in a section Wentworth did not deliver to the House, he contrasted godly MPs with bishops by suggesting the former were God's men, the latter the queen's: 'God would not vouchsafe that his Holy Spirit should all [last] session descend upon our bishops, so that the session nothing was one to the advancement of his glory. I have heard of old parliament men that the banishment of the Pope and popery and the restoring of true religion had their beginning from this House, and not from the bishops . . . It is an error to think that God's spirit is tied only to them, for the heavenly spirit saith, "First seek the kingdom of God and the righteousness thereof and all these things" – meaning temporal – "shall be given you." These words were not spoke to the bishops only but to all, and the writ, Mr. Speaker, that we are called up by is chiefly

to 'prince' to signal the queen as representing the imperial crown):

There was a message, Mr. Speaker, brought the last session to the House that we should not deal in any matters of religion but first to receive it from the bishops. Surely this was a doleful message for it was as much to say as 'Sirs, ye shall not deal in God's causes; no, ye shall in no wise seek to advance his glory. And in recompense of your unkindness God in his wrath will so look upon your doings that the chief and only cause that ye are called together for, the which is the preservation of the prince, shall have no good success.' If some one of this House had presently made this interpretation of the said message had he not seemed to have the spirit of prophecy? . . . And let it be holden for a principle, Mr. Speaker: that counsel that cometh not together in God's name cannot prosper. For God saith, 'When two or three are gathered together in my name there am I in the midst among them.'[98]

Wentworth suggests this tension will persist until MPs recognise that true service to the queen entails pre-eminently service to God. It is when the 'prince' subordinates himself to God's will that he becomes a 'king' (a godly identity); otherwise, like Nimrod, he inhabits a terrible, but fundamentally empty, majesty. (In this section of the speech and the next one Wentworth uses 'Queen' to accuse Elizabeth of particular derelictions of duty in the previous parliament; 'prince' as a neutral term to denominate a ruler who can but need not be godly; and 'king' – infrequently – to propose a godly ruler of a mixed monarchy.[99]) God's will can be read by MPs in their capacity as representing 'the nation':

[What are the consequences] if we follow not the prince's mind[?] Solomon saith the king's displeasure is a messenger of death. This is a terrible thing to the weak nature of frail flesh. Why so? For who is able to abide the fierce countenance of his prince? But if we will discharge our consciences and be true to God, our prince, and state we must have due consideration of the place and the occasion of our coming together, and especially have regard unto the matter, wherein we shall both serve God and our prince and state faithfully and not dissembling as eye pleasers, and so justly avoid all displeasures both to God and our prince. For Solomon saith in the way of the righteous there is life; as for any other way, it is the path to death. So that to avoid everlasting death and

---

to deal in God's cause, so that our commission both from God and our prince is to deal in God's causes'; *Proceedings*, p. 432.   [98] Ibid.
[99] Compare Erasmus's definitions of prince, king and tyrant in his *Education of a Christian Prince*: 'Only those who govern the state not for themselves but for the good of the state itself, deserve the title "prince". There is no more honourable title than "prince" and there is no term more detested and accursed than "tyrant" . . . Do not be satisfied just because you are called "king" or "prince". Those scourges of the earth, Phalaris and Dionysius, had those titles. Pass your own judgment on yourself. If Seneca was right, the distinction between tyrant and king is one of fact, not of terminology'; Desiderius Erasmus, *The Education of a Christian Prince*, tr. Lester K. Born (New York, 1968), pp. 160–1.

condemnation with the high and mighty God we ought to proceed in every case according to the matter and not according to the prince's mind. And now I will show you a reason to prove it perilous always to follow the prince's mind. Many times it falleth out that the prince may favour a cause perilous to himself and the whole state. What are we then if we follow the prince's mind? Are we not unfaithful unto God, our prince and state? Yes, truly, for we are chosen of the whole realm of a special trust and confidence by them reposed in us to foresee all such inconveniences.[100]

He then proceeded to specifics, signalled by his shift to 'her Majesty': 'Then I will set down my opinion herein: that is, he that dissembleth to her Majesty's peril is to be counted as an hateful enemy for that he giveth unto her Majesty a detestable Judas his kiss. And he that contraryeth her mind to her preservation, yea, though her Majesty would be much offended with him, is to be adjudged an approved lover.'[101]

Wentworth's explicit identification between national, or parliamentary, law and God's law allowed him to argue that parliament is in effect the 'head' of the body politic. It is the office of godly men consulting in parliament to arrive at a knowledge of God's will; it is then their duty to ensure that His will is effected, for the preservation of the 'prince' and the 'state'. A 'king' is one who executes 'justice': God's law interpreted by godly men (including the king) in parliament. Elizabeth's failure to execute justice, in the 1572 parliament, disallows her claim to be a king:

For the Queen's Majesty is the head of the law and must of necessity maintain the law, for by the law her Majesty is made justly our Queen and by it she is most chiefly maintained. Hereunto agreeth the most excellent words of Bracton, who saith the king hath no peer nor equal in his kingdom. He hath no equal for otherwise he might lose his authority of commanding, sithence that an equal hath no rule of commandments over his equal. The king ought not to be under man but under God and under the law, because the law maketh him a king. Let the king therefore attribute that unto the law which the law attributeth unto him, that is, dominion and power. For he is not a king in whom will and not the law doth rule, and therefore he ought to be under the law. I pray you mark the reason why my authority saith the king ought to be under the law. For, saith he, he is God's vicegerent here upon earth: that is, his lieutenant to execute and do his will, the which is law, or justice.[102]

At a later point in the speech – past the point at which he was silenced by the House – he made his meaning even more explicit. Elizabeth's continued tenure of her 'estate' depends upon her acting in accordance with the collective will of godly men:

<hr>

[100] *Proceedings*, pp. 427–8.   [101] Ibid., p. 428.   [102] Ibid., p. 429.

I beseech . . . God to endue her Majesty with his wisdom whereby she may discern faithful advice from traitorous sugared speeches, and to send her Majesty a melting, yielding heart unto sound counsel, that will may not stand for a reason. And then her Majesty [will] stand when her enemies are fallen, for no estate can stand where the prince will not be governed by advice . . . [T]he writ, Mr Speaker, that we are called up by is chiefly to deal in God's cause so that our commission both from God and our prince is to deal in God's causes . . . [W]e are incorporated into this place to serve God and all England.[103]

Wentworth was silenced before he delivered his speech in its entirety, shortly after his comments about the bishops. His meaning was evidently sufficiently clear to the House for him to be banished from parliament for a month, by order of MPs. On one level, he had overstepped the boundary between liberty and licence, to which contemporaries attached great importance, in parliamentary speech as elsewhere. On another, he had too forcefully intimated that the queen's will must be controlled, or might be ignored, by men standing in a right relationship with God and holding the office of counsellor to the 'whole realm'.

Later on the same day Wentworth appeared before a committee of the House dominated by Privy Councillors to answer for his speech.[104] The committee restricted its interrogation largely to the part of the speech he had delivered to the House, and Wentworth's response (in his account) consisted almost wholly in restating, often in the same words, the points he had earlier made to the House. What is most striking about this occasion is Wentworth's insistence that his interlocutors acknowledge his role as counsellor of the realm, thereby implicitly confirming their commitment to the godly enterprise, before he agrees to answer their questions:

Wentworth: If your honours ask me as **councillors** to her Majesty, you shall pardon me, I will make you no answer; I will do no such injury to the place from whence I came. For I am now no private person; I am a public and a **councillor** to the whole state in that place, where it is lawful for me to speak my mind freely and not for you (as **counsellors**) to call me to account for any thing that I do speak in the House. And therefore, if you ask me as **counsellors** to her Majesty, you shall pardon me; I will make no answer. But if you ask me as committees from the House, I will then willingly make you the best answer I can.[105]

---

[103] Ibid., pp. 432–3.   [104] Ibid., p. 422; T. E. Hartley, *Elizabeth's Parliaments*, pp. 132–3.
[105] *Proceedings*, p. 435, my emphasis. Wentworth uses different forms of the word 'counsel' but makes, I believe, the same distinction I have been using throughout the book. I have therefore translated his words, in the interests of clarity. The exact quotation, with the distinction as Cromwell noted it in his diary, is as follows (emphasis added): 'If your honours ask me as **councellors** to her Majesty, you shall pardon me, I will make you no answer; I will do no such

Here Wentworth seems to be arguing that he holds an office ('councillor to the whole state') that is equal in importance to the office held by his examiners, for he is a councillor to the 'whole state', while they are councillors to one constituent element, 'her Majesty'. Moreover by characterising them as 'counsellors' to her Majesty he implies that they, like the bishops, may have declined from a position of rectitude to a debased counselling function which is to advance the will of the monarch. He asks them to identify themselves, in other words, as godly, patriotic Englishmen, rather than as servants of the crown. Not surprisingly – in Wentworth's account at least – the committee immediately take his point and assert their virtue: 'We ask you as committees from the House.'[106]

CONCLUSION: SOVEREIGNTY AND PREROGATIVE

Events in the 1570s therefore problematised relations among the three estates, because they led to the politicisation of the notion of 'counsel'. These changes were signalled in one direction by the redefinition of the two houses of parliament's role as that of providing consent to legislative initiatives proposed by the queen-and-her-councillors; an interpretation made available, in the early 1570s, through theorists of parliament such as Hooker, Fleetwood and Norton. And given the perceived threat to the nation posed by Mary Stuart as queen, Catholic and Scot – views whose articulation inevitably reflected on England's own female monarch – a situation arose in which the consent of parliament (if not statutory pronouncement) could be claimed to have been attained once the most part of the 'well affected', or godly, had declared themselves once 'the nation' had spoken, whether within or outside of parliament. The high-water mark of the mixed monarchy in this manifestation was unquestionably the 1584 Bond of Association, which inaugurated a just war against Mary Stuart and led to her execution three years later. As David Cressy has shown, Burghley and Walsingham were the moving forces behind it, whatever concerns they may have had about its socially radical implications convincingly outweighed by their certainty that 'the nation' was godly, hence capable of actively creating bonds of 'fellow-

injury to the place from whence I came. For I am now no private person; I am a public and a **councellor** to the whole state in that place, where it is lawful for me to speak my mind freely and not for you (as **counsellors**) to call me to account for any thing that I do speak in the House. And therefore, if you ask me as **counsellors** to her Majesty, you shall pardon me; I will make no answer. But if you ask me as committees from the House, I will then willingly make you the best answer I can.'   [106] *Proceedings*, p. 435.

ship and society'. Burghley wrote to Walsingham that 'many sorts of persons by degrees of offices and callings are like to be parties in that society'; Walsingham assumed that 'the more public the matter is made, the better effect it is like to work'.[107]

The Bond of Association, even the execution of Mary Stuart, were made possible by the developments I have outlined in this chapter. They also suggest why law – the means by which the pronouncements of the common mind attained binding status – became the main field of contest for the remainder of Elizabeth's reign and into the reigns of her Stuart successors. For the queen had resources that she could exploit if she came to believe her participation in the mixed monarchy prejudiced her 'state' as monarch, presumably a point she reached in 1572, when she was effectively forced to abandon her absolute power to veto legislation of which she disapproved.[108] She could in effect withdraw from the copulative queen-in-parliament by drawing on variant readings of the three estates which allocated legislative competence (or sovereignty) to the monarch acting alone. Most notably, she could attempt to redefine 'prerogative' as an inalienable, and personal, right of the monarch.[109] The regime needed to have Elizabeth with them, as head of the body politic and emblem of the nation, as they mobilised 'the commonalty' to safeguard Protestantism in the 1570s and 1580s. The resulting tension helps explain the attention to redefining monarchical prerogative in the late 1570s as a means of rectifying the balance between the three estates destabilised earlier in the decade. In the first instance we therefore see it defined (by Burghley) as an attribute of the incorporated queen: 'the king . . . solely and alone is rightly said by his Prerogative to be the maker and ordainer of laws and statutes in and by his Court of Parliament, that is to say by the grave and wise counsel, advice and consent of his whole Realm.'[110]

But at a later point when, at the execution of Mary Stuart, the

---

[107] David Cressy, 'Binding the Nation: The Bonds of Association, 1584 and 1596' in *Tudor Rule and Revolution: Essays for G. R. Elton from His American Friends*, ed. Delloyd J. Guth and John W. McKenna (Cambridge, 1982), pp. 217–34, pp. 220–1. Cressy is right to reject the conventional view of the Bond as a 'desperate measure promoted by desperate men', but I think he errs in seeing it as an imposition from above, rather than a product of an increasingly widely shared commitment to the English nation as it had come to be defined and promoted by this point in Elizabeth's reign.   [108] T. E. Hartley, *Elizabeth's Parliaments*, p. 170.

[109] Powerfully conveyed through proclamation. Blair Worden provides additional evidence that the use of royal proclamations was already controversial during Elizabeth's reign, especially in its latter stages; *The Sound of Virtue: Philip Sidney's 'Arcadia' and Elizabethan Politics* (New Haven, Conn., 1996), pp. 241–2.

[110] William Lambarde, *Notes on the Procedures and Privileges of the House of Commons*, pp. 20–1.

requirement for her consent was signally overridden, Elizabeth targeted councillors – now 'certain of her judges' – who would assert that her prerogative, as queen, was above the law. That she made this 'move', and that Burghley saw its consequences as potentially signalling the death knell of the godly commonwealth, is suggested by a letter from Burghley to an anonymous correspondent, written after Mary Stuart's execution. The letter, heavily disguised through the use of cipher, code, and deliberate confusion of masculine and feminine pronouns, has been decoded and extracted by J. E. Neale as follows. (Neale's interpolations are in brackets):

> I doubt not but you understand her Majesty's great displeasure for the execution of the Scottish Queen, though justly done and most profitably for her Majesty's surety, if by mishandling since . . . it be not impaired. Poor Mr. Davison is, as you know, in the Tower, whose conscience doth only comfort him; and though her Majesty hath shown her offence to her Council that were privy to the execution, yet her offence is to me so further in some degree, as I, not having been able to appear before her with the rest, by reason of my hurt, am forbidden, or not licensed, to come to her presence to answer for myself . . . She (I know not how) is informed that by her prerogative she may cause Mr. Davison to be hanged, and that we all may be so convicted as we shall require pardon. Hereupon, yesterday, she having Mr. Justice Anderson with her and demanding question whether her prerogative were not absolute, he answered, as I hear, 'Yes.' [She had then turned on Lord Buckhurst for saying she could not hang a man against her laws, rebuking him bitterly, citing Justice Anderson. She has since] declared the judgment of Mr. Anderson to serve her purpose [and intends to consult the other judges. Burghley asks his correspondent to warn certain of them, secretly, to be careful what they reply:] I would be loath to live to see a woman of such wisdom as she is, to be wrongly advised, for fear or other infirmity; and I think it a hard time if men, for doing well afore God and man, shall be otherwise punished than law may warrant, with an opinion gotten from the judges that her prerogative is above the law.[111]

We can therefore see political exigency as a major ingredient in the emergence of the aristocratic, courtly culture revolving around the 'cult' of Elizabeth which, embryonic in the early years of the reign, dominated cultural life after the execution of Mary Queen of Scots.[112] Celebrating Elizabeth – as woman, as prince, as emblem of the nation – became a powerful means of rectifying the balance between the three estates once it became destabilised by its quest for sanctity. In the 'second' reign, the queen and her councillors enacted an elaborate masquerade in which

[111] J. E. Neale, *Elizabeth I and Her Parliaments*, pp. 141–2.
[112] Helen Hackett, *Virgin Mother, Maiden Queen: Elizabeth I and the Cult of the Virgin Mary* (London, 1995).

their assertions of Elizabeth's power functioned as counters designed to persuade her that she need not act on the opinion of the offending judges (whom Burghley saw as ungodly counsellors, acting through 'fear or other infirmity') to preserve her majesty. The masquerade allowed 'prerogative' to continue to be theorised as the means by which the king effected the common mind: '*le Roy voet*', in the sense proposed by William Fleetwood in the 1571 parliamentary debates. It provides the context for Burghley's 1593 statement to the common lawyer James Morice, applicable to Privy Councillor and Member of Parliament alike, about the role of councillor to the queen: 'If it please her to reform [abuses], it was well; if not we were to pray to God to move her heart thereunto, and so to leave the matter to God and her majesty.'[113] Rather than reflecting Burghley's political creed and making 'nonsense of the legend that Elizabeth's England was "Cecil's Commonwealth"', as J. E. Neale believed it did, it indicates the move the political establishment was prepared to make, in the latter part of Elizabeth's reign and – an important qualification – in the context of female rule, to preserve the mixed monarchy.

[113] J. E. Neale, *Elizabeth I and Her Parliaments*, p. 276.

CHAPTER 7

Rewriting the common weal: Sir Thomas Smith and the De Republica Anglorum[1]

> And consequently there may appear like diversity to be in English
> between a public weal and a common weal, as should be in Latin
> between *Res publica* and *Res plebeia*. And after that signification, if
> there should be a common weal either the commoners only must
> be wealthy, and the gentle and noble men needy and miserable, or
> else, excluding gentility, all men must be of one degree and sort,
> and a new name provided.
>
> Sir Thomas Elyot, *The Boke Named the Governour*[2]

In his 1990 article 'War and the Commonwealth in Mid-Tudor England', Ben Lowe argues that the term 'commonwealth' took on 'nuances
of meaning' over the course of the sixteenth century that did not exist at
its beginning. The earlier form ('common weal' or 'common wealth')
referred to organic, societal relationships among the estates, and their
productive interconnection for the good of all. The mid-sixteenth-
century compound form ('commonwealth') which increasingly replaced
it referred to the state, or *respublica*, and to associations among its
peoples, a development that allowed for the eventual emergence of
classical republicanism in the seventeenth century.[3] Clearly the termi-
nological shift did not signal the supersession of the older, medieval
conception of the 'common' (sometimes 'public') weal. Instead, attention to the 'commonwealth' on the part of humanists, first at Henry
VIII's court, later at Edward VI's, represented a means by which to

---

[1] I am using the vocabulary Richard Helgerson employs in *Forms of Nationhood: The Elizabethan Writing of England* (Chicago, 1992), esp. pp. 1–10.

[2] Sir Thomas Elyot, *The Book Named The Governor*, ed. S. E. Lehmberg (London, 1962).

[3] Ben Lowe, 'War and the Commonwealth in Mid-Tudor England', *Sixteenth Century Journal* 21, no. 2 (1990), pp. 171–91, p. 173.

assimilate the core values associated with the 'common weal' to England's new identity as a godly empire.

As we have seen, this project continued through the reign of Elizabeth I. It changed form dramatically with the accession after Henry VIII of his successors – Edward VI, Lady Jane Grey, Mary I, Elizabeth I. Each was perceived as incapable of exercising autonomous kingship, as a function of age, gender and/or disputable legitimacy. 'Legitimacy' itself became an elastic term, in the context of monarchical succession, and one increasingly connected to personal attributes including age, gender and confessional conviction.[4] To their other disabilities Henry VIII's successors (prior to James I) added an inability to establish a dynastic succession through heirs of their own bodies. This was a signal weakness in a hierarchical society in which blood denoted both perpetuity and virtue, and virility the means by which blood (hence civil order) was assured.[5]

Perceived monarchical incapacities inevitably promoted, in Edward's reign as in Elizabeth's, a politics of association to preserve the 'commonwealth' both as a sovereign state and as a means of grace. Yet the men who promoted this politics were, like Sir Thomas Elyot in Henry VIII's reign, uncomfortably aware that the fusion of humanism and Protestantism that promoted the godly empire could threaten order and degree – even patriarchy itself – through the egalitarian and acephalic implications of these modes of discourse. One such threat occurred with the 1549 Peasants' Rebellion, when the 'feet' of the body politic threatened to assert an egalitarian political consciousness. It was to happen again, in a different form, in 1649, when saints in arms beheaded Charles Stuart to inaugurate, literally and symbolically, the acephalous English Commonwealth.[6]

In Elizabeth's reign, Protestant apologists thus sought to reintroduce

---

[4] Howard Nenner, *The Right to Be King: The Succession to the Crown of England, 1603–1714*, Macmillan Studies in Modern History (New York, 1995), pp. 1–4, 7–12, 13–25.

[5] Sarah Hanley describes a 'biogenetic seminal theory of authority' according to which kings (but not queens) create successors who perpetuate the monarchy. This is allowed for by the contemporary reading of 'semen' and 'blood' as interchangeable terms; Sarah Hanley, 'The Monarchic State in Early Modern France: Marital Regime Government and Male Right' in *Politics, Ideology and the Law in Early Modern Europe: Essays in Honor of J. H. M. Salmon*, ed. Adrianna E. Bakos (New York, 1994), pp. 116–17.

[6] Shortly before Charles I's condemnation, Oliver Cromwell is reported to have said to Algernon Sidney 'I tell you, we will cut off his head with the crown on it'; see J. G. Muddiman, *Trial of Charles the First* (Edinburgh, n.d.), p. 70. And see Michael Walzer for the realisation that Cromwell's comment spoke to the issue of which corporation would assume headship of the body politic: 'the People of England, the Commons, the army'; *Regicide and Revolution: Speeches at the Trial of Louis XVI* (Cambridge, 1974), p. 4.

a politics of association directly descended from Edward VI's reign – as necessary under a female ruler as under a minor king – without unleashing its egalitarian or demotic potential. They did so by theorising the godly empire in a new way, as the 'mixed monarchy'. The mixed monarchy – the three estates of queen, lords and commons – proposed an incorporated crown, an association of queen and counsellors, as a mode of national identity and symbol of national election.[7] In this enterprise Tudor blood, represented by the queen, was to be hedged by the 'virtue' – a quality simultaneously spiritual and political – of her male counsellors.[8] And 'counsellor' came to be understood in a new way: as a concomitant of grace in a nation effecting true reformation. This is the context in which to locate Protestant apologetical works of the 1560s: men such as John Aylmer, John Jewel, Laurence Humphrey and John Foxe and, as we shall see, Sir Thomas Smith.

At Elizabeth's accession the need for such apologetical works was acute. At the outset Elizabeth's position as monarch was significantly weaker than her sister Mary's had been. She was the last of her line, a position that exacerbated what she identified as 'the inconstancy of the people of England', their tendency to 'mislike the present government and have their eyes fixed upon that person that is next to succeed'.[9] She gained the throne as the candidate of a Protestant interest in England which, although extremely influential, was by no means as entrenched or widely popular as historians have tended to assume, and which did not include significant elements of the nobility.[10] And at this time the English initiative ran counter to the European tide, where reforming Catholicism gave new meaning to the idea of a Church Triumphant. Finally, she was a queen regnant. She came to power in the wake of a reign that had, to contemporary eyes, shown the dire consequences, national as much as religious, of that identity – and produced a compel-

---

[7] David Norbrook cogently identifies signal continuities between Edwardian and Elizabethan politics in *Poetry and Politics in the English Renaissance* (London, 1984).

[8] An equation that testifies to the reforming commitment of the Elizabethan regime and that crucially problematised the role and status of the nobility of blood, whose 'virtue' traditionally resided in their martial competence. Good evidence that Edward's councillors feared they had got the balance between 'blood' and 'virtue' wrong comes from John Murphy, who notes the 'strange talk' during Northumberland's supremacy of making Mary Tudor regent. See 'The Illusion of Decline: The Privy Chamber, 1547–1558' in *The English Court: From the War of the Roses to the Civil War*, ed. David Starkey (London, 1987), pp. 119–46, p. 128.

[9] Maitland of Lethington's Account of His Negotiation with Elizabeth I (c. September 1561) in Mortimer Levine, *Tudor Dynastic Problems 1460–1571* (London, 1973), p. 176.

[10] Christopher Haigh, *English Reformations: Religion, Politics and Society under the Tudors* (Oxford 1993); Patrick Collinson, 'The Elizabethan Exclusion Crisis and the Elizabethan Polity', *Proceedings of the British Academy* 84 (1994), pp. 51–92, p. 56.

ling case casting doubt on the legitimacy of monarchical authority itself. Hugh Trevor-Roper understood the fragility of the Protestant nation at Elizabeth's accession, and the consequent necessity to legitimate her reign by invoking (or 'writing', in Richard Helgerson's terms) a 'continuous pedigree' – a task he sees as spurring antiquarian endeavours, and patronised in the first instance by William Cecil and Archbishop Matthew Parker:

> The rule of Queen Elizabeth must not appear to be, as foreigners saw it, the fragile authority of an insecure young woman, the last frail life of a usurping Tudor dynasty; it must appear as the natural, organic continuation of the robust, uncontested, ancient monarchy. Equally the Elizabethan Church must not appear as a whimsical, heretical innovation, an ephemeral political compromise, doomed to founder in the stress of ideological war . . . Elizabethan Englishmen [shared] the knowledge that, politically, the Queen's government, both Church and State, hung upon slender filaments and a feeble title.[11]

The continuous pedigree her apologists constructed promulgated a historical as well as a providential national identity – the Ancient Constitution as well as the Elect Nation – as two sides of the same coin in a godly empire, equally necessary as sanctions for the mixed monarchy under female rule. It also fuelled the development of a notion of 'citizen' as an identity ambiguously political and spiritual which had taken root in Edward VI's reign, in part as a means of allowing for the infusion of adult male 'virtue' into the body politic under a minor king. The language, at least, of classical republicanism became a way of describing godly Englishmen as citizens simultaneously of the True Church and of the godly nation. And in Elizabeth's reign, as in Edward's, they could be seen as men called to a *vita activa* in the service of the monarchy, to protect and defend the common weal in the absence of a king.[12]

I want to conclude by arguing the case that we should read Sir Thomas Smith's famous description of the English nation, his *De Republica Anglorum*, as responding to this national imperative in exactly these terms. Written in 1565 (although not published until 1581), the *De Republica Anglorum* promoted a vision of England that constituted a response to the conundrum posed by Elyot: how to find a 'new name' for the godly empire, now with a woman on the throne.[13] In his text

---

[11] Hugh Trevor-Roper, *Queen Elizabeth's First Historian: William Camden and the Beginning of English 'Civil History'*, Second Neale Lecture in English History (London, 1971), p. 7.

[12] J. G. A. Pocock, 'England', in *National Consciousness, History and Political Culture in Early-Modern Europe*, ed. Orest Ranum (Baltimore, Md., 1975), ch. 4, pp. 108–9.

[13] A. W. Pollard and G. R. Redgrave's *A Short Title Catalogue of Books Printed in England, Scotland, and Ireland, and of English Books Printed Abroad, 1475–1640*, 2nd edn (London, 1976–91) lists an entry

Smith sought to establish how a godly 'common weal' could maintain hierarchy (including kingship) and social order – and attain full spiritual reformation. He did so in part by claiming that in England this balancing act had already been realised through English customs and institutions, an appeal to history so successful that it has obscured the meaning of his text from subsequent historians, as it has sealed his reputation as a rationalist, secularly minded thinker.[14] Instead, like other apologists of the period, Smith endeavoured to legitimate Elizabeth, as a female ruler, and simultaneously to define the mixed monarchy as a novel form of political association. But Smith did so in ways that made his work both idiosyncratic, within the context of other apologetical literature, and, as a result, extremely influential from its first appearance in print, in 1581, until the outbreak of the civil war in the seventeenth century.

The *De Republica Anglorum* also bears investigation because of this later career. By the 1580s it had become in effect an official text of the government, as its frequent republication over the decade and into the seventeenth century suggests.[15] In this manifestation it served as ideological justification as the government – the queen and her councillors – moved to reposition the mixed monarchy as both godly and *politique*; a renegotiation that both inaugurated the aristocratic and courtly culture of Elizabeth's 'second reign' and defined its parameters.[16] Its later career thus provides an entry point for the world of late Elizabethan political culture: the world brought into existence as a direct consequence of the political engagements I have traced in the book. I want first to consider Smith's work in its 1565 context, to see how he theorises the mixed monarchy. I then want to relate its publication in the 1580s to the changed political circumstances of that decade.

---

under John Day for a 1581 published version, which evidently no longer survives. The date usually given for first publication is 1583.

[14] Stephen L. Collins, *From Divine Cosmos to Sovereign State: An Intellectual History of Consciousness and the Idea of Order in Renaissance England* (Oxford, 1989), pp. 72–5. I would use Raymond Williams's concept of 'emergent ideologies' to make it clear that my reading of Smith does not invalidate Collins's; 'Base and Superstructure in Marxist Cultural Theory' in *Problems in Materialism and Culture* (London, 1980), pp. 31–49.

[15] In Elizabeth's reign, the *De Republica* was printed in 1581, then again in 1583, 1584, 1589, 1594 and 1601 (Pollard and Redgrave, *Short Title Catalogue*). Each printed edition prominently displayed an imprimatur stating that it had been 'Seene and allowed', a peculiarity that leads Peter Herman to conclude that its publishers wished to advertise official approval of Smith's vision of the English commonwealth; '"O, 'tis a gallant king"': Shakespeare's *Henry V* and the Crisis of the 1590s' in *Tudor Political Culture*, ed. Dale Hoak (Cambridge, 1995), pp. 204–25, pp. 205–6.

[16] For this see also John Guy, 'The 1590s: The Second Reign of Elizabeth I?' in *The Reign of Elizabeth I: Court and Culture in the Last Decade*, ed. John Guy (Cambridge, 1995), pp. 1–19.

SIR THOMAS SMITH AND THE *DE REPUBLICA ANGLORUM*

By the end of the sixteenth century, and because of this changed political context, Smith's *respublica* could be tellingly defined by Gabriel Harvey as 'Smith's state' – with intimations that this was a form of political organisation with pretensions, at least, to 'absolutism'.[17] In its first manifestation, however, Smith's work had very different associations, ones that suggest that Smith, like John Aylmer and Laurence Humphrey, was engaged in defining the godly nation as a bridle upon female (and tyrannical) rule in the interests of securing the common weal. Although the actual mechanics of the transfer remain obscure, it is well known that Smith and William Harrison used the same material to describe the 'Degrees of People in the Commonwealth of England' – a politically significant element in defining a 'nation' whose collective support the regime claimed as a source of its legitimation.[18] Mary Dewar, the most recent editor of the *De Republica Anglorum* and Smith's biographer, suggests both manuscripts were to form part of Reginald Wolfe's unrealised project for a 'Universal Cosmography of the Whole World', a writing of the True Church and England's role in its history consonant with their 'maps' of England's topography and government.[19] Harrison, whose radical Protestant vision has been traced by G. J. R. Parry, worked similarly closely with John Jewel, Marian exile, bishop of Salisbury and author of the *Apology of the Church of England* (1564). Harrison incorporated material from Jewel's *Apology* into his *Description of Britain* and may have written its conclusion. And Jewel, we know, worked at the behest of William Cecil and Matthew Parker to defend the English Church that emerged from the Acts of Supremacy and Uniformity as both historically legitimated and an agent of providence.[20]

[17] Quoted in David Norbrook, *Poetry and Politics*, p. 79. Harvey was talking to Edmund Spenser, who, like others of the Essex circle, fought a rearguard action against this redefinition, most obviously in the *Faerie Queene*.

[18] William Harrison, *Description of England*, first published 1577 in Raphael Holinshed's *Chronicles*. For Harrison and the *Description* as published in the 1577 and 1587 versions of the *Chronicles* see Annabel Patterson, *Reading Holinshed's 'Chronicles'* (Chicago, 1994). For the regime's recourse to 'the nation' – and the recognition that the rhetoric became increasingly specious over the reign – see Patrick Collinson, *The Birthpangs of Protestant England: Religion and Cultural Change in the Sixteenth and Seventeenth Centuries*, 3rd Anstey Memorial Lecture, University of Kent, 1986 (London, 1988), pp. 25–7.   [19] Mary Dewar, *Sir Thomas Smith: A Tudor Intellectual in Office* (London, 1964), p. 114.

[20] G. J. R. Parry, *A Protestant Vision: William Harrison and the Reformation of Elizabethan England* (Cambridge, 1987); Sir Thomas Smith, *De Republica Anglorum* (1565), ed. Mary Dewar (Cambridge, 1982), p. 161; John Jewel, *An Apology of the Church of England* (1564), ed. J. E. Booty (New York, 1963), pp. xxxii, 121, 123, 136–7. Parry also points to Harrison's ideological affinities with the commonwealth commentators of Edward VI's reign (p. 254).

It is therefore a mistake to view Smith, or the *De Republica*, as divorced from the profound engagement with issues of spiritual and national reform and renewal characteristic of English (and European) culture at this time. Instead he – like Cecil; like Harrison's ideological progenitors Thomas Cranmer, Hugh Latimer, Nicholas Ridley; like Protector Somerset, under whom both Smith and Cecil served – saw England as a godly commonwealth and his vocation as its furtherance. The difference between men whom Geoffrey Elton sees, in Edward VI's reign, as occupying separate camps on the road to modernity was merely one of route, not destination.[21] If, in 1550, he condemned 'hotlings' who 'devise commonwealths as they like, and are angry that other men be not so hasty to run straight as their brains crow', he did so in frustration lest such devices should make the project of a godly commonwealth appear (and become) 'utopian' – socially destabilising and politically unrealisable.[22] This was common ground he shared with William Cecil, later Lord Burghley. Their ideological congruence explains not only why Cecil persevered in his efforts to gain Smith promotion to the Privy Council in the face of Elizabeth's fixed dislike, but also Smith's appointment as Burghley's successor as Secretary of State, where he served as Burghley's second self.[23]

Smith's background, particularly his political education during the reign of Edward VI, led him to long for a godly king as preserver of the commonwealth but equally to believe that godly councillors to the crown could, through their virtue and with Christ as their head, protect and defend it until such a one appeared. It was a conviction shared by other councillors who constituted the inner core of the Elizabethan Privy Council, as the vicissitudes of post-reformation English history moved them towards a bifurcated loyalty to the imperial crown as well as to the person of the reigning monarch. Most significantly, as we have seen, it informed the commonwealth theorising that flowered in Edward

---

[21] G. R. Elton, 'Reform and the "Commonwealth-men" of Edward VI's Reign' in *Studies in Tudor and Stuart Politics and Government*, vol. 3 (Cambridge, 1983), pp. 234–53, pp. 237, 252–3. J. N. King provides convincing evidence of the extent to which 'commonwealth theorising' became the *lingua franca* of the reign in *English Reformation Literature: The Tudor Origins of the Protestant Tradition* (Princeton, N.J., 1982); a point also made (and the phrase used) by M. L. Bush in *The Government Policy of Protector Somerset* (London, 1975), p. 70. For Smith's role in the Elizabethan settlement see John Strype, *The Life of the Learned Sir Thomas Smith* (Oxford, 1820), vol. I.i, II.ii pp. 392–8 and N. M. Sutherland, 'The Marian Exiles and the Establishment of the Elizabethan Regime', *Archive for Reformation History* 78 (1987), pp. 253–84, p. 281.   [22] BL MS Harley 6989, fol. 146.
[23] Sir Dudley Digges, *The Compleat Ambassador* (London, 1655), p. 54; see Mary Dewar, *Sir Thomas Smith*, chs. 11, 12 and 15. In her introduction to *De Republica Anglorum* Dewar notes that Smith's correspondence from the 1570s suggests he saw disagreements among Privy Councillors as primarily concerned with means, not ends (p. 5).

VI's reign, when associations of virtuous men preserved the empire during the king's minority, drawing on radical notions of Christian community to do so. As Smith's attack on 'hotlings' suggests, the commonwealth experiment conducted in Edward's reign initiated a line of division between visionaries and policy-men, intensely felt because of their shared premises. This was to destabilise the commonwealth consensus in Elizabeth's reign from the point at which an appeal to conscience against the queen became a feature of political debate; a point reached when Peter Wentworth and, from a different direction, Archbishop Grindal announced themselves as men of conscience in opposition to the queen in 1576.

Commonwealth ideology developed a particular identity in England that allowed it to fuse with providential and apocalyptic modes of thought in the sixteenth century and, later, to serve as a vehicle for classical republicanism in the seventeenth. It acquired these potentialities largely because of the idiosyncratic character of the Henrician Reformation, which made theocratic kingship a precondition of godly empire. But attention to issues of the 'common weal' went hand in hand with the progress of reformation throughout Europe, as religious division problematised concepts of monarchical legitimacy and authority, illegitimacy and tyranny. Such attention also arose because of the prominence of female rulers in the post-1550 European landscape, as the notion of 'tyranny' in particular took on gender-specific associations.[24] Smith was well aware of this wider context. When he described the English commonwealth in 1565 he did so while looking in the direction of both Scotland and France – he was England's ambassador to France at the time he wrote it – not only because of a powerful sense of identity with Protestant 'brothers in Christ' but also because in those countries too the brethren grappled with the problem of a body politic in which the role of head was played by a woman. This was the context in which, for example, in 1564 the Edinburgh minister John Craig could use the argument that 'every kingdom is a common wealth . . . albeit every common wealth is not a kingdom' as directly relevant to the situation of Scotland under an (ungodly) female ruler, Mary Queen of Scots.[25] It was also the context that produced François Hotman and his

---

[24] Interestingly, although Mary Dewar regards most of the emendations introduced in the 1583 print edition of *De Republica Anglorum* as 'insignificant' – largely stylistic – she instances changes in the use of the word 'tyranny' as one substantive alteration; *De Republica Anglorum*, ed. Dewar, p. 15.

[25] John Knox, *History of the Reformation in Scotland* (1566), in *The Works of John Knox*, ed. David Laing, 6 vols. (Edinburgh, 1846–64), vol. II, pp. 458–9.

attempt to identify some incorruptible essence of national Protestant character and give it institutional expression, a task that entailed, most famously in the *Francogallia*, divorcing sovereignty (or 'majesty') from the corrupting trammels of female rule.[26] Leonard Alston, the 1906 editor of *De Republica Anglorum*, was therefore astute, and I think correct, to conclude on the basis of his reading that 'intercourse between Smith and Hotman seems as likely as that between Smith and Bodin' (which historians then and now have hypothesised) and that 'Smith would have found more to approve in the *Francogallia* than in the *Six Livres.*[27]

Rather than regard Smith as a rationalist, advancing temporal and secular explanations for a society in flux, we need to consider the *De Republica Anglorum*, in its 1565 appearance, as an apologetic for the mixed monarchy in this commonwealth context. This view is consonant with Smith's stated aim of 'see[ing] who hath taken the righter, truer, and more commodious way to govern the people'.[28] This reading helps explain too his insistence that he is **describing** not 'feigning' the commonwealth of England – not following the example of 'Sir Thomas More in his *Utopia*', who invented a commonwealth 'such as never was nor never shall be', the product of 'vain imaginations [and] fantasies'. Instead he argues that his book so nakedly describes England that 'whether I writ true or not, it is easy to be seen with eyes (as a man would say) and felt with hands'.[29] And his vision of England, unsurprisingly, was of a godly nation populated by virtuous men associated in a 'common doing' productive of good order, harmony and peace – in a monarchy for the moment headed by a queen. This interpretation is supported by three related elements of Smith's vision of England: first, the social composition of the body politic; secondly, the role he attributes to women (including the queen); and, finally, his definition of sovereignty.

---

[26] Although not published until 1573, its modern editors and Hotman's modern biographer see it as a 'kind of political transmutation' of themes he first wrote about in the early 1560s. See *Francogallia*, ed. Ralph E. Giesey and J. H. M. Salmon (Cambridge, 1972), introduction, p. 23; Donald R. Kelley, *François Hotman: A Revolutionary's Ordeal* (Princeton, N.J., 1973), pp. 199, 239; and Donald Kelley, *The Beginning of Ideology: Consciousness and Society in the French Reformation* (Cambridge, 1981), p. 249.

[27] *De Republica Anglorum* (Cambridge, 1906), ed. Leonard Alston, p. xlii. Mary Dewar also notes (*Sir Thomas Smith*, p. 7) that Smith had 'little use for women and none whatsoever for Elizabeth', although she does not explain why this was the case.

[28] *De Republica Anglorum*, ed. Mary Dewar, p. 144; hereafter *DRA* and referring to Dewar's edition, unless otherwise specified.   [29] *DRA*, p. 144.

DELINEATING THE COMMONWEALTH

It is an interesting fact that slightly more than the first third of a book devoted to describing 'The manner of Government or policy of the Realm of England' consists of a general discussion of commonwealths. In this discussion Smith's emphasis is very much on the wilful and articulated nature of the commonwealth, and on the important part 'the people' (male) play in establishing and sustaining it: 'A common wealth is called a society or common doing of a multitude of free men collected together and united by common accord and covenants among themselves, for the conservation of themselves as well in peace as in war.'[30] The three kinds of commonwealth identified by Aristotle – rule by the one, the few and the many – are equally 'natural', as are 'mutations and changes of fashions of government' that transmute one form into another. What matters is that the form of government be 'according to the nature of the people, so the commonwealth is to it fit and proper'.[31] There is the suggestion that this 'common doing' preceded the forms of rule identified by Aristotle – 'The common wealth is judged by that which is most ordinarily and commonly done through the whole realm'[32] – and that the Aristotelian typology is a fairly crude analytical device applied to a protean body politic:

Now although the governments of common wealths be thus divided into three, and cutting each into two, so into six: yet you must not take that ye shall find any common wealth or government simple, pure and absolute in his sort and kind, but as wise men have divided for understandings sake and fantasied four simple bodies which they call elements, as fire, air, water, earth, and in a man's body four complexions or temperatures, as choleric, sanguine, phlegmatic, and melancholic: not that ye shall find the one utterly perfect without mixtion of the other, for that nature almost will not suffer, but understanding doth discern each nature as in his sincerity: so seldom or never shall you find any common wealth or government which is absolutely and sincerely made of the ones above named, but always mixed with another, and hath the name of that which is more and overruleth always or for the most part the other.[33]

It is at this point that Smith introduces the only chapter of the first sixteen that deals specifically with England, 'Of the name king and the administration of England'. Here he states that England is and has always been a monarchy:

---

[30] Stephen Collins, *From Divine Cosmos to Sovereign State*, pp. 72–5; *DRA*, p. 57. [31] *DRA*, p. 62.
[32] Ibid., p. 135. [33] Ibid., p. 52.

By old and ancient histories that I have read, I cannot understand that our nation hath used any other and general authority in this realm neither aristocratical, nor democratical, but only the royal and kingly majesty.

But he describes this as a 'general' authority – which I take to mean 'the name of that which . . . overruleth always or for the most part the other' – in a chapter patently introduced to insist on a 'time out of mind' pedigree for the imperial crown:

which at the first was divided into many and sundry kings, each absolutely reigning in his country, not under the subjection of other, till by fighting the one with the other, the overcome always falling to the augmentation of the vanquisher and overcomer, at the last the realm of England grew into one Monarchy. Neither any one of these kings, neither he who first had all, took any investiture of the empire of Rome or of any superior prince, but held of God and himself, his people and sword, the crown, acknowledging no prince in earth his superior, and so it is kept and held at this day.[34]

There is a strong implication in Smith's argument that the 'common doing' which forms the basis of the commonwealth imposes obligations – of oversight at least if not of direct political engagement – on 'just men', who are able to discern the common weal. In Book I.2 ('What is Just or Law in Every Common Wealth or Government'), for example, Smith indicates that the 'commandment of that part which doth rule' is to be accepted as just. Thus he is able to accept that 'that is just which is the profit of the ruling and most strong part' – Plato's repudiation of this definition notwithstanding. But he promptly undermines this assertion by noting that '[t]here is profitable and appearance of profit', intimating that the 'just man' who engages in political activity because he sees and identifies the good cannot rightfully be condemned by laws which support the partial, or misidentified, interest of the ruling part:

And as well may the ruling part command that which is not his profit, as the just man may for his just and true meaning who would amend that which is amiss, and help the common wealth, and do profit unto it. For in as much as he attempteth to do contrary to the Law which is already put, he be by the law justly condemned. If he be to be accounted justly condemned who is condemned for doing contrary to the law and the ordinance of that part which doth command.[35]

Similarly, although he acknowledges that 'it is always a doubtful and hazardous matter to meddle with the changing of the laws and government, or to disobey the orders of the rule or government, which a man doth find already established' – a resonant remark for the 1580s – his

---

[34] Ibid., p. 56.   [35] Ibid., pp. 49–50.

failure to advance the other side of the case strongly implies that the 'good and upright man, and lover of his country' will do just that:

So when the common wealth is evil governed by an evil ruler and unjust (. . . which be rather sickness of a politic body than perfect and good [estate]) if the laws be made, as most like they be always to maintain that estate: the question remaineth whether the obedience of them be just, and the disobedience wrong: the profit and conservation of that estate right and justice, or the dissolution: and whether a good and upright man, and lover of his country ought to maintain and obey them, or to seek by all means to dissolve and abolish them. Great and haughty courages hath taken one part and this made *Dion* to rise against Dionysius, and Thrasibulus against the XXX tyrants, Brutus and Cassius against Caesar, and hath been cause of many commotions in common wealths, whereof the judgment of the common people is according to the event and success: of them which be learned, according to the purpose of the doers, and the estate of the time when present.[36]

Throughout his treatise Smith also characterises the *respublica anglorum* as potentially socially inclusive, reflecting the reformation conviction that the light of the Gospel would create 'new men' throughout all ranks of the reforming commonwealth. Like other commonwealth spokesmen in Elizabeth's reign, he therefore considers social mobility (within limits) as a laudable product of England's increasing 'wealth' – of Christian virtue as well as of material prosperity. This increasing stock of virtue has transformed the social order by freeing the class of men who, because of their status as bondmen, stood outside the 'mutual society' of the commonwealth. Nowadays 'so few [bondmen] there be, that it is not almost worth the speaking',[37] because men have recognised their Christian obligations:

[H]owbeit since our Realm hath received the Christian religion which maketh us all in Christ brethren, and in respect of God and Christ *conservos*, men began to have conscience to hold in captivity and such extreme bondage him whom he must acknowledge to be his brother, and we use to term even Christian, that is, who looketh in Christ and by Christ to have equal portion with men in the Gospel and salvation.[38]

---

[36] Ibid., pp. 51–2.
[37] Ibid., p. 136. Smith also gives a more conventional account of the role of 'bondmen', in Book I. 10, pp. 57–8. In his introduction to the *DRA*, Alston suggests Smith is demonstrably wrong in the assertion I quote here, and attributes his fabrication to his 'patriotic bias' (p. xxxix).
[38] *DRA*, p. 136. I take Smith to use *conservos* here to mean that under the Christian dispensation, and especially in the godly nation, all men are equally servants (or subjects) of God and Christ, and find a powerful collective identity in that relationship. In the closing years of the century, Tommaso Campanella used the word *concives* to make a similar case. Campanella argued that Aristotle's conception of citizenry is irredeemably pagan in its elitism and hence not suitable as a model for Christian communities. He makes the case in part by drawing on St Paul (I Corinthians 12: 12–26), using the metaphor of the human body to insist on the necessary

In this spiritualised context 'more civil and gentle means and more equal' have been found to allow for the maintenance of order, in a Christian commonwealth in which virtue and obedience have replaced earlier bonds of subjection and servitude. The plenitude of virtue also explains why gentlemen can be made 'good cheap' (in William Harrison's words) in England:

> But as other common wealths were fain to do, so must all princes necessarily follow, where virtue is to honour it: and as virtue of ancient race is easier to be obtained, for the example of the progenitors, for the ability to give to their race better education and bringing up for the enraced love of tenants and neighbours to such noblemen and gentlemen, of whom they hold and by whom they do dwell. So if all this do fail (which it is great pity it should) . . . the prince and common wealth have the same power that their predecessors had, and as the husbandman hath to plant a new tree where the old faileth, to honour virtue where he doth find it, to make gentlemen, esquires, knights, barons, earls, marquises, and dukes, where he seeth virtue able to hear that honour or merits, to deserve it.[39]

Smith's equation of rank with virtue is noteworthy, characteristic of this first phase of Protestant apologetic, and far removed from the conventional interpretation of him as both describing and celebrating a static, intensely hierarchical social order.

Similarly, Justices of the Peace are drawn from the ranks of what Smith calls 'the nobility, higher and lower': an extensive social category that includes not only dukes, marquises and barons but also knights, esquires, gentlemen and 'such as be learned in the laws'. Although chosen by the prince, they in effect claim the office as due them through their political capacity, acquired 'either by increase of riches, learning, or activity and policy and government'. According to Smith, this explains why the recent English past (dates unspecified) has seen the number of JPs in each shire increase by a factor of ten – 'So many more being found, which have either will or power, both to manage and handle the affairs of the common wealth.'[40]

At other points there is detectable tension in Smith's attempt to use the language of classical antiquity to describe the godly nation. His contradictory discussion of the extent to which **all men** are included in the body politic (as we shall see, he specifically excludes women) can be

participation of all parts (including women) – under the headship of the pope. The members of the body envisaged in these Christian terms are, he says, '*concives*'. See John M. Headley, 'On Reconstructing the Citizenry: Campanella's Criticism of Aristotle's *Politics*' in *Church, Empire and World: The Quest for Universal Order, 1520–1640*, Variorum Collected Studies Series (Aldershot, Hants., 1997), pp. 29–41, p. 35.   [39] *DRA.*, p. 71.   [40] Ibid., pp. 103–4.

taken as indicating that his reading is confused in a way characteristic of apologetical discourse of the 1560s. For example, looking in the direction of the Roman republics to describe 'the fourth sort of men which do not rule' (Book I.24), Smith identifies a class equivalent to the 'Roman *capite censii proletarii* or *operae*, day labourers, poor husbandmen, yea merchants or retailers which have no free land, copyholders, all artificers as tailors, shoemakers, carpenters, brickmakers, bricklayers, masons, &c'. These men 'have no voice nor authority in our common wealth, and no account is made of them but only to be ruled, not to rule others'. But he then promptly contradicts himself, describing them as capable of holding offices even including that of constable – which, as he notes elsewhere, carries authority analogous to that which the pre-eminently just men, the Justices of the Peace, currently hold:

[Y]et [these men] be not altogether neglected. For in cities and corporate towns for default of yeomen, they are faine to make their inquests of such manner of people. And in villages they be commonly made Churchwardens, alecunners, and many times Constables, which office toucheth more the common wealth, and at the first was not employed upon such low and base persons.[41]

Elsewhere he seems to think of this fourth sort as incorporated with the yeomanry – which he presents as an honourable estate – and therefore represented through them.[42] This reading allows him to see such men as not participating directly in the political affairs of the realm, yet contributing to a political association – parliament – that embodies 'the most high and absolute power of the realm' because it draws on the virtue of the nation, the 'common doing' of godly Englishmen:[43]

[41] Ibid., pp. 76–7, 110. Patrick Collinson (*'De Republica Anglorum': Or, History with the Politics Put Back*, Inaugural Lecture, 9 November 1989 (Cambridge, 1990), p. 34) notices this paradox and ascribes it to Smith's snobbishness.

[42] For comparison see the handling of the yeomanry in the *Discourse of the Commonweal of this Realm of England* (presumed author Sir Thomas Smith; ed. Mary Dewar (Charlottesville, Va., 1969)), discussed in chapter 3 above.

[43] There is therefore a significant resemblance between Smith's understanding of parliament and the one advanced by John Hooker in the *Order and Usage* of 1572; see chapter 5 above. Both also reflect John Ponet's influence. I take issue with John Guy's view that Smith lacked Hooker's urge to assimilate the metaphor of 'counsel' to schemes for limited responsible government, making parliament 'virtually an expression of the royal prerogative' ('The Rhetoric of Counsel in Early Modern England' in *Tudor Political Culture*, ed. Dale Hoak (Cambridge, 1995), pp. 292–310, p. 303). Instead, see Brian Levack's 'The Civil Law, Theories of Absolutism, and Political Conflict in Late Sixteenth- and Early Seventeenth-Century England' in *Law, Literature, and the Settlement of Regimes*, ed. Gorden Schochet, The Folger Institute Center for the History of British Political Thought Proceedings, vol. 2 (Washington, D.C., 1990), pp. 29–48, pp. 35–6, for the view that Smith's musings led in the direction of a doctrine of parliamentary rather than royal sovereignty – and for the intimation that he might have been aware that this was where he was heading.

For every Englishman is intended to be there present, either in person or by procuration and attorneys, of what pre-eminence, state, dignity, or quality soever he be, from the Prince (be he king or queen) to the lowest person of England. And the consent of the Parliament is taken to be every man's consent.[44]

In describing relations between the elite and the commonalty in this godly commonwealth Smith clearly assumes that deference will operate. The commonalty will display their capacity for political virtue by recognising magistrates' commitment to the common weal and voluntarily remaining in obedience to the laws by which it is expressed and maintained. But in terms of relations among elite males he proposes an egalitarian model of political association, predicated on their equality as 'brothers in Christ'. This is apparent in one of the most significant passages in the book, in Book II.19, when he describes how prince, councillors and Justices of the Peace combine to reform the will of the 'popular'. (Here he shifts gears again, to read the *populus* in more conventional terms as threatening civil order.)

And commonly every year, or each second year in the beginning of summer or afterwards, (for in the warm time the people for the most part be more unruly) even in the most calm time of peace, the prince with his council chooseth out certain articles out of penal laws already made for to repress the pride and evil rule of the popular, and sendeth them down to the justices, willing them to look upon those points, and after they have met together and consulted among themselves, show to order that matter most wisely and circumspectly, whereby the people might be kept in good order and obedience after the law, to divide themselves by three or four: and so each in his quarter to take order for the execution of the said articles. And then within a certain space to meet again and certify the Prince or his privy council how they do find the shire in rule and order touching those points and all other disorders.

So far, so conventional: the prince gives life to the laws through consultation with his councillors and delegation to the lesser magistrates in the localities, who represent the princely authority in their office. At one level Smith clearly sees the exercise in this light. One reason for its efficacy is that the people 'see the chief amongst them . . . to have this special charge' from the prince. But it is interesting that the laws are those that have already been made, presumably in parliament: it is a 'new furbishing of the good laws of the realm' that the prince and his *synarchoi* are engaged in. The clear implication is that the 'just men' – now an association of prince, councillors and justices – decide which those are with reference to the common weal (and common law). And justices, as Smith has informed us, represent a fluid social category composed of men who hold office because of their personal virtue as much as because it is the king's will. In effect the 'just men' so defined are declaring the common law in a consensual and collective activity that Smith sees as uniquely English, necessary to the maintenance of the commonwealth, and always threatened by the tyrannical (or *politique*) proclivities of the prince (by this point in the discussion 'king or queen'):[45]

> There was never in no common wealth devised a more wise, a more dulce and gentle, nor a more certain way to rule the people . . . But as the invention of this, and the use and execution thereof is the most benefit that can be devised for the common wealth of England: So when it shall be misused, dissembled with, or be contemned, and come to be done *pro forma tantum*, and as they term it in France *par mainere d'acquit* only, it will be the present ruin (though not at the first apperceived) of the commonwealth. Of which the fault may be as well in the commanders for not making good choice what and how they command, as in the commanded, for not executing that which is commanded.[46]

This passage should be paired with Smith's earlier chapter (Book I.7) contrasting a king with a tyrant, where the king's share in law-making is to provide equity to fulfil the common law, and where common consent also has a substantial role to play in the legitimation of the monarch. And here, as we might expect, the *populus* again signifies a virtuous collective assembly whose preservation justifies the role of king:

> Where one person beareth the rule they define a king, who by succession or election commeth with the good will of the people to that government, and doth administer the common wealth by the laws of the same and equity, and doth seek the profit of the people as much as his own. A tyrant they name him, who by force commeth to the monarchy against the will of the people, breaketh laws already made at his pleasure, maketh other without the advice of the people, and regardeth not the wealth of his people but the advancement of himself, his faction, and kindred . . . Some men do judge the same of the kings of France . . . because that they make and abrogate laws and edicts, lay on tributes and impositions of their own will or by their private council and advice of their friends and favourers only, without the consent of the people. The people I do call that which the word *populus* doth signify, the whole body and the three estates of the common wealth: and they blame Louis XI for the bringing the administration royal of France, from the lawful and regulate reign, to this

---

[45] Compare James I on the king's role in making law: 'The King, he is the maker of [the laws] and you [parliament] are the advisors, councillors, and confirmers of them'; House of Commons, *Commons Debates, 1621*, ed. Wallace Notestein, F. H. Relf and H. Simpson, 7 vols. (New Haven, Conn., 1935), vol. II, p. 4.   [46] *DRA*, pp. 106–7.

absolute and tyrannical power and government. He himself was wont to glory and say, he had brought the crown of France *hors de page*, as one would say out of wardship.[47]

The reference to Louis XI is particularly revealing, given contemporary interpretations of this historical figure by 'resistance theorists', English, Scottish and French. As Adrianna Bakos has shown, in pamphlet literature of the 1560s and 1570s Louis XI not only symbolised the inherent flaws of monarchical government, but also, in the role of a modern-day Nimrod, dramatised the degraded position of a people that has shirked its rights and responsibilities as a sovereign community.[48]

Smith therefore describes his *respublica anglorum* as a Christian commonwealth in which 'virtue', hence some kind of civic capacity, is potentially accessible to all men (but not women), albeit differentially distributed roughly according to social standing – more precisely, in line with the social standing of men of true zeal and Protestant conviction. It is a realm in which order and degree emanate from the collective will of all men: the *populus*, who compose the 'whole body and the three estates of the common wealth'. His inability to attribute a stable identity to the *populus* is, I think, evidence of the difficulties inherent in the task he has set himself: of describing the 'mixed monarchy' brought into existence with the accession of a queen to the imperial crown.

QUEENSHIP IN THE COMMONWEALTH

What, then, of women, and more specifically the queen? Like Laurence Humphrey's, Smith's reading of England as simultaneously an aristocratic republic and a monarchy represented an innovative attempt to accommodate female rule. He too, like John Aylmer, highlighted the consensual and collective aspects of English governance as a means of guarding against the tyrannical potential of a female ruler while attempting to secure monarchical authority. In a work so intent on **describing** how 'England standeth and is governed at this day the 28 of March *Anno* 1565 in the 7th year of the reign and administration thereof by the most virtuous and noble Queen Elizabeth, daughter to King Henry the eighth', it is striking how little direct reference there is to queenship. Indeed, as Leonard Alston noticed, when Smith first comes to use the word 'monarch' in definite relationship to the king or queen of

---

[47] Ibid., pp. 53–4.
[48] Adrianna Bakos, *Images of Kingship in Early Modern France: Louis XI in Political Thought 1560–1789* (New York, 1997), esp. pp. 28–38.

England, in Book II.3, 'he finds it necessary to draw attention to fact he is doing so, as if this were in some degree a debatable point'.[49]

If we have to wait until this point in the text to find a definite reference to queenship in England, however, the ground for reading a female monarch as 'prince' –'the head, life and governor of this common wealth' – has already been well prepared in Book I, in the course of his general discussion of commonwealths.[50] The consideration of female rule in this first section, when his focus is on the historical origins of the commonwealth and before he turns his attention to England, allows him to outline the terms upon which a female ruler can be accommodated within the English polity as he describes it.

In Book I, Smith is quite categorical that women, like bondmen, can play no public role in the commonwealth.

In terms of civic capacity [only] freemen be considered . . . as subjects and citizens of the commonwealth, not bondmen who can bear no rule or jurisdiction over freemen, as they who be taken but as instruments and of the good and possessions of others. And in this consideration also we do reject women, as those whom nature hath made to keep home and to nourish their family and children, and not to meddle with matters abroad, nor to bear office in a city or common wealth no more than children and infants.[51]

It is all the more striking, given his attention to bondmen freed by the incursion of grace into the English commonwealth, that he makes no analogous move with regard to female rule in Book II.[52] Seemingly, for Smith, Elizabeth is a Tudor first and foremost, which makes her identity as 'Deborah' – a providentially legitimated ruler – of secondary importance. Instead, Smith makes his case for the legitimacy of female rule on

---

[49] *DRA*, ed. Leonard Alston, introduction, pp. xxiii–xxiv. Earlier, in Book 1.24, at the very end of his discussion of the ranks and degrees of the commonwealth, Smith refers to queenship in a passage rendered ambiguous by the handling of the trinities he invokes: 'Wherefore generally to speak of the common wealth, or policy of England, it is governed, administered and manied [maintained?] by three sorts of persons, the Prince, Monarch, and head governor, which is called the king, or if the crown fall to a woman, the Queen absolute, as I have heretofore said [although, as Alston notes, he hasn't]: In whose name and by whose authority all things be administered'; *DRA*, p. 77. [50] *DRA*, p. 88. [51] Ibid., pp. 64–5.
[52] Smith defines 'king' as follows: 'That which we call in one syllable king in english, the old english men and the Saxons from whom our tongue is derived to this day calleth in two syllables *cyning*, which whether it cometh of *cen* or *ken* which betokeneth to be able or to have power, I can not tell. The participle absolute of the one we use yet, as when we say a cunning man, *Vir prudens aut sciens*: the verb of the other as I kan, and in some places and in the older language, I kon do this, *possum hoc facere*'; *DRA*, p. 56. He does not claim that 'queen' is simply a linguistic equivalent, although this would be a logical place to do so. William Fleetwood followed the same etymology but went on to assimilate 'queen' to 'king' in this way in the *Itinerarium ad Windsor*, purporting to record a conversation between himself, Leicester and Buckhurst in the early 1570s; BL Harleian MS. 6234, fols. 10r–25v, fol. 20v.

the basis of perpetuity, political stability, and the 'marriage' of blood to counsel:

except in such case as the authority is annexed to the blood and progeny, as the crown, or duchy, or an earldom for there the blood is respected, not the age nor the sex. [In such cases women or children have the same authority in the role 'as they should have had if they had been men of full age'.] For the right and honour of the blood, and the quietness and surety of the realm, is more to be considered, than either the base age as yet impotent to rule, or the sex not accustomed (otherwise) to intermeddle with public affairs, **being by common intendment understood, that such personages never do lack the counsel of such grave and discreet men as be able to supply all other defaults.**[53]

Like John Aylmer in his *Harborowe for Faithfull and Trewe Subjects*, Smith looks to the household for a model of woman's role in the common- wealth in a way that relates directly to his endeavour to legitimate female rule.[54] Unlike Aylmer he does not advance St Paul's ruling that women can 'govern men in the house' as justification for their capacity for autonomous rule when their rule is manifestly ordained by God. He refuses to engage with the possibility of such autonomous capacity, just as he avoids recourse to the notion of a direct providential sanction. Instead he proposes marriage as a God-ordained model of office-hol- ding in which male and female conjointly exercise rule, metaphorically describing the relationship between queen and counsel that will make of the queen a 'prince':

So nature hath forged each part to his office, the man stern, strong, bold, adventurous, negligent of his beauty, and spending. The woman weak, fearful, fair, curious of her beauty and saving. Each of them excelling other in wit and wisdom to conduct those things which appertain to their office, and therefore where their wisdom doth excel, therein it is reason that each doth govern.

(His depiction of this 'natural' order also constitutes an implicit refuta- tion of the point so effectively developed by the resistance theorists: that a king, and even more a queen, is 'singular' in the exercise of political authority and hence always potentially or actually a tyrant.)

In the house and the family, therefore, we find a political model that incorporates women's capacities, if it denies them political virtue, and preserves hierarchy and degree:

[53] *DRA*, pp. 64–5, my emphasis. See Constance Jordan, 'Women's Rule in Sixteenth Century British Political Thought', *Renaissance Quarterly* 40, no. 3 (1987), pp. 421–51.
[54] Donald Kelley (*The Beginning of Ideology*, p. 71) rightly argues that conceptions of the family were fundamental to social and political theory and that intellectual historians (among others) have not fully acknowledged this centrality. See above, chapter 2, for Aylmer's attempt to legitimate female rule by fusing commonwealth and providential sanctions.

So in the house and family is the first and most natural (but a private) appearance of one of the best kinds of a common wealth, that is called *Aristocratia* where a few and the best doth govern, and where not one always: but sometime and in some thing one, and sometime and in some thing another doth bear the rule. Which to maintain for his part God hath given to the man greater wit, bigger strength, and more courage to compel the woman to obey by reason or force, and to the woman beauty, fair countenance, and sweet words to make the man to obey her again for love. Thus each obeyeth and commandeth other, and they two together rule the house . . . The house I call here the man, the woman, their children, their servants bond and free, their cattle, their household stuff, and all other things, which are reckoned in their possession, so long as these remain together in one . . . [Y]et this cannot be called *Aristocratia*, but *Metaphorice*, for it is but an house, and a little spark as it were like to that government.[55]

Elizabeth's own use of this conjugal constitutional paradigm infused it with sexual and amatory overtones, as Donald Kelley has noted – the genesis of the 'love tricks' which James Harrington saw as a powerful means by which she compensated for the political weakness of her position.[56] For the conjugal model, reinforced with the vocabulary of neoplatonic courtly love, allowed for an 'absolutist' image of counsellors', and especially courtiers', relations with the queen.[57] But this was image only, and only in the context of a 'mixed monarchy' in which political virtue continued to be a male preserve, whether expressed through collective counsel or martial exploits. For Smith, the queen 'wrapped up'[58] in this way with her counsellors is the necessary precondition for the *respublica anglorum* – the common doing of godly Englishmen – that he goes on to describe in Books II and III.

The necessity of legitimating a female ruler thus led Smith to 'feign' a commonwealth, his protestations to the contrary notwithstanding. In

[55] *DRA*, p. 59.
[56] Donald Kelley, 'Elizabethan Political Thought' in *The Varieties of British Political Thought, 1500–1800*, ed. J. G. A. Pocock (Cambridge, 1993), pp. 47–79, pp. 51–2.
[57] David Norbrook, *Poetry and Politics*, p. 118. James VI faced a particularly intractable problem with regard to his use of this language when he attained the English throne, especially because of its associations with England as a reformed realm in which, as Smith claimed, bonds of virtue and obedience replaced those of subjection and servitude. James wanted and needed to assert his political virility – yet in so doing he could be seen as claiming rights by conquest at odds with England's godly (and historical) status. See for example Lord Thomas Howard's letter to John Harington of 1611: 'You have lived to see the trim of old times, and what passed in the queen's days: These things are no more the same; your queen did talk of her subjects' love and good affections, and in good truth she aimed well; our king talketh of his subjects' fear and subjection, and herein I think he doth well too, as long as it holdeth good.' ('*Nugae Antiquae*': *Being a Miscellaneous Collection of Original Papers in Prose and Verse*, ed. Henry Harington (London, 1775), p. 126).
[58] John Stubbs's phrase, used to slightly different effect in his *Gaping Gulf*; see above, chapter 1.

Smith's commonwealth, male consensus was the order of the day at all social levels, meaning 'counsel' spoke with one voice to articulate the 'common weal' to the queen. And in the monarchical element of the *respublica anglorum* the 'prince' is a king, unless specifically counterindicated. When it is counterindicated, we can generally substitute 'crown', an office in the commonwealth, for 'king or queen', to see how Smith understands the continuity of regal majesty in a mixed monarchy headed by a queen. The evidence suggests that Smith, like François Hotman, wanted to identify 'majesty', or sovereignty, as a quality divorceable from the person of the prince. Instead he depicts it as inhering in the body politic – a capacity which can, *pars pro toto*, be represented by parliament, by the prince, or by the judicial manifestation of the Privy Council, the Star Chamber.[59]

The Star Chamber, for example, he describes as being unique, its like not to be found in any other country. Composed of the Lord Chancellor, lords and other members of the Privy Council, other lords and barons and the judges of England, it is peculiarly well equipped to deal with 'riot' – an occupational disease of the great men of the country. If the riot is proved,

> [the accused] must appear in this star chamber, where seeing (except the presence of the prince only) as it were the majesty of the whole realm before him, being never so stout, he will be abashed: and being called to answer (as he must come of what degree soever he be) he shall be so charged with such gravity, with such reason and remonstrance, and of those chief personages of England, one after another handling him on that sort, that what courage soever he hath, his heart will fall to the ground.[60]

He also made the Court of Star Chamber more broadly representative of the nobility than it had actually become, suggesting that it was composed of 'as many as will' of the Privy Council as well as other lords and barons, when he must have known that its restricted membership had been contested by the Earl of Hertford as recently as 1563.[61] And this of course was an issue of political moment, when Privy Councillors

[59] What Francis Bacon called this 'confusion of tongues' meant (as Ernst Kantorowicz notes) that 'notions such as Crown, kingdom, body politic of either the realm or the king as King were used interchangeably and often inefficiently distinguished'; *The King's Two Bodies: A Study in Medieval Political Theology* (Princeton, N.J., 1957), pp. 447–8. This was a productive ambiguity under a female ruler.   [60] *DRA*, p. 126.

[61] John Guy, 'The Privy Council: Revolution or Evolution?' in *Revolution Reassessed: Revisions in the History of Tudor Government and Administration*, ed. Christopher Coleman and David Starkey (Oxford, 1986), pp. 59–86, pp. 81–2.

were unrepresentative of the old nobility, in terms of their social status and religious identity.

Similarly his description of the 'marvellous good order' which prevails in the House of Commons gives us an egalitarian assembly in which collective reason is exhibited through a 'perpetual oration'. In this idealised location, the Speaker symbolises parliament itself; he is 'as it were the mouth of them all', in an assembly so virtuous that degree has been forsworn:[62]

In the disputing is a marvellous good order used in the lower house. He that standeth up bareheaded is understood that he will speak to the bill. If more stand up, who that first is judged to arise, is first heard, though the one do praise the law, the other dissuade it, yet there is no altercation. For every man speaketh as to the speaker, not as one to another, for that is against the order of the house. It is also taken against the order, to name him whom you do confute, but by circumlocution, as he that speaketh with the bill, or he that spake against the bill, and gave this and this reason, doth not satisfy but I am of the contrary opinion for this and this reason. And so with perpetual oration not with altercation, he goeth through til he do make an end . . . So that in such a multitude, and in such diversity of minds, and opinions, there is the greatest modesty and temperance of speech that can be used.[63]

He also deliberately glosses over the relationship of the Speaker to the crown – another explicitly political issue, as we saw in the 1572 parliamentary debates – intimating that the best-qualified candidate assumes the role in a mystical process that 'the prince's will' contributes to but does not cause. MPs 'are willed [presumably by Privy Councillors] to choose an able and discreet man to be as it were the mouth of them all, and to speak for and in the name of them, and to present him so chosen by them to the prince'.[64] (By 1589, in contrast, the third edition of the *De Republica* – published twelve years after Smith's death, although still as if written and amended by him alone – asserted that the Speaker is 'appointed by the King or Queen, though accepted by the assent of the House'.[65])

Finally, it is significant that his chapter on parliament, represented as the 'most high and absolute power of the realm of England' because it denotes the common consent of the nation, is the point at which the 'prince' is explicitly identified as potentially a queen:

For every Englishman is intended to be there present, either in person or by procuration and attorneys, of what pre-eminence, state, dignity, or quality

[62] Vernon Snow, *Parliament in Elizabethan England: John Hooker's 'Order and Usage'* (New Haven, Conn., 1977), pp. 168–9.   [63] *DRA*, p. 82.   [64] Ibid., p. 80.
[65] *DRA*, ed. Leonard Alston, p. 154.

soever he be, from the **Prince (be he king or queen)** to the lowest person of England. And the consent of the Parliament is taken to be every man's consent.[66]

His subsequent description of monarchical authority – in Book II.3, 'Of the Monarch King or Queen of England' – occurs **after** his chapters on parliament, a location that entitles us to read the prince as 'the life, the head and the authority of all things that be done in the realm of England' insofar as he (or she) is ruling *politice* – as the mystical head of the body politic. Smith therefore refers 'majesty' to the office of the prince as representing the body politic. It is the office, not the person, to whom Englishmen give their reverence. He also implies that only Englishmen can comprehend, hence attain to, this level of abstraction, with its concomitant potential for civic virtue:

> To be short the prince is the life, the head and the authority of all things that be done in the realm of England. And to no prince is done more honour and reverence than to the **king and queen of England**, no man speaketh to the prince nor serveth at the table but in adoration and kneeling, all persons of the realm be bareheaded before him: insomuch that in the chamber of presence where the cloth of estate is set, no man dare walk, yea though the prince be not there, no man dare tarry there but bareheaded. This is understood of them of the realm: for all strangers be suffered there and in all places to use the manner of their country such is the civility of our nation.[67]

DE REPUBLICA ANGLORUM AND THE 1580S

Sir Thomas Smith died in 1577. After that, his book took on a life of its own. The first printed edition of *De Republica Anglorum* that survives appeared in 1583, six years after his death, and featured changes to the text that Smith himself is unlikely to have made.[68] An amended version of the *Discourse of the Common Weal* also appeared in print at this time, a conjunction that leads Mary Dewar to posit Sir Thomas Smith as its author. Dewar also advances a simple answer for the appearance in print of these two canonical commonwealth texts. She hypothesises that the manuscripts came into the possession of Sir Thomas Smith's nephew, William Smith, who published them both, after first revising the *Discourse* to take account of events in Elizabeth's reign, and specifically the recoinage of 1560–1.[69]

[66] *DRA*, p. 79.   [67] Ibid., p. 88, my emphasis.
[68] Mary Dewar argues there is 'overwhelming' textual evidence that Smith himself did not correct, revise or amend the *De Republica* in any way (*Sir Thomas Smith*, pp. 110–14).
[69] See Dewar's preface to her edition of *A Discourse of the Commonweal of This Realm of England*, p. xviii.

This is plausible as far as it goes, but it does not go far enough, especially in view of the significance of these two texts in their earlier incarnations in manuscript as exemplars, respectively, of the Edwardian commonwealth and the Elizabethan mixed monarchy. It does not explain the editorial care taken with the text of the *De Republica* in its first three print editions, or the increasingly dogged attribution of the whole work to 'Sir Thomas Smith, Knight, Doctor of both lawes, and one of the principall Secretaries unto two most worthy Princes, King Edward and Queen Elizabeth'. Clearly the anonymous editor[70] of the 1583 edition went over Smith's text with a fine tooth comb, making multiple changes on every page, and it is therefore odd that his name did not appear on the title page. The 1589 edition (now, in English, *The Common-Wealth of England*) moved even further from the manuscript version, introducing revisions designed to address the issue of law and monarchical authority directly and taking Elizabeth's queenship as a given. Moreover, in tenor and at points in substance the 'new additions' it contained contradicted aspects of Smith's manuscript text – yet the book continued to be presented as if it were entirely written by Sir Thomas Smith.[71]

How then are we to understand the meaning of the *De Republica Anglorum* as it circulated in the 1580s? I think we need to see its publication history as evidence of a strategy adopted at this point by the queen and her councillors. They sought to proselytise for the mixed monarchy as the regime moved inexorably in a *politique* direction to protect itself against the threat to its authority posed by Catholicism at home and abroad and by 'faction' (now 'Puritans') in league with Protestant brethren, especially in the Netherlands. It did so in the wake of political developments of the 1570s, which, as we saw, dangerously destabilised the mixed monarchy by increasingly self-conscious appeals to the godly commonwealth latent within it.

In particular, from the mid-1570s those developments allowed for the emergence of the notion of conscience as a key term in political debate. Stuart E. Prall argues that it was Christopher St Germain who, during Henry VIII's reign, introduced the word 'conscience' into English legal vocabulary, hence political discourse, as a means of 'bridling' the

---

[70] Or editors – Leonard Alston suggests that the 1584 edition may have had a different editor; *DRA*, ed. Alston, p. lii.
[71] Leonard Alston also repudiates the attribution to Smith on stylistic grounds; *DRA*, ed. Alston, pp. 148, 151.

imperial king.[72] Under a female ruler, and largely owing to the exertions of the resistance theorists, 'conscience' acquired a particular valence as a correlative of (male) political virtue and therefore as a capacity that was simultaneously individual and collective.[73] 'Conscience' could be conceived of as representing 'the nation' or 'the country', and standing in opposition to a 'politic' hierarchy seduced and corrupted by the queen. In Elizabeth's reign this point had demonstrably been reached by 1576, the year which witnessed Peter Wentworth's famous parliamentary oration on 'free speech' and, from a different direction but in the same terms, Archbishop Grindal's refusal to enact the queen's will in suppressing prophesyings. By this point both 'free speech', as Wentworth used the term, and prophesyings symbolised manifestations of the collective wisdom of the realm informed by grace – and stymied by the queen. Yet the language of providential legitimation – God working through His handmaid, Elizabeth – remained the most effective means of mobilising support for a regime increasingly narrowly based and unrepresentative, under a queen increasingly regarded as at best an equivocal Deborah, at worst a tyrant.[74]

In these circumstances *De Republica Anglorum* spoke to the attempt on the part of Privy Councillors (and the queen) to position their government as both godly and the sole support of order, to harness 'zeal' to the constraints of 'policy'. This marriage occurred as political necessity forced first the regime, and eventually the queen herself, to adopt ever more radical expedients to preserve the mixed monarchy. The most radical expedient of all was the regime's recourse to the 'commonwealth' as an acephalous body politic – the common doing of godly men – as a means of enacting 'justice' against Mary Queen of Scots, in the first instance regardless of its consequences for (Elizabeth's) monarchical authority. This stance was signalled initially by the Bond of Association of 1584, which encouraged 'all [male] subjects . . . to prosecute to the death, as far as lay in their power, all those that should attempt any thing against the Queen'.[75]

It is not coincidental that the Bond, presented as emanating from the will of 'the nation', brought in its wake the most intensive undertaking on the part of Burghley and his colleagues to establish interregnal conciliar structures in which power would emanate from the acephalous

---

[72] Stuart E. Prall, 'The Development of Equity in Tudor England', *American Journal of Legal History* 8 (1964), pp. 1–19, p. 3.   [73] See above, chapter 3.

[74] Patrick Collinson, *The Birthpangs of Protestant England*, pp. 25–7; John Guy, 'The 1590s', p. 16.

[75] William Camden, *The History of the Most Renowned and Victorious Princess Elizabeth Late Queen of England* (London, 1615), ed. Wallace T. MacCaffrey (Chicago, 1970), pp. 170, 190.

body politic to preserve the offices of the crown in the event of the queen's death. It is noteworthy, for example, that Thomas Digges's treatise outlining plans for a 'Grand Council' to govern in conjunction with parliament in the event of Elizabeth's death – described by Digges as 'a cause to immortalize your Majesty's fame and renown with all posterity, being the first Estate Royal that ever in England established so rare a provision' – was endorsed by Burghley: 'Mr. Digges discourse upon the Association.'[76] In its rhetoric the Bond attempted to square another circle: to appropriate the powerful image of God's persecuted people, generalise it to 'the nation', and assimilate it to a male hierarchical structure symbolised by, but not including, the queen. This was a position forced on the queen's councillors by her refusal to accede to legislation condemning Mary Queen of Scots to death for treason in 1572, and the resulting failure of the political nation to carry its point in parliament during the 1570s.

And what of the queen's role with regard to the Bond of Association? Elizabeth professed to know nothing about it until a copy of it reached her in 1586 – coincidentally when, engaged in the same game but at a different political moment, she sought to preserve her monarchical authority by securing Mary Stuart's assassination rather than her public execution. Was the Bond then an occasion, like others earlier in the reign, when Elizabeth's councillors acted to mobilise the political nation in their capacity as godly Englishmen, on her behalf and against her will, in the hope that the resulting political pressure would persuade her to adopt a course of action they deemed necessary to the state? This is the interpretation that Patrick Collinson advances. He notes that Walsingham inserted the following into the form letter declaring allegiance to the Bond drafted by Burghley and suggests readers should substitute 'we would' for 'her majesty would' to unlock the full meaning of the text:

Your lordship shall not need to take knowledge that you received the copy from me, but rather from some other friend of yours in these parts: for that her Majesty would have the matter carried in such sort as this course held for her [safety] may seem to [come more] from the particular care of her well affected subjects than to grow from any public direction.[77]

But a convincing case can be made that in this instance Walsingham's insertion can be taken, if not quite at face value, at least as pointing to a

[76] J. E. Neale, *Elizabeth I and Her Parliaments*, 2 vols. (London, 1957), pp. 45–8; Michael Pullman, *The Elizabethan Privy Council in the 1570s* (Berkeley, Calif., 1971), p. 242.
[77] Patrick Collinson, 'The Monarchical Republic of Queen Elizabeth I', *Bulletin of the John Rylands University Library of Manchester* 69, no. 2 (1986–7), pp. 394–424, p. 416.

collusive relationship between the queen and her Privy Councillors in
the realm of policy that became a feature of English politics in the 1580s,
as the queen and her councillors closed ranks to ensure Mary Queen of
Scots' death – 'extinction', in the words of contemporaries – **and** the
maintenance of monarchical authority. Arguably, by 1584 Elizabeth
herself had determined that Mary posed too great a threat to her own
tenure of the English throne to be allowed to live, because of the threat
of deposition by her Protestant subjects mobilising to secure the godly
commonwealth.[78] Mary's agent Englefield certainly saw the Bond of
Association as signalling the regime's intention to 'take away [Mary's]
life', and he specifically associated Elizabeth with her councillors'
intention:

[I]t is to be considered, that the queen of England and her council, having first,
by printed libels, published the queen of Scotland to be a confederate practiser
[in a treasonable conspiracy] against the queen and the realm of England;
having also contrived and set forth a new form of *association* or *confederacy*,
whereby all men shall swear and subscribe to resist and pursue all that shall
pretend a right in succession in the crown of England; and now lastly, having
changed the place of her abode and keepers, by removing her from the custody
of the earl of Shrewsbury, and putting her into the hands of base and obscure
heretics . . . it is by these doings very probable, and in effect manifest to such as
have had experience of the English government, that the queen and council of
England have made a secret resolution, not only to deprive and disinherit the
said queen of Scotland, but also to ruin her person, and take away her life.[79]

From at least 1584, if not earlier, Elizabeth must have been engaged
in complex negotiations with her Privy Councillors as to how that
high-risk political outcome, the necessity for which they could agree on,
could be achieved in a form satisfactory to their different political
agendas. In these negotiations the Bond of Association had an important role to play. From Elizabeth's point of view, it suggested a means by
which Mary could be assassinated by a private association of men

---

[78] In 1579 Elizabeth evidently believed that the attempt to link her proposed marriage to the duc
d'Anjou with the establishment of the succession had her deposition as a hidden agenda.
According to the Spanish ambassador, Mendoza, she 'ha[d] been given to understand that as
soon as a successor is appointed they will upset her'; *Calendar of State Papers, Spanish, 1568–79*, pp.
692, 703, cited in Blair Worden, *The Sound of Virtue: Philip Sidney's 'Arcadia' and Elizabethan Politics*
(New Haven, Conn., 1996), p. 184.

[79] John Strype, *Annals of the Reformation and Establishment of Religion . . . during Queen Elizabeth's Happy
Reign*, 7 vols. (Oxford, 1824), vol. III.i, p. 359. Ambassadors during Elizabeth's reign were aware
that their intentions could diverge and of the resulting power dynamic. According to Michael
Pulman, the Spanish ambassador de Spes reported on one occasion that Elizabeth had been
overruled by a unanimous council; and in 1603 the Venetian ambassador complained that
'[t]hese lords of the council behave like so many kings'; *The Elizabethan Privy Council*, pp. 238,
209–10.

without her own direct involvement, thereby preserving (her) kingly majesty, albeit at the risk of depicting her as impotent in the exercise of her queenship.[80] For the queen and her councillors – the government – it represented a means of focusing the support of 'the nation' on the queen – without explicit reference to providential rhetoric. The risk here was that the task – the protection of one queen through the destruction of another – would unleash levelling propensities in the body politic, or, despite that omission, at least make the pressure for a full and godly reformation unstoppable. For Elizabeth's godly council-lors, headed by Burghley and Walsingham, the Bond of Association represented the first stage in their long-term strategy to insist that Mary's trial and execution must be 'public': conducted, and seen to be conducted, by the majesty of the 'state', the three estates embodied in parliament.[81] The risk here was and remained, until the point when William Davison forced (?) the queen's hand by delivering Mary's signed execution warrant to the Privy Council, that Elizabeth would withdraw from the agreement. They feared, rightly, that she would continue to hold out for – indeed invite – a private resolution to the matter in the form of assassination, even having accepted the premise that political necessity made Mary's death imperative. For if Elizabeth's survival, political or physical, required Mary's 'extinction', she clearly feared that the monarchical principle that she embodied would not survive Mary's execution at the instigation of the state.[82]

There was, inevitably, signal continuity between the politics of the Bond of Association and those that led to the trial and execution of Mary Queen of Scots in 1586–7. In both, the queen's role was similarly equivocal. In 1586, Elizabeth first publicly recognised the existence of the Bond of Association, now a useful counter in her attempt to secure Mary's 'private' assassination rather than a public execution. At the same time she broke with precedent by not attending the opening of the 1586 parliament, summoned specifically to arrange for Mary's judicial

---

[80] Allison Heisch, 'Queen Elizabeth I: Parliamentary Rhetoric and the Exercise of Power', *Signs: Journal of Women in Culture and Society* 1, no. 1 (1975), pp. 31–55, pp. 46–7.

[81] See J. E. Neale, *Elizabeth I and Her Parliaments*, pp. 114–15, 139–40.

[82] William Camden writes that the following epitaph was set up near Mary's tomb after her execution, and very quickly taken down: 'A princess accomplished with royal virtues and a royal soul, having many times (but in vain) demanded her royal privilege, is by barbarous and tyrannical cruelty extinct . . . and by one the same wicked sentence is both Mary Queen of Scots doomed to a natural death, and all surviving kings, being made as common people, are subjected to a civil death. A new and unexampled kind of tomb is here extant, wherein the living are enclosed with the dead: for know, that with the sacred ashes of saint Mary here lieth violate and prostrate the majesty of all kings and princes'; *The History of the Most Renowned and Victorious Princess Elizabeth*, p. 289.

execution – perhaps in an attempt to render its proceedings illegitimate by 'uncoupling' herself from her counsellors. Instead the crown went into commission, in effect, when a committee of three Privy Councillors (including Burghley) deputised on her behalf. Significantly, they omitted to mention the usual limitations placed on the privilege of free speech to the assembled MPs, an omission that, given the parliamentary history of the 1570s, amounted to a coded appeal to MPs to bring their consciences to bear upon the matter in hand.[83] The queen's absence allowed the male political nation to enact justice without mercy, hence civic virtue uninformed by a monarchical prerogative – mercy – claimed by Elizabeth and vouchsafed her, as monarch, by John Aylmer's reading of the mixed monarchy in 1559 and disallowed in the parliamentary debates of the 1570s.

   This reading of the evidence gains additional support from the behaviour of the queen and her councillors at this climactic moment of Elizabeth's reign. In the run-up to the execution, Elizabeth first sought to amend the petition of both houses calling for Mary's death (drafted by Burghley) to include a reference to the Bond of Association. When this failed she tried to manipulate the men she claimed as her 'creatures' – Leicester and Whitgift – to argue the case for murder to Burghley and Walsingham.[84] When that failed, when once again, as in 1572, she found herself stymied by a solid front among her councillors, she appealed to William Davison to break ranks and do the deed himself. According to J. E. Neale, at least three times Elizabeth spoke to him 'of a course [murder] that had been propounded unto her by one of great place'. When he argued the councillor line, she told him that 'wiser men than he were of another opinion', a strategy she had adopted in the 1570s and similarly to no avail.[85] Most revealing of all is the interpretation of Mary's execution that Burghley provided after the event, in a letter to James VI's councillors warning against James's plans for revenge. For in this action, the acme of commonwealth ideology in Elizabeth's reign, 'the state', not the queen, had been God's instrument:

he taking arms against this realm in revenge of an action so necessarily done by general consent, for the safety of her majesty's person and this state, and

---

[83] J. E. Neale, *Elizabeth I and Her Parliaments*, p. 106.
[84] Robert P. Shephard, 'Royal Favorites in the Political Discourse of Tudor and Stuart England', Ph.D. Dissertation, Claremont Graduate School, Calif. (1985), p. 149.
[85] J. E. Neale, *Elizabeth I and Her Parliaments*, pp. 114–15, 139–40. I am following Neale's account, but I disagree with his conclusion that Elizabeth was led to this position by irresponsible councillors (p. 105).

accompanied with that justice, as all the world may be judges of the honourable and upright proceedings used in that behalf. It can no way be avoided, but he must be said to oppose himself to the course of justice; and so consequently to the judgment of God himself, **whose minister this state was in the execution thereof.**[86]

As I suggested in chapter 1, the Bond should be read as drawing on, if not responding to, Thomas Sampson's 'book', written at the same time, which proposed a '*holy league* with the living God . . . to be entered into, both by prince and people', with the specific object of overriding 'politic laws' (including manifestations of the queen's will) that would allow for Mary's succession, even her continued survival.[87] The regime's strategy therefore entailed endeavouring to appeal to a higher law without promoting what had hitherto been its concomitant, commitment to fundamental ecclesiastical reform – a prospect that, by this point, threatened political revolution. Once Mary's execution had been secured, the exigencies of this position required a complex, and high-risk, renegotiation of the basis of the mixed monarchy. It entailed presenting the queen as the symbolic embodiment of Protestant England, she and it as threatened by faction and sedition (the province of minorities) both within and without the realm, and responding to the **necessity** this position imposed. This move heralded the 'increasingly claustrophobic atmosphere' of the latter stages of Elizabeth's reign, dominated by plots, conspiracies and repression, as well as the emergence of the notion of political necessity as a higher law: *necessitas non habet legem.*[88]

CONCLUSION

As I have argued above, Smith's original text was by no means as narrowly descriptive of Tudor customs and institutions as later historians have assumed. It derived quite specifically from the 'commonwealth' attempt to accommodate a female ruler which characterised apologetics of the 1560s. But because of the radicalisation of English politics that had occurred in the 1570s, Smith's weighting of hierarchical and egalitarian elements in his *respublica* could be used to support the *politique* (and repressive) renegotiation of commonwealth ideology which

[86] John Strype, *Annals*, vol. iii.i, p. 549, my emphasis.
[87] Thomas Sampson, *A supplication, to be exhibited to our sovereign lady, queen Elizabeth, to the honourable lords of her most honourable privy-council, and to the high court of the parliament* (1584), in John Strype, *Annals*, vol. iii.ii, pp. 284–5.   [88] John Guy, 'The 1590s', p. 18.

dominated the last decades of Elizabeth's reign. This transformation explains its print career – when Smith's *respublica anglorum* was presented as the official version of the English commonwealth – as well as Gabriel Harvey's reference to the battlefield of England in the 1590s as 'Smith's state'. It provides a classic example of 'text as event' which J. G. A. Pocock has described.[89]

By the 1580s, legitimating the mixed monarchy no longer entailed defining England as a sovereign nation of godly men bridling a queen through commitment to the imperial crown, although that intention and reading of their role remained paramount among old guard Privy Councillors. Instead a new political alignment emerged, the product of the unstable marriage between two reactive strands among the elite. Each proposed an alternative conception of sovereignty and the crown. One asserted the sovereign capacity of the crown, defined in aristocratic terms as an association of the few, explicitly or implicitly allied against the demotic potential of the many, a conception that allowed for the naturalisation of divine right and absolutist conceptions of monarchy.[90] The other argued the case for godly councillors playing a *politique* role at the level of the crown, on behalf of a 'state' composed of godly men whose political virtue was displayed by their loyalty to the queen: the 'mixed monarchy' as it was played out in the second reign. In its official capacity, the *De Republica* formed part of the defence of 'policy' as providence acting through the queen and her (godly) councillors, exclusively defined – a move that buttressed monarchical authority as the preserver of degree, monarchical as a species of aristocratic authority, and that ushered in the culture and politics of the last years of the reign.

Couched in the language of the 1560s, Smith's text played a useful role in advancing this new conception, because it presented England as both commonwealth and kingdom. It therefore exhibited traits that made it fruitfully ambiguous in the 1580s. Smith's recourse to republican rather than providential language as a means of legitimating female rule allowed 'conscience' to be redefined as the recognition by virtuous men of their civic responsibilities, on behalf of the queen and her

---

[89] Texts 'act upon the languages in which they are performed: as they perform they inform, injecting new words, facts, perceptions, and rules of the game; and, whether gradually or catastrophically, the language matrix becomes modified by the acts performed in it'; J. G. A. Pocock, 'Texts as Events: Reflections on the History of Political Thought' in *Politics of Discourse: The Literature and History of Seventeenth Century England*, ed. Stephen N. Zwicker and Kevin Sharp, (Berkeley, Calif., 1987), pp. 21–34, p. 29.

[90] J. P. Sommerville, 'Richard Hooker, Hadrian Saravia, and the Advent of the Divine Right of Kings', *History of Political Thought* 4 (1983), pp. 229–45.

councillors.[91] Secondly, Smith's uncertainty about the social boundaries of the commonwealth – a common feature of apologetical works of the 1560s – meant that his *respublica* could be read as exclusive (an aristocrat republic) and inclusive (a godly nation). Like many other cultural products of the 1580s, including the Bond of Association itself, the print editions of the *De Republica* exploited ambiguities available in the language of 'common weal' to encourage an equal commitment on the part of all men to the godly nation – but a godly nation now presented as in existence, under threat, and represented by the image of the queen.[92]

In these reinterpretations, of course, Smith himself had no role to play. He stood instead as an exemplar of the godly and patriotic councillors whose commitment to the common weal ensured a right relationship with king, country and the law. As such he could symbolically represent Elizabeth's councillors of the 1580s and 1590s – increasingly disparaged as 'favourites', sycophants dependent on the erratic will of a tyrannical queen – who claimed to be his political heirs. In its print career it equally represented a move away from the notion of parliament as the location and visible expression of royal majesty – a quality pertaining equally to the realm and the ruler – which had been allowed for in Smith's original work and explored and exploited in the radical context of the 1570s.

The shift is well exemplified in what Mary Dewar acknowledges to be one major change between the manuscript and 1583 print edition of the *De Republica*. It occurs in Book II.2, 'The Form of Holding the parliament', when Smith gives an account of the Chancellor's words on the last day of parliament. The manuscript version suggests a mystical union between the prince and the body politic, such that the prince becomes participant and executor of the collective reason arrived at through the 'perpetual oration' that is parliament:

[He] sayeth that the Prince hath well viewed and weighed what hath been moved and presented and debated amongst the Lords and them [the Commons] and thereupon will show his mind that the doings might have perfect life and accomplishment by his princely authority, and so have the whole consent of the realm.[93]

But by 1583 the 'Prince' is an autonomous agent whose will (guided by his councillors) enacts, and in so doing perfects, the common wisdom of the realm. The printed edition reads:

[91] See, for example, George Whetstone's *The English Myrror* (London, 1586), especially p. 199.
[92] For the terms 'inclusive' and 'exclusive' see Richard Helgerson, *Forms of Nationhood*, pp. 8–9.
[93] *DRA*, p. 84.

and that he for his part is ready to declare his pleasure concerning their proceedings, whereby the same may have perfect life and accomplishment by his princely authority, and so have the whole consent of the realm.[94]

The new status of the *De Republica* – indeed the attempt to redefine the articulation and enactment of the 'common weal' as the prerogative of the queen (and her councillors) – was not uncontested. The ways in which it was contested provide further evidence for the reading I have advanced here. In closing I want to point to two instances where the contest was made explicit. The first occurred as part of the struggle between common law and prerogative courts to appropriate 'conscience' in the form of equity which developed in the late 1580s.[95] At this point a debate arose over equity: the right to enlarge or restrict the letter of the law (that is, statute law) in order to enact perfect justice. Christopher St Germain had introduced the concept of equity in his analyses of the nature of law and the role of the Chancery at the time of the Henrician Reformation; Edmund Plowden had argued in the early years of Elizabeth's reign that the common law tradition equally admitted of equitable principles. Both men can be seen as attempting, in an imperial England, to define true justice as something other than merely the will of the king.[96] (It was in this context that St Germain introduced the word 'conscience' into English legal vocabulary.[97])

By the late 1580s, the location of equity had become a political issue, as a result of the growing antagonism between common law and prerogative jurisdictions. The common law position – set out by Edward Hake in *'Epieikeia': A Dialogue on Equity in Three Parts* – was that, because the common law itself was founded on equity, the Chancery's unique distinction was not that it was a court of equity, but rather that it was a prerogative court. In that court the Chancellor acted for the prince as 'keeper of the King's conscience', as Christopher Hatton defined himself in 1587.[98] But Hake regarded this connection less as ensuring perfect justice than as a means through which the monarch exercised a purely personal power: 'For in the help which the Chancery giveth, the decree

---

[94] *DRA*, Dewar's 'Introduction', p. 16.
[95] A contest possibly inaugurated in the parliament of 1584 where, according to William Camden, some MPs 'proposed a new oath to be taken by the bishops in the Chancery and the King's Bench, viz that they should act nothing contrary to the common law of England'. Camden leaves it open as to whether they acted in the interest of 'innovation or reformation' (*The History of the Most Renowned and Victorious Princess Elizabeth*, p. 190).
[96] John Guy, *Christopher St German on Chancery and Statute* (London, 1985).
[97] Stuart E. Prall, 'The Development of Equity in Tudor England', pp. 14, 3.
[98] Edward Hake, *'Epieikeia': A Dialogue on Equity in Three Parts* (London, 1587?), ed. D. E. C. Yale, with preface by Samuel E. Thorne (New Haven, Conn., 1953), see Thorne's preface, pp. vii–viii.

or sentence thereof is compulsory *ad personam* and not *ad rem*, as at the common law it is . . . It bindeth not the right but bindeth the person to obedience.' His discussion throughout makes it clear not only that he is aware of the political and constitutional issues at stake in the definition of equity but also that, as Prall concludes, he actually regards Chancery as the place 'where the prince ruled through his conscience in the absence of law'.[99]

In pursuit of his quarry, Hake cited Sir Thomas Smith as an example of an authority who had got it wrong:

> Sir Thomas Smith . . . in his book [*De Republica*] . . . doth make mention of diverse exceptions of the civil law as *metus, doli male, minoris aetatis*, etc. All which when they shall happen with us (sayeth he) we must be holpen therein by the Lord Chancellor, whom he resembleth to the Praetor in the old civil law, even as though the help of those matters were so lacking in our written law as that the same were not supplied by the *epieikeia* of the same law. But the professors of our common law do well know that in every of those cases of exception as in infinite others the law alloweth several pleas, as *infancy, coverture, non compos mentis, threats, duress, nient lettered, averment de fraude*, etc.[100]

But was he reacting to the 1565 version of the *De Republica*? Or was he drawing attention the to 'new additions' of 1589, which explicitly referred 'absolute' law to the person of the prince, so that he could refute them?[101] In 1565 Sir Thomas Smith had identified English common law as equivalent to *jus civile* in other kingdoms, and saw the Chancellor as the 'just man' whose conscience would follow the law, in this point manifestly occupying the same ideological terrain as St Germain and Plowden:

> To the . . . question of the chancery, this I answer: That our law which is called of us the common law as ye would say *Jus civile*, is and standeth upon . . . *Jus summum*: and their maxims be taken so straitly that they may not depart from the tenor of the words even as the old civil law was. And therefore as that lacked the help of a *Praetor* (which might *moderari illud jus summum*, give actions where none was, mitigate the exactness and rigour of the law written, give exceptions, as *metus, doli mali, minoris aetatis*, &c. for remedies, and maintain always *aequum & bonum*): the same order and rank holdeth our chancery, and the chancellor hath the very authority herein as had the *Praetor* in the old civil law before the time of the Emperors . . . And for so much as in this case he is without remedy in the common law, therefore he requireth the chancellor according to equity and

---

[99] Ibid., p. 126; Stuart E. Prall, 'The Development of Equity in Tudor England', p. 18.
[100] Edward Hake, *Epieikeia*, pp. 50–1.
[101] Leonard Alston notes that these additions were printed in the 1589 edition but appear to have been composed earlier in the decade.

reason to provide for him and to take such order as to good conscience shall appertain. And the court of the chauncery is called of the common people the court of conscience, because that the chancellor is not strained by rigour or form of words of law to judge but *ex aequo* and *bono*, and according to conscience.[102]

In 1565 Smith could assume the Chancellor would enact equity with regard to the common law because he could not imagine that the Chancellor might become (or be perceived to be) a favourite of the queen, hence an adjunct to her will.[103] Yet this was the situation that had arisen with Christopher Hatton's appointment to that position in 1577, a situation seemingly reflected in the 'new additions'. In the 1589 edition of the *De Republica* – still attributed to Sir Thomas Smith – this passage is directly followed by an assertion that perfect equity, hence justice, resides in the conscience of the prince and is voiced by the Chancellor in Chancery, the court of his/her conscience:

Out of this court, as from the person of the Prince come all manner of original writs ... The matter in this court are all causes wherein equity and extremity of law do strive and where the rigour of laws have no remedy, but conscience and the moderation of *Summum jus* hath sufficient. And here it is to be noted, that conscience is so regarded in this court, that the laws are not neglected, but they must both join and meet in a third, that is, in a moderation of extremity.[104]

Finally – and here we can see commonwealth ideology eliding into a potentially radical oppositional stance – there is the case of William Harrison's use of Smith in the 1587 version of his *Description of England*, included in the edition of Holinshed's *Chronicles* of that year. Here we can see an attempt to reassert the role of parliament as the locus of grace in the godly nation by drawing on commonwealth ideology of the 1560s and 1570s. In 1587 Harrison inserted a new chapter, 'Of the High Court of Parliament and Authority of the Same', into his *Description of England*, a chapter that he claimed was largely taken from Sir Thomas Smith's *De Republica*. In fact, as Annabel Patterson has shown, the passages differ crucially, in ways that suggest that Harrison might have wanted to draw attention to the ambiguities of Smith's work, exploited by the regime in the 1580s, in order to force a reconsideration (a reformation?) of the conflation of commonwealth and kingdom at its heart.[105] Smith had opened his chapter, the first of the second book, with the announcement that '[t]he most high and absolute power of the realm of England, is in

[102] *DRA*, pp. 93–4.   [103] See Robert P. Shephard, 'Royal Favorites', pp. 113–18.
[104] *DRA*, ed. Alston, p. 156.   [105] Annabel Patterson, *Reading Holinshed's 'Chronicles'*, pp. 103–4.

the Parliament'. He went on to define parliamentary powers, in the course of portraying parliament as 'absolute' because it embodied the consent of the 'whole realm', as an incorporated body:

> The Parliament abrogateth old laws, maketh new, giveth orders for things past, and for things hereafter to be followed, changeth rights, and possessions of private men, legitimateth bastards, establisheth forms of religion, altereth weights and measures, giveth form of succession to the crown, defineth of doubtful rights, whereof is no law already made, appointeth subsidies, tailes, taxes, and impositions, giveth most free pardons and absolutions, restoreth in blood and name as the highest court, condemneth or absolveth them whom the Prince will put to that trial: And to be short, all that ever the people of Rome might do either in *Centuriatis comitiis* or *tributis*, the same may be done by the parliament of England, which representeth and hath the power of the whole realm both the head and the body.[106]

Harrison's 'borrowage' dropped Smith's portrayal of parliament as the visible embodiment of the three estates of the realm, shifting his focus specifically to 'this house' – the House of Commons. As Patterson shows, he gave 'this house' a new first function – that of deposing kings – and, by condensing Smith's long list, 'rendered Parliament's actions more important than those who perform them, more grandly and simply constitutional' ('majestic' would be more apt).[107] He also envisaged parliament in the terms we encountered in John Hooker's *Order and Usage* of 1572: as a body in which the House of Commons could be taken, *pars pro toto*, to represent the assembly and by extension the 'common weal'.[108] Immediately after the phrase 'absolute power', Harrison wrote:

> This house hath the most high and absolute power of the realm, for thereby kings and mighty princes have from time to time been deposed from their thrones, laws either enacted or abrogated, offenders of all sorts punished, and corrupted religion either disannulled or reformed, which commonly is divided into two houses or parts.

Harrison appealed to Smith – by this point dead for ten years – to accuse the regime of declension, of sacrificing 'zeal' to policy in ways that threatened England's godly status. He did so by arguing that he gives the correct reading of the *respublica anglorum*, claiming he copied Smith 'almost word for word', manifest evidence to the contrary. His reading was grounded in the shared perception of England as a commonwealth

[106] *DRA*, pp. 78–9.   [107] Annabel Patterson, *Reading Holinshed's 'Chronicles'*, pp. 103–4.
[108] For Hooker see above, chapter 6.

of grace, which he argues he and Smith and other godly men still in government shared, and which the regime have betrayed:[109]

As Sir Thomas Smith doth deliver and set them down, whose only direction I use, and almost word for word in this chapter, requiting him with the like borowage as he hath used toward me in his discourse of the sundry degree of estates in the common-wealth of England, which (as I hope) shall be no discredit to his travail.[110]

Patterson cannot assess the tone that Harrison adopted to acknowledge his use of Smith's work – whether it is 'testy, joking, or generous'. I would argue it is mildly embittered – the response of a godly Englishman confronting a regime entrammelled in, and seemingly colluding with, the coils of necessity that defined the last decades of Elizabeth's reign. This was the necessity that elevated monarchical authority, even in the person of a queen, and equally disallowed the Christian fellowship that seemed to sustain it, at the beginning of the reign, when both Smith and Harrison described how grace could preserve the *respublica* in order, yet redeem it from degree.[111]

---

[109] This reading is consonant with the depiction of Harrison presented by G. J. R. Parry in *A Protestant Vision* and with Annabel Patterson's explanation for the career of Holinshed's *Chronicles* in its 1587 version in her *Reading Holinshed's 'Chronicles'*, to which I am obviously very much indebted. The 1587 version of the *Chronicles* occupies much the same ideological terrain as Smith's *De Republica*. Its strange career in the late 1580s, which Patterson draws attention to, speaks partly to the fact that its authors were, like Harrison, determined to express their sense of the regime's declension, but were, unlike Smith, able to revise their text to update the code in which they did so. The censorship farrago of 1587 also shows how difficult it was for Privy Councillors themselves to determine the acceptable overlap between that earlier ideological configuration and the defence of policy they were committed to in the 1580s. Patterson is quite right to argue the reasonableness of the Privy Council's action in attempting to revise the text in a way that would make it suitable for their purposes. But where she sees 'inefficacy', in its 'failure to notice those parts of the project prior to the "Continuation" that were equally obnoxious to governmental policy and prestige' (pp. 238–9), I see evidence of their own profound ambivalence.

[110] Annabel Patterson, *Reading Holinshed's 'Chronicles'*, p. 103.

[111] It is important to bear in mind that Harrison himself, like other godly Englishmen, could shift his ground when it appeared men of 'zeal' became antinomian, the province of men who 'will obey no law at all' and who therefore jeopardised the existence of an ordered society. Parry (*Protestant Vision*, pp. 169–72) indicates that Harrison reached this point in the 1590s, when he no longer regarded parliament as the consensual focus for the common weal – hence analogous to government in Old Testament Israel – but as the speaking engine of anarchic interests, packed (significantly) with '**young** burgesses, picked out of purpose to serve some secret turn'.

Afterword

> In the span of forty years an individual has been transposed into a symbol.
>
> Roy Strong, *Portraits of Queen Elizabeth I*[1]

Elizabeth's accession to the English throne in 1558 posed a crisis of legitimacy to the English political nation, in large part because of her gender. Henry VIII transformed the meaning of kingship by defining England as an empire and himself (and his assumed successor 'kings of this realm') as Supreme Head of the Church of England, in the larger European context of Protestant reformation. The regnal sequence after his death and before Elizabeth's accession of a boy king and two queens (Lady Jane Grey and Mary I) of disputable legitimacy greatly complicated that legacy. It invested imperial identity – now seen as necessary to secure Protestantism as well as to preserve England's autonomous status as a nation – in weak vessels. That tainted sequence inevitably implicated religious conviction in political ideology in new ways.

At Elizabeth's accession this pre-history made it necessary for the queen and her apologists to innovate in order to legitimate her rule. They did so most obviously by exploiting elements of a conception of imperial rule first adumbrated in Henry VIII's reign: they identified the nation as elect, and appealed to godly men to act as citizens on behalf of the imperial crown.[2] They also followed John Aylmer in defining monarchical authority as 'mixed'. This was the term used to imply that the realm (and Protestantism) would be secured through a marriage of the commonwealth and the person of the ruler at the level of the crown: a marriage symbolised by her (or his) coronation. The exact meaning of this marriage remained undefined, but contentious, as long as what

---

[1] Roy Strong, *Portraits of Queen Elizabeth I* (Oxford, 1963), p. 3, contrasting the 1592 Ditchley portrait with the anonymous portrait of Elizabeth as a young girl.
[2] Quentin Skinner, *The Foundations of Modern Political Thought*, 2 vols. (Cambridge, 1978), vol. II, *The Age of Reformation*, pp. 65–108.

J. G. A. Pocock calls the 'monarchy of counsel' remained in existence.[3] But in Elizabeth's reign the mixed monarchy posited a political configuration in which the virtue of the male political nation could be seen as constraining, with God's oversight and in the interest of England's imperial identity, the tyrannical proclivities of a female ruler.

This model of political engagement succeeded in allowing for forty years of rule by a female monarch. This was no mean achievement in a culture profoundly hostile to the exercise of political authority by a woman. But it simultaneously, and irretrievably, altered contemporary conceptions of monarchical authority in ways that problematised the exercise of imperial kingship by Elizabeth's successors. Above all, it provided the seedbed for the 'explosion of civic consciousness' that J. G. A. Pocock rightly sees, not as a consequence of the English civil wars, but rather as their precedent and precondition.[4] Citizens were indeed 'concealed within subjects', as Patrick Collinson remarks; so were saints.[5] But the concealment remained effectual throughout Elizabeth's reign in large measure because, during that time, men were subject to a woman. It was the fate of Elizabeth's successor kings to preside over a marriage of those distinct identities – one which privileged the citizen over the subject in the service of Christ the King – in sufficient numbers of godly men to make the conduct of monarchy impossible, at least for a time.

Four elements of the creation of the mixed monarchy were particularly significant in defining English political culture during Elizabeth's reign and into the reigns of her Stuart successors. First, recourse to providentialism – God's guiding and sustaining hand immediately manifest in English national history – proved to be the most effective means of legitimating a female ruler by this point in the Tudor succession. Providentialism simultaneously encouraged the articulation of a national Protestant identity that was potentially inclusive in social terms and, as a consequence, a politics rooted in prophetic discourse. In Elizabeth's reign the identities of godly individual and prophet were gendered male, in part (though not exclusively) as a means of controlling their radical implications. England became the Elect Nation, English-

[3] J. G. A. Pocock, 'A Discourse of Sovereignty: Observations on the Work in Progress' in *Political Discourse in Early Modern Britain*. ed. Nicholas Phillipson and Quentin Skinner (Cambridge, 1993), pp. 377–428, pp. 395–6.
[4] J. G. A. Pocock, 'England' in *National Consciousness, History, and Political Culture in Early-Modern Europe*, ed. Orest Ranum (Baltimore, Md., 1975), ch. IV, p. 103.
[5] Patrick Collinson, *'De Republica Anglorum': Or, History with the Politics Put Back*, Inaugural Lecture, 9 November 1989 (Cambridge, 1990), p. 25.

men became 'God's Englishmen' – and Elizabeth became 'Deborah', a profoundly ambiguous and polemically weighted image of monarchical authority.

Secondly, the attempt to legitimate a Protestant queen transformed the 'problem of counsel' – that well-established humanist topic – by infusing the notion of 'counsel' with providential, as well as gender, significance. This transformation of debate about relations between the king and his councillors in a monarchical setting had three main political effects. It tended to detach the role of 'councillor' from moorings in birth or office, by implication its status as a function, directly or indirectly, of the king's will. It simultaneously recalibrated the relative weighting of the monarch's will as against councillors' judgement (at points when these could be seen to conflict) in ways that enhanced, in the first instance, the political status of the Privy Council. It also privileged rectitude – 'godliness', in Protestant parlance – as a key element in determining who should be called to counsel the queen, thereby proposing a model of election at the heart of the imperial crown.

Thirdly, Elizabeth's reign made canonical a gendered reworking of the identity of 'king-in-parliament' advanced by Henry VIII as a means of legitimating his status as imperial ruler. 'Queen-in-parliament', an identity first mooted in Mary I's reign, was not simply its equivalent in the context of a female incumbent of the crown. Instead it developed as a means of conceptualising (and constraining) a female ruler. 'Queen-in-parliament' denoted a mystical marriage celebrated between the queen and her estates at her coronation. This marriage effected the queen's incorporation in a political body signified as male and read as possessing virtue, ambiguously moral and political, sufficient to preserve the realm, and the monarch in a right relationship to it. In Elizabeth's reign, as in Mary's, the doctrine of queen-in-parliament advanced the idea that the crown was a public office ordained to preserve the 'common weal', and focused attention on the crown as separable from the person of the ruler. It also promoted the authority of parliament as a literal manifestation of the nation's body politic, simultaneously producing contested readings – primarily between the House of Lords and the House of Commons, later in the reign between the Houses of Parliament and opinion 'out of doors' – as to which estate voiced the common weal in the godly nation.

Finally, attention to monarchical government at this stage of Protestant reformation, and in the context of female rule, allowed for the return to political significance of a commonwealth ideology recognisably descended from the one that had flourished during Edward VI's reign. Notions of Christian egalitarianism took on new, and gendered, political significance in a godly nation where men might define themselves as having a civic capacity as brothers in the body of Christ, as being God's subjects as well as the queen's, and might see themselves as called by their peers (ambiguously men of virtue or peers of the realm), prophets or brothers – or by God Himself – to political action on behalf of an elect nation that included the queen – whether with or against her will. Inevitably, this configuration led, in England as in her sister nation Scotland, to the perception that a 'commonwealth' and a 'kingdom' might be two different things: that the 'commonwealth' might exist as a potential capacity within the 'kingdom', in the form of godly men whom political necessity might conjoin into a political body charged with preserving the common weal.[6] This political configuration reached its apogee with the 1584 Bond of Association, the means by which godly men from throughout the ranks of the political nation covenanted to preserve the commonwealth from the threat to its existence posed by Mary Queen of Scots. This was a covenant on behalf of the nation and in opposition to the queen's will. It led, in two years' time, to Mary's execution, when Elizabeth at last bowed to political necessity announced and enacted by godly Englishmen as God's will – in the service of the state.

For contemporaries, however, this political configuration proved deeply troubling. At some level it made of the (political) 'body' a 'head': a monstrosity in nature that threatened monarchy itself as well as the maintenance of order and hierarchy. The fears that it engendered are equally part of the political discourse of the reign. They inform especially the politics of reaction which followed the execution of Mary Queen of Scots and which transformed the political landscape in the period after 1585.

The new *status quo* that developed after 1585 is identifiable in the regime's attempt to mobilise support for the imperial crown by translating Elizabeth into a symbol of God's grace made available to the state, and a political agent, as queen, in that role. In this attempt we see a sleight of hand analogous to the indeterminate use of 'Supreme Head' and 'Supreme Governor' in the early years of the reign, this time one that proposed acceptance of Elizabeth as a 'sanctified icon' and Virgin Queen – as a statement of allegiance to the Protestant godly nation and

[6] J. H. Burns, *Lordship, Kingship, and Empire: The Idea of Monarchy 1400–1525*, The Carlyle Lectures, 1988 (Oxford, 1992), pp. 150–1.

the imperial crown.[7] Reaction to the spectre of political radicalism and social instability inherent in the earlier programme dictated that the resulting appeal should be ambiguous. On the one hand it should be couched in such a way that it would appear to be (and at one level would be) inclusive, in motivating Englishmen to embrace an identity as subjects, of the queen and of the crown, and to display this identity through unqualified obedience to the state. On the other hand it should allow scope for the inclusion among the ranks of political actors of men both godly and noble; the latter especially an increasingly contentious term.

The intricacies of this political configuration explain distinctive features of late Elizabethan political culture. There was a peculiar intensity to the disillusionment and self-disgust to which courtiers in the early modern period were 'endemically prone'.[8] Its expression became, in some cases, an oblique means of announcing ideological purity – distinguishing one's zealous soul from the carapace of a *politique* man in the context of the court. The period also witnessed the rise to political significance of the cult of Tacitism and, more generally, the fascination with hidden, emblematic and tacit forms of behaviour that we associate with the period: the idea that reality is covert, masquerades under false pretences and needs to be decoded if its true meaning is to be deciphered.[9] In this age, as Elizabeth told William Lambarde, 'the wit of the fox is everywhere on foot' – an assertion that at this point (and very likely on this occasion) often justified appeals to the triad characteristic of late sixteenth-century European political culture: scepticism, Stoicism and *raison d'état*.[10] Its particular formation, in England, owes much to its genesis in the context of female rule.

Providentialism as a legitimating strategy was not abandoned in the climate of reaction, however. Its persistence is one indication of the continuity in political culture that existed over Elizabeth's reign, as well as the extent to which the innovative became normative by its end. Instead it was used by the government to maintain the 'commonalty' (now distanced from the elite) in obedience to the queen and state –

---

[7] For this sleight of hand see above, chapter 1. Helen Hackett notes, accurately and unsurprisingly, that in Elizabeth's early reign the queen 'applied the iconography of sanctified virginity to herself with more seriousness than did her subjects'; *Virgin Mother, Maiden Queen: Elizabeth I and the Cult of the Virgin Mary* (London, 1995), p. 71.

[8] J. G. A. Pocock, 'A Discourse of Sovereignty', pp. 380–1.

[9] See for example Perez Zagorin, *Ways of Lying: Dissimulation, Persecution and Conformity in Early Modern Europe* (Boston, Mass., 1990), pp. 103–4, 255, 272, 310.

[10] Richard Tuck, *Philosophy and Government 1572–1651* (Cambridge, 1993), p. xiii.

except when it seemed that God might indeed speak in unequivocal terms to His Englishmen, in a language that all men might understand.[11] Then the old relationship, in which God spoke and was interpreted by His Englishmen for the benefit of the nation, could be resumed – as it was to be again, during the English Revolution. This is the thrust of James Aske's expressed reason for writing, in the wake of the Armada triumph of 1588, his *Elizabetha Triumphans* (and one reason for the enormous political significance of that event). At first, 'having intelligence of the commonness of ballads, with books to this purpose, I resolved myself to bestow this my pamphlet on the fire'. But then he realised his duty as a godly man and member of the elite and decided to publish. In other words, he felt he could run the risk of ridicule – 'dispraise' – by his peers for engaging in providential discourse (and in ballad form), secure in the knowledge that God had spoken so resoundingly that both discourse and *genre* could and should be re-appropriated by the elite, instead of 'let[ting] . . . broken tales, told in plain ballads, express the unspeakable acts, and wondrous overthrows had against the Pope by this our royal queen and her (by this made famous) island'.[12]

Efforts to promote loyalty to the state through providential readings of the 'sanctified icon' produced equivocal effects during the latter part of the reign, certainly among the elite. In 1585 William Lambarde, godly man, lawyer and antiquarian, wrote to Burghley urging him and his fellows to discharge their duties as councillors by imparting the spirit of God to Elizabeth 'till she hath yielded to the thing that concerneth her safety and high honour' – becoming the head of the 'poor people' of the Netherlands, 'to beat down the tyranny of Spain'. He suggested that the Protestant stance adopted by the queen (and the regime?) has been nothing but show, in effect a false idol that will no longer effectually conduce to political stability or the maintenance of her 'state'. Her reputation has been 'kept in tune these twenty seven years by one policy': the **appearance** of Protestant rectitude. Now, however, 'the date is out'. She must 'show herself openly', if she is to avoid the fate that befell her sister. Her 'mask' – her appeal to God's providence and reason of state – 'argueth fear and no policy, howsoever it may be covered or pretended'.[13]

And by the 1590s the Cambridge theologian William Perkins found it

---

[11] I am deliberately emphasising 'men' here.
[12] James Aske, *Elizabetha Triumphans* (London, 1588), 'To the Gentle Reader'.
[13] Letter from William Lambarde to Burghley, 1585, in John Nichols, *The Progresses and Public Processions of Queen Elizabeth*, 3 vols. (London, 1823), vol. 3, pp. 554–6.

necessary to write a tract for 'the common protestant', explaining the
differences between 'us and the Church of Rome' – a quite extraordinary necessity, given the sustained attention to publicly defining the
godly nation as the antithesis of the Roman Church which informed
government polemic throughout the reign.[14] Significantly, as Helen
Hackett has shown, Perkins followed this up in a later work by denounc-
ing the Catholic cult of the Virgin Mary (by now resonant in the English
imperial context) as improperly elevating a queen above a king – Mary
over her son Jesus Christ.[15] In the closing years of the reign, then,
Perkins used a gendered image of monarchy to make a Calvinist case
concerning imperial kingship and simultaneously to challenge the
queen and the regime.

The reaction that fuelled the political dynamics of the period after
1585 undoubtedly enhanced Elizabeth's monarchical authority and
hence her political autonomy.[16] It did not, however, eradicate or even
significantly affect the culturally entrenched convictions concerning
female rule, or substantially undermine the 'mixed monarchy' invented
to mitigate their political consequences. After 1585, as from Elizabeth's
accession, protecting the imperial crown continued to be understood as
legitimating and constraining a female ruler, in anticipation of a (godly)
king. Instead, the period of reaction introduced a far more complicated
brand of conviction politics. Most obviously, it brought centre-stage the
attempt to demonise and marginalise Catholics and 'Puritans' as equally
threatening to the queen and to the state – and hence to the godly
nation. This agenda might at first glance look like the one proposed by
Elizabeth to her councillors in 1584, when she argued that religious zeal
of whatever complexion threatened the crown, her monarchical authority and order itself ('I pray you, look unto such men . . . Both these
[Papists and Protestants] join together in one opinion against me, for
neither of them would have me to be Queen of England').[17] This was a
telling assertion, given contemporary fears of social instability. But in
fact the regime's agenda differed signally from the queen's by identifying the state as a means of grace (hence constituting a higher author-

---

[14] William Perkins, *A Reformed Catholike* (London, 1597), quoted in Helen Hackett, *Virgin Mother, Maiden Queen*, p. 202, and discussed by her (pp. 202–6). Hackett suggests (p. 202) that Perkins's work reveals a fear among Puritans in the 1590s that the Church of England was actually 'slipping back towards' the Church of Rome. For Perkins see also G. J. R. Parry, *A Protestant Vision: William Harrison and the Reformation of Elizabethan England* (Cambridge, 1987), pp. 122–4.
[15] William Perkins, *A Warning Against the Idolatrie of the last times* (London, 1601), discussed by Helen Hackett, *Virgin Mother, Maiden Queen*, pp. 202–6.
[16] Wallace MacCaffrey, *Queen Elizabeth and the Making of Policy, 1572–1588* (Princeton, N.J., 1981), pp. 251–2. [17] See above, chapter 1.

ity than the monarch), the state as separable from the person of the monarch, and godly men as those loyal to the queen on its behalf.[18] Common ground between the two agendas therefore positioned the queen and her councillors in an intermittently contested relationship – the same dynamic as had characterised their relationship from her accession, but played out on a different field.

Like Howard Nenner, then, I take issue with J. E. Neale's assertion that Elizabeth's tenure of the imperial crown successfully laid to rest any doubts about the practicability of a female monarch, and that from fairly early in her reign.[19] Neale, although nearer to the mark in his reading of Elizabeth's reign than his best-known critics, was, I think, demonstrably wrong on this point. Far from persuading Englishmen of the acceptability of queenship, Elizabeth's reign actually made the exercise of imperial kingship, even by a fully adult male, intensely problematical. Revising our understanding of the relationship between the queen and her subjects shows that the problem of kingship that emerged under the Stuarts was very directly related to the solutions to the problem of queenship explored during Elizabeth's forty years on the throne.

In this regard James VI and I's actions in 1612 in response to the death of his son and heir, Henry Stuart, are revealing; and particularly striking in view of the fact that he still had another male heir in the person of his son Charles.[20] He first asked parliament to naturalise his son-in-law, the Elector Palatine, a request that, as Nenner notes, implied doubt as to whether his own daughter, Elizabeth (the Elector's wife), would or should take the throne, and whether her place in the succession could be secure without confirming legislation. Moreover, James's request was worded in language that expressed concern specifically for the Elector's issue, rather than Elizabeth's, or the issue of Elizabeth and her husband.

---

[18] It would appear that the exigencies of Elizabeth's position, as a woman and a monarch, allowed her to use the term 'state' in what Quentin Skinner (*Foundations of Modern Political Thought*, vol. II, esp. pp. 352–3, 356–7) calls a 'recognisably modern way' earlier than her male contemporaries. She did so as a concomitant of the sceptical grounds on which she repudiated providentialism as a means to legitimate her rule. The evidence dates from as early as 1559, for example in her annotations of John Knox's letter of that year (BL Add. MS. 32,091, fols. 167–9). What is striking, however, is how limited support for her stance, and her definition, was, even in the period after 1585.

[19] Howard Nenner, *The Right to be King: The Succession to the Crown of England, 1603–1714*, Macmillan Studies in Modern History (New York, 1995), pp. 36–7.

[20] I am attempting not to depict James as an Englishman in recounting this episode, but rather to position him as shaped by the Scottish experience of female rule in the sixteenth century, and as responding to the demonstrable values, beliefs and concerns of his English subjects as he attempted to secure the English crown for the Stuart interest.

It is 'ironic', Nenner says, that 'this most outspoken advocate of inde-
feasible hereditary right [James I] was likely to have compromised his
own daughter's place in the order of the succession', in the interest of
securing England's imperial crown. But I must disagree with his view
that it is 'hard to credit' the obvious conclusion that James would have
welcomed a place in the succession for the issue of the Elector from a
subsequent marriage, even in preference to the heirs of his own blood.[21]
In fact this conclusion is easy to credit once we recognise that James's
quest was for the (preferably legitimate, preferably adult) male offspring
of an adult male ruler – a response to the spectre of female rule as
inevitable in James's reign as it had been at every stage in English history
from Henry VIII's assumption of the imperial crown. And as this
episode suggests, for most Englishmen, queenship remained at the end
of Elizabeth's reign, as it had been from its beginning, an anomalous
condition whose continuance threatened the existence of the godly
nation and the imperial crown, if not that of the state called into being
over the reign to preserve both.

[21] Howard Nenner, *The Right to be King*, pp. 65, 275.

Bibliography

PRIMARY SOURCES

The STC numbers given after certain texts refer to A. W. Pollard and G. R. Redgrave, *A Short-Title Catalogue of Books Printed in England, Scotland, and Ireland, and of English Books Printed Abroad, 1475–1640*, 3 vols., 2nd edn (London, 1976–1991).

Alberti, Leon Battista, *On Painting*, tr. John R. Spencer (New Haven, Conn., 1976).

Aristotle, *The Politics*, ed. Stephen Everson (Cambridge, 1988).

Aske, James, *Elizabetha Triumphans* (London, 1588).

Aylmer, John, *An Harborowe for Faithfull and Trewe Subjects, agaynst the late blowne Blaste, concerninge the Government of Wemen* (Strasbourg, 1559), STC 1004.

Bacon, Sir Francis, 'Sir Francis Bacon His Apologie, in Certaine Imputations Concerning the late Earle of Essex' (London, 1604), in *The Collected Works of Sir Francis Bacon*, ed. James Spedding, 14 vols. (London, 1868), vol. 10, pp. 139–160.

  'Letter of Advice to Queen Elizabeth' (1584?), in *The Collected Works of Sir Francis Bacon*, ed. James Spedding, 14 vols. (London 1868), vol. 8, pp. 47–57.

The Bardon Papers: Documents Relating to the Imprisonment and Trial of Mary Queen of Scots, ed. Conyers Read, Camden Third Series vol. xvii (London, 1909).

Beale, Robert, 'A Treatise of the Office of a Counsellor and Principall Secretarie to her Majestie' (1592), in *Mr. Secretary Walsingham and the Conduct of Elizabethan Foreign Policy*, ed. Conyers Read (Oxford, 1925), vol. 1, pp. 423–43.

Blundeville, Thomas, tr., *A very brief and profitable Treatise declaring how many counsells, and what maner of Counselers a Prince that will govern well ought to have* (London, 1570).

Bullinger, Heinreich, *A Confutation of the Popes Bull* (London, 1572).

Cabala, Sive Scrinia Sacra, Mysteries of State and Government: in Letters of Illustrious Persons and Great Matters of State (London, 1663).

Camden, William, 'Discourse Concerning the Prerogative of the Crown' (1615?), ed. Frank Smith Fussner, 'William Camden's "Discourse Concerning the Prerogative of the Crown"', *Proceedings of the American Philosophical Society* 101 (1957), pp. 204–15.

The History of the Most Renowned and Victorious Princess Elizabeth Late Queen of England, (London, 1615), ed. Wallace T. MacCaffrey (Chicago, 1970).

Cecil, William [presumed author], *The Execution of Justice in England* (London, 1583), in *The Harleian Miscellany*, ed. T. Park and W. Oldys, 12 vol. (London, 1808–11), vol. 1, pp. 490–513.

Certaine Questions Demanded and Asked by the Noble Realm of England, of her true natural children and Subjects of the Same (Wesel, 1555), STC 9981.

Clapham, John, *Certain Observations Concerning the Life and Reign of Queen Elizabeth* (1603), in *Elizabeth of England*, ed. Evelyn Plummer Read and Conyers Read (Philadelphia, 1951).

A Collection of State Papers relating to Affairs in the Reign of Queen Elizabeth, From the Year 1571 to 1596, ed. William Murdin (London, 1759).

The Commentaries and Reports of Edmund Plowden, originally written in French and now faithfully translated into English (London, 1779).

Cowell, John, *The Interpreter* (London, 1607).

Digges, Dudley, *The Compleat Ambassador* (London, 1655).

A Discourse upon the exposition and understanding of Statute (London, 1567–71?), ed. S. Thorne (San Marino, Calif., 1942).

Elizabeth I, *The Letters of Queen Elizabeth*, ed. G. B. Harrison (London, 1935).

Elyot, Sir Thomas, *The Book Named The Governor*, ed. S. E. Lehmberg (London, 1962).

The Image of Governance (1541), in *Four Political Treatises by Sir Thomas Elyot*, ed. Lillian Gottesman, Scholars' Facsimiles and Reprints (Gainsville, Fl.. 1967).

Erasmus, Desiderius, *The Education of a Christian Prince* (1516), tr. Lester K. Born (New York, 1968).

Faunt, Nicholas, 'Discourse Touchinge the Office of Principall Secretarie of Estate etc.' (1592), ed. Charles Hughes, *English Historical Review* xx (1905), pp. 499–508.

Fleetwood, William [presumed author], *Itinerarium ad Windsor*, BL Harleian MS 6234, fols. 10r–25v.

Fortescue, Sir John, *De Laudibus Legum Anglia* (London, 1471), ed. S. B. Chrimes (Cambridge, 1949).

Foxe, John, *Acts and Monuments of these latter and perilous days* (1563), ed. George Townsend, 8 vols. (London, 1843–9).

Gardiner, Stephen [presumed author], *A Discourse on the Coming of the English and Normans to Britain* (1553–5), ed. and tr. as *A Machiavellian Treatise by Stephen Gardiner*, by Peter Samuel Donaldson (Cambridge, 1975).

Geneva Bible, a facsimile of the 1560 edition, ed. Lloyd E. Berry (Madison, Wisc., 1969).

Gilbey, Anthony, *An Admonition to England and Scotland to call them to Repentance* (Geneva, 1558), in *The Works of John Knox*, ed. David Laing, 6 vols. (Edinburgh,1846–64).

Goodman, Christopher, *How Superior Powers Oght to be Obeyed* (1558), The Facsimile Text Society (New York, 1931).

Greville, Fulke, *The Life of Sidney* (London, 1652), in *The Prose of Fulke Greville Lord Brook*, ed. Mark Caldwell (New York, 1987).

Hake, Edward, '*Epieikeia*', *A Dialogue on Equity in Three Parts* (London, 1587?), ed. D. E. C. Yale with preface by Samuel E. Thorne (New Haven, Conn., 1953).

Hales, John, *A Declaration of the Succession of the Crown Imperial of England* (London, 1563).

An Oration of John Hales to the Queenes Majestie, and delivered to her Majestie by a certain Noble man, at her first entrance to her reign (1559?), in John Foxe, *Acts and Monuments of Matters . . . happening in the Church*, 3 vols. (London, 1641), vol. 3, pp. 976–9.

Hall, Arthur, *A Letter on the Origin and Antiquity of Parliament, with Advice to a Member for His Conduct Therein*, (1579), in *Miscellanea Antiqua Anglicana* (London, 1815).

Harington, Sir John, '*Nugae Antiquae': Being a Miscellaneous Collection of Original Papers in Prose and Verse*, ed. Henry Harington (London, 1775).

A Tract on the Succession of the Crown (1602), ed. Clements Markham (London, 1880).

Hentzner, Paul, *Travels in England During the Reign of Queen Elizabeth* (1603?), tr. Horace Walpole (London, 1797).

Hilliard, Nicholas, *A Treatise Concerning the Arte of Limning* (1598?), ed. R. K. R. Thornton and T. G. S. Cain (Ashington, Northumberland, 1981).

Hooker, John, *Order and Usage* (1572), in *Parliament in Elizabethan England: John Hooker's 'Order and Usage'*, ed. Vernon Snow (New Haven, Conn., 1977).

Hotman, François, *Francogallia* (1573), ed. Ralph E. Giesey and J. H. M. Salmon (Cambridge, 1972).

House of Commons, *Commons Debates, 1621*, ed. W. Notestein, F. H. Relf and H. Simpson, 7 vols. (New Haven, Conn., 1953).

Howard, Henry (Earl of Northampton), *Answer to Stubbs' Book against Queen Elizabeth's Marriage with Francis, Duke of Alençon* (1580), in *John Stubbs's 'Gaping Gulf' with Letters and Other Relevant Documents*, ed. Lloyd E. Berry (Charlottesville, Va., 1968), pp. 28–32.

Humphrey, Laurence, *De Religionis Conservatione et Reformatione Vera* (1559), tr. Janet Kemp, Appendix to 'Laurence Humphrey, Elizabethan Puritan: His Life and Political Theories', Ph.D. Dissertation, West Virginia University (1978).

The Nobles or of Nobility. The Original nature, duties, rights, and Christian institutions thereof (London, 1563), STC 13964.

James I, *Basilikon Doron. Or His Majesties Instructions to his dearest sonne, Henry the Prince* (London, 1603), in *The Political Works of James I*, ed. C. H. McIlwain (London, 1965).

Jewel, John, *An Apology of the Church of England* (1564), ed. J. E. Booty (New York, 1963).

Knox, John, *The First Blast of the Trumpet against the monstrous regiment of Women*

(1558), ed. Edward Arber (London, 1878).

History of the Reformation in Scotland (1566), in *The Works of John Knox*, ed. David Laing, 6 vols. (Edinburgh, 1846–64).

The Political Writings of John Knox: The First Blast of the Trumpet Against the Monstrous Regiment of Women and Other Selected Works, ed. Marvin A. Breslow (Washington, D.C., 1985).

The Works of John Knox, ed. David Laing, 6 vols. (Edinburgh, 1846–64).

Lambarde, William, *Notes on the Procedures and Privileges of the House of Commons* (1587), ed. P. L. Ward (London, 1977).

'Archeion' or, a Discourse upon the High Courts of Justice in England (London, 1635), ed. Charles H. McIlwain and Paul L. Ward (Cambridge, Mass., 1957).

Law and Politics in Jacobean England: The Tracts of Lord Chancellor Ellesmere, ed. Louis A. Knafla (Cambridge, 1977).

Leicester's Commonwealth: The Copy of a Letter Written by a Master of Art of Cambridge (1584) and Related Documents, ed. D. C. Peck (Athens, Ohio, 1985).

Leslie, John, bishop of Ross [pseud. Morgan Philippes], *A Treatise Wherein is Declared, that the Regiment of Women is conformable to the lawe of God and Nature* (London, 1571), STC 15506.

A Treatise of Treasons against Queene Elizabeth, and the Crowne of England (Louvain, 1572), STC 7601.

Lodge, Edmund, *Illustrations of British History, Biography and Manners in the Reigns of Henry VIII, Edward VI, Elizabeth and James I*, 3 vols. (London, 1791).

Merbury, Charles, *A Briefe Discourse of Royal Monarchie, as of the Best Common Weale* (London, 1581), STC 17823.5.

Mulcaster, Richard, *The Quenes Maiesties Passage through the Citie of London to Westminster the Day before her Coronation* (London, 1559), ed. James M. Osborn (New Haven, Conn., 1960).

Naunton, Sir Robert, *'Fragmenta Regalia'; being A History of Queen Elizabeth's Favourites* (Edinburgh, 1808).

Nichols, John, *The Progresses and Public Processions of Queen Elizabeth*, 3 vols. (London, 1823).

Parker, Matthew, *Correspondence*, ed. J. Bruce and T. Berowne (Cambridge, 1853).

Patrizi, Francesco, *A Moral Methode of civile Policie . . . Abridged oute of the Comentaries of the Reverende and famous clerke, Franciscus Patricius, Byshop of Caieta in Italye*, tr. Richard Richard (London, 1576), STC 19475.

Perkins, William, *A Reformed Catholike* (London, 1597).

A Warning Against the Idolatrie of the last times (London, 1601).

Policies to reduce this realm of England unto a prosperus wealthe and estate (1549), in *Tudor Economic Documents*, 3 vols., ed. R. H. Tawney and E. Power (London, 1924), vol. 3, pp. 311–45.

Ponet, John, *A Shorte Treatise of politike power, and of the true Obedience which subjects owe to kings and other civil Governours, with an Exhortacion to all true naturall Englishmen* (1556), in *The English Experience*, no. 484 (Amsterdam, 1972).

Proceedings in the Parliaments of Elizabeth I, vol. 1: *1558–1581*, ed. T. E. Hartley

248 *Bibliography*

(Leicester, 1981).

Puritan Manifestos: A Study of the Origin of the Puritan Revolt, ed. W. H. Frere and C. E. Douglas (London, 1907).

Raleigh, Sir Walter, *Maxims of State* (London, 1651).

Seyssel, Claude de, *The Monarchy of France* (1519), tr. J. H. Hexter, ed. Donald R. Kelley (New Haven, Conn., 1981).

Shakespeare, William, *King Richard II* (1595), ed. Andrew Gurr (Cambridge, 1984).

    King Henry V (1599), ed. Andrew Gurr (Cambridge, 1992).

Sidney, Sir Philip, *Miscellaneous Prose*, ed. Katherine Duncan-Jones and Jan Van Dorsten (Oxford, 1973).

    The Complete Works of Sir Philip Sidney, ed. Albert Feuillerat (Cambridge, 1968).

Smith, Sir Thomas, *De Republica Anglorum* (1565; London, 1583), ed. Leonard Alston (Cambridge, 1906).

    De Republica Anglorum (1565; London, 1583), ed. Mary Dewar (Cambridge, 1982).

    Dialogue concerning the Queen's marriage (1560), in John Strype, *The Life of the Learned Sir Thomas Smith* (Oxford, 1820), Appendix III, pp. 187–259.

    [presumed author] (1549), *A Discourse of the Commonweal of This Realm of England*, ed. Mary Dewar (Charlottesville, Va., 1969).

Starkey, Thomas, *An Exhortation to the People* (London, 1536).

Staunford, Sir William, *Exposition of the King's Prerogative* (London, 1567), STC 23213.

Strype, John, *Annals of the Reformation and Establishment of Religion and other various occurrences in the Church of England during Queen Elizabeth's Happy Reign; together with an appendix of original papers of state, records and letters*, 7 vols. (Oxford, 1824).

    The Life of the Learned Sir Thomas Smith (Oxford, 1820).

Stubbs, John, *The Discoverie of a Gaping Gulf Whereinto England is like to be Swallowed by an other French mariage, if the Lord forbid not the banes . . .* (1579), in *John Stubbs's 'Gaping Gulf' with Letters and Other Relevant Documents*, ed. Lloyd Berry, (Charlottesville, Va., 1968).

A Treatise concerning suits in the Chauncery by Subpoena, in *A Collection of Tracts Relative to the Law of England, from Manuscripts*, ed. Francis Hargrave (Dublin, 1787).

A Treatise of the Maisters of the Chauncerie, in *A Collection of Tracts Relative to the Law of England, from Manuscripts*, ed. Francis Hargrave (Dublin, 1787).

Tudor Constitutional Documents 1485–1603, ed. Joseph Robson Tanner (Cambridge, 1940).

Tudor Royal Proclamations, ed. Paul L. Hughes and James F. Larkin, vol. II (New Haven, Conn., 1969).

Tudor Tracts 1532–1588, ed. A. F. Pollard (London, 1903).

Whetstone, George, *The English Myrror* (London, 1586).

SECONDARY SOURCES

Adams, Simon, 'Eliza Enthroned? The Court and Its Politics' in *The Reign of*

Elizabeth I, ed. Christopher Haigh (London, 1984), pp. 55–78.
'The Protestant Cause: Religious Alliance with the European Calvinist Communities as a Political Issue in England, 1585–1630', D.Phil. Dissertation, Balliol College, Oxford (1972–3).
Alford, Stephen, 'William Cecil and the British Succession Crisis of the 1560s', Ph.D. Dissertation, University of St Andrews (1996).
Alsop, J. D., 'The Act for the Queen's Regal Power, 1554', *Parliamentary History* 13, no. 3 (1994), pp. 261–76.
'Innovation in Tudor Taxation', *English History Review* 99, no. 390 (1984), pp. 83–93.
Alvin, John and West, Thomas G., eds., *Shakespeare as Political Thinker* (Durham, N.C., 1981).
Amussen, Susan Dwyer, *An Ordered Society: Gender and Class in Early Modern England* (New York, 1988).
'"The Part of a Christian Man": The Cultural Politics of Manhood in Early Modern England' in *Political Culture and Cultural Politics in Early Modern England: Essays Presented to David Underdown*, ed. Susan D. Amussen and Mark A. Kishlansky (Manchester, 1995), pp. 213–33.
Anglo, Sydney, 'Crypto-Machiavellism in Early Tudor England: The Problem of the *Ragionamento dell'advenimento delli Inglesi, et Normani in Britannia*', *Renaissance and Reformation* 14, no. 2 (1978), pp. 182–93.
Images of Tudor Kingship (London, 1992).
Spectacle, Pageantry and Early Tudor Policy (Oxford, 1969).
Archambault, Paul, 'The Analogy of the "Body" in Renaissance Political Literature', *Bibliothèque d'Humanisme et Renaissance* 29 (1967), pp. 21–53.
Art and History: Images and Their Meaning, ed. Robert I. Rotberg and Theodore K. Rabb (Cambridge, 1988).
Aston, Margaret, *The King's Bedpost: Reformation and Iconography in a Tudor Group Portrait* (Cambridge, 1993).
Axton, Marie, *The Queen's Two Bodies: Drama and the Elizabethan Succession* (London, 1977).
Bakos, Adrianna, *Images of Kingship in Early Modern France: Louis XI in Political Thought 1560–1789* (New York, 1997).
Bann, Stephen, *The Invention of History: Essays on the Representation of the Past* (Manchester, 1990).
Barrell, John, *The Political Theory of Painting from Reynolds to Hazlitt: 'The Body of the Public'* (New Haven, Conn., 1986).
Barroll, Leeds, 'The Court of the First Stuart Queen' in *The Mental World of the Jacobean Court*, ed. Linda Levy Peck (Cambridge, 1991), pp. 191–208.
Baskerville, E. J., 'John Ponet in Exile: A Ponet Letter to John Bale', *Journal of Ecclesiastical History* 37, no. 3 (1986), pp. 442–7.
'A Religious Disturbance in Canterbury, June 1561: John Bale's Unpublished Account', *Historical Research: The Bulletin of the Institute of Historical Research* 65, no. 158 (1992), pp. 340–8.
Basnett, Susan, *Elizabeth I: A Feminist Perspective*, Berg Women's Series (Oxford,

1988).

Bates, Catherine, *The Rhetoric of Courtship in Elizabethan Language and Literature* (Cambridge, 1992).

Baxandall, Michael, *Patterns of Intention: On the Historical Explanation of Pictures* (New Haven, Conn., 1985).

Beer, Barrett L., 'John Ponet's *Short Treatise of Politike Power* Reassessed', *Sixteenth Century Journal* 21, no. 3 (1990), pp. 373–83.

Belsey, Catherine and Belsey, Andrew, 'Icons of Divinity: Portraits of Elizabeth I' in *Renaissance Bodies: The Human Figure in English Culture c. 1540–1660*, ed. Lucy Gent and Nigel Llewellyn (London, 1990), pp. 11–35.

Bergeron, David, 'Elizabeth's Coronation Entry (1559): New Manuscript Evidence', *English Literary Renaissance* 8 (1978), pp. 3–8.

English Civic Pageantry 1558–1642 (London, 1971).

Berry, Lloyd, *John Stubbs's 'Gaping Gulf' with Letters and Other Relevant Documents* (Charlottesville, Va., 1968).

Berry, Philippa, *Of Chastity and Power: Elizabethan Literature and the Unmarried Queen* (London, 1989).

Bevington, David, *Tudor Drama and Politics: A Critical Approach to Topical Meaning* (Cambridge, Mass., 1968).

Black, Antony, *Monarchy and Community: Political Ideas in the Later Conciliar Controversy 1430–1450*, Cambridge Studies in Medieval Life and Thought (Cambridge, 1970).

Bouwsma, William, *'Concordia Mundi': The Career and Thought of Guillaume Postel (1510–1581)* (Cambridge, Mass., 1957).

Bowler, Gerald, ' "An Axe or an Acte": The Parliament of 1572 and Resistance Theory in Early Elizabethan England', *Canadian Journal of History* 19, no. 3 (1984), pp. 349–59.

'Marian Protestants and the Idea of Violent Resistance to Tyranny' in *Protestantism and the National Church in Sixteenth Century England*, ed. Peter Lake and Maria Dowling (London, 1987), pp. 124–43.

Brockwell, Charles W., 'Answering' The Known Men": Bishop Reginald Pecock and Mr. Richard Hooker', *Church History* 49 (1980), pp. 133–46.

Burke, Peter, *The Fabrication of Louis XIV* (New Haven, Conn., 1992).

The Historical Anthropology of Early Modern Italy: Essays on Perception and Communication (Cambridge, 1987).

Burns, J. H., 'George Buchanan and the Anti-Monarchomachs' in *Political Discourse in Early Modern Britain*, ed. Nicholas Phillipson and Quentin Skinner (Cambridge, 1993), pp. 3–22.

Lordship, Kingship, and Empire: The Idea of Monarchy 1400–1525, The Carlyle Lectures, 1988 (Oxford, 1992).

'*Regimen Medium*: Executive Power in Early-Modern Political Thought' (unpublished paper).

The True Law of Kingship: Concepts of Monarchy in Early-Modern Scotland (Oxford, 1996).

Bush, M. L., *The Government Policy of Protector Somerset* (London, 1975).

Bushnell, Rebecca W., *Tragedies of Tyrants: Political Thought and Theater in the English Renaissance* (Ithaca, N.Y., 1990).
The Cambridge History of Political Thought 1450–1700, ed. J. H. Burns (Cambridge, 1991).
Campbell, Lorne, *Renaissance Portraits: European Portrait-Painting in the Fourteenth, Fifteenth and Sixteenth Centuries* (New Haven, Conn., 1990).
Cannadine, David and Price, Simon, eds., *Rituals of Royalty: Power and Ceremonial in Traditional Societies* (Cambridge, 1987).
Cargill Thompson, W. D. J., *Studies in the Reformation: Luther to Hooker* (London, 1980).
Cerasano, S. P. and Wynne-Davies, Marion, eds., *Gloriana's Face: Women, Public and Private, in the English Renaissance* (New York, 1992).
Christian, Margaret, 'Elizabeth's Preachers and the Government of Women: Defining and Correcting a Queen', *Sixteenth Century Journal* 24, no. 3 (1993), pp. 561–76.
Cohen, Abner, 'Political Anthropology: The Analysis of the Symbolism of Power Relations', *Man* 4 (1969), pp. 215–35.
Coleman, Christopher and David Starkey, eds., *Revolution Reassessed: Revisions in the History of Tudor Government and Administration* (Oxford, 1986).
Collins, Stephen, *From Divine Cosmos to Sovereign State: An Intellectual History of Consciousness and the Idea of Order in Renaissance England* (Oxford, 1989).
Collinson, Patrick, *The Birthpangs of Protestant England: Religious and Cultural Change in the Sixteenth and Seventeenth Centuries*, 3rd Anstey Memorial Lecture, University of Kent, 1986 (London, 1988).
'De Republica Anglorum': Or, History with the Politics Put Back*, Inaugural Lecture, 9 November 1989 (Cambridge, 1990).
'The Elizabethan Exclusion Crisis and the Elizabethan Polity', *Proceedings of the British Academy* 84 (1994), pp. 51–92.
The Elizabethan Puritan Movement (London, 1967).
From Iconoclasm to Iconophobia: The Cultural Impact of the Second English Reformation, The Stenton Lecture, University of Reading (Reading, 1986).
Godly People: Essays on English Protestantism and Puritanism (London, 1983).
'The Monarchical Republic of Queen Elizabeth I', *Bulletin of the John Rylands University Library of Manchester* 69, no. 2 (1986–7), pp. 394–424.
'Puritans, Men of Business and Elizabethan Parliaments', *Parliamentary History* 7, no. 2 (1988), pp. 187–211.
The Concise Dictionary of National Biography, 3 vols. (Oxford, 1992).
Conrad, Frederick William, 'A Preservative Against Tyranny: The Political Theology of Sir Thomas Elyot', Ph.D. Dissertation, Johns Hopkins University, Baltimore, Md. (1988).
Corts, Paul R., 'Governmental Persuasion in the Reign of Queen Elizabeth I, 1558–1563', Ph.D. Dissertation, Indiana University, Bloomington, Ind., (1971).
Crane, Mary Thomas, '"Video et Taceo": Elizabeth I and the Rhetoric of Counsel', *Studies in English Literature* 28 (1988), pp. 1–15.

Cressy, David, 'Binding the Nation: The Bonds of Association, 1584 and 1596' in *Tudor Rule and Revolution: Essays for G. R. Elton from his American Friends*, ed. D. J. Guth and J. W. McKenna (Cambridge, 1982), pp. 217–34.
'Describing the Social Order of Elizabethan and Stuart England', *Literature and History* 3 (1976), pp. 29–44.
Croft, Pauline, 'Robert Cecil and the Early Jacobean Court' in *The Mental World of the Jacobean Court*, ed. Linda Levy Peck (Cambridge, 1991), pp. 134–47.
Cropper, Elizabeth, 'The Beauty of Women: Problems in the Rhetoric of Renaissance Portraiture' in *Rewriting the Renaissance: The Discourses of Sexual Difference in Early Modern Europe*, ed. Margaret W. Ferguson, Maureen Quilligan and Nancy J. Vickers (Chicago, 1986), pp. 175–90.
Cuddy, Neil, 'The Revival of the Entourage: The Bedchamber of James I, 1603–25' in *The English Court: From the War of the Roses to the Civil War*, ed. David Starkey (London, 1987), pp. 173–225.
Davis, Natalie Zemon, 'Women on Top' in *Society and Culture in Early Modern France* (Stanford, Calif., 1965), pp. 124–51.
Dawson, Jane E. A., 'Revolutionary Conclusions: The Case of the Marian Exiles', *History of Political Thought* 11, no. 2 (1990), pp. 257–72.
'The Two John Knoxes: England, Scotland and the 1558 Tracts', *Journal of Ecclesiastical History* 42, no. 4 (1991), pp. 556–76.
Day, J. F. R., 'Death be Very Proud: Sidney, Subversion, and Elizabethan Heraldic Funerals' in *Tudor Political Culture*, ed. Dale Hoak (Cambridge, 1995), pp. 179–203.
Dean, David, 'Image and Ritual in the Tudor Parliaments' in *Tudor Political Culture*, ed. Dale Hoak (Cambridge, 1995), pp. 243–71.
Dewar, Mary, 'The Authorship of the *Discourse of the Commonweal*', *Economic History Review* 19 (1966), pp. 388–400.
Sir Thomas Smith: A Tudor Intellectual in Office (London, 1964).
Dolan, Frances E., *Dangerous Familiars: Representations of Domestic Crime in England, 1550–1700* (New York, 1994).
Donaldson, Peter S., *Machiavelli and Mystery of State* (Cambridge, 1988).
'Bishop Gardiner, Machiavellian', *Historical Journal* 23, no. 1 (1980), pp. 1–16.
Doran, Susan, *Monarchy and Matrimony: The Courtships of Elizabeth I* (London, 1996).
Dowdall, H. C., 'The Word "State"', *Law Quarterly Review* 39 (1923), pp. 98–125.
Duncan-Jones, Katherine, 'Sidney and Titian' in *English Renaissance Studies Presented to Dame Helen Gardner in Honour of Her Seventieth Birthday*, ed. John Carey (Oxford, 1980), pp. 1–11.
Dunham, William Huse, Jr, 'Regal Power and the Rule of Law: A Tudor Paradox', *Journal of British Studies* 3, no. 2 (1964), pp. 24–56.
Dunlop, Ian, *Palaces and Progresses of Elizabeth I* (London, 1962).
Eccleshall, Robert, *Order and Reason in Politics: Theories of Absolute and Limited Monarchy in Early Modern Europe* (Oxford, 1978).
Edgerton, Samuel Y., Jr, *The Renaissance Rediscovery of Linear Perspective* (New

York, 1975).

Eggert, Katherine, 'Nostalgia and the Not Yet Late Queen: Refusing Female Rule in *Henry V*, *English Literary History* 61 (1994), pp. 523–50.

Eisenstein, Elizabeth, *The Printing Press as an Agent of Change* (Cambridge, 1979).

Elias, Norbert, *The Court Society*, tr. Edmund Jephcott (Oxford, 1983).

Elton, Geoffrey, 'Arthur Hall, Lord Burghley and the Antiquity of Parliament' in *Studies in Tudor and Stuart Politics and Government*, 4 vols. (Cambridge, 1983), vol. III, pp. 254–73.

The Parliament of England, 1559–1582 (Cambridge, 1986).

'Reform and the "Commonwealth-Men" of Edward VI's Reign' in *Studies in Tudor and Stuart Politics and Government*, 4 vols. (Cambridge, 1983), vol.III, pp. 234–53.

The Tudor Constitution: Documents and Commentary, 2nd edn (Cambridge, 1982).

Esler, Anthony, *The Aspiring Mind of the Elizabethan Younger Generation* (Durham, N.C., 1966).

Fenlon, Dermot, '*Machiavelli and Mystery of State* by Peter S. Donaldson', *Historical Journal* 19 (1976), pp. 1019–23.

Forte, Paul E., 'Richard Hooker's Theory of Law', *The Journal of Medieval and Renaissance Studies* 12, no. 2 (1982), pp. 122–58.

Freedberg, David, *The Power of Images: Studies in the History and Theory of Response* (Chicago, 1989).

Frye, Roland Mushat, 'Ways of Seeing in Shakespearean Drama and Elizabethan Painting', *The Shakespeare Quarterly* 31 (1980), pp. 323–42.

Frye, Susan, *Elizabeth I: The Competition for Representation* (Oxford, 1993).

'The Myth of Elizabeth at Tilbury', *Sixteenth Century Journal* 23, no. 1 (1992), pp. 95–114.

Fumerton, Patricia, '"Secret" Arts: Elizabethan Miniatures and Sonnets' in *Representing the English Renaissance*, ed. Stephen Greenblatt (Los Angeles, Calif., 1988), pp. 93–133.

Gaunt, William, *Court Painting in England from Tudor to Victorian Times* (London, 1980).

Gent, Lucy and Llewellyn, Nigel, eds., *Renaissance Bodies: The Human Figure in English Culture c. 1540–1660* (London, 1990).

Gilliam, Elizabeth and W. J. Tighe, 'To "Run with the Time": Archbishop Whitgift, the Lambeth Articles, and the Politics of Theological Ambiguity in Late Elizabethan England', *Sixteenth Century Journal* 23, no. 1 (1992), pp. 325–40.

Gilman, Ernest B., *Iconoclasm and Poetry in the English Reformation: Down Went Dagon* (Chicago, 1986).

Ginzburg, Carlo, 'High and Low: The Theme of Forbidden Knowledge in the Sixteen and Seventeen Centuries', *Past and Present* 73 (1976), pp. 28–41.

Graves, M. A. R., 'Managing Elizabethan Parliaments' in *The Parliaments of Elizabethan England*, ed. D. M. Dean and N. L. Jones (Oxford, 1990), pp. 37–64.

Graziani, Rene, 'The "Rainbow Portrait" of Queen Elizabeth I and Its

Religious Symbolism', *Journal of the Warburg and Courtauld Institutes* 35 (1972), pp. 247–59.

Greaves, Richard L., 'Concepts of Political Obedience in Late Tudor England: Conflicting Perspectives', *Journal of British Studies* 22, no. 1 (1982), pp. 23–34.

Greenblatt, Stephen, 'Invisible Bullets: Renaissance Authority and Its Subversion, *Henry IV* and *Henry V*, in *Political Shakespeare: New Essays in Cultural Materialism*, ed. Jonathan Dollimore (Manchester, 1994), pp. 18–47.

ed., *Representing the English Renaissance* (Berkeley, Calif. 1988).

Gunn, S. J., 'Literature and Politics in Early Tudor England', *Journal of British Studies* 30 (1991), pp. 216–21.

Guy, John, *Christopher St German on Chancery and Statute*, Selden Society (London, 1985).

'The "Imperial Crown" and the Liberty of the Subject: The English Constitution from Magna Carta to the Bill of Rights' in *Court, Country, and Culture: Essays in Honor of Perez Zagorin*, ed. Bonnelyn Kunze and Dwight Brautigan (New York, 1992), pp. 65–88.

'The Henrician Age' in *The Varieties of British Political Thought 1500–1800*, ed. J. G. A. Pocock (Cambridge, 1993), pp. 13–46.

'The Privy Council: Revolution or Evolution?' in *Revolution Reassessed: Revisions in the History of Tudor Government and Administration*, ed. Christopher Coleman and David Starkey (Oxford, 1986), pp. 59–86.

'The Rhetoric of Counsel in Early Modern England' in *Tudor Political Culture*, ed. Dale Hoak (Cambridge, 1995), pp. 292–310.

'The 1590s: The Second Reign of Elizabeth I?' in *The Reign of Elizabeth I: Court and Culture in the Last Decade*, ed. John Guy (Cambridge, 1995), pp. 1–19.

Tudor England (Oxford, 1988).

ed., *The Tudor Monarchy* (London, 1997).

Hackett, Helen, *Virgin Mother, Maiden Queen: Elizabeth I and the Cult of the Virgin Mary* (London, 1995).

Haigh, Christopher, *English Reformations: Religion, Politics and Society under the Tudors* (Oxford, 1993).

ed., *The Reign of Elizabeth I* (London, 1984).

Haller, William, *Foxe's Book of Martyrs and the Elect Nation* (London, 1963).

Hanley, Sarah, 'Engendering the State: Family Formation and State Building in Early Modern France', *French Historical Studies* 16, no. 1 (1989), pp. 4–27.

The 'Lit de Justice' of the Kings of France: Constitutional Ideology in Legend, Ritual and Discourse (Princeton, N.J., 1983).

'The Monarchic State in Early Modern France: Marital Regime Government and Male Right' in *Politics, Ideology and the Law in Early Modern Europe: Essays in Honor of J. H. M. Salmon*, ed. Adrianna E. Bakos (New York, 1994).

Harding, Alan, 'The Origins of the Concept of the State', *History of Political Thought* 15, no. 1 (1994), pp. 57–72.

Hartley, T. E., *Elizabeth's Parliaments: Queen, Lords and Commons 1559–1601* (Manchester, 1992).

Haskell, Francis, *History and Its Images: Art and the Interpretation of the Past* (New

Haven, Conn., 1993).

Hasler, P. W., ed., *The House of Commons 1558–1603*, The History of Parliament, 3 vols. (London, 1981).

Headley, John M., *Church, Empire and World: The Quest for Universal Order, 1520–1640*, Variorum Collected Studies Series (Aldershot, Hants., 1997).

Healey, Robert M., 'Waiting for Deborah: John Knox and Four Ruling Queens', *Sixteenth Century Journal* 25, no. 2 (1994), pp. 371–86.

Heisch, Allison, 'Queen Elizabeth I and the Persistence of Patriarchy', *Feminist Review* 4 (1980), pp. 45–54.

'Queen Elizabeth I: Parliamentary Rhetoric and the Exercise of Power', *Signs: Journal of Women in Culture and Society* 1, no. 1 (1975), pp. 31–55.

Helgerson, Richard, *Forms of Nationhood: The Elizabethan Writing of England* (Chicago, 1992).

Self-Crowned Laureates: Spenser, Johnson, Milton, and the Literary System (Berkeley, Calif., 1983)

Herman, Peter C., '"O, 'tis a gallant king": Shakespeare's *Henry V* and the Crisis of the 1590s' in *Tudor Political Culture*, ed. Dale Hoak (Cambridge, 1995), pp. 204–25.

Hind, Arthur M., *Engraving in England in the Sixteenth and Seventeenth Centuries: A Descriptive Catalogue with Introductions*, Part I: The Tudor Period (Cambridge, 1952).

Hinton, R. W. K., 'Husbands, Fathers and Conquerors', *Political Studies* 15, no. 3 (1967), pp. 291–300, and 16, no. 1 (1968), pp. 55–67.

Hoak, Dale, 'Rehabilitating the Duke of Northumberland: Politics and Political Control, 1549–53' in *The Mid-Tudor Polity c. 1540–1560*, ed. Jennifer Loach and Robert Tittler (London, 1980), pp. 29–51.

ed., *Tudor Political Culture* (Cambridge, 1995).

'Two Revolutions in Tudor Government: The Formation and Organisation of Mary I's Privy Council' in *Revolution Reassessed: Revisions in the History of Tudor Government and Administration*, ed. Christopher Coleman and David Starkey (Oxford, 1986), pp. 87–115.

Hobsbawm, Eric and Ranger, Terence, eds., *The Invention of Tradition* (Cambridge, 1983).

Holtgen, Karl Josef, 'The Reformation of Images and Some Jacobean Writers on Art' in *Functions of Literature: Essays Presented to Erwin Wolff*, ed. U. Broich, T. Stemmler and G. Stragmann (Tubingen, 1984), pp. 119–46.

Horie, Hirofume, 'The Origin and the Historical Context of Archbishop Whitgift's "Orders" of 1586', *Archive for Reformation History* 83 (1992), pp. 240–57.

Hudson, Winthrop S., *The Cambridge Connection and the Elizabethan Settlement of 1559* (Durham, N.C., 1980).

John Ponet (1516?–1556): Advocate of Limited Monarchy (Chicago, 1942).

Jackson, Richard A., 'Peers of France and Princes of the Blood', *French Historical Studies* 7, no. 1 (1972), pp. 27–43.

James, Mervyn, *Society, Politics and Culture: Studies in Early Modern England* (Cambridge, 1986).

Jardine, Lisa, *Reading Shakespeare Historically* (London, 1996).

Jenkins, Marianna, *The State Portrait: Its Origins and Evolution*, Monographs on Archaeology and Fine Arts III, College Art Association of America in conjunction with the Art Bulletin (Chicago, 1947).

Johnston, Theodore E., 'A Persuasive Plenty: Copia in the English Renaissance Parliament', Ph.D. Dissertation, Arizona State University, Phoenix, (1990).

Jones, Ann Rosalind, 'Nets and Bridles: Early Modern Conduct Books and Sixteenth Century Women's Lyrics' in *The Ideology of Conduct: Essays on Literature and the History of Sexuality*, ed. Nancy Armstrong and Leonard Tennenhouse (London, 1987), pp. 39–72.

Jones, Norman, 'Parliament and the Political Society of Elizabethan England' in *Tudor Political Culture*, ed. Dale Hoak (Cambridge, 1995), pp. 226–42.

Jordan, Constance, *Renaissance Feminism: Literary Texts and Political Models*. (Ithaca, N.Y., 1990).

'Woman's Rule in Sixteenth-Century British Political Thought', *Renaissance Quarterly* 40, no. 3 (1987), pp. 421–51.

Kantorowicz, Ernst H., *The King's Two Bodies: A Study in Medieval Political Theology* (Princeton, N.J., 1957).

'Mysteries of State: An Absolutist Concept and Its Late Medieval Origins', *Harvard Theological Review* 48 (1955), pp. 65–91.

Kelley, Donald R., *The Beginning of Ideology: Consciousness and Society in the French Reformation* (Cambridge, 1981).

'Civil Science in the Renaissance: The Problem of Interpretation' in *The Languages of Political Theory in Early-Modern Europe*, ed. Anthony Pagden (Cambridge, 1987), pp. 57–78.

'Elizabethan Political Thought' in *The Varieties of British Political Thought, 1500–1800*, ed. J. G. A. Pocock (Cambridge, 1993), pp. 47–79.

François Hotman: A Revolutionary's Ordeal (Princeton, N.J., 1973).

'Ideas of Resistance before Elizabeth' in *Law, Literature, and the Settlement of Regimes*, ed. Gordon Schochet, The Folger Institute Center for the History of British Political Thought Proceedings, vol. 2 (Washington, D.C., 1990), pp. 5–28.

'"Jurisconsultus Perfectus": The Lawyer as Renaissance Man', *Journal of the Warburg and Courtauld Institutes* 51 (1988), pp. 84–102.

Kemp, Janet, 'Laurence Humphrey, Elizabethan Puritan: His Life and Political Theories', Ph.D. Dissertation, West Virginia University, Morgantown, West Virginia (1978).

Kenyon, J. P., *The History Men: The Historical Profession in England since the Renaissance* (London, 1983).

'Queen Elizabeth and the Historians' in *Queen Elizabeth I: Most Politic Princess*, ed. Simon Adams (London, 1984), pp. 52–5.

King, John N., *English Reformation Literature: The Tudor Origins of the Protestant Tradition* (Princeton, N.J., 1982).

'The Godly Woman in Elizabethan Iconography', *Renaissance Quarterly* 38 (1985), pp. 41–84.

'Queen Elizabeth I: Representations of the Virgin Queen', *Renaissance Quarterly* 43, no. 1 (1990), pp. 30–74.

'The Royal Image, 1535–1603' in *Tudor Political Culture*, ed. Dale Hoak (Cambridge, 1995), pp. 104–32.

Tudor Royal Iconography: Literature and Art in an Age of Religious Crisis (Princeton, N.J., 1989).

Kingdon, Robert M., 'Calvinism and Resistance Theory, 1550–1580' in *The Cambridge History of Political Thought 1450–1700*, ed. J. H. Burns (Cambridge, 1991), pp. 193–218.

'William Allen's Use of Protestant Political Argument' in *From the Renaissance to the Counter-Reformation: Essays in Honour of Garrett Mattingly*, ed. Charles H. Carter (London, 1966), pp. 164–78.

Knappen, M. M., *Tudor Puritanism: A Chapter in the History of Idealism* (Gloucester, Mass., 1963).

Koenigsberger, H. G., Mosse, G. L. and Bowler, G. Q., *Europe in the Sixteenth Century* (London, 1968; 2nd edn, 1989).

Lake, Peter, 'The Significance of the Elizabethan Identification of the Pope as Antichrist', *Journal of Ecclesiastical History* 31, no. 2 (1980), pp. 161–78.

Laski, Harold J., *Studies in the Problem of Sovereignty* (New Haven, Conn., 1917).

Lee, Maurice, Jr, *James Stewart, Earl of Moray: A Political Study of the Reformation in Scotland* (Westport, Conn., 1953).

Lee, Patricia-Ann, '"A Body Politique to Governe": Aylmer, Knox and the Debate on Queenship', *The Historian* 52, no. 2 (1990), pp. 242–61.

Lepschy, Anna Laura, *Tintoretto Observed: A Documentary Survey of Critical Reactions from the Sixteenth to the Twentieth Century* (Ravenna, 1983).

Leslie, Michael, 'The Dialogue between Bodies and Souls: Pictures and Poesy in the English Renaissance', *Word and Image* 1 (1985), pp. 16–30.

Levack, Brian P., *The Civil Lawyers in England 1603–1641: A Political Study* (Oxford, 1973).

'The Civil Law, Theories of Absolutism, and Political Conflict in Late Sixteenth- and Early Seventeenth-Century England' in *Law, Literature, and the Settlement of Regimes*, ed. Gordon Schochet, The Folger Institute Center for the History of British Political Thought Proceedings, vol. 2 (Washington, D.C., 1990), pp. 29–48.

Levin, Carole, 'John Foxe and the Responsibilities of Queenship' in *Women in the Middle Ages and Renaissance: Literary and Historical Perspectives*, ed. Mary Beth Rose (Syracuse, N Y, 1986), pp. 113–33.

The Heart and Stomach of a King: Elizabeth I and the Politics of Sex and Power (Philadelphia, 1994).

Levine, Mortimer, *The Early Elizabethan Succession Question, 1558–1568* (Stanford, Califor., 1966).

Tudor Dynastic Problems 1460–1571 (London, 1973).

Levy, F. J., 'Francis Bacon and the Style of Politics' in *Renaissance Historicism:*

Selections from English Literary Renaissance, ed. A. F. Kinney and D. S. Collins (Boston, 1987), pp. 146–67.

'The Theatre and the Court in the 1590s' in *The Reign of Elizabeth I*, ed. John Guy (Cambridge, 1995), pp. 274–300.

Levy Peck, Linda, 'Kingship, Counsel and Law in Early Stuart Britain' in *The Varieties of British Political Thought, 1500–1800*, ed. J. G. A. Pocock (Cambridge, 1993), pp. 80–115.

Lewis, S. J., 'An Instrument of the New Constitution: The Origins of the General Warrant', *Journal of Legal History* 7, no. 3 (1986), pp. 256–72.

Lightman, Harriet, 'Queens and Minor Kings in French Constitutional Law', *Proceedings of the Annual Meeting of the Western Society for French History* 9 (1981), pp. 26–36

Limon, Jerzy, *The Masque of Stuart Culture* (Newark, Del., 1990).

Loach, Jennifer, *Parliament and Crown in the Reign of Mary Tudor* (Oxford, 1986).

Loades, David, *Politics and the Nation 1450–1660* (Oxford, 1974).

Lommel, Andreas, *Masks: Their Meaning and Function* (London, 1972).

Lotman, Yuri and Uspensky, B. A., 'On the Semiotic Mechanisms of Culture', *New Literary History* 9 (1977–8), pp. 211–32.

Lowe, Ben, 'War and the Commonwealth in Mid-Tudor England', *Sixteenth Century Journal* 21, no. 2 (1990), pp. 171–91.

Luxton, Imogen, 'The Reformation and Popular Culture' in *Church and Society in England: Henry VIII to James I*, ed. Rosemary O'Day and Felicity Heal (Basingstoke, Hants., 1977), pp. 57–77.

MacCaffrey, Wallace, 'The Anjou Match and the Making of Elizabethan Foreign Policy' in *The English Commonwealth 1547–1640*, ed. Peter Clark, A. G. R. Smith and Nicholas Tyacke (New York, 1979), pp. 59–76.

'Patronage and Politics under the Tudors' in *The Mental World of the Jacobean Court*, ed. Linda Levy Peck (Cambridge, 1991), pp. 21–35.

Queen Elizabeth and the Making of Policy, 1572–1588 Princeton, N.J., 1981).

The Shaping of the Elizabethan Regime (Princeton, N.J., 1969).

McCoy, Richard C., 'Lord of Liberty: Francis Davison and the Cult of Elizabeth' in *The Reign of Elizabeth I*, ed. John Guy (Cambridge, 1995), pp. 212–28.

'The "Wonderfull Spectacle" and Obscure Ordo Progress of Elizabeth I's Coronation' in *Law, Literature, and the Settlement of Regimes*, ed. Gordon Schochet, The Folger Institute Center for the History of British Political Thought Proceedings, vol. 2 (Washington, D.C., 1990), pp. 99–112.

McGiffert, Michael, 'Covenant, Crown, and Commons in Elizabethan Puritanism', *Journal of British Studies* 20, no. 2 (1981), pp. 32–52.

McIlwain, C. H., ed., *The Political Works of James I* (New York, 1965).

Mack, Phyllis, 'Feminine Behavior and Radical Action: Franciscans, Quakers, and the Followers of Gandhi', *Signs: Journal of Women in Culture and Society* 11, no. 3 (1986), pp. 457–77.

McLaren, A. N., 'Delineating the Elizabethan Body Politic: Knox, Aylmer and the Definition of Counsel, 1558–1588', *History of Political Thought* 17, no. 2

(1996), pp. 224–52.

'Prophecy and Providentialism in the Reign of Elizabeth I' in *Prophecy: The Power of Inspired Language in History 1300–2000*, ed. Bertrand Taithe and Tim Thornton, Themes in History (Stroud, Glos., 1997), pp. 31–50.

Maclean, Ian, *The Renaissance Notion of Woman: A Study in the Fortunes of Scholasticism and Medical Science in European Intellectual Life* (Cambridge, 1980).

Maitland, F. W., 'Elizabethan Gleanings' in *Selected Historical Essays of F.W. Maitland*, ed. Helen M. Cam (Cambridge, 1957), pp. 211–46.

Manley, Lawrence, *Literature and Culture in Early Modern London* (Cambridge, 1995).

Marcus, Leah S., 'Erasing the Stigma of Daughterhood: Mary I, Elizabeth I, and Henry VIII' in *Daughters and Fathers*, ed. Lynda E. Boose and Betty S. Flowers, (Baltimore, Md., 1989), pp. 400–17.

'Shakespeare's Comic Heroines, Elizabeth I, and the Political Uses of Androgyny' in *Women in the Middle Ages and Renaissance: Literary and Historical Perspectives*, ed. Mary Beth Rose (Syracuse, N.Y., 1986), pp. 135–53.

Mayer, Thomas F., *Thomas Starkey and the Commonweal: Humanist Politics and Religion in the Reign of Henry VIII* (Cambridge, 1989).

Mendle, Micheal, *Dangerous Positions: Mixed Government, the Estates of the Realm, and the Making of the 'Answer to the xix propositions'*, (Tuscaloosa, Ala., 1985).

Montrose, Louis, 'The Elizabethan Subject and the Spenserian Text' in *Literary Theory/Renaissance Texts*, ed. Patricia Parker and David Quint (Baltimore, Md., 1986), pp. 303–40.

'"Shaping Fantasies": Figurations of Gender and Power in Elizabethan Culture' in *Representing the English Renaissance*, ed. Stephen Greenblatt (Berkeley, Calif., 1988), pp. 31–64.

Moore, Tod, 'Recycling Aristotle: The Sovereignty Theory of Richard Hooker', *History of Political Thought* 14, no. 3 (1993), pp. 345–59.

Morgan, Victor, 'Whose Prerogative in Late Sixteenth and Early Seventeenth Century England?' in *Custom, Courts and Counsel: Selected Papers of the 6th British Legal History Conference*, ed. Albert K. R. Kiralfy and Michele Slatter (London, 1985).

Morris, Christopher, 'Machiavelli's Reputation in Tudor England' in *Machiavellismo e Antimachiavellici nel Cinquecento*, Atti del Convegno di Perugia 30 (Florence, 1969).

Mosse, George L., *The Struggle for Sovereignty in England from the Reign of Queen Elizabeth to the Petition of Right* (New York, 1968).

Muddiman, J. G., *Trial of Charles the First* (Edinburgh, n.d.).

Murphy, John, 'The Illusion of Decline: The Privy Chamber, 1547–1558' in *The English Court: From the War of the Roses to the Civil War*, ed. David Starkey (London, 1987), pp. 119–46.

Neale, J. E., 'The Commoners' Privilege of Free Speech in Parliament' in *Historical Studies of the English Parliaments*, ed. E. B. Fryde and E. Miller, (Cambridge, 1970), vol. 2, pp. 147–76.

Elizabeth I and Her Parliaments, 2 vols. (London, 1957).

The Elizabethan House of Commons (London, 1949).

Queen Elizabeth I (London, 1934; repr. 1952).

'Sir Nicholas Throckmorton's Advice to Queen Elizabeth on Her Accession to the Throne', *English Historical Review* 65 (1950), pp. 91–8.

Nenner, Howard, *The Right to Be King: The Succession to the Crown of England, 1603–1714*, Macmillan Studies in Modern History (New York, 1995).

Norbrook, David, *Poetry and Politics in the English Renaissance* (London, 1984).

Oakley, Francis, 'Christian Obedience and Authority, 1520–1550' in *The Cambridge History of Political Thought 1450–1700*, ed. J. H. Burns (Cambridge, 1991), pp. 159–92.

O'Day, Rosemary, 'Hugh Latimer: Prophet of the Kingdom', *Historical Research: The Bulletin of the Institute of Historical Research* 65, no. 158 (1992), pp. 258–76.

Oestreich, Gerhard, *Neostoicism and the Early Modern State* (Cambridge, 1982).

Orlin, Lena, *Private Matters and Public Culture in Post-Reformation England* (New York, 1994).

Packull, Werner O., 'The Image of the "Common Man" in the Early Pamphlets of the Reformation (1520–1525)', *Historical Reflections* 12, no. 2 (1985), pp. 253–77.

Pagden, Anthony, ed., *The Languages of Political Theory in Early-Modern Europe* (Cambridge, 1987).

Parry, G. J. R., *A Protestant Vision: William Harrison and the Reformation of Elizabethan England* (Cambridge, 1987).

Patterson, Annabel, *Censorship and Interpretation: The Conditions of Writing and Reading in Early Modern England* (Madison, Wis., 1984).

Reading Holinshed's 'Chronicles' (Chicago, 1994).

'The Very Name of the Game: Theories of Order and Disorder', *South Atlantic Quarterly* 86, no. 4 (1987), pp. 519–43.

Peardon, Barbara, 'The Politics of Polemic: John Ponet's *Short Treatise of Politic Power* and Contemporary Circumstances 1553–1556', *Journal of British Studies* 22, no. 1 (1981), pp. 35–49.

Pearson, A. F. Scott, *Thomas Cartwright and Elizabethan Puritanism 1535–1603* (Cambridge, 1925).

Peltonen, Markku, *Classical Humanism and Republicanism in English Political Thought 1570–1640*, Ideas in Context (Cambridge, 1995).

Phillips, James E., Jr, 'The Background of Spenser's Attitude toward Women Rulers', *Huntington Library Quarterly* 5 (1941), pp. 5–32.

'George Buchanan and the Sidney Circle', *Huntington Library Quarterly* 12 (1948–9), pp. 23–56.

Phillipson, Nicholas and Skinner, Quentin, eds., *Political Discourse in Early Modern Britain* (Cambridge, 1993).

Plett, Heinrich, 'Aesthetic Constituents in the Courtly Culture of Renaissance England', *New Literary History* 14 (1982–3), pp. 597–621.

Plucknett, T. F. T. 'Ellesmere on Statutes', *Law Quarterly Review* 40 (1944), pp. 242–9.

Pocock, J. G. A., *The Ancient Constitution and the Feudal Laws: English Historical Thought in the Seventeenth Century* (Cambridge, 1957); reissued in 1987 as *The Ancient Constitution and the Feudal Law: A Reissue with a Retrospect.*

'The Concept of a Language and the *Métier d'historien*: Some Considerations on Practice' in *The Languages of Political Theory in Early-Modern Europe*, ed. Anthony Pagden (Cambridge, 1987), pp. 19–38.

'Contingency, Identity, Sovereignty' in *Uniting the Kingdom? The Making of British History*, ed. Alexander Grant and Keith J. Stringer (London, 1995), pp. 292–302.

'A Discourse of Sovereignty: Observations on the Work in Progress' in *Political Discourse in Early Modern Britain*, ed. Nicholas Phillipson and Quentin Skinner (Cambridge, 1993), pp. 377–428.

'England' in *National Consciousness, History, and Political Culture in Early-Modern Europe*, ed. Orest Ranum (Baltimore, Md., 1975), ch. IV.

The Machiavellian Moment: Florentine Political Thought and the Atlantic Republican Tradition (Princeton, N.J., 1975).

Politics, Language and Time: Essays on Political Thought and History (New York, 1973).

'The State of the Art' in *Virtue, Commerce, and History* (Cambridge, 1985), pp. 1–33.

'Texts as Events: Reflections on the History of Political Thought' in *Politics of Discourse: The Literature and History of Seventeenth Century England*, ed. Stephen N. Zwicker and Kevin Sharp (Berkeley, Calif., 1987), 21–34.

ed., *The Varieties of British Political Thought 1500–1800* (Cambridge, 1993).

'*Vous Autres Européens* – Or Inventing Europe', *Filozovski Vestnik* 14, no. 2 (1993), pp. 141–58.

Pollard, A. W. and Redgrave, G. R., *A Short-Title Catalogue of Books Printed in England, Scotland, and Ireland, and of English Books Printed Abroad, 1475–1640*, 3 vols., 2nd edn (London, 1976–91).

Pomeroy, Elizabeth W., *Reading the Portraits of Queen Elizabeth I* (New Haven, Conn., 1989).

Potter, Mary, 'Gender Equality and Gender Hierarchy in Calvin's Theology', *Signs: Journal of Women in Culture and Society* 11, no. 4 (1986), pp. 725–39.

Prall, Stuart E., 'The Development of Equity in Tudor England', *American Journal of Legal History* 8 (1964), pp. 1–19.

Pulman, Michael, *The Elizabethan Privy Council in the 1570s* (Berkeley, Calif., 1971).

Pye, Christopher, 'The Sovereign, the Theatre, and the Kingdome of Darknesse: Hobbes and the Spectacle of Power', *Representations* 8 (1984), pp. 85–106.

Redworth, Glyn, *In Defence of the Church Catholic: The Life of Stephen Gardiner* (Oxford, 1990).

Robertson, Karen, 'The Body Natural of a Queen: Mary, James, *Horestes*', *Renaissance and Reformation* 26, no. 1 (1990), pp. 25–36.

Roper, Lyndal, '"The Common Man", "The Common Good", "Common Women": Gender and Meaning in the German Reformation Commune',

Social History 12, no. 1 (1987), pp. 3–21.

Roston, Murray, *Renaissance Perspectives in Literature and the Visual Arts* (Princeton, N.J., 1987).

Rowen, Herbert H., '"L'État, C'est à Moi": Louis XIV and the State', *French Historical Studies* 2, no. 1 (1961), pp. 83–98.

Rubenstein, Nicolai, 'The History of the Word *Politicus* in Early-Modern Europe' in *The Languages of Political Theory in Early-Modern Europe*, ed. Anthony Pagden (Cambridge, 1987), pp. 41–56.

Sacks, David Harris, 'Private Profit and Public Good: The Problem of the State in Elizabethan Theory and Practice' in *Law, Literature, and the Settlement of Regimes*, ed. Gordon Schochet, The Folger Institute Center for the History of British Political Thought Proceedings, vol. 2 (Washington, D.C., 1990), pp. 121–42.

Salmon, J. H. M., *The French Wars of Religion in English Political Thought* (Oxford, 1959).

Samuel, Raphael, 'Art, Politics and Ideology', *History Workshop* 6 (1978), pp. 101–6.

Schama, Simon, 'The Domestication of Majesty: Royal Family Portraiture, 1500–1800' in *Art and History: Images and Their Meaning*, ed. Theodore K. Rabb and Robert I. Rotberg (Cambridge, 1988), pp. 155–84.

Schmitt, Charles B., *John Case and Aristotelianism in Renaissance England* (Montreal, 1983).

Schochet, Gordon J., *Patriarchalism in Political Thought: The Authoritarian Family and Political Speculation and Attitudes Especially in Seventeenth-Century England* (Oxford, 1975).

Scott, Mary Augusta, *Elizabethan Translations from the Italian* (Boston, Mass., 1916).

Shephard, Amanda, 'Gender and Authority in Sixteenth Century England: The Debate about John Knox's *First Blast of the Trumpet against the Monstrous Regiment of Women*', Ph.D. Dissertation, University of Lancaster, (1990).

Shephard, Robert P., 'Royal Favorites in the Political Discourse of Tudor and Stuart England', Ph.D. Dissertation, Claremont Graduate School, Claremont, Calif. (1985).

Skinner, Quentin, *The Foundations of Modern Political Thought*, 2 vols. (Cambridge, 1978).

  'Meaning and Understanding in the History of Ideas' in *Meaning and Context: Quentin Skinner and His Critics* ed. James Tully (Cambridge, 1988), pp. 29–67.

  'Motives, Intentions, and the Interpretation of Texts', *New Literary History* 3 (1972), pp. 393–408.

  'The Origins of the Calvinist Theory of Revolution' in *After the Reformation: Essays in Honour of J. H. Hexter*, ed. Barbara C. Malament (Philadelphia, 1980), pp. 309–30.

  'The State' in *Political Innovation and Conceptual Change*, ed. Terence Ball, James Farr and Russell L. Hanson, Ideas in Context (Cambridge, 1989; repr.

1995), pp. 90–131.

Slack, Paul, 'Poverty and Social Regulation' in *The Reign of Elizabeth I*, ed. Christopher Haigh (London, 1984), pp. 221–42.

Smith, Edward O., Jr, 'Crown and Commonwealth: A Study in the Official Elizabethan Doctrine of the Prince', *Transactions of the American Philosophical Society* 66, no. 8 (1976), pp. 3–51.

Smuts, Malcolm, 'Cultural Diversity and Cultural Change at the Court of James I' in *The Mental World of the Jacobean Court*, ed. Linda Levy Peck (Cambridge, 1991), pp. 99–112.

Snow, Vernon, *Parliament in Elizabethan England: John Hooker's 'Order and Usage'* (New Haven, Conn., 1977).

Sommerville, J. P., 'Richard Hooker, Hadrian Saravia, and the Advent of the Divine Right of Kings', *History of Political Thought* 4 (1983), pp. 229–45.

Stafford, Pauline, 'More Than a Man, Or Less Than a Woman? Women Rulers in Early Modern Europe', *Gender and History* 7, no. 3 (1995), pp. 486–90.

Starkey, David, 'Court History in Perspective' in *The English Court: From the War of the Roses to the Civil War*, ed. David Starkey (London, 1987), pp. 1–24.

ed., *Rivals in Power* (London, 1990).

Stern, Virginia, *Gabriel Harvey: His Life, Marginalia and Library* (Oxford, 1979).

Stone, Lawrence, *The Crisis of the Aristocracy 1558–1641*, abridged edn (Oxford, 1977).

Strong, Roy, *The English Icon: Elizabethan and Jacobean Portraiture* (London, 1969). *Portraits of Queen Elizabeth I* (Oxford, 1963).

Sutherland, N. M., 'The Marian Exiles and the Establishment of the Elizabethan Regime', *Archive for Reformation History* 78 (1987), pp. 253–84.

Talbert, Ernest William, *The Problem of Order: Elizabethan Political Commonplaces and an Example of Shakespeare's Art* (Chapel Hill, N.C., 1962).

Teague, Frances, 'Queen Elizabeth in Her Speeches' in *Gloriana's Face: Women, Public and Private, in the English Renaissance*, ed. S. P. Cerasano and Marian Wynne-Davies (London, 1992).

Tennenhouse, Leonard, 'Strategies of State and Political Plays: *A Midsummer Night's Dream, Henry IV, Henry V, Henry VIII*' in *Political Shakespeare: New Essays in Cultural Materialism*, ed. Jonathan Dollimore (Manchester, 1994), pp. 109–28.

Thorne, S. E., *Essays in English Legal History* (London, 1985).

Tierney, Brian, 'Medieval Foundations of Elizabethan Political Thought' in *Law, Literature, and the Settlement of Regimes*, ed. Gordon Schochet, The Folger Institute Center for the History of British Political Thought Proceedings, vol. 2 (Washington, D.C., 1990), pp. 1–4.

Todd, Margo, *Christian Humanism and the Puritan Social Order*, Ideas in Context (Cambridge, 1987).

Toews, John E., 'Intellectual History after the Linguistic Turn: The Autonomy of Meaning and the Irreducibility of Experience', *American Historical Review* 92, no. 4 (1987), pp. 879–907.

Trevor-Roper, Hugh, *Queen Elizabeth's First Historian: William Camden and the Beginnings of English 'Civil History'*, Second Neale Lecture in English History (London, 1971).

Tuck, Richard, *Philosophy and Government 1572–1651* (Cambridge, 1993).

Tully, James, 'The Pen is a Mighty Sword: Quentin Skinner's Analysis of Politics' in *Meaning and Context: Quentin Skinner and His Critics*, ed. James Tully (Cambridge, 1988), pp. 7–25.

Ullman, Walter, *Medieval Political Thought* (London, 1965).

Vasoli, Cesare, 'Francesco Patrizi and the "Double Rhetoric"', *New Literary History* 14 (1982–3), pp. 539–51.

Viroli, Maurizio, *From Politics to Reason of State: The Acquisition and Transformation of the Language of Politics 1250–1600* (Cambridge, 1992).

Walzer, Michael, 'The Communitarian Critique of Liberalism', *Political Theory* 18, no. 1 (1990), pp. 6–23.

Regicide and Revolution: Speeches at the Trial of Louis XVI (Cambridge, 1974).

Weisner, Merry E., *Women and Gender in Early Modern Europe*, New Approaches to European History (Cambridge, 1993).

Weiss, Penny A., *Gendered Community: Rousseau, Sex and Politics* (New York, 1993).

Whigham, Frank, 'Interpretation at Court: Courtesy and the Performer–Audience Dialectic', *New Literary History* 14 (1982–3), pp. 623–39.

White, Hayden, *The Context of the Form: Narrative Discourse and Historical Representation* (Baltimore, Md., 1987).

Williams, Raymond, 'Base and Soperstructure' in *Problems in Materialism and Culture* (London, 1980), pp. 31–49.

Williamson, Arthur H., *Scottish National Consciousness in the Age of James VI: The Apocalypse, the Union and the Shaping of Scotland's Public Culture* (Edinburgh, 1979).

Wood, Neal, 'Avarice and Civil Unity: The Contribution of Sir Thomas Smith', *History of Political Thought* 23, no. 1 (1997), pp. 24–42.

Woods, Susanne, 'Spenser and the Problem of Women's Rule', *Huntington Library Quarterly* 48, no. 2 (1985), pp. 40–58.

Woolf, D. R., 'The "Common Voice": History, Folklore and Oral Tradition in Early Modern England', *Past and Present* 118 (1988), pp. 26–52.

'The Mental World in Tudor and Early Stuart England', *Canadian Journal of History* 27, no. 2 (1992), pp. 341–52.

'Speech, Text, and Time: The Sense of Hearing and the Sense of the Past in Renaissance England', *Albion*, 18, no. 2 (1986), pp. 159–94.

'Two Elizabeths? James I and the Late Queen's Famous Memory', *Canadian Journal of History* 20, no. 2 (1985), pp. 167–91.

Worden, Blair, *The Sound of Virtue: Philip Sidney's 'Arcadia' and Elizabethan Politics* (New Haven, Conn., 1996).

Wormald, Jenny, 'James VI and I, *"Basilikon Doron"* and *The Trew Law of Free Monarchies*: The Scottish Context and the English Translation' in *The Mental World of the Jacobean Court*, ed. Linda Levy Peck (Cambridge, 1991), pp. 36–54.

Wright, Pam, 'A Change in Direction: The Ramifications of a Female House-
    hold, 1558–1603' in *The English Court: From the War of the Roses to the Civil War*,
    ed. David Starkey (London, 1987), pp. 147–72.
Zagorin, Perez, *Ways of Lying: Dissimulation, Persecution and Conformity in Early
    Modern Europe* (Boston, Mass., 1990).
Zeefeld, William Gordon, *Foundations of Tudor Policy* (Cambridge, Mass., 1948).

Index

IDEAS IN CONTEXT

Edited by QUENTIN SKINNER (*General Editor*),
LORRAINE DASTON, DOROTHY ROSS AND JAMES TULLY

Titles marked with an asterisk are also available in paperback